THE SCIENCE OF WRITING
THEORIES, METHODS,
INDIVIDUAL DIFFERENCES,
AND APPLICATIONS

THE SCIENCE OF WRITING
THEORIES, METHODS, INDIVIDUAL DIFFERENCES, AND APPLICATIONS

C. Michael Levy
University of Florida

Sarah Ransdell
Florida Atlantic University

Editors

Routledge
Taylor & Francis Group
NEW YORK AND LONDON

First Published by
Lawrence Erlbaum Associates, Inc., Publishers
10 Industrial Avenue
Mahwah, New Jersey 07430

Transferred to Digital Printing 2009 by Routledge
270 Madison Avenue New York, NY 10016
2 Park Square Milton Park, Abingdon Oxon OX14 4RN

Cover design by Gail Silverman

Library of Congress Cataloging-in-Publication Data

The science of writing: Theories, methods, individual differences, and applications / edited by C. Michael Levy and Sarah
Ransdell
     p. cm.
    Includes bibliographical references and index.
    ISBN 0-8058-2108-2 (c) ISBN 0-8058-2109-0 (p)
                             96-84604
                                CIP

Publisher's Note
The publisher has gone to great lengths to ensure the quality
of this reprint but points out that some imperfections in the
original may be apparent.

CONTENTS

INDIVIDUAL DIFFERENCES AND APPLICATIONS

PREFACE

In 1978 Lee Gregg and Erwin Steinberg organized an interdisciplinary conference at Carnegie Mellon University to assess what research had already shown and to describe what research was then ongoing. One legacy of that meeting was the collection of papers that Gregg and Steinberg assembled into a book titled *Cognitive Processes in Writing*. Its publication in 1980 was a watershed event. It served as an extremely influential source of ideas that guided a great deal of the research in the field of writing for the next 15 years.

About a year ago, while discussing the considerable historical significance of *Cognitive Processes in Writing*, we realized that despite the impressive increase in writing research that occurred since its publication, no book had appeared during this time that captured the state of our knowledge about writing in the same way. We therefore explored with some of the contributors to the Gregg and Steinberg book — and many others, as well — whether they also felt that there had been enough development to warrant another collective snapshot of the field. The consensus was that the time was ripe.

It was clear that a great deal of important work in writing was now being done by people all over the globe, most of whom had never actually met the others. It wasn't feasible for us to assemble these researchers at a traditional conference to discuss their current thinking and data. So we used the technology that has only recently become generally available (principally, World Wide Web browsers over the Internet) that would enable us to mount an extended, virtual conference. With everyone connected electronically, every collaborator could participate in the evolution of ideas that could emanate from laboratories in any of eight countries involved, simulating the exchange of ideas that is a hallmark of face-to-face conferences. We hoped that such electronic collaboration would foster cohesiveness to the book.

This book is divided into three sections. The first seven chapters capture some of the most recent thinking about the theoretical underpinnings of writing. Here, in chapter 1, Hayes presents his revision of the theory he first described with Flower in the first chapter of Gregg and Steinberg. The major differences from the earlier model are an emphasis on the central role of working memory, visual and spatial information, motivation and affect, and a reorganization of the cognitive processes involved. In chapter 2, Hayes and Nash discuss a theory for understanding planning and includes some methods for improving the analysis of planning data. Kellogg introduces his model of working memory in writing in chapter 3. This theory allows for the simultaneous activation of formulation (planning and translating), execution (programming and executing), and monitoring (reading and editing) systems of text production, as long as the demands placed on the central executive do not exceed working memory capacity. In chapter 4, Grabowski presents a regulation theory of writing which, like Hayes' and Kellogg's models, emphasizes the importance of working memory constraints. Regulation theory focusses on pragmatic context that "regulates" writing at three hierarchical levels: declarative and procedural memory, auxiliary systems which enhance coherence and consistency with audience needs, and an encoding mechanism. Chapter 5 introduces some evidence from our own labs that link writing quality, as measured by the Six-Subgroup Quality Scale, writing fluency, and individual differences in working memory, as measured by complex span tasks. Reading span and writing quality were found to account for over a third of the variance in reading comprehension skill suggesting a general capacity explanation of working memory in the language domain. In chapter 6, Rijlaarsdam and van den Bergh highlight the importance of the dynamics of composing and summarize central questions for writing process research such as, the nature of the general pattern of cognitive activities, changes in subject differences in the probability of various activities over time, and the generalizability of temporal patterns across writing assignments. Sharples focuses in chapter 7 on writing as creative design, providing a context in which to resolve some apparent inconsistencies in studies of writing: writing as demanding, but sometimes seemingly effortless, writing as analytic, and yet synthetic, writing as involving deliberate planning, and yet full of chance discovery. Thus, the chapters in this seciton place a stress on writing in context, working memory constraints, and the interaction among cognitive subprocesses, and the focus in each on providing explicit frameworks for testing explanatory hypotheses about writing. These theories should serve as guidelines for those conducting research on writing processes, as well as for those, including composition instructors and students of writing, who seek to better understand writing success. Psychology of language students would also benefit from learning about these new theoretical developments as written language production currently receives cursory attention in most textbooks at best.

The next six chapters focus on new tools and techniques that have promise for helping us to study writing processes in exquisite detail at levels not previously possible. In chapter 8, we introduce the concept of writing signatures, robust and uniquely individual patterns of time on specific writing subprocesses. The method that makes this possible disambiguates among subprocesses by capturing keystrokes and speech and playing them back in real-time. Severinson Eklundh introduces S-notation in chapter 9. This is an interactive, computer-based method for tracing a writer's revisions on-line. S-notation is unique in providing an automatic record of a writing session where revisions appear explicitly in the text produced. Torrance, Thomas and Robinson illustrate in chapter 10 a system for coding writing protocols in order to determine the nature of strategic and automatic processes in idea generation. The system provides criterion for identifying new propositions, content form plans, rhetorical elements, elements from the assignment, and evaluation. Van den Bergh and Rijlaarsdam demonstrate in chapter 11 the use of multilevel models to study the dynamics of composing processes and includes explicit guidelines for data preparation, manipulation, analysis, and interpretation using these modeling techniques. In chapter 12, Janssen, van Waes, and van den Bergh provide experimental data using a key capturing program which bears on the question of reactivity in thinking-aloud protocol data. They found that thinking-aloud has larger effects on complex "knowledge transforming" writing than on simple "knowledge telling." Chapter 13 concludes the section on writing tools and techniques. Here, Sanders and van Wijk present a text analysis system named PISA for determining how hierarchical text structure contributes to understanding conceptual processes in writing. All of these tools — writing signatures, S-notation, multilevel modelling, Keytrap, and PISA — may be relevant to those interested in the cognitive processes involved in any complex behavior that is difficult to observe "first-hand." Many of these tools are available from the authors for those who would like to try them in their research or for those who would simply like to better understand their own writing behavior.

The last section of this book showcases six approaches to studying individual differences and to studying writing in natural environments. Chapter 14 is unique in this volume for its emphasis by Levin, Share, and Shatil on the development of literacy in preschoolers and how it is related to early attempts at writing. A longitudinal study finds significant correlations between level of writing, early literacy, vocabulary, and IQ (Ravens) and concludes that preschoolers' early attempts at writing are important precursors to literacy. In chapter 15 Madigan, Linton, and Johnson show how individual differences in writing apprehension are more be a consequence of negative self-talk rather than poor writing skills. This "pain without gain" finding should be relevant not only to writing researchers, but to all who may feel apprehensive about their own writing or have students with this problem. Van der Geest presents in chapter 16 some answers to those who would like to study writing in "real-life" contexts but find it methodologically challenging. This chapter questions the traditional limits of case study research and suggests by example that explanation rather than just exploration is possible when studying writers at work. Britton describes in chapter 17 three methods for rewriting expository instructional text to improve its learnability: the coherence revision method, the diagnosis-treatment revision method, and the method of good examples. Chapter 18 portrays the investigations by Grahan and Harris of the effectiveness of teaching writing strategies and self-regulation procedures for students who find learning and writing challenging. This chapter should be of interest to composition instructors, as well as those who do educational research. Finally, in chapter 19, Reece reports research on three techniques for reducing the demands of writing: outlining, planned dictation, and a Listening Word Processor. The latter two speech-based composition methods were found to be superior, especially for very young writers and those intellectually or learning-challenged.

While we have tried to encompass as much of the exciting ongoing work in writing research as we could, we are the first to admit that this book is not all-inclusive. Writing research is now a global endeavor, and we simply are not aware of all of the good work currently underway. Many active workers whose thinking we hoped to include in this volume had previous commitments that prevented them from contributing a chapter.

The title of our book, *The Science of Writing: Theory, Methods, Individual Differences, and Applications*, probably implies different things to different people. The book was designed with a wide audience in mind. We initially set out to provide a sorely needed resource book for researchers and scholars in writing. Somewhere along the way, we realized that the most productive approach might be to write so that those outside the academic establishment could also readily participate in this attempt to capture our understanding of writing at this particular moment. Composition instructors, and those that teach writing in applied settings have much to contribute to this field. Professional writers, poets, critics, as well as the nascent novelists can all help address the question of whether researchers' conjectures about writing contain more than a kernel of truth. Finally, researchers, scholars, and writers of our future, that is, today's students, should find this book accessible and informative, particularly graduate and advanced undergraduate students in cognition, psychology of language, or psychology of writing courses.

Finally, we acknowledge Larry Erlbaum and Judi Amsel at LEA, whose enthusiasm got this project off the ground in a hurry and Kathleen O'Malley who nurtured the project through the final stages of production. We express our thanks to Linda Flynn and Shauna Kai for their editorial assistance, and to Pamela Marek and Joseph Lea for their many constructive comments and careful attention to detail. We are extremely grateful to Michael Weilbacher for helping us to establish the virtual conference and a WWW home page that only our collaborators could access, to the trustees of the Norman Shulevitz Foundation for their contributions to our research program, and to Ellie Levy and Brett Laursen for their constant and total support of everything we do. Without our collaborators, there would be no book. So we say *bravo* to them for producing wonderful chapters that will provide more than enough interesting and important ideas to keep a vigorous writing research community busy past the turn of the century.

— C. Michael Levy
— Sarah Ransdell
March, 1996

THEORIES OF WRITING AND FRAMEWORKS FOR WRITING RESEARCH

— 1 —
A NEW FRAMEWORK FOR UNDERSTANDING COGNITION AND AFFECT IN WRITING

John R. Hayes
Carnegie Mellon University

Alan Newell (1990) described science as a process of approximation. One theory will replace another if it is seen as providing a better description of currently available data (pp. 13-14). Nearly 15 years have passed since the Hayes-Flower model of the writing process first appeared in 1980. Since that time a great many studies relevant to writing have been carried out and there has been considerable discussion about what a model of writing should include. My purpose here is to present a new framework for the study of writing — a framework that can provide a better description of current empirical findings than the 1980 model, and one that can, I hope, be useful for interpreting a wider range of writing activities than was encompassed in the 1980 model.

This writing framework is not intended to describe all major aspects of writing in detail. Rather, it is like a building that is being designed and constructed at the same time. Some parts have begun to take definite shape and are beginning to be usable. Other parts are actively being designed and still others have barely been sketched. The relations among the parts — the flow of traffic, the centers of activity — although essential to the successful functioning of the whole building, are not yet clearly envisioned. In the same way, the new framework includes parts that are fairly well developed — a model of revision that has already been successfully applied, as well as clearly structured models of planning and of text production. At the same time, other parts (such as the social and physical environments), though recognized as essential, are described only through incomplete and unorganized lists of observations and phenomena — the materials from which specific models may eventually be constructed.

My objective in presenting this framework is to provide a structure that can be useful for suggesting lines of research and for relating writing phenomena one to another. The framework is intended to be added to and modified as more is learned.

The 1980 model

The original Hayes-Flower (1980) writing model owes a great deal to cognitive psychology and, in particular, to Herbert Simon. Simon's influence was quite direct. At the time Flower and I began our work on composition, I had been collaborating with Simon on a series of protocol studies exploring the processes by which people come to understand written problem texts. This research produced cognitive process models of two aspects of written text comprehension. The first, called UNDERSTAND, described the processes by which people build representations when reading a text (Hayes & Simon, 1974; Simon & Hayes, 1976), and the second, called ATTEND, characterized the processes by which people decide what is most important in the text (Hayes, Waterman, & Robinson, 1977). It was natural to extend the use of the protocol analysis technique and cognitive process models to written composition.

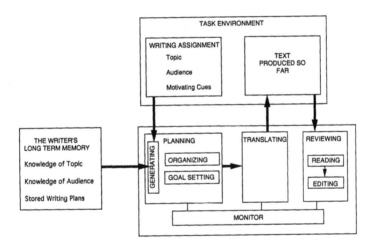

Figure 1.1. The Hayes-Flower model proposed in 1980.

Figure 1.1 shows the Hayes-Flower model as it was originally proposed (Hayes & Flower, 1980). Figure 1.2 is a redrawing of the original model for purposes of graphic clarity. It is intended to better depict the intended relations in the original rather than as a substantive modification. In the redrawing, memory has been moved to indicate that it interacts with all three cognitive writing processes (*planning, translating,* and *revision*) and not just with planning — as some readers were led to believe. The names of the writing processes have been changed to those in more current use. Certain graphic conventions have been clarified. The boxes have been resized to avoid any unintended implication of differences in the relative importance of the processes. Arrows indicate the transfer of information. The process-subprocess relation has been indicated by including subprocesses within superprocesses. In the 1980 model, this convention for designating subprocesses was not consistently followed. In particular, in the original version, the monitor appeared as a box parallel in status to the three writing process boxes. Its relation to each process box was symbolized by undirected lines connecting it to the process boxes. As is apparent in the 1980 paper (pp.19-20), the monitor was viewed as a process controlling the subprocesses: planning, sentence generation, and revising. Thus, in Figure 1.2, the monitor is shown as containing the writing subprocesses.

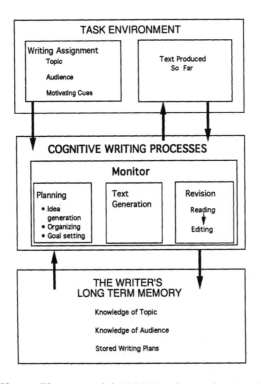

Figure 1.2. The Hayes-Flower model (1980) redrawn for clarification.

The model, as Figures 1.1 and 1.2 indicate, had three major components. First is *the task environment*; it includes all those factors influencing the writing task that lie outside of the writer's skin. We saw the task environment as including both social factors, such as a teacher's writing assignment, as well as physical ones such as the text the writer had produced so far. The second component consisted of the cognitive processes involved in writing. These included planning (deciding what to say and how to say it), translating (called text generation in Figure 1.2, turning plans into written text), and revision (improving existing text). The third component was the writer's long-term memory, which included knowledge of topic, audience, and genre.

General organization of the new model

Figure 1.3 shows the general organization of the new model. This model has two major components: the task environment and the individual. The task environment consists of a social component, which includes the audience, the social environment, and other texts that the writer may read while writing, and a physical component, which includes the text that the writer has produced so far and a writing medium such as a word processor. The individual incorporates *motivation and affect, cognitive processes, working memory,* and *long-term memory.*

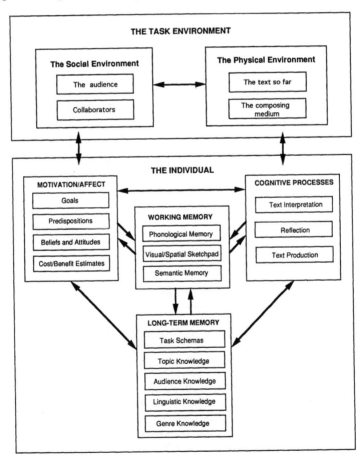

Figure 1.3. The general organization of the new model.

In the new model, I group cognition, affect, and memory together as aspects of the individual; I depict the social and physical environments together as constituting the task environment. Thus, rather than a social-cognitive model, the new model could be described as an individual-environmental model.

In what follows, I will say more about modeling the individual aspects of writing than about the social ones. This is because I am a psychologist and not a sociologist or a cultural historian. It does not mean that I believe any of these areas is unimportant. Rather, I believe that each of the components is absolutely essential for the full understanding of writing. Indeed, writing depends on an appropriate combination of cognitive, affective, social, and physical conditions if it is to happen at all. Writing is a communicative act that requires a social context and a medium. It is a generative activity requiring motivation, and it is an intellectual activity requiring cognitive processes and memory. No theory can be complete that does not include all of these components.

There are four major differences between the old model and the new: First, and most important, is the emphasis on the central role of working memory in writing. Second, the model includes visual-spatial as well as linguistic representations. Scientific journals, schoolbooks, magazines, newspapers, ads, and instruction manuals often include graphs, tables, or pictures that are essential for understanding the message of the text. If we want to understand many of the texts that we encounter every day, it is essential to understand their visual and spatial features. Third, a significant place is reserved for motivation and affect in the framework. As I will show, there is ample evidence that motivation and affect play central roles in writing processes. Finally, the cognitive process section of the model has undergone a major reorganization. Revision has been replaced by text interpretation; planning has been subsumed under the more general category, reflection; translation has been subsumed under a more general text production process.

The task environment

The social environment

Writing is primarily a social activity. We write mostly to communicate with other humans. But the act of writing is not social just because of its communicative purpose. It is also social because it is a social artifact and is carried out in a social setting. What we write, how we write, and who we write to is shaped by social convention and by our history of social interaction. Our schools and our friends require us to write. We write differently to a familiar audience than to an audience of strangers. The genres in which we write were invented by other writers and the phrases we write often reflect phrases earlier writers have written. Thus, our culture provides the words, images, and forms from which we fashion text. Cultural differences matter. Some social classes write more than others (Heath, 1983). Japanese write very different business letters than Americans. Further, immediate social surroundings matter. Nelson (1988) found that college students' writing efforts often have to compete with the demands of other courses and with the hurly burly of student life. Freedman (1987) found that efforts to get students to critique each others' writing failed because they violated students' social norms about criticizing each other in the presence of a teacher.

Although the cultural and social factors that influence writing are pervasive, the research devoted to their study is still young. Many studies are, as they should be, exploratory in character and many make use of case study or ethnographic methods. Some areas, because of their practical importance, are especially active. For example, considerable attention is now being devoted to collaborative writing both in school and in the workplace. In school settings, collaborative writing is of primary interest as a method for teaching writing skills. In a particularly well-designed study, O'Donnell, Dansereau, Rocklin, Lambiote, Hythecker, and Larson (1985) showed that collaborative writing experience can lead to improvement in subsequent individual writing performances. In workplace settings, collaboration is of interest because many texts must be produced by work groups. The collaborative processes in these groups deserve special attention because, as Hutchins (1995) showed for navigation, the output of group action depends on both the properties of the group and those of the individuals in the group. Schriver (in press) made similar observations in extensive case studies of collaboration in document design groups working both in school and industry.

Other research areas that are particularly active are socialization of writing in academic disciplines (Greene, 1991; Haas, 1987; Velez, 1994), classroom ethnography (Freedman, 1987; Sperling, 1991), sociology of scientific writing (Bazerman, 1988; Blakeslee, 1992; Myers, 1985), and workplace literacy (Hull, 1993).

Research on the social environment is essential for a complete understanding of writing. I hope that the current enthusiasm for investigating social factors in writing will lead to a strong empirical research tradition parallel to those in speech communication and social psychology. It would be regrettable if antiempirical sentiments expressed in some quarters had the effect of curtailing progress in this area.

The physical environment

In the 1980 model, we noted that a very important part of the task environment is the text the writer has produced so far. During the composition of any but the shortest passages, writers will reread what they have written apparently to help shape what they write next. Thus, writing modifies its own task environment. However, writing is not the only task that reshapes its task environment. Other creative tasks that produce an integrated product cumulatively such as graphic design, computer programming, and painting have this property as well.

Since 1980, increasing attention has been devoted to the writing medium as an important part of the task environment. In large part, this is the result of computer-based innovations in communication such as word processing, e-mail, the World Wide Web, and so on. Studies comparing writing using pen and paper to writing using a word processor have revealed effects of the medium on writing processes such as planning and editing. For example, Gould and Grischowsky (1984) found that writers were less effective at editing when that activity was carried out using a word processor rather than hard copy. Haas and Hayes (1986) found searching for information on-line was strongly influenced by screen size. Haas (1987) found that undergraduate writers planned less before writing when they used a word processor rather than pen and paper.

Variations in the composing medium often lead to changes in the ease of accessing some of the processes that support writing. For example, on the one hand, when we are writing with a word processor, including crude sketches in the text or drawing arrows from one part of the text to another is more difficult than it would be if we were writing with pencil and paper. On the other hand, word processors make it much easier to move blocks of text from one place to another, or experiment with fonts and check spelling. The point is not that one medium is better than another, although perhaps such a case could be made, but rather that writing processes are influenced, and sometimes strongly influenced, by the writing medium itself.

As already noted, when writers are composing with pen and paper, they frequently review the first part of the sentence they are composing before writing the rest of the sentence (Kaufer, Hayes, & Flower, 1986). However, when writers are composing with a dictating machine, the process of reviewing the current sentence is much less frequent (Schilperoord, in press). It is plausible to believe that the difference in frequency is due to the difference in the difficulty of reviewing a sentence in the two media. When writing with pen and paper, reviewing involves little more than an eye movement. When composing with a dictating machine, however, reviewing requires stopping the machine, rewinding it to find the beginning of the sentence, and then replaying the appropriate part.

The writing medium can influence more than cognitive processes. Studies of e-mail communication have revealed interesting social consequences of the media used. For example, Sproull and Kiesler (1986) suggested that marked lapses in politeness occurring in some e-mail messages (called flaming) may be attributed to the relative anonymity the medium provides the communicator.

Such studies remind us that we can gain a broader perspective on writing processes by exploring other writing media and other ways of creating messages (such as dictation, sign language, and telegraphy) that do not directly involve making marks on paper. By observing differences in process due to variations in the media, we can better understand writing processes in general.

The individual

In this section I discuss the components of the model that I have represented as aspects of the individual writer: working memory, motivation and affect, cognitive processes, and long-term memory. I will attend to both visual and verbal modes of communication.

Working memory

The 1980 model devoted relatively little attention to working memory. The present model assumes that all of the processes have access to working memory and carry out all nonautomated activities in working memory. The central location of working memory in Figure 1.3 is intended to symbolize its central importance in the activity of writing. To describe working memory in writing, I draw heavily on Baddeley's (1986) general model of working memory. In Baddeley's model, working memory is a limited resource that is drawn on both for storing information and for carrying out cognitive processes. Structurally, working memory consists of a central executive together with two specialized memories: a "phonological loop" and a visual-spatial "sketchpad." The phonological loop stores phonologically coded information and the sketchpad stores visually or spatially coded information. Baddeley and Lewis (1981) likened the phonological loop to an inner voice that continually repeats the information to be retained (e.g., telephone numbers or the digits in a memory span test). The central executive serves such cognitive tasks as mental arithmetic, logical reasoning, and semantic verification. In Baddeley's (1986) model, the central executive also performs a number of control functions in addition to its storage and processing functions. These functions include retrieving information from long-term memory and managing tasks not fully automated or that require problem solving or decision making. In the writing model, I represent planning and decision making as part of the reflection process rather than as part of working memory. Further, I specifically include a semantic store in working memory because, as I discuss later, it is useful for describing text generation. Otherwise, working memory in the writing model is identical to Baddeley's model of working memory.

Useful experimental techniques have been developed for identifying the nature of the representations active in working memory. In particular, tasks that make use of phonologic representations such as the memory span task are seriously interfered with when the individual is required to repeat an arbitrary syllable (e.g., la, la, la, etc.). This procedure is called *articulatory suppression*. Similarly, tasks that make use of visual/spatial representation such as interpreting spatial direction are interfered with when the individual is required to engage in spatial tracking tasks (e.g., monitoring the position of a visual or auditory target). These techniques could be useful for identifying the roles of visual and phonological representations in reading and writing tasks.

Motivation

Few doubt that motivation is important in writing. However, motivation does not have a comfortable place in current social-cognitive models. The relatively low salience of motivational concerns in cognitive theorizing is in striking contrast to earlier behaviorist thinking, which provided an explicit and prominent theoretical role to motivation (see, for example, Hull, 1943). Hilgard (1987) believed that cognitive theorists have not attended to motivation because their information-processing models are not formulated in terms of physiological processes. It is these processes that give rise to the basic drives.

I find this explanation unconvincing for the following reason: Cognitive psychologists have been interested in human performance in areas such as reading, problem solving, and memory. The motivations underlying such performances have never been adequately accounted for by the behaviorists or by anyone else in terms of basic drives. Cognitive psychology's failure to account fully for motivation in these complex areas of human behavior is not unique.

Actually, cognitive psychologists, following the lead of the Gestalt psychologists, took an important step in accounting for the effects of motivation by recognizing that much activity is goal directed. Powerful problem-solving mechanisms such as means-ends analysis and hill climbing are built on this recognition (see Hayes, 1989, chapter 2). Despite the success of such mechanisms in providing insight into a number of important behaviors, much more needs to be understood about motivation and affect. In the following section, I discuss four areas that I believe are of special importance for writing.

1. THE NATURE OF MOTIVATION IN WRITING. Motivation is manifest, not only in relatively short-term responses to immediate goals, but also in long-term predispositions to engage in certain types of activities. For example, Finn and Cox (1992) found that teachers' ratings of fourth-grade students for engagement in educational activities correlated strongly with the achievement scores of those students in the first three grades. Hayes, Schriver, Hill, and Hatch (1990) found that students who had been admitted to college as "basic" writers engaged much less in a computer-based activity designed to improve their writing skills than did "average" and "honors" students. In particular, the basic students attended fewer training sessions than did the average and honors students. Further, when basic students did attend training sessions, they spent less time attending to the instructional materials than did the average and honors students.

Research by Dweck (1986) suggests that the individual's beliefs about the causes of successful performance are one source of such long term predispositions. Dweck compared students who believed that successful performance depended on innate and unchangeable intelligence with those who believed that successful performance depended on acquirable skills. She found that these two groups of students responded very differently to failure. The first group tended to hide failure and to avoid those situations in which failure was experienced. In contrast, the second group responded to failure by asking for help and by working harder. One can imagine that if students believe that writing is a gift and experience failure, they might well form a long-term negative disposition to avoid writing.

Palmquist and Young (1992) explored in college students the relation between the belief that writing is a gift, on the one hand, and the presence of writing anxiety, on the other. They found that students who believed strongly that writing is a gift had significantly higher levels of writing anxiety and significantly lower self-assessments of their ability as writers than other students.

2. INTERACTION AMONG GOALS. Activities that are successfully characterized by means-end analysis typically have a single dominant goal. In writing, there are many situations, however, that involve multiple goals which interact with each other to determine the course of action. For example, the college students described by Nelson (1988) had goals to write papers for their classes but often those goals were set aside because of competition with other goals. If a writer has a goal, that does not mean the goal will necessarily lead to action.

Writers typically have more than one goal when they write (Flower & Hayes, 1980). For example, they may want both to convey content and also to create a good impression of themselves, or they may want to convey information clearly but not to write a text that is too long, or they may want to satisfy a first audience but not offend a second. Van der Mast (1996) studied experts writing policy documents for the Dutch government. He found that writers employ explicit linguistic strategies for creating texts that are ambiguous about issues on which members of the audience have conflicting interests. In all of these cases, the text will be shaped by the writer's need to achieve a balance among competing goals.

3. CHOICE AMONG METHODS. Even for situations in which the goals are specified, motivational factors can additionally influence action by influencing strategy selection. If a person wants to get from one place to another or to compute the answer to an arithmetic problem, the person can still make choices about what strategies should be used to reach that goal. Siegler, Adolph, and Lemaire (1995) studied strategy choice in a variety of situations. In one situation, infants who had just learned to walk were trying to reach their mothers on the other side of a ramp. To reach her, the infants could traverse the ramp by walking, or by crawling forward or backward, prone or supine. Siegler et al. found that experienced infants chose their strategy on the basis of the steepness of the slope, choosing to walk when the slope was small but choosing other strategies when the slope was large.

In a second study, Siegler et al. studied the choice of strategy for solving arithmetic problems among elderly people. Participants could solve problems by retrieving the answers from memory, by pencil-and-paper calculation, or by calculator. Siegler et al. found that the choice of strategy depended on the difficulty of the problem. The more difficult the problem, the more likely it was that the participants would use the calculator.

Thus, motivation may be seen as shaping the course of action through a kind of cost-benefit mechanism. Even when the overall goal of an activity is fixed, individuals will select the means that, in the current environment, is least costly or least likely to lead to error. This mechanism appears to shape overt as well as reflective actions. In a recent study by Kenton O'Hara (in press) at the University of Cardiff, participants were asked to solve a puzzle using a computer interface. The experimenter manipulated the interface so that it was either easy or difficult to make moves. At first, individuals using the difficult interface spent more time between trials than those using the easier interface. However, with practice, those using the hard interface rapidly decreased their time between trials until they were responding more quickly than those with the easy interface.

In another study, O'Hara compared two groups who had practiced for five trials either on the hard or the easy interface. Both groups were then transferred to a third interface. Those trained on the hard interface solved problems in fewer steps and with shorter solution times than those trained on the easy interface. O'Hara's results suggest that:

- people who use the hard interface reflect more before making a move about what move is most likely to lead to solution,
- they do so because the cost of reflection is more likely to be outweighed by its benefits — a reduction in the number of steps to solution — when the cost of each step is high, and
- increased reflection leads to increased learning and improved performance in solving the problems.

The studies of Siegler et al. (1995) and O'Hara (1996) indicate that changes in the task environment can have significant impact on the costs of both overt and reflective activities and can thereby influence the way in which tasks are carried out. In the case of writing, changes in the writing media such as those already discussed can influence the cognitive processes involved in carrying out writing tasks. Designers of word processing systems and other writing media should understand that system characteristics can have significant impact on writing processes.

4. AFFECTIVE RESPONSES IN READING AND WRITING. Earlier I mentioned that students who believe both that they are poor writers and that writing is a gift are likely to experience writing anxiety. Reading and writing have a number of other affective consequences as well.

Schriver (1995) studied reader's affective responses to manuals for consumer electronic products such as video cassette recorders and telephone answering machines. In a first study, she asked 201 consumer electronic customers where they placed the blame when they had difficulty understanding the instructions for electronic products they bought: on the manual, on the machine, on the manufacturer, or on themselves. Across both genders and across all age groups (from under 20 to over 60), readers blamed themselves for more than half of the problems they experienced. In a second study, Schriver collected thinking-aloud protocols from 35 participants as they were using manuals to help them carry out typical tasks with consumer electronics products. Analysis of the comments that the participants made as they worked, again indicated that they blamed themselves for their difficulties in more than half of the cases (52%).

Schriver found that people were right in about a third of the cases in which people blamed themselves. They had misread or misused the manual. However, in two thirds of the cases, the manual was clearly at fault. The information was either unintelligible, missing, or incorrectly indexed. The tendency of people to blame themselves when they read poorly designed instructional texts may well lead them to believe they are not competent readers of such materials and therefore make them reluctant to read it. We should very seriously consider whether a comparable problem exists in students reading school texts.

Note that people respond affectively not just to the linguistic aspects of a text but to the graphic features as well. Wright, Creighton, and Threlfall

(1982), Redish (1993), and Schriver (1996) all noted that if a text is unappealing in appearance, then people frequently decide not to read it.

A developing body of research indicates that the act of writing about stress related topics can have important affective consequences. A number of researchers in the field of health psychology have conducted studies on the use of writing to reduce stress. In a typical study, a group of people subject to stress (e.g., unemployed people, or students entering college) are divided at random into experimental and control groups. Both groups are asked to write for about 20 minutes on each of 3 to 5 days. The experimental group is asked to write about a stress-related topic, for example, "Getting laid off" or "Coming to college." The control group is asked to write on a neutral topic such as "What I did today." Then the groups are compared on some stress-related variables such as doctor visits, immune levels, or symptoms of depression. Pennebaker and Beall (1986) found that participants asked to write about traumatic experiences showed a significant drop in health center visits as compared to control groups. Greenberg and Stone (1992) found similar results. Pennebaker, Kiecolt-Glaser, and Glaser (1988) found that experimental participants showed enhanced immune function after the last day of writing compared to controls.

These results are still controversial. Some researchers have failed to find positive effects of writing on mental health. Further, when writing is compared with face-to-face discussion, the effects of discussion are usually found to be more powerful.

Cognitive processes

There is a fairly popular view in the field of literacy studies in the United States that social/cultural studies are "in" and cognitive studies are "out." Many feel it is no longer appropriate to do cognitive analyses of writing. Comments such as "We've done cognition" are pronounced with a certain finality.

There are two reasonable arguments that might lead to abandoning cognitive studies of writing. First, one might argue that all there is to know has already been learned about the relation of writing to topic knowledge, to language structure, to working memory capacity, and so on, and, therefore, no further investigations are necessary. However, this argument would not be easy to defend. Second, one might argue that all of the issues that can be investigated through cognitive measures such as working memory capacity or reading level are better or more conveniently studied through social factors such as race, class, or gender. The validity of this position certainly has not been demonstrated nor is it likely to be.

The real reason for the current rejection of cognitive methods is an unfortunate tendency to faddishness that has plagued English studies in the United States, the locus of much research on writing, though certainly not all or necessarily the best work. It is a sort of professional "7-year itch," a kind of collective attention deficit that has nothing to do with scientific progress. Just as we would think a carpenter foolish who said, "Now that I have discovered the hammer, I am never going to use my saw again" so we should regard a literacy researcher who says, "Now that I have discovered social methods, I am never going to use cognitive ones again." Our research problems are difficult. We need all available tools, both social and cognitive. Let's not hobble ourselves by following a misguided fad.

In this model, I propose that the primary cognitive functions involved in writing are text interpretation, reflection, and text production.

Text interpretation is a function that creates internal representations from linguistic and graphic inputs. Cognitive processes that accomplish this function include reading, listening, and scanning graphics. *Reflection* is an activity that operates on internal representations to produce other internal representations. Cognitive processes that accomplish reflection include problem solving, decision making, and inferencing. *Text production* is a function that takes internal representations in the context of the task environment and produces written, spoken, or graphic output. It was important to include spoken language in a writing model because spoken language can provide useful inputs to the writing process in the form of content information and editorial comment. In the case of dictation, speech is the output medium for the composing process. Further, for many writers, the process of planning written sentences appears to be carried out, either vocally or subvocally, in the medium of speech.

I assume that the cognitive processes involved in writing are not bound solely to writing but are shared with other activities. For example, I assume that the text-interpreting activities involved in writing overlap with those involved in reading novels and understanding maps; that the reflective activities involved in writing overlap with those involved in solving mystery stories and arithmetic puzzles; and that the text-producing activities involved in writing overlap those used in ordinary conversation and drawing. In addition, I assume that working memory and long-term memory resources are freely shared among both cognitive and motivational processes involved in writing.

Replacing Revision With Reading

Hayes, Flower, Schriver, Stratman, and Carey (1987) reported an extensive series of studies of revision in expert and not so expert adults. These studies led to the model of revision shown in Figure 1.4. Central to this model is the evaluation function — a process that is responsible for the detection and diagnosis of text problems. We postulated that this evaluation function was similar to the process of reading comprehension as described by Just and Carpenter (1980).

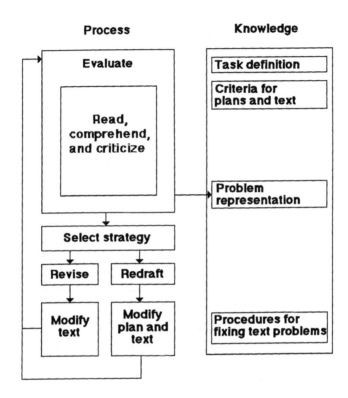

Figure 1.4. The revision process. (From Hayes et al., 1987. Reprinted with permission Cambridge University Press.)

Figure 1.5 shows an adaptation of the Just-Carpenter model for our tasks. The important feature of this model is that it shows reading comprehension as a process of constructing a representation of the text's meaning by integrating many sources of knowledge — from knowledge of word patterns and grammatical structures to factual knowledge and beliefs about the writer's intent. Also represented in Figure 1.5 is the observation that when we read to comprehend, we do not attend much to text problems. That is, we try to form a clear internal representation of the text's message but we are rarely concerned with stylistic issues. When we have problems in comprehending a text, we try to solve those problems and then, most usually, forget them. Consequently, when readers are reading for comprehension, their retrospective reports about text difficulty tend to be very incomplete. However, when we read to revise, we treat the text quite differently. We are still concerned with the text's message, but now we are also concerned with bad diction, wordiness, and poor organization — features of the text that we may not have attended to when we were reading for comprehension. In revision tasks, people read not only to represent the text's meaning but more importantly they read to identify text problems. With the extra goal of detecting problems, the reviser reads quite differently than does the reader who is simply reading for comprehension, seeing not only problems in the text but also opportunities for improvement that do not necessarily stem from problems. Our model for reading to evaluate a text is shown in Figure 1.6.

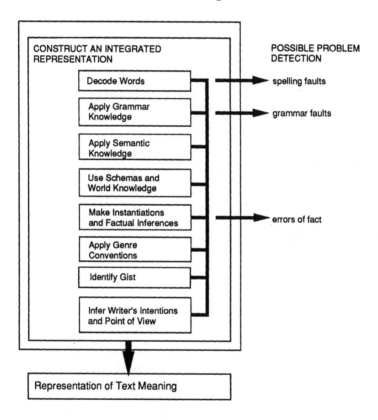

Figure 1.5. Cognitive processes in reading to comprehend text. (From Hayes et al., 1987. Reprinted with permission of Cambridge University Press).

Our model of revision, then, had a form of reading built in. Before it was constructed, I was concerned that revision did not seem to fit comfortably as a basic process in the writing model. Recognizing that the revision model included reading as a subpart suggested that revision would more naturally be thought of as a composite of more basic processes, in particular, a composite of text interpretation, reflection, and text production.

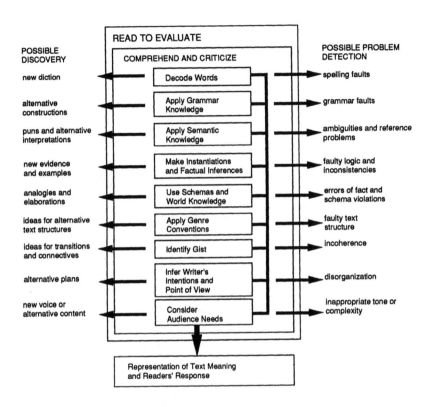

Figure 1.6. Cognitive processes in reading to evaluate text. (From Hayes, et al. 1987. Reprinted with permission of Cambridge University Press).

To understand revision, it is not enough to identify the underlying processes involved. It is also necessary to understand the control structure that determines how these processes are invoked and sequenced. I propose the following provisional model for that control structure. First, the control structure for revision is a task schema. By task schema I mean a package of knowledge, acquired through practice, that is useful for performing the task and is retrieved as a unit when cues indicating the relevance of the schema are perceived. This package of knowledge might be thought of as a set of productions — that is, condition-action rules — that mutually activate each other. People's knowledge of arithmetic shows evidence of being organized in task schemas for solving particular classes of problems. A person may hear just the first few words of a problem (e.g., "A river boat...") and be able to retrieve the problem category ("river current" problems), the nature of the information to be provided (the speed of the boat upstream and downstream), the question to be asked (What would the boat's speed be in still water?) and the kinds of mathematical procedures needed to find the answer.

The control structure for revision is a task schema that might include some or all of the following:

- A goal: to improve the text.
- An expected set of activities to be performed: evaluative reading, problem solving, text production.
- Attentional subgoals: what to pay attention to in the text being revised, what errors to avoid.
- Templates and criteria for quality: criteria for parallelism, diction, and so on.
- Strategies for fixing specific classes of text problems.

Figure 1.7 suggests how the components of the revision process might be organized.

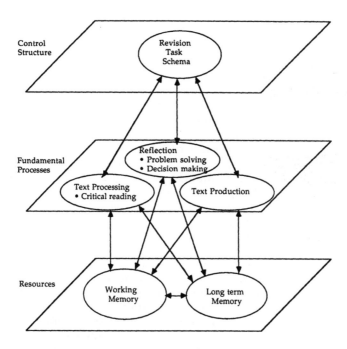

Figure 1.7. A model of revision.

The following example illustrates how this model may be applied. In a protocol study, Hayes, Flower, Schriver, Stratman, and Carey (1987) observed that college freshmen tended to focus their revision activities on problems at or below the sentence level but that more experienced writers attended both to local and global problems. There are a number of reasons one might propose to account for this failure to revise globally. First, the writer's basic revision processes may be inadequate. For example, the reading process may fail to detect global problems. Second, as Bereiter and Scarlamalia (1987) suggested, the writer may lack sufficient working memory to coordinate the basic revision processes. For example, the writer may see the global problems in the text but may be unable to keep the problems in focus while trying to fix them. Third, the writer's task schema may be at fault. For example, as Wallace and Hayes (1991) hypothesized, the control structures of freshman writers simply may not include the goal to attend to global problems.

To test the control structure hypothesis, Wallace and Hayes (1991) designed 8 minutes of instruction that demonstrated the difference between global and local revision, and urged students to revise both globally and locally. The authors reasoned that 8 minutes of instruction might modify the control structure by changing students' definition of the revision task but would be unlikely to cause changes in the basic revision processes or in the functioning of working memory. Wallace and Hayes (1991) then compared revisions produced by a group of freshmen who had received the instruction, the experimental group, with those of a control group that had been instructed simply to make the original text better. The experimental group outperformed the control group both in number of global revisions and in the holistically assessed quality of the revision. These results suggest two conclusions: First, the control structure for revision can be modified by a brief instructional prompt. Second, the control structure plays an important role in determining the nature and quality of revision performance.

Reading as a central process in writing

As discussed previously, reading to evaluate the text is a central component of revision. Poor text evaluation skills, such as Hayes et al. (1987) report, must surely lead to poor revisions. In addition to reading to evaluate, two other kinds of reading play important roles in writing: *reading source texts* and *reading to define tasks*.

READING SOURCE TEXTS. Usually, we think of source texts as providing writers with content, that is, with topic information that any competent reader would infer from the source text. However, if writers are not competent readers, if they oversimplify or misunderstand the source texts, their own texts that interpret or summarize those source texts are likely to suffer. For example, Zasloff (1984) studied a group of student writers who were asked to summarize an essay with the form "Others hold Position A but I hold Position B." Some of the students misread the essay to mean that the author held Position A. As a result, these students received very poor grades for their written summaries. Spivey (1984) found that students who wrote more adequate summaries tended to score better on reading tests than did students who wrote less adequate summaries. Chenoweth (1995) found that nonnative speakers of English had particular difficulty in identifying the main points of an essay, suggesting that these students may not be responding appropriately to textual cues that indicate the relative importance of information.

However, the reading of source texts is not simply an activity that provides readers with topic knowledge. Readers may form at least three different representations when they read: a representation of the topic discussed, a representation of the writer's persona, and a representation of the text as a spatial display.

REPRESENTATIONS OF THE WRITER'S PERSONA. In addition to forming a representation of the topic of the text, readers may also form another and quite different representation as they read — a representation of the writer's personality. Hatch, Hill, and Hayes (1993) asked judges to read college application essays and to identify personality traits of the authors. They found that the judges showed substantial agreement in the personality traits they attributed to the authors. In a second study, Hatch et al. (1993) found that these personality judgments predicted whether or not college admission personnel would vote to admit the author of the application essay to college. Thus, for these texts at least, the reader's representation of the author appeared to play an important role in the functioning of the text. Finally, Hatch et al. (1993) showed that readers' judgments of the writer's personality could be influenced in predictable ways by modifying the style of the text in ways that left the content substantially unchanged. For example, in one of the texts, a student described a play that she and her friends had produced. When that text was modified by replacing the word "we" with the word "I," there was a sharp reduction in judgments of the author as "likable" and "sensitive to others."

Hill (1992) asked undergraduates to rate the personality traits of writers who would write pro or con essays on a controversial topic (legalization of drugs). He found that the ratings were far more positive for the writer who agreed with the rater's own position than for the writer who did not. Schriver, Hayes, and Steffy (1994) asked primary and secondary school students to make judgments about the text, the graphics, and the author of drug education brochures. They found that the students often perceived the writers as people who would not be credible communicators. For example, students characterized the writers as people who got their information from books rather than from experience, and as people who were different from themselves in age and social class.

These results suggest that the reader's representation of the author can play an important role in the way readers respond to a text. Indeed, in some cases, the acceptance of a writer's argument may depend more on how the writer comes across as a person than on the logical quality of the argument itself.

REPRESENTATIONS OF THE TEXT AS A SPATIAL DISPLAY. Even when texts consist simply of sequences of sentences without any obvious graphic features such as pictures, tables, and graphs, they still have important spatial features. For example, Rothkopf (1971) found that individuals reading from multiple printed texts showed significant incidental memory for the spatial location in the text of information they read. Readers showed better than chance recall of where the information was located both on the page and within the text. Haas and Hayes (1986) found that readers formed a less precise spatial image of the text when they read one page at a time from a computer screen than from a two-page spread in hardcopy. In addition, they provided evidence linking readers' spatial images of the text to their success in searching for information in the text.

Bond and Hayes (1984) asked readers to paragraph text passages from which the original paragraphing marks had been removed. In one condition, the original texts were otherwise unchanged; in other conditions, the original texts were degraded by replacing categories of words (e.g., nouns) with Xs. In the most extreme condition, all of the words were replaced with Xs. The result was that readers showed greatest agreement in paragraphing with the undegraded texts. However, they still showed significant agreement even when all of the words had been replaced by Xs. To account for their data, Bond and Hayes (1984) proposed a model of paragraphing that included both linguistic and spatial features of the text.

READING TO UNDERSTAND THE TASK. Reading to understand the writing task is another important function that reading serves for the writer. It is a specialized reading genre that shapes writers' interpretation of writing tasks in school and at work. Success in carrying out this activity in school seems to depend on skill in interpreting terms such as "describe," "argue," and "interpret." In many school writing tasks, and possibly in other writing tasks as well, a text is judged inadequate because the writer has done the wrong task. For example, when assigned to analyze an article, students often respond by summarizing it. Chenoweth (1995) reported a study of this sort of reading in which students were shown exam questions together with an answer a student had written in response to the question. The task was to select one of four items of advice about how to improve the answer. Teachers and students differed systematically in the answers they chose. Students tended to prefer the suggestion to improve the mechanics. In contrast, teachers preferred the suggestion to make the answer more responsive to the question.

Reading, then, takes on a central role in the new model. It is seen as contributing to writing performance in three distinct ways: reading for comprehension, reading to define the writing task, and reading to revise. The quality of writers' texts often depends on their ability to read in these three ways.

From planning to reflection

In the 1980 model, planning played a prominent role in our thinking about writing and about writing pedagogy. Indeed, planning was the only reflective process that was explicitly included in that model. Since that time, consideration of the available data has convinced me that other reflective processes should be included in the model and that they are organized as follows: problem solving (including planning), decision making, and inferencing.

PROBLEM SOLVING. People engage in problem solving when they want to achieve a goal but do not know as yet what steps will achieve it. Problem solving is an activity of putting together a sequence of steps to reach a goal. In writing, problem solving constitutes a substantial part of any but the most routine composing activities. It may take the form of chaining together a sequence of phrases to form a sentence or of claims to form an argument. It may involve constructing a graph to make a point or it may involve creating a plan for an essay or a book.

In cognitive science, planning is treated as one of several problem solving methods (see Hayes, 1989). Chapter 2 (this volume) presents a theoretical treatment of planning processes in adults together with a taxonomy of these planning processes and a critical review of some of the literature on planning in writing. The most important conclusion we drew from this review was that although several studies showed strong positive correlations between the time spent planning and the quality of the texts, these correlations were confounded with time on task. When time on task was taken into account, the correlations between planning and text quality were generally nonsignificant. These observations do not suggest that planning is unimportant, but they do suggest that we placed too much emphasis on planning in the 1980 model.

Writers, especially student writers, are often required to do writing tasks for which they do not yet have a fully adequate task schema. When this occurs, writers must rely on their general problem-solving and decision-making skills to manage the writing task. It is in such cases that writers engage in process planning described by Hayes and Nash (chapter 2 in this volume).

DECISION MAKING. People engage in decision making when they evaluate alternatives to choose among them. Like problem solving, decision making is also an important component of all but the most routine writing tasks. Many writing tasks are ill-defined problems, that is, they are problems that cannot be solved unless the writer makes a number of *gap-filling* decisions (Reitman; 1964). For example, if students are asked to write an essay on a controversial topic, they will have to make decisions about what perspective to take, what sources to read, what points to emphasize, how to order those points, how to deal with conflicting views, and so on. In fact, the writers have so many gap-filling decisions to make in writing such an essay that if two students were to submit the same essay, there would be a strong presumption of plagiarism.

If gap-filling decisions are especially important for creating first drafts, evaluative decisions are especially important for revision. When revising, writers must decide whether or not the text is adequate on a variety of dimensions including diction, tone, clarity, effect on audience, and so on. For example, they must answer questions such as "Is this graph clear?", "Is this language appropriate for teenagers?", and "Is this phrase better than that one?"

Difficult writing tasks often require writers to do a substantial amount of problem solving or decision making. Document design tasks may require the designer to produce alternative designs that satisfy complex sets of spatial and linguistic constraints and then to evaluate the relative merits of the designs. As yet, though, relatively little research has been devoted to the complex problem solving and decision making processes that go on in writing.

INFERENCING. Inferencing is a process by which new information is derived from old. It may or may not be goal directed, and it may be conscious or unconscious. Inferencing is important in both reading and writing. For example, as Braddock (1992) pointed out, readers often infer the main point of a paragraph when that point is not explicitly stated in the text. Similarly, writers often make inferences about the knowledge and interests of their audiences. Clearly, inferencing is an important process that allows readers and writers to make useful extensions of available information. However, in some cases, readers may extend given information in surprising ways. For example, Stein (1992), studying a phenomenon of "elaboration," found that readers may draw inferences from reading that are both idiosyncratic and consequential.

Stein asked readers to imagine themselves as jurors, to read transcripts of a murder trial, and to make judgments as to the degree of guilt of the defendant in the trial. The case involved a fight between a victim who was stabbed to death by the defendant after the victim had threatened the defendant with a razor. In debriefing, participants revealed that their decisions had been influenced by idiosyncratic representations of the crime situation. For example, one participant, who voted for acquittal on the basis of self defense, had represented the defendant as being unable to avoid the victim because his escape routes were cut off by brick walls. In fact, the trial transcript said nothing about walls. Another participant, who voted for first-degree murder, thought that stabbing was far too strong a response to being threatened with a razor. When asked to draw the razor, she represented a small disposable safety razor, a type that might cause a nick but certainly not a fatal wound.

Notice that there appears to be a strong visual/spatial component in these representations. The fact that the first participant was making inferences about spatial locations of people and objects suggests that his representation included a mental image of the scene. Similarly, the second participant's description of the size and shape of the razor also suggests a mental image. The presence of a visual-spatial component is consistent with the reports of a number of the other participants in Stein's study. For example, one participant reported that the bar mentioned in the transcript (but not described) looked like one with which he was familiar.

If visual representations play an important role in reflecting about texts, as Stein's observations suggest, we need to be alert to the functional properties of these representations. Studies by Paivio (1971) and Bower (1972) indicate that visual and verbal inputs are represented in different ways in memory. Further, studies indicate that these differences in representation can influence the way in which people use the inputs in making inferences and in solving problems. For example, Santa (1977) showed participants a display and asked them to say whether or not it had the same elements as a display they had studied earlier. In some cases, the displays showed an array of geometrical figures and in other cases, an array of names of geometrical figures. He found that some matching problems were easier with visual/spatial input but that others were easier with verbal input indicating that the visual and verbal representations were being processed differently. In a study of physics problem solving, Larkin and Simon (1987) found that visual-spatial inputs were sometimes better than verbal inputs because the visual inputs supported powerful visual inference procedures but the verbal inputs did not. Clearly, if we are to understand how texts are understood and how they are best designed, we have to attend both their verbal and their visual features.

Although reflective processes may be carried on for extended periods without input or output, they are often interleaved with input and output processes. For example, in library research, individuals may alternate between reading paragraphs and summarizing them, and, in brainstorming, individuals may alternate between generating ideas and writing them down.

Text production

Kaufer, Hayes, and Flower (1986) conducted series of studies of competent and advanced adult writers that provided several insights into the processes involved in text generation. Protocol data revealed that writers produce text not in whole sentences but, rather, in sentence parts. Sentence parts were identified either by a pause of twp or more seconds or by a grammatical discontinuity indicating that the current language represents a revision of earlier language. On average, writers produced about three sentence parts for each sentence of the final text. The average length of these parts was 7.3 words for competent writers and 11.2 words for advanced writers. However, variability in the size of sentence parts was large. In some cases, a sentence part might consist of a single word. In other cases, the same writer might produce a sentence part that consisted of several clauses or a whole sentence.

Generally, sentences were composed from left to right with more than 90% of sentence parts being added at the leading edge of the sentence — that is, the word farthest from the beginning of the sentence that has been produced so far. Writers frequently reread the sentence produced so far, prior to adding a sentence part to an incomplete sentence. About a third of the sentence parts ended at clause boundaries, which is more than would be expected by chance. When sentence parts are produced, they are evaluated and may be rejected either for semantic or syntactic problems. When a sentence part is accepted, writers often appear to search for an appropriate meaning for the next part in the sentence. Thus, the content of the sentence may not be fully determined before the writer begins to produce syntactically complete sentence parts. Kaufer et al. also provided evidence indicating that sentence production was about equally facilitated by prior knowledge of a sentence's meaning and prior knowledge of its grammatical structure. Further, they found that these two facilitative effects, knowledge of syntax and semantics, were independent of each other.

In what follows, I propose a provisional model of text production that draws heavily on the theoretical ideas and empirical results of Kaufer et al. According to this model, text is produced as follows: Cues from the writing plan and from the text produced so far are used to retrieve a package of semantic content. This content is stored in working memory but not in the articulatory buffer. (This may correspond to what Garrett, 1976, described as the "message level" in his model of speech production.) A surface form to express this content is then constructed and stored in the articulatory buffer. Garrett's (1980) observations on "word exchange" errors (e.g., "the room to my door" for "the door to my room") suggest that the construction process may sometimes operate on more than one clause at a time (p. 193). When all of the content is expressed or when the capacity limit of the articulatory buffer is reached, the sentence part is articulated either vocally or subvocally. If all of the current content has been expressed, then the writer may show evidence of searching for new content. If the articulated sentence part is positively evaluated, then it is written down and the process is repeated. If it is rejected, a new sentence part is constructed and evaluated.

As studies of pausing during composing have indicated (Matsuhashi, 1981; Schilperoord, in press), working memory demands are especially high following clause boundaries. Thus, the limit of the articulatory buffer is more likely to be exceeded at clause boundaries than at other places. For this reason, the model predicts that sentence parts will also be somewhat more likely to end at clause boundaries than at other places. In addition, experience in writing and, more generally, experience with language should reduce the amount of memory required for constructing sentence parts from content. Therefore, writers who have more language and writing experience should write longer sentence parts than other writers.

The following hypotheses may be derived from this model:

1. Secondary tasks that involve the phonological loop, such as the continuous repetition of a syllable string, should interfere seriously with text production. In particular, such secondary tasks will reduce the rate at which text is produced, the average length of the sentence parts produced, and the cohesion of the text that is produced.

2. The length of sentence parts produced should increase as the writer's experience with the language increases. For example, writers who are learning a new language would be expected to produce short sentence parts. (Observations by Friedlander, 1987, on Chinese students writing in English provide some support for this hypothesis.)

Long-term memory

Writing simply would not be possible if writers did not have long-term memories in which to store their knowledge of vocabulary grammar, genre, topic, audience, and so on. I will discuss three topics: task schemas, knowledge of audience, and the impact of extended practice as they relate to LTM.

TASK SCHEMAS. Task schemas, such as the schema for revision already discussed, are packages of information stored in long-term memory that specify how to carry out a particular task. Typically, task schemas will include information about the goals of the task, the processes to be used in accomplishing the task, the sequencing of those processes, and criteria for evaluating the success of the task. Adults may be expected to have schemas for tasks such as reading graphs, writing business letters, reading a textbook, editing, and so on.

Task schemas are usually activated by environmental stimuli. For example, the editing schema may be triggered by a misspelled word. However, schemas may also be activated by reflection. For example, thinking about a topic may remind us that we have failed to credit the work of a colleague in a paper and thus trigger revision.

KNOWLEDGE OF AUDIENCE. When people are writing to friends or acquaintances, they can draw on a history of personal interaction to decide what to say and how to say it. However, when writers address audiences they do not know personally, they have no such experience to rely on. Writers are sometimes urged to role-play the audience, that is, to "get inside the skin" of the audience and to try to experience the message as the audience would. To do so would be quite a complex representational act. Protocols of people who are writing for an audience of strangers rarely reveal this sort of complex representation of the audience. Rather, what one sees are not very frequent occasions in which the writer considers whether or not a particular text feature is appropriate for the audience. For example, the writer may say of a teenage audience, "I wonder if this is too racy for them?" or, of a child audience "Will they know this word?" When writers show evidence of considering the audience at all, they appear to consider them in a limited and one-dimensional way.

Observations such as these, together with the traditional belief that experts have difficulty writing for novices, led Hayes, Schriver, Spilka, and Blaustein (1986) to hypothesize that writers may use themselves as their primary model for the audience. That is, for example, that they will judge a text unclear for the audience if and only if it is unclear for them.

To explore this hypothesis, Hayes et al. (1986) asked participants to read a difficult text and to underline parts of the text that would be unclear to another reader. Participants in the experimental condition were given information immediately prior to making judgments of difficulty that clarified a number of points in the text. Participants in the control condition were not given this information. The result was that compared to participants in the control condition, the experimental participants were significantly less likely to identify those points that had been clarified for them as being unclear for others. The participants, then, did appear to be using themselves as models for the imagined reader.

If writers do use themselves as models for the audience, it is easy to understand why experts have trouble writing clear instructions for novices. Writing clear instructions has been a major practical problem for the consumer electronics industry where engineers often write user manuals. Swaney, Janik, Bond, & Hayes (1991) showed that the clarity of instruction manuals could be improved significantly by providing writers with think-aloud protocols of real users trying to use the manuals. This technique, called Protocol-Aided Revision, allowed writers to supplement the knowledge that they would ordinarily use to model the audience with data reflecting the responses of audience members.

Schriver (1987) showed that exposure to user protocols can provide writers with knowledge about readers that is generalizable to new readers and new genre. Schriver constructed a sequence of 10 lessons in which readers first predicted reader difficulties with a passage from a computer manual and then read a protocol of a person trying to use the manual. Using a pre-post paradigm, she showed that students who completed these lessons were significantly better at anticipating readers' difficulties with popular science texts than were controls who received traditional training in anticipating audiences' needs.

THE IMPACT OF EXTENSIVE PRACTICE. In addition to topic knowledge and audience knowledge, writing practice provides people with other sorts of knowledge that are useful in writing. For example, with increased experience, writers may acquire more effective writing strategies, more refined standards for evaluating text, more facility with specific genre, and so on. Indeed, writing experience is widely assumed to be essential for the development of high levels of writing skill.

The literature on expert performance provides some useful insights into the relation of practice and writing skill. In a landmark study, Chase and Simon (1973) provided evidence that skill in chess depends on a very large store of knowledge of chess patterns. They estimated that a grand master chess player had at least 50,000 chess patterns stored in memory. They noted that chess players typically take 10 years or more to acquire such chess knowledge. Following this lead, Hayes (1985) conducted biographical studies to determine if famous composers also required long periods of practice before they began to produce the works for which they were famous. He examined the lives of 76 composers to determine when each had begun the serious practice of music. He then determined how long after this beginning date each of the composer's major works had been written. (A major work was defined as one for which at least five independent recordings were available.)

Hayes found that almost none of the major works were written in the first 10 years after the beginning of practice. From about 10 to 20 years after the beginning of practice, there was a rapid increase in the production of major works. From 20 years to about 45 years, productivity remained fairly stable at about one work every 3 years. Hayes then carried out a parallel study in which he examined the lives of 131 painters. In this case, the criterion of a major work was inclusion in one of a set of general histories of art. The results for the painters were quite similar to those for the composers. Wishbow (1988) conducted a parallel study of 66 English and American poets, defining a major work as one included in the *Norton Anthology of Poetry*. Her results closely paralleled those found for composers and painters.

These three studies indicate that even very talented individuals require a long period of practice before they can produce notable works of music, art, or poetry. Many years of practice may also be required to attain expert performance in any of the genres of writing.

Conclusions

The new writing framework I have presented here is intended to provide a more accurate and more comprehensive description of available observation than was provided by the Hayes-Flower (1980) model. The major changes in focus in the new framework are: greater attention to the role of working memory in writing, inclusion of the visual-spatial dimension, the integration of motivation and affect with the cognitive processes, and a reorganization of the cognitive processes which places greater emphasis on the function of text interpretation processes in writing.

In addition, the new framework includes new and more specific models of planning, text production, and revision and proposes a number of testable hypotheses about writing processes.

I hope that the new framework provides a clearer and more comprehensive description of writing processes than did the earlier model. However, it will have served its function if it stimulates new research and discussion.

Acknowledgments

The author wishes to express thanks to Karen A. Schriver for her many critical readings of this manuscript and for her extensive help in its preparation. The author is also greatly indebted to Michael Levy, Sarah Ransdell, Gert Rijlaarsdam, and Eliza Beth Littleton for many helpful comments. In addition, the author would like to recognize the stimulating discussions and collegial support provided by his many friends at the Center for Language and Communication, University of Utrecht, where much of this manuscript was written.

— 2 —
ON THE NATURE OF PLANNING
IN WRITING

John R. Hayes
Carnegie Mellon University

Jane Gradwohl Nash
Stonehill College

Researchers investigating the nature of cognition have had a long-standing interest in the process of planning and its consequences. Researchers in written composition have shared this interest but, in many cases, have used the term *planning* quite loosely. Indeed, *planning* has been used so broadly that its meaning is often little different from *thinking*. In addition, distinctions among terms such as *plan, planning,* and *goal* are not made clear.

In this chapter, we have attempted to provide a description of planning in writing that is reasonably precise and that allows us to characterize the relations among various treatments of planning in the writing literature. In our discussion, we will draw ideas about planning from the fields of cognitive psychology and computer science as well as from empirical studies of writers. We will begin with a general discussion of planning as a cognitive process important in a variety tasks. Then we will focus more specifically on planning in writing. This chapter covers the nature of plans and planning; planning methods; multiple planning environments, layering, and metaplanning; interleaving planning and action; planning in a changing environment; and matching theory to data.

The nature of plans and planning

Planning as preparation for action

The maxim, "Look before you leap," is an exhortation to plan — to think before acting. Planning is a kind of preparatory reflection. In describing planning, it is important to notice that there are two rather different sorts of reflection that people may engage in when planning. First, people may reflect on the *means* they will use to achieve their goal. For example, when planning to leap, people may be most concerned with the sequence of steps they are going to take before they launch themselves into space. Similarly, in planning a trip from one city to another, the planner may specify a sequence of roads to travel and turns to take. On the other hand, planners may be more concerned with clearly specifying the *goal* of their action. For example,

designer may sketch many alternative ideas for a poster before choosing the version to be produced. The figure represents the planning process as having explored many blind alleys (solid circles) and have produced a new, more refined specification of the goal (a more elaborate building). The open circles mark a sequence of steps that the planner believes will lead to the goal.

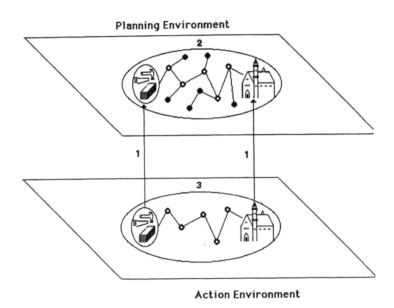

Figure 2.1. Steps in planning.

The combination of the (better specified) goal and the sequence of steps (the means) to achieve that goal is called a *plan*. The plan may be viewed as a set of suggestions for how the task should be accomplished in the action space. These suggestions may concern the goal to be accomplished (e.g., "The paper should describe the economic factors leading to the civil war.") or they may concern the actions to be taken. Suggestions for action might include reading specified sources, discussing a specified list of topics, or doing other things useful for completing the task (e.g., "Holing up" in the library).

The plan may be embodied in any of a number of media. For example, in chess, where planning is conducted in thought, the plan is stored in memory. In design, where planning makes heavy use of sketches on paper, the plan is typically a drawing. In writing, plans often consist of both internal and external components. For example, certain goal specifications may be stored in memory (e.g., "keep it simple") and others (e.g., the topic outline) may be recorded in writing, especially if they might be hard to remember. The plan, then, may be either a mental construct, a physical artifact, or a combination. Planning is a cognitive activity but the resulting plan may be either a mental artifact, a physical artifact, or a blend of the two.

PLANS AS CONTROL STRUCTURES. When planning is complete, the plan is used to help in carrying out the original task in the action environment (indicated by 3 in Figure 2.1). Miller, Galanter, and Pribram (1960) describe plans as control structures, that is, as structures that convey information to control some other process. Control may be *tight* or *loose*. An example of a very tight control structure is a computer program. The control structure is very tight in the sense that the computer performs exactly those actions specified by the program and no others. In interpreting the *control structure* metaphor, though, it is important to understand that most plans are loose rather than tight control structures. Thus, it seems more natural to say that plans guide action rather than control it.

Typically, then, the plan is not fully in control of action. Rather, plans provide suggestions for action — suggestions that may be accepted, rejected, or modified as action proceeds. Certainly, writing plans are frequently modified in the course of execution. Topics may be added, deleted, combined, or otherwise modified as the writer tries to translate the initial plan into prose. Indeed, the activity of writing sometimes suggests new ideas which lead to radical changes in the writing plan (see the section on planning in a changing environment).

Whereas plans are control structures, not all control structures are plans. If we are to accept the common sense notion that plans are the result of planning and that planning is an intentional activity, then many control structures are not plans. For example, the genetic structures that control instinctive behaviors (such as the migration of birds) are not plans because they did not result from an intentional process.

WHY PLANNING IS USEFUL. Why should people bother to plan? There are at least two very practical justifications for planning. First, planning can greatly reduce the cost of carrying out an action. By choosing an inexpensive medium for the planning environment, the planner can search for a way to carry out the task — exploring blind alleys and dead ends — in a way that is less costly than searching in the action environment. For example, an architect may explore a design problem in the planning environment by drawing sketch after sketch, testing and rejecting one possibility after another before beginning to build. Carrying out the same exploration in the action environment (i.e., constructing alternative buildings) would be very expensive of time and materials.

The savings that can be realized through planning may be temporal as well as material. For example, planning a trip with the aid of airline timetables can reduce the time travelers spend in layovers between flights. The PERT chart scheduling method (Garsch, 1985) is a planning procedure for reducing the amount of time required to complete a task.

The second way planning can be useful is by providing flexibility in the choice of problem solving strategies. Some problem solving strategies may be available in the planning environment that are not available in the action environment. For example, although one cannot take a trip backwards, one can plan it backwards. The primary advantage of planning in chess is flexibility. It is illegal to explore alternative moves on the chess board. Once a move is made, it cannot be taken back. However, players can try out as many alternative mental moves as they care to.

Planning methods

In this section, we will discuss three frequently employed planning methods: planning by abstraction, planning by analogy, and planning by modeling. We discuss methods first from a general cognitive process perspective and then focus more specifically on how these methods can be used in writing. These planning methods differ from one another in the way they represent the task in the planning environment.

Planning by abstraction

One of the most commonly discussed planning methods, planning by abstraction, might be characterized as planning in which only some aspects of the problem, usually the most important or critical aspects, are represented in the planning environment. For example, an architect planning a hotel will typically begin with very crude drawings that take into account only the most abstract properties of the structure to be built. The architect may draw circles to indicate the general positions of the major units (e.g., the registration area, dining areas, kitchen, guests rooms, recreation areas, etc.) with arrows indicating traffic flow. These drawings provide no hint either of the shape or the appearance of the structures to be built. Later in the design process, drawings become progressively more detailed and specific until the final drawings become, literally, blueprints for construction.

Perhaps the best-known application of planning by abstraction in the artificial intelligence literature is the work of Sacerdoti (1974). Sacerdoti was concerned with providing a planning procedure for a robot that had the task of moving objects from place to place in a suite of rooms. To move an object from one place to another, the robot first had to plan a path so that it could reach the object to be moved and another path from the object to the object's destination. This involved finding a path through adjacent rooms connecting the robot's initial location, the object's initial location, and the object's destination, determining if there are doorways connecting the rooms, and dealing with any closed doors and furniture that may block the way. To solve this problem by abstraction, the first step would be to simplify the task. One way to do this would be to concentrate on the problem of identifying the sequence of rooms and to forget, for the moment, about the problems of doorways, closed doors, and inconveniently placed furniture. Once this simplified problem has been solved and a promising path has been identified, the path can be used as a plan to guide the solution of the original problem.

An important feature of planning by abstraction as Sacerdoti (1974) has described it is that tasks are simplified by dropping the less critical features and retaining the more critical ones. Thus, planning by abstraction tends strongly to be *top-down* planning, that is, planning shaped primarily by the top-level goals of the task. In the case of Sacerdoti's ABSTRIPS program, planning proceeds from the most important goal to the next most important goal and on down to the least important goal.

The effectiveness of planning by abstraction comes from its ability to reduce the amount of search required to find a solution to the original problem. Top-down planning does so by applying the following commonsense heuristic: "If an alternative doesn't meet the most important criteria for success, then it probably isn't worth checking how well it does on the less important criteria." Thus, if a room is not connected to the one where the goal is, it is not worth checking to see whether or not its door is locked.

Writers often use planning by abstraction when they are generating ideas for topics to be included in their texts and when they are trying to provide an organization for those ideas. When carrying out these activities, writers usually represent potential topics by brief names that capture the most important feature of the topic. For example, a writer may want to discuss complex questions of policy relating to an issue but represent this topic simply as "policy questions." When writers create topic outlines, they rely primarily on the topic names and ignore the details associated with those topics. For example, a writer may decide to have "policy questions" follow "definition of issues" without detailed examination of either topic. The names of the topics may be thought of as pointers to packages of information in the writer's memory. A topic outline may be thought of as a list of such pointers. As Flower and Hayes (1984) pointed out, a writing plan may consist simply of a list of such topic pointers although it may include other things as well.

Because topic outlines are abstract, a major cost in writing is the effort involved in turning abstract topic designations into formal written text. If writers had to write out every idea in formal language before deciding whether or not it should be included in the final text, that would entail an enormous amount of wasted effort. Planning can reduce the total effort involved in writing by reducing the amount of written text devoted to exploring blind alleys and false starts.

Planning by analogy

In some cases, the act of representing one task reminds us of another similar task that has already been carried out. The procedure for doing the second task may then prove useful as a plan for doing the first without the need of further problem solving activity in the planning environment.

Kohler (1940) reported a very interesting study of planning by analogy, which shows it is very sensitive to factors in the task environment that may influence the planner's attention. Kohler asked people to solve an equation that involved multiplying 21 x 19. When the participants reached their conclusion, Kohler pointed out to them, apparently as an aside, that 21 x 19 is the same as $(20 + 1)(20 - 1)$ and that this in turn is the same as 400 - 1. Later in the experiment, Kohler asked the participants to solve an equation which involved multiplying 32 x 28. This product could be calculated, by analogy to the first problem, as $(30 + 2)(30 - 2)$, which equals 900 - 4. In one condition, the participants solved visual puzzles in the interval between solving these two algebra puzzles. In the second condition, the participants solved other algebra problems in the interval. Kohler found that most people in the first condition (73%) solved the problem using the analogy but that relatively few people in the second condition (26%) did so. The participants who failed to solve by analogy had not forgotten the trick they had been shown. They all remembered it when asked. They simply had not thought spontaneously to apply it.

Kohler's (1940) experiment demonstrates both that analogy can be an important planning method and that a person's tendency to make use of analogy depends critically on the immediate situation (the task environment).

Writers use planning by analogy when they base a plan for one text on the plan for another. Writers plan by analogy when they make use of genre. For example, in writing a scientific article or a business letter, the writer has a template available that specifies many of the features of the text's language and structure. Story grammars such as those of Stein and Glenn (1979) and Thorndyke (1977) are intended to describe the template for simple stories.

Planning by analogy is abstract in the sense that the analogy does not specify all aspects of the action to be taken and, indeed, may specify only a few of them. For example, in the Kohler (1940) study, it is not the specific numbers in the source problem that are important but rather their relation. In the case of writing, most genre specify only a few of the decisions the writer has to make. The difference between planning by analogy and planning by abstraction is that in planning by analogy, the plan is borrowed whereas in planning by abstraction, the plan is created afresh.

Planning by modeling

Planning by abstraction gains its power by representing the original task in simplified form in the planning environment. In contrast, planning by modeling gains its power by representing the original task inexpensively in the planning environment without necessarily reducing its complexity. For example, low speed aircraft wings are sometimes designed by examining the performance of small scale wing models in wind tunnels. This method is useful because wing design depends relatively little on scale — a good shape for a wing is good both for small wings and big ones — but cost depends critically on scale. It is much less expensive to build a small wing than a big one.

Another example of planning by modeling is the practice of using small-scale models to evaluate the appearance of an architectural project. A small-scale model of a building viewed at 5 feet can convey useful information about what the finished building will look like from 1,000 feet, but at much less cost. Proportion depends relatively little on scale but, again, cost depends critically on scale. Planning by modeling is common in games such as chess and bridge. When chess players plan moves mentally, they try to represent everything that bears on the success of that move in the real game. To leave out a piece or fail to consider a possible reply could be disastrous.

Writers use planning by modeling very frequently in the process of composing sentences. Characteristically, writers will compose sentences mentally before they write them down (Kaufer, Hayes, & Flower, 1986). The language that is composed mentally is not simpler or less complete than the language that is written down. But it is composed in a medium that requires less effort than visible writing.

DIFFERENCES BETWEEN THIS VIEW OF PLANNING AND THAT OF NEWELL AND SIMON. Although we have generally adhered to Newell and Simon's (1972) cognitive architecture, our characterization of planning differs somewhat from theirs. For Newell and Simon, the first step in planning is "... abstracting by omitting certain details of the original objects and operators..." (p. 429). Thus, planning for Newell and Simon is what we have called *planning by abstraction*. We have chosen not to require abstracting as a criterion for planning for two reasons. We wanted to provide a slightly more general characterization of planning to include cases such as the sentence generation and chess examples above for which abstraction does not seem to be the most important aspect of the planning process. More important, though, we wanted to emphasize that abstraction is just one of several ways in which planning may increase economy and flexibility in carrying out tasks.

Multiple planning environments, layering, and metaplanning

By the definition of planning that we have adopted, when planning occurs, there must be at least two distinct task environments or spaces: one for planning and one for action. However, there is no reason to limit planning to a single environment. In fact, a number of artificial intelligence programs make effective use of multiple planning environments. MOLGEN (Stefik, 1981a, 1981b) and MACHINIST (C. Hayes, 1987) each have two planning environments, and ABSTRIPS (Sacerdoti, 1974) allows for an unlimited number of planning environments.

MOLGEN, a program for designing genetics experiments, has three layers. The lowest layer is the action or laboratory environment. The methods available in this environment are actions to be taken by a laboratory technician, such as killing the unwanted bacteria in a culture. The next layer above, the design environment, is the first planning environment. The methods available in this environment are actions to be taken by an experiment designer such as testing a prediction or searching for an unusual genetic feature. The top layer is the strategy environment. The methods available in this environment concern the choice of general problem-solving strategies, such as whether to wait for more information or make an informed guess. The strategy environment contains no knowledge of genetics, only knowledge of general problem-solving strategies. The environments in MOLGEN are layered in the sense that each layer has a major impact on what the layer below it does. Thus, the strategy layer provides a plan for how the design layer will construct a plan. Stefik (1981a) called this planning to plan "metaplanning."

ABSTRIPS (Sacerdoti, 1974) was designed to plan paths for a robot moving objects around in a suite of rooms. The program allows for planning in an unspecified number of planning environments arranged in a hierarchy of levels of abstraction. The top layers are the most abstract and take into account only a few features judged to be the most important ones, (e.g., whether two rooms are adjacent to each other). Lower levels are less abstract in the sense that, in addition to the features considered by the higher levels, they also consider less important features such as whether doors between rooms are open or closed.

Multiple planning environments need not be layered. For example, MA-CHINIST (C. Hayes, 1987) has two planning environments that are not layered with respect to each other. MACHINIST creates plans for machining blocks of metal in much the same way human machinists do. One of MA-CHINIST's planning environments is concerned with squaring, that is, with choosing three sides of the block to smooth. The other environment is concerned with choosing the order in which cuts should be made in the block. Plans are made independently in these two environments (they can be made in either order) and then combined into a final plan for machining the block. We call planning environments such as those used in MACHINIST *parallel* rather than layered.

Scardamalia, Bereiter, and Steinbach (1984) proposed parallel planning environments for written composition. They describe them as follows:

> We may conceive of composition planning as taking place in two types of problem spaces. One type, the content space, is made up of knowledge states that may be broadly character-ized as beliefs. It is the kind of space in which one works out opinions, makes moral decisions, generates inferences about matters of fact, formulates causal explanations, and so on. Content spaces thus have wide use in daily life and are by no means limited to composition planning. The other type of problem space, the rhetorical space, is specifically tied to text production. The knowledge states to be found in this kind of space are mental representations of actual or intended text — representations that may be at various levels of abstraction from verbatim representations to representations of main ideas and global intentions...the goal states in the rhetorical space are plans [sic] for achieving various purposes in com-position. (pp. 175-176)

According to Scardamalia, Bereiter, and Steinbach (1984), these two spaces interact with each other through processes which take information in each space and create related goals in the other space. For example, the be-lief (in the content space) that one had been overcharged might lead to the rhetorical goal of convincing a merchant to make restitution. This rhetorical goal, in turn, might lead the writer to search in the content space for factual evidence to support an argument to the merchant.

Scardamalia et al. (1984) used this model of parallel but interacting planning environments to account for expert-novice differences in composition. They suggested that for both expert and novice writers, there are connections from the content space to the rhetorical space but in novices, the connections in the other direction are missing. That is, the two planning environments are parallel for experts but layered for novices. They claim that, as a consequence, novice writers tend to present ideas in the order they were thought of rather than in an order adapted to the audiences needs. Further, when they revise, they make only cosmetic changes that can be made entirely in the rhetorical space.

We find this model a very interesting one. However, we have some reservations about the adequacy of the model to account for the expert-novice differences referred to earlier. First, much reorganization that is observed in expert writing could result from operations that happen in the content space. For example, much of the reorganization of ideas occurring in the protocol quoted in Hayes and Flower (1980) can be attributed to the writer's attempt to create hierarchical structure rather than the result of audience considerations. Second, we would expect that at least some reorganization of topic order could occur within the rhetorical space. Changing the order of topics to suit the audience need not always involve rethinking of the topical content. Third, some of the differences between expert and novice writing may well result from differences between these groups in their ability to consider the audience when writing. That is, experts and novices may differ not only in the connections between spaces but in the nature of the spaces themselves. These three considerations lead us to wonder how much of the observed expert-novice differences are likely to be accounted for by the proposed dual planning space model.

Interleaving plans and action

In some tasks, such as arranging a wedding or a conference, planning must be substantially complete before the action starts. One does not do a bit of planning, then a bit of wedding, then a bit more planning, and so on. In other tasks such as writing and computer programming, though, planning and action are often interleaved. Lansman, Smith, and Weber (1990) examined the interleaving of planning and action in 18 adult writers whose task was to compose expository essays using a computer based writing system. To measure the extent of interleaving, Lansman et al. computed the proportion of planning time that preceded each minute of writing and averaged that proportion over all minutes of writing for each writer. If writers did all of their planning before doing any writing, then this index would have been 1.0. However, if the writer did a little planning, then a little writing, and so on (that is, if planning and writing were thoroughly interleaved) the index could approach .5. Among their 18 writers, Lansman et al. observed indices ranging from .98 to .58 with an average of .78. Although there were large individual differences (the writers exhibited degrees of interleaving that spanned almost the entire range of possibility), most writers engaged in a substantial amount of interleaving.

There are at least two major reasons that would lead a planner to interleave planning and action. First, the planner might want to get information about how the plan is working out so far. Many planned actions have uncertain consequences. When several such actions are chained together, the uncertainty is multiplied. Checking frequently to see what the consequences of the plan have been is a very effective way to keep planning on track.

Another major reason to interleave plan and action is to overcome memory limitations. When the planning is done internally, say in visual or auditory imagery, the planner will have difficulty remembering long plans. Thus, memory limitations can force the interleaving of plan and action. Composing sentences provides a familiar example. Many have had the experience of losing a brilliantly conceived sentence because it could not be written down quickly enough. The usual planning environment for composing sentences is auditory imagery. Kaufer et al. (1986) found that writers typically plan no more than 6 to 10 words before writing them down.

Planning in a changing environment

Changes caused by the activity of planning

In many cases, the activity of planning changes its own environment and can, therefore, influence the way in which planning proceeds. For example, the act of planning may bring items of information to the planners' attention that they may not have previously thought about at the same time. This can lead the planner to discover relations or contradictions among ideas that have importance for planning. Hayes (1990) described a writer who, during planning, discovered a contradiction in her beliefs about the topic she was writing about. Resolving that contradiction became the central issue in a subsequent composing episode.

Planners may also formulate information during planning in a way that facilitates the later stages of planning. Working in a planning environment of pencil and paper, designers often draw sketches of alternative design ideas and later use those sketches to decide which of the ideas is best. Ballay et al. (1984) described an example of an industrial designer who makes four sketches of alternative designs for later consideration.

Planners may make decisions during planning that constrain the later stages of planning. The part of the plan that has been developed early often has an important influence on subsequent planning. For example, suppose a client has asked an architect to design a modern office building that fits on a specified lot and provides a specified amount of office space for a particular business. This is clearly an ill-defined task because, to create such a design, the architect has to make a very large number of decisions such as specifying the organization of the space and the placement of stairs and elevators, as well as the treatment of the windows and the style of the lobby. The later stages of planning in tasks such as these is very likely to be influenced by decisions the architect has made earlier in planning. Thus, early decisions about the placement of elevators is likely to influence later decisions about the organization of office space.

In some cases, planning may lead to plan evaluation before any attempt has been made to execute the plan. As Hayes, Flower, Schriver, Stratman, and Carey (1987) pointed out, a writer may create a plan for a text and then evaluate and reject it before any attempt has been made to execute it. For example, Kaufer, Hayes, and Flower (1986) observed a writer who proposed early in planning to present a sequence of examples and then, long before either plan or text had been written down, changed the plan on the grounds that what he had proposed to say would be boring. Thus, the results of planning can directly influence the course of planning because plans can be evaluated before they are translated into action.

Ballay et al. (1984) described a designer who discovered while evaluating a crude model of a proposed design that the design discriminated against left-handed people. By evaluating the plan, the designer was alerted to the issue of handedness, which then became an important criteria by which to judge later designs.

These examples show not only that planning can influence itself but also that it is an activity that can change the way the planner thinks about an issue. It can lead to the reorganization of topic information, to the discovery of relations and contradictions among the writer's ideas, and to the modification of standards for quality that the planner applies to the current task and to later tasks. In these respects, planning is similar to other reflective activities such as critiquing and revising. All of these activities can lead to discovery and increased understanding.

Changes caused by interleaving plan and action

The planner's reason for interleaving planning and action may be to relieve strains on memory or to get information about how the plan is working, but the act of interleaving may have other effects as well. Actions taken during interleaving may reveal relevant but unanticipated information or it may actually change the world in ways that are important for planning. We will discuss these effects in greater detail in the sections below.

WHEN TASK EXECUTION CHANGES THE TASK ENVIRONMENT. Writing, industrial design, and computer programming are examples of tasks producing outputs that become an important part of the task environment. For example, in planning what to write next, writers frequently consult the text they have just written for ideas about how to proceed. Kaufer, Hayes, and Flower (1986) showed that in composing sentences, writers frequently reread the beginning of an incomplete sentence in order to get a "running start" in composing the next segment. Writers appear to use the text written so far to remind them of the constraints imposed by what has already been written. Thus, the writer's prior output becomes an important part of the task environment and influences planning of the next text segment.

We will call tasks such as these *construction tasks*. Specifically, construction tasks are tasks that produce their output gradually with considerable interleaving of plan and action, and the output influences subsequent planning.

As writers, designers, and programmers produce new output as they work on a task, they are continually changing the task environment. These changes stimulate new ideas and, as a result, invention may be stimulated continuously throughout the course of these tasks. Indeed, it has been observed both in writing (Hayes et al., 1987) and design tasks (Ballay et al., 1984) that invention occurs continually in these tasks right up to the moment when the final drawing or final draft is complete. Many creative tasks such as writing, painting, and designing scientific studies are construction tasks.

WHEN TASK EXECUTION REVEALS UNANTICIPATED INFORMATION. In many cases, the act of carrying out a task leads us to notice new task-relevant information. For example, while we are revising an article, the reading we do in the course of fixing óne problem may reveal other problems that also need to be fixed. Similarly, as Hayes-Roth and Hayes-Roth (1979) observed, if individuals are doing a series of errands, they may discover in the course of doing one errand that others can be accomplished at the same time. Such unanticipated information could influence planning by leading planners to modify their representations of the available resources or of the goal specification.

Hayes-Roth and Hayes-Roth (1979) claimed that behavior of the sort described earlier illustrates a distinct planning method that they have called *opportunistic planning*. Opportunistic planning, in their view, differs from other planning methods because it is "bottom up," by which they mean that it is, at least in part, event driven. They contrasted opportunistic planning to planning by abstraction, which they characterized as "top down," that is, driven most strongly by the "top level" or most important goals. The reader should note that top-down planning is not logically opposite to bottom-up planning as Hayes-Roth and Hayes-Roth defined that term. The opposite of top-down planning would be planning driven by the least rather than the most important goals. There is no reason to believe that events need be relevant only to the least important goals.

The events that drive opportunistic planning are events such as we discussed earlier — changes due to planning or to the interleaving of planning and action. We feel that it is unnecessary and potentially confusing to postulate a distinct planning method, as Hayes-Roth and Hayes-Roth (1979) did, to describe planning in a changing environment. It is more parsimonious to characterize such behavior as reflecting the impact of new information from a changing environment on familiar planning methods for the following reasons:

1. Human activities are quite generally influenced by new information. Not only is planning influenced by unanticipated events but so are numerous forms of problem solving, so is reading, so is talking, so is singing, and so on. It seems more parsimonious to recognize that human activities are very generally responsive to the environment than it is to define new methods such as opportunistic planning, opportunistic reading, opportunistic singing, and so forth.

2. It seems that what Hayes-Roth and Hayes-Roth described as unique about opportunistic planning is opportunistic but it is not planning. Suppose that we meet a friend on the street who is just returning from a shopping trip

on which she purchased a purse and a pair of shoes. She tells us that she had set out to buy the purse but that she had "just run across" the shoes. It seems unreasonable to say that our friend had been opportunistically planning to buy the shoes because her behavior in buying the shoes shows none of the features that characterize planning. There was no looking ahead. There was no prior thought about what kind of shoes to buy or where to look for them. The purchase was certainly opportunistic, but there seems to be no more reason to call it planning than to say that a person who tripped while going down stairs opportunistically planned to break a leg.

Matching theory to data

Types of planning for writing

In analyzing planning in writing, many researchers distinguish among categories of planning. Although these distinctions are potentially very useful, they contribute to the current confusion in planning research because researchers do not agree about what the categories should be or how they should be named. In this section, we propose a set of planning categories that is based both on the literature and on our theoretical analysis of planning. We then use our category system as a template to describe the relations among the planning categories used by various researchers. Later, we use this template to compare results across studies.

A TAXONOMY OF PLANNING. First, we distinguish process planning from text planning. Process planning is focused on the writer and how the writer intends to carry out the writing task (e.g., "I'm going to write this tomorrow," or "First, I'll read the text through, then, I'll edit it."). In contrast, text planning is focused on what is being written — its content, its form, its impact on the audience (e.g., "I'll tell them about my job", "Let's organize this as pros and cons", and "I'll make them [the audience] think I'm one of them."). The hallmark of a text planning statement is that it says something about what the planned text will be like.

Within text planning, it is very important to distinguish between abstract text planning and language planning. Abstract text planning employs the method of analogy or abstraction. In conceptual planning, the writer proposes ideas for the text without specifying the particular language to be used (e.g., "Talk about the difficulty of choosing courses," "Tell them about the problems associated with age," "Do it like an interview," or "Make it friendly"). Language planning employs the method of modeling and produces grammatical text. Typically, writers will plan a string of words, often a clause or two, in thought or in speech, and then write them down verbatim. Data from Hayes and Flower (1980) and Kaufer, Hayes, and Flower (1986) suggest that abstract text planning leads to the production of ideas, notes, and outlines that need to be expanded greatly to produce a finished text. In contrast, language planning leads directly to text.

The connection between language planning and text production often appears to be so close that one might question whether or not a valid distinction can be made between them. However, there is at least one kind of writing that appears to involve text production without language planning. Specifically, free writing (Elbow, 1973) appears to results in text without the prior representation of language in thought or speech. If true, one would expect that free writing would not suffer from articulatory interference (see chapter 1).

Flower and Hayes (1980) distinguished two kinds of abstract planning: planning to do and planning to say. They defined *planning to do* as planning that addresses the writer's rhetorical problem of shaping the text to meet the needs of the writer, the reader, and a purpose. In contrast, they defined *planning to say* as planning that creates an abstract or simplified version of the information to be conveyed. Carey et al. (1989) used essentially the same categories but have renamed them *rhetorical planning* and *content planning*. Within rhetorical planning, they included planning for structure, genre, audience, focus, tone, style, ethos, and so on. Burtis, Bereiter, Scardamalia, and Tetroe (1983) identified a very closely related category they called conceptual planning, which they defined as planning dealing with "goals, strategies, organization, and the like" (p. 163).

The real distinction between these categories is not that one is rhetorical and the other is not. Choice of content can be just as rhetorical as choice of organization. Nor is one category more conceptual than the other. In both cases, the planner is dealing in abstractions. Therefore, we have chosen to label these categories *non-content planning* and *content planning*, which reflect what judges actually attend to when they make the distinction, namely, the presence or absence of content. We have tried to identify a more descriptive label for noncontent planning but have concluded that as it is used by Burtis et al. (1983) and by Carey et al. (1989), it really is a residual category.

The top part of Figure 2.2 shows the relation of the planning categories we propose to distinguish. The bottom part of the figure shows the relations among planning categories as they are described by various researchers. We tried to be conservative in interpreting the articles cited in Figure 2.2. For example, we left columns blank for some articles because the corresponding planning categories were not discussed in these articles. On the other hand, in interpreting Hayes and Flower (1980), we have included language planning in the translation process because these authors specifically identify a planning process distinct from abstract text planning within the translation process (see Hayes & Flower, 1980, Figure 1.8). Similarly, the category "content generation," which Burtis et al. (1983) define as the planning of "material intended for actual use in the text" (p. 163), clearly includes both content planning and language planning.

Planning measures

Most studies of planning have made use of one or more of four kinds of data: think-aloud protocols (Bereiter & Scardamalia, 1987; Hayes & Flower, 1980), pause duration (Gould, 1980; Matsuhashi, 1981), planning notes (Nelson, 1988; Spivey & King, 1987), and retrospective reports (Burtis et al., 1983; Schumacher et al., 1984). The method most generally useful for the study of planning is the *think-aloud protocol*. With this method, participants are asked to say whatever comes into their minds as they perform a task.

Think aloud protocols provide more detailed data about planning processes than any of the other methods. However, there are several problems with the method that make it desirable, where possible, to use it in conjunction with other methods. First, protocols can be reactive. That is, the act of speaking aloud may have some impact on the writing process. For example, a recent study by Stratman and Hamp-Lyons (in press) indicates that the activity of thinking aloud may interfere with editing. Second, like other methods, protocols are incomplete. People cannot articulate everything that crosses their minds. Conjoining protocols with other methods can help to fill in the blanks.

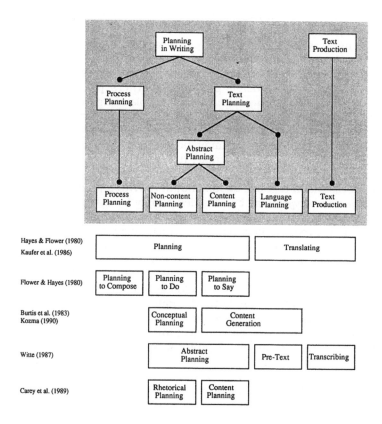

Figure 2.2. The taxonomy of planning types proposed in this article compared to the taxonomies of various authors.

Assumptions underlying the analysis of *pause durations* are that pauses reflect planning and that longer pauses indicate more planning (Gould, 1980; Matsuhashi, 1981). To measure pause duration, the researcher observes or videotapes the writer at work and measures pauses in writing activity throughout the task. Pausal data collected in this way can be used to test hypotheses about where planning is most likely to occur in the writing process. For example, the researcher might be interested in knowing if pauses tend to occur at clause boundaries. An advantage of pausal data is that it is relatively nonreactive. Writers may be bothered by the presence of the researcher, but, at least, they do not have to talk continuously while writing. The major disadvantage of pausal data is that writers who are pausing are not necessarily planning. As writers, we know that pauses are often occupied by daydreaming or other distractions from the task at hand. The occurrence of a pause, then, is rather indirect evidence that planning has occurred. A second disadvantage of pausal data is that even when pauses do correspond to planning, the pause provides few clues about what is being planned or what kind of planning is involved.

The writer's written notes and outlines provide external evidence of planning processes. Researchers — including Spivey (1984), Spivey and King (1987), and Nelson (1988) — have found that judges can very reliably assess the extensiveness of these visible products of writers' planning. However, as think-aloud protocol evidence attests, not all planning activity results in a written product. External *planning notes*, then, provide very credible evidence for some planning activities but may fail to provide evidence of some others. Of more concern, this measure may be more sensitive to some kinds of planning than to others. In particular, it may be more sensitive to abstract text planning such as organizing and brainstorming than to language planning, which results in text but usually not in a written plan.

Retrospective reports may be obtained simply by asking participants who have just performed a task to comment on their performance. However, participants' uncued recollections tend to be incomplete and are subject to distortion. It is generally more effective to provide the participant with cues to support their recall of the performance. For example, Schumacher et al. (1984) obtained good results by having participants report while they view videotapes of themselves in the act of writing. Retrospective reports can serve as a very valuable supplement to think aloud protocols by providing the researcher with an opportunity to probe for information not mentioned in the protocol. For example, a writer may reject information from a source text but not say why during a think-aloud protocol. A retrospective report might reveal that the writer thought the author of the source text was not credible (e.g., "He sounds like a health food nut.").

Which method is most appropriate will depend on the goals of the study and the circumstances under which it is conducted. Often, it is useful to use more than one method so that results can be compared.

Interpreting empirical writing studies

It is important to be clear about the definitions of key terms, but it is also important, and perhaps even more important, to be clear about what inferences can validly be drawn from research studies. In this section, we will focus on both correlational and experimental studies of abstract planning in writing. (Most studies of planning in writing are studies of abstract planning.) In correlational studies, researchers describe naturally occurring relationships without attempting to manipulate them. An example would be a study in which researchers observed how much time students spent planning an essay without attempting to influence that time, and related the planning time to the quality of the resulting essay. In experimental studies, in contrast, the researchers make changes in order to observe the effects of those changes. An example would be a study in which researchers encourage one group of students to spend extra time planning while encouraging another group to plan as they ordinarily do, and compare the quality of essays written by the two groups. Both correlational and experimental studies pose problems of interpretation. We will illustrate some of these problems by discussing studies of both kinds that address an empirical issue of considerable significance for pedagogy, the relation of planning to text quality.

Correlational studies

The central problem in interpreting correlational studies is keeping in mind that correlation does not imply causation. If A and B are correlated, there may or may not be a causal relation between A and B. The correlation might be caused by any of a multitude of third factors called *confounding variables*. For example, shoe size happens to be correlated with writing ability. This surprising correlation comes about not because shoe size causes writing ability but because both are related to a third factor, age. Very young children, who tend not to write well, also have very small feet.

Carey et al. (1989) carried out a study of 12 writers in which the researchers related the quantity and kind of planning events revealed in verbal protocols prior to writing with the quality of the final product. They found that the quality of the final text was strongly correlated with the quantity (r = .655) and quality (r = .874) of their initial planning. The authors, as they should have been, were quite cautious in interpreting these results. The correlations could have come about because high quantity and high quality of planning cause high text quality. Such an interpretation might suggest a writing pedagogy focusing on the teaching of planning. However, this interpretation is not required by the data because there are a number of other plausible interpretations. Later, we will discuss confounding variables that might account for such correlations, but will mention one here that is particularly salient in protocol studies: verbal ability. The correlations could have come about because fluent writers may also be fluent speakers. That is, people who are good at writing about their jobs (that was the task in the Carey et al. study) may also be good at talking about their planning in think-aloud protocols.

That verbal ability might be an important factor influencing correlations between measures of planning and measures of text quality is suggested by some intriguing observations of Ruth Lebovitz at the University of Illinois at Chicago. Lebovitz (personal communication) asked one group (n = 50) to plan to write on Topic A and a second group (n = 55) to write on Topic B. After 20 minutes of planning, roughly half of each group was asked to write on Topic A and the other half on Topic B. Thus, there were four groups of participants in the study: those who planned to write on Topic A and wrote on Topic A, those who planned to write on Topic A and wrote on Topic B, those who planned to write on Topic B and wrote on Topic A, and those who planned to write on Topic B and wrote on Topic B. Lebovitz found a significant correlation ($r = .23$, $p < .05$) between quality of plan and quality of essay over all four groups. The most surprising aspect of the study was that the correlations were just as high (actually, they were somewhat higher) when the writers planned and wrote on different topics as when they planned and wrote on the same topic. Thus, in the Lebovitz study at least, all of the correlation between plan quality and essay quality could be accounted for by a confounding variable such as verbal ability.

In a study of 60 6th through 10th grade students writing from sources, Spivey and King (1987) found that the quality of the text was significantly correlated with the quality of the writers' written plans ($r = .39$). Spivey and King clearly recognized that the relation between planning and writing quality might be other than causal. They suggested that the differences between more and less successful participants might "...be due to differences in effort expended on the task as well as to cognitive factors..." and noted that the more successful participants "...were making more elaborate plans and were spending more time" (p. 22). This observation points out a problem that often arises when researchers focus on the impact of just one of several processes that might influence task performance. Variables that change overall task performance such as motivation or fatigue could lead to parallel changes in each of the subprocesses involved in the task. Thus, more motivated students may spend more time on library research, on planning, on crafting sentences, and on revision than less motivated students. We would expect to find positive correlations between each of these processes and text quality. Looking only at the positive correlation between planning and text quality and not at the similar positive correlations for other processes, we might lead us to think that there was something special about planning. Worse, we might be inclined to advise students to emphasize planning in their writing when it would be better to advise them to do more of everything, that is, to work harder.

In both the Carey et al. (1989) study and the Spivey and King (1987) study, the relation between planning and text quality is confounded with a third factor — verbal ability in the first case and time-on-task in the second. Confounding is a problem because it complicates the interpretation of observed relation. For example, in the Spivey and King (1987) study, increasing time-on-task might plausibly improve text quality. If planning is positively related to time-on-task, then a positive relation between planning and text quality might just be a "tag along" effect. How, then, can we disentangle the relation between planning and text quality from the effects of time-on-task? One way would be to hold time-on-task constant. That is, we could observe the relation between planning and text quality in a group of writers, all of whom spent the same amount of time-on-task. Unfortunately, studies of this sort are often hard to arrange and, in addition, imposing time constraints may distort the writing process. A more practical approach is to use the technique of partial correlation. Partial correlation allows us to use the correlations among three factors that are changing together to estimate what the correlation between any two of them would be if the third were held constant.

In particular, we can use the three pairwise correlations among text quality, planning, and time-on-task to estimate what the correlation between text quality and planning would be if time-on-task were held constant.

Spivey and King (1987) reported the correlations between time-on-task and text quality (r = .50) and between time-on-task and planning (r = .36) as well as the correlation between planning and text quality. Given this information, we have calculated that the partial correlation between text quality and planning with time held constant in the Spivey and King data is .26. Because this value is not statistically significant, we cannot conclude with confidence that the quantity of planning is associated with text quality. Thus, the significant correlation between planning and text quality reported earlier (r = .39) appears to be due at least in part to the association between planning and time-on-task.

In an earlier study of 40 adult writers writing from sources, Spivey (1984) found a small non-significant correlation (r = .11) between the extensiveness of written plans and the quality of the text. The partial correlation with time on task held constant was r = -.05. Here again, there is no strong evidence of a positive relation between quantity of planning and text quality.

In another interesting study of writing from sources, Nelson (1988) measured holistic essay quality, time on task, and three indices of written planning. The indices were notes-extensiveness, a measure of the quantity of the writer's notes; notes-processing, a measure of the extent to which the writer reinterprets source materials when making notes; and plans-elaborateness, a measure of written plans very similar to that used by Spivey (1984) and Spivey and King (1987). Nelson found that the holistic quality of the text correlated .46 with notes-extensiveness, .54 with notes-processing, .59 with plans-elaborateness, and .69 with time-on-task. These correlations were significant at the .05, .01, .005, and .0005 levels, respectively. However, Nelson found that the partial correlations between holistic quality and the planning indices with time-on-task held constant were -.24, -.06, and .16 respectively, none of them statistically significant.

The conclusion to be drawn from these examples is that the strong relation between writing quality and planning that may be observed in correlational studies should be interpreted with caution. First, a strong correlation between text quality and planning may be illusory. Confounding variables, such as time-on-task, can create the appearance of a special relation when none exists. When confounding variables are suspected, the technique of partial correlation may allow us to account for their effects. Second, correlations do not imply causation. If people who write well plan a lot, that does not imply that teaching people to plan a lot will help them to write well. As noted previously, shoe size happens to be correlated with writing ability. This does not imply that a writing pedagogy based on foot exercises would be effective.

In addition to studying the impact of the total amount of planning on text quality, the Carey et al. (1989) study also explored the relation between types of planning and text quality. After observing that text quality was strongly correlated both with the total number of initial planning statements (r = .655) and with the number of content planning statements (r = .654), these authors examined the balance between content and rhetorical planning in the total.[2] They found that as the quality of the text increased, the proportion of content plans in the total decreased. The correlation between text quality and percentage of content plans was -.366. This led the authors to suggest, cautiously, that content plans are not as effective for producing high quality texts as are rhetorical plans:

> Our results, while by no means conclusive, suggest that less successful writers' emphasis on "content planning" (as opposed to rhetorical planning) result in texts which are less well adapted to the audience and which do not manifest a clear rhetorical purpose or organizational structure — that is, texts weaker on rhetorical as opposed to content features. (p. 17)

These are not unreasonable suggestions but they don't follow from the observations. Carey et al. (1989) showed that the poorer writers did little content planning and even less rhetorical planning. In contrast, the better writers did both more content planning and more rhetorical planning. On the basis of data on 12 writers reported in Carey et al. (1989), we compared the numbers of planning statements produced by the six poorer and the six better writers. On average, the six poorer writers produced 7.8 content plans and 3.8 rhetorical plans (67% of all plans were content plans). In contrast, the better writers produced 26.5 content plans and 18.7 rhetorical plans (59% of all plans were content plans). On the basis of these observations, one cannot tell if the differences between the groups depend more on content plans or rhetorical plans. The partial correlation between text quality and the amount of rhetorical planning with total planning held constant is -.09. The corresponding partial correlation for content planning is .12. It would appear, then, that the Carey et al. data does not support a conclusion that content planning is less effective for promoting text quality than rhetorical planning.

EXPERIMENTAL STUDIES. Unlike correlational studies, experimental studies can provide the sort of evidence about causal relations that is important for theory and essential for the design of pedagogy. Scardamalia and Bereiter (1985) studied the effects that facilitating advance planning had on the quality of essays written by 6th grade students. All of the students were asked to plan before beginning to write but they were to take no written notes as they did so. They were also asked to think aloud as they planned. Planning was facilitated for the 18 experimental writers by presenting them with planning cues in the form of cards with sentence openers such as "My next point..." and "An even better idea is..." In one version of the procedure, the experimenter listened as the student planned aloud and, at opportune times, presented the student with a card selected with a view to raising the level of the students' reflective thinking. In other versions, the cards were presented either by the writers themselves or by a peer. The 20 control subjects did not receive planning cues.

---

[2] Carey et al.'s rhetorical planning corresponds to what we have called *noncontent planning*.

The essays of the experimental group were found to show significantly more "reflective thought" than those in the control group. Thus, the researchers' effort to facilitate planning had some impact on the character of the students' writing. However, there was almost no difference in text quality between the experimental and the control group.

Schriver (1988) studied the effect of a planning procedure she called *goals elaboration* on writing quality. Forty undergraduate professional writing students were randomly assigned to the experimental or the control condition. Both groups were asked to read a five-page research summary and then to write a plan and compose a one-page handout based on the plan. The purpose of the handout was to advise freshmen about the use of computers for composing papers. Students in the control group were instructed to plan as they ordinarily did. Students in the experimental group were asked to set goals in each of the following categories: audience, client, self, text structure, and language. The goals elaboration procedure was intended to encourage that aspect of planning here called *further specification of the goal*.

Schriver classified the writers' plans as either *goal setting* or as *content generation*.[3] As Table 2.1 shows, the experimental group produced more than three times as many goal setting plans as the control group. However, the control group produced nearly four times as many content plans as the experimental group. Overall, though, the groups did not differ significantly in the total amount of planning they did. Schriver's instructions, then, clearly had an effect on the way writers planned but not on the amount they planned. When the 40 handouts were holistically evaluated for features such as audience adaptation and use of provided information, no differences between experimental and control group were found.

Table 2.1
Numbers of plans in Schriver's study

	Goal setting	Content generation	Total
Experimental	18.4	5.3	23.7
Control	5.7	20.5	26.2

Kozma (1991) studied the impact of both computer based planning tools and planning prompts on the process and product of college student's writing. The participants were 21 students in introductory composition courses and 20 students in advanced writing courses. All of the students composed using a computer. There were three software conditions. In the first condition, writers were provided just with the software package that all writers used. In the second condition, writers were provided, in addition, with an online outliner that allowed them to arrange the sequence and subordination of ideas. In the third condition, writers were provided with the software package together with an online organizer, a graphic display that allowed them to

---

[3] These categories correspond closely to what we have called, respectively, *noncontent planning* and *content planning*.

construct relations among ideas and to arrange them spatially in tree and node-and-link structures. In addition, these writers were assigned either to a *prompt* or to a *no-prompt* condition. In the prompt condition, writers received reminders to plan in categories such as topic, audience, and goal.

Kozma measured writing processes by collecting think aloud protocols and classifying the planning events, following Burtis et al. (1983), as either *conceptual planning* or *content generation.*[4] He found that the planning tools and the planning prompts both significantly increased the proportion of conceptual planning that the writers did. However, these changes in the proportion of conceptual planning did not result in improved compositions. The correlation between the proportion of time spent on conceptual planning and quality rating was -.06. Further, neither the writing tools nor the writing prompt had significant main effects on writing quality.

Kellogg (1988) conducted experiments measuring the impact on writing process and text quality of two techniques widely recommended for promoting planning: preparing an outline and writing a rough draft. In the first experiment, 36 college students were asked to prepare a written outline prior to writing and another 36 were not. In addition, half of each of these groups was asked to prepare a rough draft before producing their polished draft and the other half was not asked to produce a rough draft.

Kellogg employed an interesting technique for assessing writing processes. He interrupted writers at frequent but unpredictable intervals and asked them to report whether, at that moment, they were planning, translating, reviewing, or doing something else. With this technique, he was able to establish that the draft condition had only a minor effect on the writers' process (a small reduction in reviewing) and that the outline condition had a major effect (an increase in translating). Kellogg found that outlining significantly improved text quality but that the draft condition had no effect on text quality.[5]

In his second experiment, Kellogg attempted to determine whether or not the effect of outlining depended on writing the plan down. He asked one group of 20 college writers to prepare written outlines; another group of 20 was asked to prepare mental outlines. A third group of 20 served as controls. Kellogg found that preparing written and mental outlines had very similar effects on writing processes. Both resulted in increases in translating. Further, preparing written and mental outlines had similar effects on text quality. Both conditions resulted in essays of significantly better quality than the no-outline condition but not significantly different from each other.

In both of these studies, note that requiring students to outline increased time-on-task both directly and indirectly. As Table 2.2 shows, students in the

---

[4] Conceptual planning corresponds to what we have called noncontent planning and content generation to a combination of what we have called content and language planning.

[5] In another study, Kellogg (1990) also found that an opportunity to outline prior to writing improved text quality but that a similar opportunity to use a graphic clustering procedure did not.

outlining condition not only devoted extra time to outlining, they also wrote longer than students in the control condition. As a result, total time-on-task was very much larger in the outlining conditions than in the control conditions. Further, the extra time was by no means all planning time. Kellogg's process data suggests that students required to do initial outlining devoted a much smaller proportion of their time to planning during writing than did the control subjects. In consequence, the proportions of total task time devoted to planning were about the same in control and outline conditions.

Table 2.2
Writing and outlining times in Kellogg's studies

	Outlining time	Writing time	% of writing spent in planning	Total time	% total time spent in planning
Study 1					
Control	0	21.0	40	21.0	40
Outline	8.6	28.2	26	36.8	43
Study 2					
Control	0	26.5	34	26.5	34
Outline	7.5	29.9	23	37.4	38

Planning, time-on-task, and writing quality

Our analysis of these studies indicates that text quality is strongly and positively related to time-on-task (Kellogg, 1988; Nelson, 1988; Spivey, 1992; Spivey & King, 1987). This finding has some direct implications for teaching. Nelson (1988) found that students often spend much less time on their writing assignments than their teachers expect them to. This implies not only that students will, on average, produce poorer quality essays than they might, but, more important, that they will fail to face and solve the writing problems their writing assignments pose. Thus, writing instruction will suffer. Researchers need to pay much more attention to motivation than they have in the past. We need to understand better how to engage students in writing tasks.

Many of the studies revealed a strong and positive relation between text quality and the amount of abstract planning (Carey et al., 1989; Kellogg, 1988; Nelson, 1988; Spivey, 1992; Spivey & King, 1987). However, in all of the studies that measured both planning and time-on-task, the effect of planning on text quality could be attributed entirely to time-on-task (Kellogg, 1988; Nelson, 1988; Spivey, 1992; Spivey & King, 1987). Thus, there was no evidence in these studies that writers who spent a larger proportion of their time planning were more successful than those who spent a smaller proportion. This result does not mean that planning is useless. Rather, it means that planning is neither more, nor less, valuable than other writing activities (such as sentence generation and revising) the writers might choose to engage in.

Many of the studies we analyzed did not distinguish between *content* and *noncontent planning* (Kellogg, 1988; Nelson, 1988; Spivey, 1992; Spivey & King, 1987), which might bring concern that our conclusions fail to reflect differences between these two types of planning. Indeed, Carey et al. (1989) claimed that noncontent planning is more strongly associated with text quality than is content planning. But reanalysis of the Carey et al. (1989) data reveals no support for this claim. Further, the studies of Schriver (1988) and Kozma (1991) failed to find any advantage of content planning over other forms of planning. At present, then, there is no evidence to suggest that noncontent planning contributes more to text quality than does content planning.

Before we analyzed these planning studies, it seemed reasonable to believe that planning was especially important among writing processes in the sense that writers would be well advised to spend more of their time on abstract planning and less on other processes. It seemed as plausible to believe that people plan too little as it was to believe that they exercise too little. It was surprising, therefore, when analysis failed to reveal any advantage for writers who devoted a larger proportion of their time to planning over those who devoted a smaller proportion.

What can be made of this result? One possible interpretation is that the balance of writing processes does not matter and any writer could mix writing processes in a wide variety of proportions with equal success. However, it is more plausible to believe that the balance of processes does matter but that the appropriate balance varies from writer to writer and from situation to situation. We assumed that writers make judgments about how much effort to devote to each writing process on the basis of their perception of the nature of the task and on their assessment of their topic knowledge and their writing skills. Although these judgments may be imperfect, they are at least based on the writer's own situation. When writers are told to plan more, they may well find that there is only so much planning that they know how to do. We find support for the position that writers are making judgments about the appropriate balance of processes in the observation that writers in Kellogg's (1988) study who were required to plan before writing "compensated" by devoting a smaller proportion of their writing time to planning than they would otherwise have done. We interpret this compensation as reflecting the writers' judgments about how much planning is appropriate for them in doing that task. Though their judgments may be imperfect, writers may be better advised to rely on their own sense of their writing situation to determine an appropriate balance among writing processes than to depend on an unconditional imperative to plan more.

We note that our analysis does not apply to process planning or to language planning and it does not suggest that it is useless to teach people better planning techniques. It does suggest, however, that it is useless to push writers to do more abstract planning without teaching them to do it better.

Perhaps the most important conclusion to draw from these results is methodological. Research focusing on a single writing process without sufficient attention to its context within the total writing activity may well yield misleading results. Thus, the observation that more successful writers do more planning than less successful ones might well be misinterpreted if one did not notice that the more successful writers also did more library research and spent more time drafting and revising.

Conclusions

In this chapter, we have outlined a theoretical framework for understanding planning, defined a set of general planning methods, emphasized the interaction of planning and environment, proposed a list of planning types that occur in writing, and suggested procedures for improving the analysis of planning data. Hopefully, this chapter can help writing scholars to communicate about planning and to become clearer about what we know and, especially, what we do not know.

Acknowledgments

The authors wish to express thanks to Karen A. Schriver, Joachim Grabowski, Michael Levy, Sarah Ransdell, Kenneth Kotovsky, Caroline C. Hayes, and Herbert A. Simon for many helpful comments.

— 3 —
A MODEL OF WORKING MEMORY
IN WRITING

Ronald T. Kellogg
University of Missouri — Rolla

The influential model of writing by Hayes and Flower (1980) focused on the cognitive factors involved in composition. Although it succeeded in laying the foundation for a cognitive theory of text production, it drew criticism for failing to address the affective (Brand, 1989) and social (Nystrand, 1989) dimensions of writing. A recent revision of the model has broached these concerns and underscored the need to consider how working memory supports cognition in writing (Hayes, chapter 1 in this volume).

In writing, reading, and other cognitive tasks, working memory makes use of knowledge and experiences stored in long-term memory. It serves both as a short-term store and as a limited capacity system for processing information in cognitive tasks, thus wedding theories of memory and attention. As a writer plans ideas, translates these ideas into sentences, types the sentences on a word processor, and monitors all these activities, many demands are made on temporary storage and processing capacity. This chapter explores how working memory supports this orchestration.

First, I note the assumptions made here about the nature of writing and working memory. These assumptions link the proposed model to findings on speech production and the comprehension of speech and text as interpreted from the perspective of Baddeley's (1986) constructs of working memory. Next, the basic processes of three systems of language production are reviewed: the formulation of ideas and linguistic expression; the motor execution of speech, handwriting, or typing; and the monitoring of these production systems. Each system involves two basic processes and numerous subprocesses. I follow this sketch with a proposal regarding the demands made by the basic processes on the central executive, the phonological loop, and the visuo-spatial sketchpad resources of working memory. Before concluding the chapter, I turn to the writing research that partially tests the model's predictions and suggests directions for further research.

Key assumptions

One assumption of the present approach is that speaking, listening, reading, and writing use some common components (Brown, McDonald, Brown, & Carr, 1988). There are also differences in the components involved, in that reading uses vision and listening audition. As Grabowski notes in chapter 4, writing and speaking differ both for social/pragmatic reasons and for processing reasons, but it is still plausible that the formulation, comprehension, and editing components of monitoring are shared in speaking and writing. Further, the formulation system of language production — the planning of ideas and their translation into sentences — presumably is used in both speaking and writing. By assuming common components in various uses of language, the extensive experimental literature on reading, speech comprehension, and speech production may advance our theories of writing, as well. Here I draw on such work to fashion a tentative model of the relation between working memory and writing.

The other assumption is that working memory includes separate resources for the processing of phonological information; visual and spatial information; and centralized tasks such as reasoning, problem solving, and decision making. Baddeley's (1986) influential model fits this bill, but then so do alternative models of working memory (Cowan, 1995; Schneider & Detweiler, 1987). Because the Baddeley model has already been extended to work on reading, listening, and speaking (Gathercole & Baddeley, 1993), it seemed the logical choice here.

Baddeley and his colleagues distinguish two specialized slave systems from a multipurpose, limited-capacity system called the *central executive*. One slave system — the *phonological loop* — is dedicated to the storage and processing of auditory and verbal information. The *visuo-spatial sketchpad*, in contrast, stores and processes visual and spatial information. These slave systems can operate independently of the central executive, although they are limited in how much information they can process. When task demands for the storage of phonological information, for example, become too great for the slave system to handle, then central resources can be called on to aid successful performance. Indeed, the central executive plays several roles (Gathercole & Baddeley, 1993). Whenever a task demands sustained effort, controlled processes draw on the central executive. Examples include problem solving, mental calculation, and reasoning. The central executive also plays regulatory roles. For example, whenever competing behaviors are simultaneously elicited by the environment, the central executive selects the motor schemas that take precedence. It intervenes to inhibit some schemas and activate others to ensure smooth, responsive, and appropriate behavior.

A model of working memory in writing

Systems and basic processes

Figure 3.1 shows the model proposed here. This model distinquishes formulation, execution, and monitoring systems of text production (Brown et al., 1988). These are, in essence, superordinate categories of language production processes. Each of these systems involve two basic level processes. For instance, formulation consists of planning ideas and translating them into sentences. The flow of information is indicated by arrows between basic processes and entire systems. Thus, the output of planning is input for translating, and the output of translating may then be sent to programming in the execution system. However, outputs of planning and translating are also fed forward for editing prior to the execution of motor movements, contrary to the Brown et al. model. Corrections in each of these basic processes may thus be made before handwriting, typing, or dictating take place.

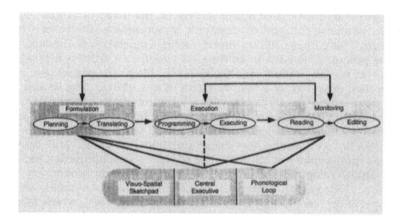

Figure 3.1 The resources of working memory used by the formulation, execution, and monitoring system.

The model must not be construed to imply that writers first formulate a text as a whole, execute it, and then monitor it. Rather, the model allows for the simultaneous activation of formulation, execution, and monitoring, as long as the demands placed on the central executive do not exceed capacity limitations. Interaction among systems is also fundamental to the proposed model. For example, some kinds of editing that take place prior to execution and editing may also call for renewed planning and translating. The model further assumes that the execution of a word or phrase may take place simultaneously with the formulation of new material or monitoring of already written material. This is possible only because execution can, when well-practiced, proceed virtually automatically. The basic processes of formulation and monitoring, on the other hand, are in many respects controlled and effortful.

Subprocesses

For clarity and convenience, Figure 3.1 does not show a further subordinate level of analysis, the several subprocesses that comprise each basic process. The subprocesses are briefly mentioned, but the demands of the basic processes on working memory, the chief concern here, can be explained without detailing the subprocesses.

PLANNING AND TRANSLATING. As used here, to *plan* is to set goals for one's actions, to think up ideas related to the goals, and to organize the ideas in ways that guide future actions (see chapters 1 and 2 in this volume for a more restrictive use of the term). The outputs of planning may be propositional representations that are readily handled by the process of linguistic translation (Flower & Hayes, 1984). Yet, they may also emerge as abstractions, images, and feelings that defy easy translation. In struggling to translate these into intelligible sentences, the writer's editing processes typically reject the outputs and prompt further planning.

In expressing ideas as complete sentences, the writer activates semantic, syntactic, phonological, and orthographic subprocesses (Badecker, Hillis, & Caramazza, 1990; Bock, 1982; Garrett, 1976). Translation is the amalgam of linguistic processes needed to convert an idea into a written message. The literature on speech production often refers to this as the planning of speech, which is then executed by a motor system of articulation. The writing literature at times saves the term *planning* for the intensive conceptual, nonlinguistic work that characterizes so many writing tasks. The linguistic work — translation — includes selecting lexical units, building a syntactic frame, phonologically representing the lexical units in the frame, and converting phonemes into graphemes, all the levels of representation needed for written motor output. Adopting the terms of Garrett's speech production model, translation of ideas into sentences entails functional, positional, and phonetic levels of representation. It excludes the message level, which is a product of planning, and the articulatory level, which is a product of motor programming.

It is commonplace for planning to be accompanied by partial translation but without overt execution. The inner speech of Vygotsky (1962) corresponds to just such partial translation. Word meanings and their phonological representations make up such speech, but its syntactic structure is sketchy. As Vygotsky described it, "Inner speech is to a large extent thinking in pure word meanings. It is a dynamic, shifting, unstable thing, fluttering between word and thought" (p. 149).

A related internal dialogue is Witte's (1987) pre-text, a further developed form of inner speech on both lexical and syntactic levels. Writers might try out sentences mentally and edit them before preceding to execution. Pre-text represents a tentative translation, what Witte aptly called "'the last cheap gas' before writers commit themselves to extended written text" (p. 398). Both inner speech and pre-text, then, allow a writer to plan and tentatively translate ideas before beginning a first draft.

On occasion, the writer may program and execute degraded output resulting from partial translation. Personal notations, networks, diagrams, lists, and topical outlines are externalized plans that have undergone only partial translation. They carry meaning for the writer, but little if any for a reader. They may combine visual symbols along with words, abbreviations, and single letters. The lexical work is impoverished and the syntactic work is skirted altogether. In contrast to scribbling ideas and organizational schemes, generating an acceptable, meaningful sentence demands all the key subprocesses.

PROGRAMMING AND EXECUTING. The output of translation is programmed for use by the appropriate motor system in handwriting, typing, or dictating. In dictation, the complex muscle movement system of speech is activated, including programs for controlling laryngeal vibration, airflow, and articulation (MacKay, Wulf, Yin, & Abrams, 1993). In typing, arm, hand, and finger movements require similar intricate, rapid control. Through high speed videotaping of skilled typists, Norman and Rumelhart (1983) revealed the striking parallelism involved, describing it as "a fluid set of motions, of fingers moving in many directions at once" (p. 47). At the extreme, champion typists can execute up to 200 words per minute, with an average interval between key strokes of only 60 milliseconds.

The programming and muscle execution subprocesses differ depending on the output mode. In handwriting, for instance, the size of the letters and their allographic form must be selected. This abstract specification of letter form is one of three subprocesses (Van Galen, 1990). Force parameters must be set and the necessary motor units recruited as well. The precision-grip execution process entails motor commands, muscle movements, and feedback mechanisms (Shepard, 1994). Central or reafference feedback, proprioceptive feedback, and sensory feedback from the environment each play a part. Only the later kind of feedback is explicitly represented in Figure 3.1, showing how visual information gained in reading provides corrective information to the execution system. Controlling legibility depends in part on such sensory feedback (Brown et al., 1988).

READING AND EDITING. Monitoring involves reading and editing. In reading, the author engages several subprocesses in recognizing words, comprehending sentences, establishing coherence among sentences, and building global discourse structures (e.g., Carr & Levy, 1990; Gernsbacher, 1992; Just & Carpenter, 1992). Reading well is probably best regarded as a necessary, but not sufficient, condition for writing well.

Ransdell and Levy note in chapter 5 of this volume that individual differences in reading comprehension correlate significantly, albeit moderately, with variations in assessments of writing mechanics, organization, and overall quality. The specific aspects of reading ability that relate to writing abilities change with cognitive development. For young children beginning to read, knowledge of phonics and spelling correlates positively with writing achievement, whereas older, more proficient readers reveal correlations between knowledge of vocabulary and discourse structure (Shanahan, 1984).

Editing is seen as a comparison between a writer's intentions and the output of a given basic process. A mismatch between the two initiates feedback either to the process in question or to earlier processes. Editing is analogous to the evaluation function that detects and diagnoses problems in a text in the revision model of Hayes, Flower, Shriver, Stratman, and Carey (1987).

It is important to note that editing takes numerous specific forms. Speed, legibility, and spacing on the page of handwriting are edited and correction signals fed back to the execution system. Localized errors in formulation, such as spelling and diction, are also monitored. Other editing is global, as in paragraph and text organization problems. Still other kinds fall in between these extremes, as in a sentence structure problem or the failure to establish a cohesive link between adjacent sentences. Assessments of the quality of written text typically include measures of both local and global textual problems (e.g., see chapters 5 and 15 in this volume).

The timing of editing

The bidirectional arrow between formulation and monitoring represents that editing can occur both before and after a sentence is programmed and executed. Writers can in theory edit ideas, organizational schemes, writing goals, and sentences heard as inner speech or pre-text before execution. Editing may also occur after the writer has read the sentence, paragraph, or larger units of text already produced. Such editing after execution may be juggled with production or delayed until after a writer has completed a section of text.

One factor influencing how and when the outputs of formulation are monitored is the prewriting and drafting strategy adopted by the writer. With Elbow's (1981) strategy of free writing, both premonitoring and monitoring concurrent with text production are minimized. An effort is made to plan, translate, program, and execute continuously without any monitoring at all. Only after a draft is completed does the writer step back and read the product and initiate editing. At the other extreme is the polished draft strategy combined with heavy planning during prewriting (e.g., preparing a detailed outline). Writers may engage in both extensive premonitoring of ideas, organization, and sentences plus try to monitor each sentence as it is executed. They aim to generate a first draft that is as polished and complete as possible.

Thus, it is not necessary to hear or read an error before initiating changes. At the same time, there is no doubt that hearing or reading what one has to say powerfully shapes subsequent output from the formulation system. Speaking and particularly writing enable the discovery of new ideas and organizational schemes, a process well-known in the writing literature as knowledge transformation (Bereiter & Scardamalia, 1987).

Demands on working memory

Now that the basic processes of formulation, execution, and monitoring have been described, it is time to consider the demands they make on working memory. The lines connecting each system with the components of working memory in Figure 3.1 indicate a demand by at least one basic process. For example, the formulation system places major demands on the central executive, as well as the slave components. As we will see in this section, planning theoretically demands the resources of the visuo-spatial sketchpad and the central executive and translating the phonological loop and the central executive (see Table 3.1). The demands of each system are detailed next.

FORMULATION. The formulation system presumably places the heaviest burden on working memory, as shown in Table 3.1. To begin, writers plan by visualizing ideas, organizational schemes, supporting graphics, appearances of the orthography and layout, and then they engage the visuo-spatial sketchpad. Creating ideas (Shepard, 1978) and recalling them from long-term memory (Paivio, 1986) can invoke visual imagery. Further, planning in all of its facets engages the central executive (Gathercole & Baddeley, 1993). Generating ideas, trying out various organizational schemes, or debating the appropriate tone to establish for a particular discourse community are labor intensive aspects of composition (Flower & Hayes, 1980). The often difficult work of thinking through what one is trying to say, in theory, draws heavily on the limited pool of central capacity.

Table 3.1

The resources of working memory used by the six basic processes of writing

| Basic Process | Working Memory Resource | | |
	Visuo-Spatial Sketchpad	Central Executive	Phonological Loop
Planning	✓	✓	
Translating		✓	✓
Programming		✓	
Executing			
Reading		✓	✓
Editing		✓	

Translating an idea into an acceptable sentence involves the phonological loop. This occurs when writers covertly talk to themselves in the form of inner speech or pre-text as they are generating sentences, using their "inner voice" (Baddeley & Lewis, 1981). Phonological representations of the words selected in a syntactic frame are stored in the short-term store of the loop. It is presumably this storage that gives rise to the phrases, clauses, and sentences of pre-text or more sketchy representations of inner speech. Subvocal articulation of these representations prolongs their availability for covert editing. Alternatively, the representations may be further processed for immediate execution, such as happens when writers type sentences seemingly as fast as they think of them.

Disruption of the translation process has been observed in apraxic and dyspraxic patients who make phonemic and other linguistic mistakes in speech. Such patients also are impaired in memory span tests and fail to show the phonological similarity and word length effects normally seen in these tests (Waters, Rochon, & Caplan, 1992). They behave as do normal individuals under conditions of articulatory suppression. In contrast, anarthric patients, whose speech difficulty lies in the execution of the speech motor musculature, appear to possess an intact phonological loop based on memory performance characterisitics (Baddeley & Wilson, 1985).

In addition to the phonological loop, translating also demands resources of the central executive when the writer must struggle to find just the right words and sentence structures. Long pauses and high degrees of expended cognitive effort suggest the involvement of the central executive in these cases. Translation is typically viewed as automatic in conversational speech (Bock, 1982), with syntactic processing in particular thought of as modular (Fodor, 1983). In writing, at least certain situations call for effortful translation, such as when a writer must compose a polished final draft on the first attempt. The model assumes, then, that involvement of the central executive in translation varies with the demands of the task at hand.

One piece of evidence for central capacity involvement is that the greater one's working memory capacity, the better one can select lexical items for use in a sentence (Daneman & Green, 1986; McCutchen, Covill, Hoyne, & Mildes, 1994). This would not be expected if semantic and phonological subprocesses were entirely automatic. Further evidence is that sentence generation interferes with the simple reaction times to a secondary probe presented concurrently (Kellogg, 1988). Such interference would not be expected if translation were fully automatic. Although planning ideas typically demands the most cognitive effort as reflected in reaction time interference, translating sentences from the ideas is still effortful for adult writers composing essays.

EXECUTION. Typing and handwriting presumably make demands only on the central executive and these are minimal when the skills are well practiced. For a novice, the demands of behavioral output can be substantial. Novel activities of all kinds require the central executive to control the schemas used in motor output. For example, handwriting demands more capacity than speaking in young children, but both modes of output demand little capacity by early adulthood (Bourdin & Fayol, 1994). It is the programming, not the executing, of muscle movements that demands central capacity in the present model.

The dotted line shown in Figure 3.1 symbolizes the light demands of well-practiced execution. Presumably, for one skilled in longhand or typing, the degree of load placed on the central executive is normally slight and dwarfed by the demands stemming from formulation and monitoring. Slight demands of programming motor output remain even in skilled individuals, as seen in the following study.

Brown et al. (1988) manipulated the availability of sentences in the formulation system by visually presenting them to be copied in one case and requiring their recall in another. They also manipulated the execution and — perhaps — monitoring systems by stressing speed of handwriting in one case and legibility in another. They found that the legibility or execution accuracy was affected by both the availablility and stress manipulations. When formulation must rely on memory retrieval, legibility decreased and both corrected and uncorrected errors increased. This implied interference in the execution system as a result of a direct manipulation of the difficulty of formulating sentences. It seemed unlikely that the decrement came from the monitoring system because both corrected and uncorrected errors showed the same advantage for copying as opposed to recalling the sentences.

Brown et al. interpreted this result to mean that formulation drew capacity away from execution under the difficult recall conditions. Probably, if writers had to compose sentences from scratch, rather than recall them, then even more capacity would be shunted to the formulation system. Interestingly, when the instructions stressed speed over accuracy, legibility decreased markedly as the demands for rapid execution increased, but the accuracy of the content of the sentences failed to decline. It appears as if the formulation system is "protected from deterioration due to demands placed on execution" (p. 56). Thus, the results of Brown et al. suggest that formulation demands are critical and take priority over execution demands on the central executive. The more general point is that execution appears to consume at least a small degree of central capacity even for a college student skilled in handwriting.

MONITORING. Reading, one basic process of the monitoring system, is thought to require the resources of both the phonological loop and the central executive (Gathercole & Baddeley, 1993; Gernsbacher, 1992; Just & Carpenter, 1992). Consequently, the monitoring system is shown in Figure 3.1 as making demands on both components of working memory. However, the most significant demand stems from editing, not reading, and that demand falls on the central executive. Generally, it would seem that reading one's own writing is greased because of all the planning and translation that preceded. Comprehending another writer's text calls for inferences that are transparent to the author. Conversely, seeing errors in another writer's text is seemingly easier, because the reading process is heavily driven from the top down when working with recently self-generated text (Daneman & Stainton, 1993). More importantly, editing takes so many forms, ranging from the detection of a motor programming error to a revision in the organization of ideas in a text. Although the forms of editing probably vary in their individual demands, taken together they should make heavy demands on the central executive.

Brown et al. (1988) found that errors in content and in the syntax and cohesion of text decreased as the demands of formulation increased. Having to recall sentences from memory, as opposed to reading and transcribing them, yielded more failures in monitoring, in other words. This result implies that monitoring depends on limited central capacity and suffers when the formulation demands grow. Interestingly, only the syntactic and cohesive errors fluctuated with the speed versus accuracy manipulation. Both verbatim and gist scoring of content errors failed to change as the instructions stressed speed over legibility. One interpretation of these findings is that editing of semantic content takes precedence over syntax and textual cohesion when demands for rapid execution place a strain on the central executive.

Relevant writing research

Explicit assumptions about how the three systems affect the rate and quality of language production are needed to test the model. *Fluency*, measured as the words produced per unit of composition time, presumably varies directly with the rate of information processing within all three systems. *Words per minute* (wpm) of composition time provides an average measure of fluency, one that includes all the pause time as well as time actually spent in execution.

In contrast, the quality of the document as measured by holistic ratings or alternative methods of subjective assessment are not directly dependent on processing rates. Formulating thoughts and sentences well is not the same as formulating them rapidly. Holistic quality depends on the effectiveness of the formulation and monitoring systems and the feedback between them. This claim assumes that handwriting legibility or typographical errors are not distorting conceptual and rhetorical judgments. Assuming these execution issues are removed, then predictions about quality and fluency differ in the present model.

Output modes

One prediction that follows from the model's assumptions is that the output mode — longhand, word processor, or dictation — should vary in fluency albeit not at the extremes suggested by execution rates alone. Gould (1978) noted that people can speak memorized material at a rate of about 200 wpm, but can write it in longhand at only 40 wpm. Typing rates of 60 – 90 wpm are not unusual among professional secretaries (Gentner, 1983). So when formulation and monitoring time are minimized, there are striking differences in fluency owing to the different execution rates of these output modes. These differences should remain when the formulation and monitoring systems are challenged by original composition. But in such a case pauses during formulation and monitoring should greatly slow the rates of text production below maximum execution rates.

Gould's (1978) data on fluency for experienced writers composing business letters indicate that handwriting (12.1 wpm) is reliably slower than dictating (20.9 wpm). These are based on total writing time that includes all pauses. *Speaking*, defined as dictation meant to be heard rather than read, is still faster (29.3 wpm), but still far below the maximum speaking rate for memorized text. Card, Robert, and Keenan (1984) replicated Gould's procedures for handwriting and extended them to composing on a word processor (display-based editor as opposed to a line editor). The mean for handwriting (12.0 wpm) and the word processor (12.2 wpm) were virtually identical. Unlike professional secretaries, their experienced writers typed about as fast as they could write in longhand. Especially fast typists tended to achieve higher fluency on a word processor than in longhand. However, the reliability of the observed difference was not reported and was doubtful given the small sample size of fast versus slow typists ($n = 4$).

A second prediction of the model is that holistic quality should not differ for longhand and word processors in composing a draft. This assumes that judges examine a typed copy of the text so that handwriting legibility is not at issue. Also, it assumes that the number of drafts produced and the use of spelling checkers and other editing aids are not confounding factors (Kellogg, 1994). A third output mode, dictation, presents an interesting case because of its lack of a visual record of the developing text. It is similar to handwriting with invisible ink, although not identical in that one can replay dictated material. In theory, dictation and invisible longhand disrupt feedback to the formulation system gained from reading and editing and so should disrupt quality.

The results from several experiments with adult writers confirm that longhand and word processors do not differ reliably on measures of text quality, such as holistic subjective judgments (Card et al., 1984; Haas, 1989; Kellogg & Mueller, 1994; Ransdell & Levy, 1994). However, contrary to the model's expectations, dictation and invisible writing in Gould's (1978) experiments also yielded the same quality as longhand. Other research indicates that invisible writing does in fact decrease quality for both experienced and inexperienced writers (Hull & Smith, 1983), although it had no reliable impact on fluency, in accordance with the present model.

One difference in the studies of invisible writing is that Gould's participants wrote routine business letters of less than 100 words, whereas Hull and Smith's writers produced persuasive essays of 200 to 500 words. Another is that in Gould's study a second, corrected draft was produced and judged, not the original draft as in the Hull and Smith study. To the extent that substantive errors were caught in the drafts from dictation and invisible writing, the predicted negative impact of disrupting feedback would be hard to detect. Additional work is needed, however, to resolve the discrepancy in outcomes.

Strategy effects

Five of the basic processes presumably make demands on the central executive. Only the execution of motor movements is assumed to take place entirely automatically. Although one skilled in longhand or typing places a minimal load on motor programming during execution, the demands of planning, translating, reading, and editing are formidable in many writing situations. Theorists have long emphasized that these processes often overload attentional capacity (Flower & Hayes, 1980) and measurements of the cognitive effort expended during writing bear out this point (Kellogg, 1994).

Strategies that funnel central capacity to one or two processes, rather than many, should improve their functioning with regard to both effectiveness and rate. The model predicts gains in both text quality and fluency as a result. One consequence of preparing an outline before beginning a first draft of an essay appears to be a reduction in overload, allowing writers to focus the capacity of the central executive on translating (Kellogg, 1988). Both the quality of the resulting essay and the rate of language production during drafting increased reliably in the outline condition compared to a no outline, control condition.

The relevance of this outcome to the proposed model hinges on the assumption that outlining indeed helps writers by focusing attention on translation. As discussed in detail in Kellogg (1994), this along with their organizational benefits underlie the outlining effect. In chapter 2, Hayes and Gradwohl-Nash offer an alternative, time-on-task explanation of the outlining effect. As they correctly observe, extra time spent planning means more time engaged in the task. It could be this extra time that accounts for the benefit of outlining. They present evidence that it is time on task that correlates with quality, not planning time alone. Writing quality need not correlate with the time spent planning in all its forms, but time-on-task may not fully explain the outlining benefit. Total time on task was equated in the clustering and outlining conditions of Kellogg (1990). Yet it turned out that the prewriting time spent outlining enhanced essay quality, whereas the same time devoted to clustering — a network-based plan — had no effect. Clustering resulted in the same essay quality as a no prewriting, control condition that spent less total time on the task.

Another strategy-based experiment varied the simultaneous demands made on formulation and monitoring as college students generated ideas for an essay (Glynn, Britton, Muth, & Dogan, 1982). The unordered propositions condition allowed the writers to focus on generating ideas. The ordered propositions condition increased the demands on planning by requiring that the ideas be organized as well as generated. The mechanics free condition added the requirement of translating the organized ideas in sentences, without regard for mechanical problems. Lastly, the polished sentences condition added reading and editing demands as well as translating and organizing demands. The number of ideas generated by the writers declined systematically across these four conditions as the task demands increased.

Capacity differences

A further implication of the heavy demands that writing places on the executive is that individual differences in central capacity ought to correlate with writing skill. Researchers have identified low and high capacity college students based on Daneman and Carpenter's (1980) reading span test and found that high span writers produce texts of superior quality (Madigan, Holt, & Blackwell, 1993; Madigan, Johnson, & Linton, 1994; McCutchen et al., 1994). Reading span requires not only the retention of items, but simultaneous processing of information. There is some controversy about what this test actually measures (Engle, Cantor, & Curullo, 1992) and whether it necessarily correlates with writing quality (Ransdell & Levy, 1995). But, if one assumes that reading span and related processing/storage tests measure the general capacity of the central executive, then such results, if they stand up in future research, are readily interpretable within the present model.

Finally, Benton, Kraft, Glover, and Plake (1984) examined the correlation between writing ability and how well an individual retains 4 letters in order while shadowing digits so as to prevent subvocal rehearsal (Benton, Kraft, Glover, & Plake, 1984). According to Baddeley's (1986) model, the ordered letters task primarily assessed retention in the phonological store. By contrast, other tests in the Benton et al. study required the reordering and recalling of 5 letters, reordering the 10 words of a scrambled sentence, or reordering the 12 sentences of a scrambled paragraph. Because these reordering tasks called for both storage of information beyond the meager limits of the phonological store and the manipulation of that information in working memory, they presumably provided valid measures of central capacity. Benton et al. reported that, in fact, only these reordering tests yielded reliable differences in performance between good and poor writers. This outcome suggests that central executive functioning is more predictive of writing ability than variations in phonological storage ability.

Irrelevant speech

Irrelevant speech occupies the phonological loop. The model predicts that such speech should disrupt translating and reading processes. But planning, programming, executing, and editing ought to be immune from such disruption. Compared to the central executive, the phonological loop plays a more restricted role in the functioning of the formulation and monitoring systems.

One study suggests that taking the phonological loop out of action has a modest impact on writing performance. Madigan et al. (1994) reported that irrelevant speech decreased slightly, but reliably, holistic judgments of the quality of essays written by college students. The small effect size is consistent with the hypothesis that irrelevant speech disrupts only translating and reading. A more massive effect on quality ratings would be expected if planning and editing were disrupted in addition.

Simultaneous articulation

Another way to occupy the phonological loop is continuous, repetitive articulation of a syllable (la, la, la...) or a well-learned sequence (1, 2, 3, 1, 2, 3...). Unlike irrelevant speech, this load demands the rehearsal loop as well as the phonological store. It should also implicate the central executive to a slight degree in that overt responding draws central resources in programming output. So, the present model predicts that such continuous articulation should disrupt writing more than irrelevant speech, but less than dual tasks that heavily consume central capacity.

No study seems to have examined the effect of simultaneous irrelevant articulation on writing. However, a few studies have assessed whether the articulation of relevant information during composition — verbal protocols — disrupts the production rate (Janssen, van Waes, & van den Bergh, chapter 13 in this volume; Ransdell, 1994). This work suggests that fluency suffers when writers think aloud, generating fewer words and clauses per minute and pausing more between clauses and paragraphs. The model predicts that verbal protocols should at a minimum load the phonological loop and disrupt the quality and fluency of translation. More work on these issues is needed.

Loading the central executive

Holding 6 digits in working memory loads the central executive, on the assumption that the phonological loop can store only about 3 digits (Baddeley, 1986). When writers typed a visually presented sentence, the time to initiate the transcription increased reliably while retaining 6 digits compared with a no-digit control condition (Jeffery & Underwood, 1995). This disruption of fluent typing is consistent with the assumption that reading the stimulus and then programming and executing the response (and monitoring the output) require central capacity.

When required to formulate rather than transcribe sentences, Jeffery and Underwood found the writers coped with the added demand by trading off quality and fluency. That is, they actually took less time to initiate sentence generation in the 6-digit condition, but produced less semantically complex sentences as well. This pattern, which Power (1985) also found for spoken sentence generation, is troublesome for the proposed model. It predicts that loading the central executive should hinder fluency to the greatest degree when sentence formulation is called for in addition to execution and monitoring. But this outcome would only be expected when the semantic complexity and other quality aspects of sentences were equated across conditions.

Brown et al. (1988) manipulated the load on working memory as writers recalled sentences from memory and wrote them in longhand. In the irrelevant speech condition, speech was played with instructions to ignore it. In the easy concurrent task condition, the writers listened to the speech and recalled aloud the word that just preceded a signal word. In the hard concurrent task condition, they recalled the word that occurred two words before the signal. Whereas the first condition merely loaded the phonological loop, the other two presumably placed varying demands on the central executive. The words written per second declined systematically and reliably across the three conditions, in accordance with the present model (.38, .33, and .29 WPS). A silent control condition was not included but should place only slightly higher than an irrelevant speech condition.

A second manipulation of the load on the central executive primarily altered execution demands (Madigan, Holt, & Blackwell, 1993). A normal keyboard for a word processor was used in one condition, but in a second the keyboard was rearranged for two letters. The letter *o* was reassigned to the "2" key and the letter *a* to the "9" key. So in typing these vowels, the college-level writers had to "hunt and peck" rather than type automatically.

The quality of text, as reflected in holistic ratings, relies only on the formulation and monitoring systems. In contrast, fluency depends on the execution as well as the formulation and monitoring systems and so should have been affected by the reassignment condition. The results revealed a strong effect on fluency in the direction expected here. Word production times for the first three words of a clause were assessed and found to be markedly slower in the reassigned key condition, especially on the first word. Holistic quality judgments were unaffected by key reassignment.

Conclusions

The proposed model specifies the demands made by the formulation, execution, and monitoring systems on working memory. The model assumes that the output of the formulation system feeds forward to the monitoring system and the output of monitoring feeds back to both formulation and execution. The formulation system presumably makes the heaviest demand on working memory in that planning and translating require the visuo-spatial sketchpad, the phonological loop, and central capacity. The programming and execution of muscle movements — particularly when the skill is extensively practiced — makes the least demands. A writer's fluency presumably depends on all three systems, whereas the resulting content and stylistic qualities of the text vary with the functioning of the formulation and monitoring systems. Effects of output mode, writing strategies, capacity differences, irrelevant speech, simultaneous articulation, and loads on the central executive are generally consistent with the model.

The existing literature is plainly not up to the task of fully testing the model. However, the literature does suggest ways in which the model appears to have merit and areas of controversy. Its feedback assumptions require further tests using invisible writing, for example. Also, the methods of loading working memory in specific ways and then examining their effects on the output of one or more systems or basic processes should be explored further.

Baddeley's approach to working memory has borne fruit in understanding memory, reading, and the comprehension and production of speech. Extending it to writing is a plausible step. Of ultimate interest to the field of cognitive psychology is whether Baddeley's version of working memory is superior to competing approaches. It seems likely that data on all forms of language use, as well as on memory and thinking, can best resolve this issue.

Acknowledgments

Preparation of this chapter was supported by a grant from the University of Missouri Research Board. I thank Joachim Grabowski, Robert Madigan, Michael Levy, and Sarah Ransdell for their comments on earlier drafts.

— 4 —
WRITING AND SPEAKING: COMMON GROUNDS AND DIFFERENCES TOWARD A REGULATION THEORY OF WRITTEN LANGUAGE PRODUCTION

Joachim Grabowski
University of Mannheim

In order to be fundamentally complete, a psychological theory of written language production must consider a wealth of subprocesses. These subprocesses include the following:

- The acquisition of knowledge
- The situation-dependent and goal-dependent retrieval of knowledge from memory
- The (inferring) construction of information
- The linearization of information that is cognitively provided
- The translation of these prelinguistic cognitive structures into topically and grammatically appropriate sentences
- The choice and inflection of words
- The graphemic and finally grapho-motoric realization of written traces of behavior

This list is almost certainly not exhaustive.

Although significant and extensive theories have been developed so far (e.g., Beal, 1990; Bereiter & Scardamalia, 1987; Hayes & Flower, 1980; U. Guenther, 1993; Molitor, 1987; Vipond, 1993; Wallesch, 1983; see also K. B. Guenther & H. Guenther, 1983; Herrmann & Grabowski, 1995; Jakobs, 1995), psychology lacks a comprehensive and integrated theory of written language production in all its aspects. Furthermore, language production is always part of the general dynamics of human behavior. People write (or speak) because they want to achieve particular goals in particular situations in a particular way, or because they cannot achieve them in nonlinguistic ways. Consequently, language production should not (only) be reconstructed as the outcome of separate subsystems, but its theoretical reconstruction must show the greatest possible compatibility with the relevant processes investigated in general psychology (i.e., with perceptive, cognitive, motivational and emotional processes).

In this chapter, we first elucidate some ways in which writing may be considered, and opposed to speaking, from a systemic perspective. This discussion leads to the distinction between mere social and pragmatic coincidences (for which writing does not necessarily need to be treated different from speaking) and process-related necessities, which call for a writing-specific psychological explanation. Then a regulation theory of language production is introduced that has already been elaborated for speech production (Herrmann & Grabowski, 1994). This raises two questions: What kinds of situations make people write? And, how are some of the peculiarities of the writing process to be dealt with in our theoretical framework? Finally, we concentrate on early cognitive processes of language production, that is, on the relation between the — by cognition — potentially available information in long-term memory, the — by retrieval — actual available information in working memory, and the — by selection in the course of language production — information, thematized in observable texts. We discuss the variable load of working memory, which serves as the central control of the language production process, during the speaking process and during the writing process. (See, e.g., Bourdin & Fayol, 1994; Kellogg, 1994; Kellogg, chapter 3 in this volume for further research on writing related to working memory.)

What does writing really mean?

In psychology as well as in linguistics, the description of writing, in particular when compared with speaking, is by no means uniform (e.g., Coulmas, 1985; Klein, 1985; Olson, 1977). Rather, there are variety of ways in which writing and speaking are characterized and described. For example, Ludwig (1980) distinguished between "script," "written utterance," "written communication," "written language," and "language in the written mode." This section focuses on three of these aspects (cf. Herrmann & Grabowski, 1994, p. 21; Klein, 1985; Koch & Oesterreicher, 1988). The discussion is restricted to the synchronic characteristics of written and oral language production, but recognizes the significant implications of the history of language and culture on the development of script, writing, and the modes of recording and documentation (Miller, 1991).

Writing as analogy of articulation

Written characters can be regarded as the attempt to represent the sound units of a language as visible and surviving symbols (Gelb, 1963). Script is either alphabetic or syllabic, depending on whether single sounds or consonant-vowel compounds are being symbolized (cf. H. Guenther, 1988; Miller, 1991). (Logographic script needs different reflections.) In this respect, speakers' knowledge of the written composition of linguistic units provides them with a subjective theory about the phonemic and phonetic features of their language, independent of and distant from the developmental history of orthography. For example, it is sometimes difficult to cure even graduate students of the conviction that "sh" contains two letters, but represents one phoneme. Speakers also like to believe that "kernel" and "colonel" must be pronounced somewhat differently and must therefore be acoustically distinguishable. German speakers are surprised when they learn that double consonants at the end of a syllable indicate the shortness of the preceding vowel and do not indicate a stronger pronounciation of the consonant. These phenomena may have their roots in the fact that people learn speech (without formal instruction) before they learn to write; furthermore, a basis of the theoretical understanding of language is acquired at the time they learn to write (with formal instruction) and not before. Therefore, when people think about language, they confuse orthography with pronunciation. Phenomena like ambisyllabicity (Kahn, 1980; Ramers, 1992) or co-articulation (Lindblom, 1982) show the absence of clear segmentation; therefore, they can be only partially represented, even in optimized phonetic transcription systems like the International Phonetic Alphabet. Apart from this, languages are known to be different with respect to their correspondence between sounds and characters (i.e., with respect to their orthography providing an appropriate subjective theory of phonetic speech). Orthographical reforms are often aimed at raising the correspondence, or at least at standardizing the relation between graphemes and phonemes. However, such undertakings are unpopular, because reducing the difference between what speakers know explicitly and what they do automatically would mean updating their idea of language and discarding a quite inappropriate subjective theory. This observation leads to the next aspect.

Writing as a norm

Writing, when compared to speaking, can be seen as a more standardized system which must be acquired through special instruction. Mastery of this standard system is an important prerequisite of cultural and educational participation and the maintenance of one's rights and duties. Morphological and grammatical textbooks, as long as they follow written language, are always in conflict between description and prescription. The fact that writing is more standardized than speaking allows for a higher degree of sanctions when people deviate from that standard. Literate users of their language know the standards of written language and should — along with all other considerations about appropriate language production that also hold for speaking — generally pursue the metagoal of obeying these standards when they write. (This is also true for particular oral situations, such as official or institutionalized settings like exams or lectures, where people try to speak "ready for printing.") Standardization of writing facilitates communication in cases when dialect renders oral understanding difficult. (In Germany, where dialects are based on different stages of language development, this can be a severe problem.) The characteristic features of maintaining the standard — as provided by school grammar or by particular national institutes — include the production of syntactically correct sentences, the command of all tenses, and the selection or rejection of particular words.

However, technological development shows that the standardization of written language seems not to be a necessary feature of writing, but comes from canonical contexts of language use. Thus, the objective of saving resources in telegraphy led to the development of telegram style; here, without the risk of sanctions, even the most elementary morphological and syntactical rules are suspended. In communication via electronic mail, a new writing culture has developed beyond where written messages do not obey the written language standards. This observation leads to the next aspect.

Writing as a medium of communication

Writing and speaking can be considered to be different media of communication with different features, different possibilities of use, and different functions (Henning & Huth, 1975). As a rule, writing does not require temporal and spatial co-presence of the participants because it is recorded (Dimter, 1981). However, careful analysis shows that this is merely a question of social and pragmatic coincidences and not a rule that follows from a necessary connection (cf. Herrmann & Grabowski, 1994). In the first place, it is the writing-related necessities that call for particular psychological explanation, whereas the cases where speaking and writing could, in principle, mutually substitute should be treated within a common framework of language production.

Writing and speaking have several characteristics in common, although from everyday experience, they might be assigned to one or the other. First, the processes of speaking and writing can be executed without leaving physical traces of behavior at all. For example, individuals can (even under water) make speaking movements with their mouth, and partners can deduce the words from the course of these visible movements. There is a written equivalent to this example: In Japanese, there are many words that sound identical (homophones). While talking, these are disambiguated by speakers who enscribe the relevant character on their hand with a finger. This leaves no lasting visible trace, but demands that listeners must, in order to understand, form the impression of the logographic character in their mind. So, communicative writing does not necessarily imply recorded products.

Second, normal speaking (i.e., modulating a stream of air) is volatile, due to physical reasons. Likewise, writing can also be volatile, dependent on the carrier of the behavioral traces. Imagine a child in a car, who writes with a finger "Ben is stupid" on the steamed-up windshield. Once the ventilator is turned on, the writing disappears. Similarly, when you write something with your toe in the sand, it may immediately be gone with the wind.

Next, speaking is only perceptible within range. Its differentiation decreases the further away the hearer is. The same is true of writing. The perceptible range of speaking increases with volume and differentiated articulation; the perceptible range of writing increases with the size and graphic differentiation of the characters.

People sometimes speak just for themselves, without a communication partner. People sometimes write something down for themselves, without an addressee. You can have an oral dialogue with somebody, and you can interchange written notes with somebody. You can speak to several people at the same time (e.g., during a lecture), and you can write for several people at the same time (e.g., a teacher on the blackboard).

You can speak so softly that only one particular partner can understand you. For example, you can whisper something directly into somebody's ear. You can write with letters so small that only your immediate neighbor can read them, or you can show your written message to one person while concealing it from another.

Speaking as well as writing is possible in the dark or when it is noisy. But oral language production does not work well when it is noisy, and written language production does not work well in the dark; this is because the control channel — hearing or seeing, respectively — is not available. The significant differences are in comprehension because, in the case of noise little or nothing is heard, and in the case of darkness little or nothing is seen. (A modified analysis is needed for the Braille script, because its reception is managed through physical contact rather than distance senses.)

Execution of writing as well as speaking is sequential in time, producing one physical element after the other. In oral as well as written communication, production and reception may occur at the same time. Partners hear immediately what speakers say, but they can also look at the sheet on which the writers are writing. (The spread of soundwaves and light needs time. In this respect, language production and reception is never effected simultaneously, but with negligible latency.)

Written as well as spoken products can be recorded. For example, in one case a cassette recorder is needed, in the other case a pencil and a suitable surface is needed. In both cases, it is possible afterward to transport the record elsewhere and make it available to the receiver at another time. In both cases, it is possible to make the linguistic product available to different receivers, simultaneously or one after the other.

For both writing and speaking, media have been developed that make it possible to connect participants that are at different places. This connection is designed to permit on-line communication that is both simultaneous and interactive (e.g., telephone, or talk mode on the computer).

Thus, the different habits and uses of speech and writing in everyday communcation result from goal-related and situation-related appropriateness or, in a different theoretical context, from their variable functionality and practicability. They are not merely the outcome of the physical and medial properties of speech and writing. Among these aspects is, for example, the language producers' calculation of expenditure, and their anticipation of the situation and of the receivers' needs. Without claiming completeness, the following is a list of four of the differences between writing and speaking that might guide the producers' choice of either to write or to speak.

First, if individuals do not suffer from hoarseness or spasmic vocal chords, speaking is less costly than writing. Lower costs of speaking concern production and its prerequisites as well as initiation of the partner's sensory attention. With writing, addressees must be brought to direct their visual attention to a particular place, whereas soundwaves reach the listeners within a certain range, whatever sensory orientation they take up in the moment.

Second, the air, being the carrier of the acoustic trace of behavior, is almost always available; the same is not true of possible carriers of visual traces. On the other hand, the traditional writing implements are, with respect to the conservation of the linguistic product, technologically less complicated than acoustical stores.

Third, except when you write with your foot, writing needs at least one of your hands, whereas you can speak while having your hands otherwise busy.

Finally, language producers know that there are different conditions of reception for the hearer and the reader, respectively. Written text may be read repeatedly and in any order. With spoken language, the listener is bound more to the speaker's sequence and speed. As a rule, reading is more tightly bound to the characteristics of the writing process than hearing is bound to the characteristics of the speaking process. This is not only due to the different technological developments, but also because of the different physical (energetic) preconditions and the different sensory features involved in hearing and seeing. (For example, in perception, simultaneous presentation of visible things is processed better than simultaneous presentation of acoustical stimuli.) Why do people keep letters when they seldom keep tapes from their telephone answering machine? Is it because language producers use letters and do not use the listeners' answering machine when they are conveying messages that are important or possess sentimental value? Or, is it easier or more likely to produce such messages in written form, due to the different cognitive characteristics of the writing process, compared to the speaking process? In the few cases where speakers have succeeded in forming their words memorably, and if records exist, they have become part of our cultural heritage (e.g., Martin Luther King's speech "I had a dream," J. F. Kennedy's German words, "Ich bin ein Berliner," or important sports reports). It is still unclear why, on the whole, written records are preserved for lengthy periods compared to spoken records. The social status of writing and speaking, as well as the different conservation and documentation technologies may be important factors here (as, indeed, might the process itself).

For the production of scientific text, physical and social characteristics of writing and speaking and their conservation have always played an important role. However, it is necessary to make the distinction between the choice of the mode of utterance when text is being produced, and the fact that in science written texts are distributed and recorded. For example, the use of computers is an issue worth investigating in respect to the production of publications and the preparation of talks. Investigation could elucidate the process-related interrelations between the distribution medium and the production channel (e.g., you can write a talk, or you can dictate a paper). For text production, technological innovations have always been used to rehearse phrasing and thematic succession, to permit re-reading or re-hearing, and to change and restructure utterances with the minimum of effort. For writing, this process began with crossing out and erasing. Next, dictaphones with a marking device enabled the producer to delete, restructure and change existing parts of text; however, this had the limitation that the final linearization of the acoustic product was not available. Dictating, typing, and rewriting could be repeated in successive cycles. In addition, cutting out script and mounting it was helpful. Certainly, a new quality — of facility, not necessarily of content — is reached with text processors. These encourage the producer to edit text more easily, because the current state of text is immediately available on the screen or on a printout. In this respect, the computer is the carrier of a virtual written trace, which can be realized when needed (except in the case of system failure).

All three of these aspects of writing — articulation analogy, norm, and medium of communication — have in common that they focus on the general system of language and the way in which individuals encounter it. In contrast, a central characteristic of general psychology is the objective of theoretically reconstructing the psychological interior of the individual. What are the cognitive, motivational, affective, perceptive, and other processes that control the generation of an observable linguistic product? We are far away from a theory that would explain all determinants of these products perfectly. However, in the area of oral language production, we have organized some of the important factors and their interaction into a regulation theory of speaking (Herrmann & Grabowski, 1994), which demonstrates the usefulness of our approach with empirical studies. These relate to selected categeories of utterance — naming, localizing, requesting, reporting and narrating (Rummer, Grabowski, & Vorwerg, 1995). The following sections elaborate this theory for language production in general and for writing in particular.

A regulation theory of language production

Production of oral or written language serves, like other kinds of behavior, for the regulation of the speaker/writer system (S/W system), which may be considered the general cognitive system of individuals under a language-related perspective (Herrmann, Grabowski, Graf, & Schweizer, in press). Regulation means aligning actual values with desired values, refering to cybernetic systems like refrigerators. Language is produced only if the information about actual and desired values, represented in the S/W system at a given time, is such that the system is expected to be successfully regulated. The subsystem where the information is available, called *focus memory*, is the declarative part of central control. The procedural part of central control, called *central executive*, continually executes comparisons between the actual and the desired state of the system. If above-threshold differences exist, and these match the conditional parts (IF parts) of language production operators, then the executive parts of these operators (THEN parts) are instantiated and the corresponding processes are initiated.

The model of language production described here (see Figure 4.1) has three levels: (a) the aforementioned central control with its declarative (focus memory) and procedural (central executive) parts, the conception of which follows the idea of attention-consuming central control as a part of working memory (Baddeley, 1986; Gathercole & Baddeley, 1993); (b) the auxiliary systems (see explanation later, which are, again, conceptualized for language-related processes and do not equal Baddeley's articulatory loop and visuo-spatial sketchpad); (c) the encoding mechanism. Together, these levels form a hierarchical system with vertical feedback. In other words, a higher level adjusts a lower level, but not vice versa (hierarchy). The lower, and therefore dependent and subordinate. levels continually inform the higher levels about their activities (vertical feedback).

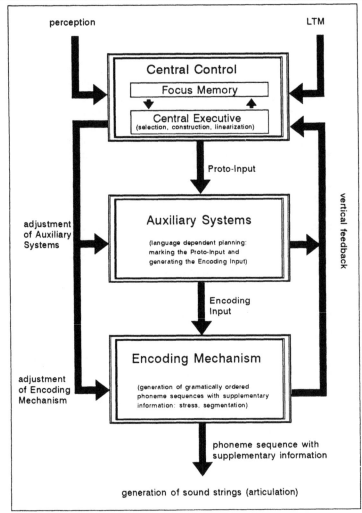

Figure 4.1. A graphical representation of the regulation theory of written language production.

In the case of language production, the processes initiated and guided by central control do three things: They select from information in focus memory (and from information retrieved from long-term memory) the information units that are to be verbalized (selection). When necessary, these information units are modified, e.g., by inferences (construction), and eventually are brought into sequence (linearization). The selected, constructed, and linearized output of central control, which is similar to Levelt's (1989) preverbal message (and which is not very deeply analyzed there), serves as the proto-input of the auxiliary systems, where markings are added in order to ensure coherence; an appropriate choice of tense, aspect, and mood; and an appropriate prosodic emphasis. Part of the auxiliary systems is also the discourse protocol. Here, the speaker's already produced linguistic output and the partner's utterances are continually maintained (Hjelmquist, 1984; Sachs, 1967). The discourse protocol interacts intensively with the other subsystems. The marked output of the auxiliary systems is the input to the encoding mechanism. The encoding mechanism generates phoneme sequences, or grapheme sequences, respectively, by applying grammatical schemata and generating word forms that fit the transferred concepts (Herrmann & Grabowski, 1993).

Execution of processes at the level of central control demands attentional resources, whereas the levels of the auxiliary systems and the encoding mechanism are largely automatic. (Speakers, or writers, are, as a rule, not conscious of the processes on these levels.) Consequently, four idealized control modes of the language production system are distinguished, which differ according to two factors: the flexibility of focus information, and the attentional consumption, both being either high or low, and thus leading to 2 x 2 = 4 types of control mode (Herrmann, & Grabowski, 1995; Rummer, Grabowski & Vorwerg, 1995). These differ in the specific involvement of central control in planning processes, as opposed to the mere execution of procedural schemata, and in the way the auxiliary systems are pre-adjusted; because of this, they also differ in susceptibility to disturbances, interferences, and intrusion. However, this is not the place to repeat our typology of control modes (see Power, 1985; Rummer, 1995; Rummer & Grabowski, in press, for experimental support).

Writing as system regulation

Within the framework of the structure of assumptions explained in the previous section, the treatment of writing raises two questions: Under which conditions do people choose written language production, as opposed to speaking, as a means of system regulation that leads to goal-related success? That is, how is the information in focus memory (actual values and desired values) structured when writing operations are triggered? And assuming that writing is chosen in order to achieve one's goals, what are the peculiarities of the way the mechanisms involved in the language production process function? This section provides answers to the first question; the second question is treated in subsequent sections.

We assume four things in the field of individual communication: The set of informational constellations in focus memory that trigger written language production and the set of informational constellations that trigger oral language production are not identical. Neither of these is a proper subset of the other; the union of both sets is a proper subset of the set of all possible informational constellations in focus memory. The intersection of both sets is not empty. From this, we make the following three conclusions: There are informational states of focus memory that can be successfully regulated either by written or by oral language production. There are informational states of focus memory that cannot be successfully regulated by written or oral language production. Writing when compared to speaking extends the set of situations in which language production allows for successful system regulation. Elsewhere, some conditional categories are mentioned that lead one to use the telephone (Herrmann & Grabowski, 1994, p. 464). Here, we describe the conditions of choosing writing for system regulation, thus answering the previous first question and delimiting the field in which writing research necessarily applies.

ABSOLUTE RESTRICTIONS. All kinds of partner-oriented oral language production depend on one of the following conditions: The speaker and hearer are at the same place at the same time (face-to-face communication). The addressee makes a phone number available, the speaker knows it, and the addressee is close enough to the phone at the moment the speaker tries to make contact. The addressee disposes of the necessity for temporal copresence by providing a device for speech recording (automatic answering machine). If none of these preconditions exist, and language producers cannot effect one of these conditions, they can still write. But, writing itself is not enough; success depends on the existence of the world wide postal service. Incidentally, this could also be used to send a tape-recorded message. However, given the comparably easy conditions for physical conservation of written traces (discussed earlier), it is evident that the written transmission of messages requires the lowest amount of preconditions: You simply need to know the addressee's name, a place where he or she will be at least once in a certain period of time, or where the addressee made contingencies for incoming mail. (In general, this is one's mailbox, but it could also be an agreement to have sent on, or it is an electronic mailbox that might also be forwarded to a different place — if the term *place* remains applicable at all.)

ECONOMY OF SYSTEM REGULATION. Different costs and advantages are involved when the language producer either talks or writes to the addressee. For the producer, it is less expensive to send a letter or electronic mail than to make a phone call. However, the partner's response to mail is, in most cases, received later than is the case with phone calls. For the producer, writing might be more costly with respect to the time needed, but it can be carried out at any time almost completely independent of the present circumstances, of the partner's willingness to communicate, and of the partner's communication devices being in operation or not. (A note sometimes gets through to the busy boss much easier than a person.) If you were asked to give your roommate a message, you can leave a note and thus relieve the strain of your own memory. A note with your name and address left on the windshield of a car you have damaged saves waiting time; on the other hand, it may be more advisable to orally apologize with the goal of calming the victim down and keeping your subsequent costs as low as possible. Whether or not language is produced, and whether the oral or written mode is used, is often decided by a calculation of expense and return.

CONVENTIONS AND SOCIAL NORMS. For certain categories of linguistic utterances, it is a matter of custom, or at least advisable, to produce writing. Depending on your relation to the bereaved, you offer your condolences in writing. We often add a card to a birthday present even if it is accompanied by oral congratulations. In certain situations, you offer your business card and would never give an account of where you come from and who you work for. Writing allows one to communicate without sanctions in situations where it is imperative not to produce sounds (e.g., during lessons, during church attendance, or in formal situations when one person is making an address.) Incidentally, during a lecture, it is safer to write, "He is talking stuff and nonsense!" on your neighbor's notepad rather than to whisper it into the individual's ear, a little bit too loud so that other people can hear it. Written messages, being conserved language, do not require the recipient's immediate attention. Therefore, even in case of the addressee being a colleague who is working in the office next door, consideration and the intention not to bother, may bring you to ask via electronic mail rather than directly addressing the colleague about having lunch together. Moreover, many situations exist in which legal validity requires written language, for example, notice to quit, purchase agreements, or wedding ceremonies. At least in the German legal system, many of these acts can also be undertaken orally, but when they are fixed in writing, they are easier to prove.

INTERIM GOALS. Writing can assist oral language production or, indeed, nonlinguistic behavior in the pursuit of a goal, not by achieving the goal but by moving closer to it; for example, a written request to attend a meeting. It should be emphasized again that language production generally serves, in the first place, for the regulation of the S/W system (i.e., to achieve a stable state in the cognitive system), and not for the transmission of messages. The desired values, with which actual values are to be aligned by language production, refer predominantly to states outside the world of language; language production is often not more than one means among others for system regulation.

INSTRUMENTALITY. For certain goals, writing is more or less suitable than speaking. Unpleasant things are sometimes better written than said. In many cases, the written product appears more formal, or more distant, than speaking. Writing allows addressees to have more freedom, because they is not forced to react immediately. On the other hand, persuasion and surprise attacks are effected more easily through speaking. Writing, although it can be supplemented with pictures or graphics, lacks the nonverbal parts of language that may be useful to achieve goals. Writers cannot adapt the progress of their utterances to the partner's reaction to previous utterances. In a lecture, speakers often consider a mixture of oral and written language (i.e., on a blackboard, on transparencies) as instrumental in order to illustrate their topic in the best possible way. When instructing students in very formal and abstract topics, teachers often simultaneously speak and write the same thing (with formulae). Finally, if you want to meet strangers at the airport, it is hardly useful to call their name, simply because it is too loud there and it would be even louder if everybody would do so. Thus, in this situation, people carry written signs with the name on it.

COORDINATE AND SUPERORDINATE GOALS. In most cases, the partner knows which ways of communication would have been available for the speaker, whether or not they have been chosen. Therefore, the speaker can pursue a goal just by deciding to write or to speak, whatever the contents may be. You are not compelled to overcome your shyness when you declare your love in writing. You show your special attentiveness to friends when you pin a note on their apartment door instead of leaving a message on the answering machine — this implies that you have made an effort. Recall the example of inviting a colleague for lunch via electronic mail, thus showing that the partner's concentration is respected. As a last example in this context, writing with chalk on a slate and smudging it immediately afterward can serve the coordinate goal of keeping the group of potential receivers of a message under control (e.g. in situations where people might be bugged).

When there is a discrepancy between actual and desired values in the S/W system, which calls for system regulation, a decision is made about whether language production would be instrumental at all, and, if it is, which form of language production would lead to maximum instrumentality. First, this decision is based on the information (as it is represented in the system) about the current situation, as previously illustrated. Second, it is based on one's previous experiences. Third, it is based on one's general knowledge about the world. The decision also takes into consideration coordinate and superordinate goals. We tried to particularly emphasize that, in a great number of situations, instrumental language production can, in principle, be either oral or written.

With the production of scientific utterances, the institutional context requires, in most cases, the final product to be either oral or written. For example, lectures call for the production of spoken texts, whereas the documentation and distribution of theories, ideas and results is, nowadays, canonized in writing. And scholars know the problem with conferences when submitting a talk proposal (which requires speaking) and earning a poster presentation (which requires writing and drawing). However, the mode in which a text is produced does not need to be determined by the required form of the final product. People often write the manuscript for a lecture, which they conceive as instructions for their spoken language production. Conversely, you can dictate an entire textbook, which is not typed out before the end of the language production process. Thus, depending on whether the researcher pursues the product or the process of language production, the identical field of investigation can be concerned with either speaking or writing — with all their related cognitive processes. (See also the distinction between oral language and spoken language; Antos, 1982.)

Characteristics of the writing process

Assume that, in a situation, written language production appears to be the appropriate means of instrumental system regulation. How is the process of written language production to be characterized (cf. Herrmann & Grabowski, 1995)?

Several decades ago, linguistic studies employed statistical means and showed that oral and written linguistic products (results of language production) differ in several respects (e.g., Horowitz & Newman, 1964; Portnoy, 1973). For example, written utterances were proved to be longer than oral ones, and so forth. In these studies, however, the channel of utterances, the situation in which language is produced, and the content of communication often remained confounded (Grabowski-Gellert, 1989). When, for example,

Hidi and Hildyard (1983) partially resolved this confounding, they showed that the composition of utterances is determined more by the content-related factor "account of a story versus account of a commentary" than by the factor "oral vs. written mode of utterance." Furthermore, linguistic research on text types (Dimter, 1981; Guelich & Raible, 1975) showed that either the written or the oral mode is only occasionally a defining feature of text types. For the most part, there are just probabilistic coincidences.

In order to approach those characteristics of the language production process that are necessarily related to the choice of the written mode and therefore can be unambiguously attributed to the fact that writing processes (and not speaking processes) are operating, writing must be separated from all the aforementioned situation-related and goal-related coincidences. One appropriate means to reach the desired clarity is to compare writing with speaking in conditions that are comparable in regard to the situation, the goals and the partner. Several phenomena are generally considered to belong to the typical features that differentiate between speaking and writing and their underlying processes. However, in keeping with the analyses in the section *Writing as a Medium of Communication*, for a large part of these phenomena, an adequate explanation can be found in the field of the cognitive triggers of language production processes, that is, in the field of informational constellations in focus memory. Consequently, investigation of these phenomena is a question of the general language production process and not a question of writing as such. For example, many of the peculiarities observed with the use of deictic expressions (Grabowski & Miller, 1996), or with the situation-dependent specification of names for objects (Carroll, 1985), are based on identical or different situation contexts of the communicators or on the available or nonavailable mutual knowledge about the partner's situation context; these are not just based on the mode of utterance. A comparison of descriptions or instructions (which are addressed to a partner and produced via telephone, via electronic mail, via answering machine, or via letter) would tell us which peculiarities in the use of referential expressions are based on the choice of the spoken or written mode, and which are based on the partners being temporally and spatially co-present or not.

Asume it is the very same language production system that produces, from case to case, oral or written utterances; consequently, also assume that the preterminal levels of process (i.e., all levels that precede vocal or graphomotoric execution) are not separate modules specific to speaking or writing (Velichkovsky, 1994). People definitely succeed in "oralizing" written language when communicating via electronic mail, or, on the other hand, in dictating cooking recipes ready for printing. At all its levels, down to the encoding mechanism, the language production system is characterized by great flexibility and fine tuning between the subsystems involved. The following sections enumerate and discuss some candidates for those peculiarities of the process that are specific for writing.

People have strategic and process knowledge about how certain types of utterance are to be produced instrumentally, or how they should be produced according to norms and conventions (cf. Herrmann, 1983, for verbal request; Rummer, Grabowski, & Vorwerg, 1995, for event-related reports).

Here, the initiation of the process of written language production can join with particular pre-adjustments of the auxiliary systems and the encoding mechanism. These writing-specific preadjustments affect, among other things, the choice and instantiation of particular grammatical schemata and the inhibition of other ones (e.g., ellipses), the use of all tenses, and the means of emphasizing and sometimes also the choice (or inhibition) of certain word forms.

For written language production, the interaction of the auxiliary systems is different, as compared to speaking. Certain means for processing the proto-input before it is passed on to the encoding mechanism are inhibited, whereas other means are activated. For example, if the proto-input commands special emphasis of a particular concept, this can, in the case of speaking, make the auxiliary systems add marks that instruct the encoding mechanism to generate a cleft sentence. Alternatively, the auxiliary systems can command the encoding mechanism to put the corresponding word in the first position of a sentence (e.g., by putting the sentence in the passive voice); or to put stress on the corresponding word (e.g., by raising the volume); or to locally modify the pace of speaking (e.g., by pausing before the relevant word); or to use a combination of these means. In the case of writing, only the generation of cleft sentences and the modification of word order are available from these means; additional means are graphical emphasis (italics, underlining, font size) or, possibly, dashes — these are, in some cases, equivalent to temporal delays in the progression of speech. The functions of intonation contour and accent, which help to disambiguate the syntactic relations of phrases in speaking, must be compensated for in writing by word order and often also by the more precise choice of grammatical schemata (e.g., obeying the canonical subject-object order).

Punctuation marks play a special role in written language production. They can be used in three different functions that do not necessarily concur. In their grammatical use, they indicate the formal type of the sentence (declarative, interrogative, or imperative). Secondly, punctuation marks can symbolize intonation: the question mark after declarative sentences like "You like it?" or the exclamation mark after interrogative sentences with imperative intention, like "Could you mow the meadow now!" Question and exclamation marks are also used in order to express the producer's certainty or uncertainty about the content of the utterance, or to express the producer's estimation of the given facts. Thirdly, punctuation marks are used to mark the illocution of a sentence, such as when exclamation marks are used to indicate directives (Searle, 1969).

The problem of the necessity for compensation of nonverbal-nonvocal means, although it seems to be a writing-specific problem at first glance, concerns the general situation determinants of language production. Here, nonverbal-nonvocal means refer to, for example, a smile to show the producer's attitudes on the content of an utterance, a frown to show one's doubts about correct understanding, or a gesture as the deictic referent of "that big." These determinants result from whether or not the communication partners can see and/or hear one another, and, respectively, whether or not they mutually know whether their partner can see and/or hear them; they do not genuinely concern writing. On the one hand, many of these nonverbal means are not available in phone calls as well. On the other hand, as mentioned earlier, there are situations where writing is the instrumental choice of behavior, although both partners are temporally and spatially co-present and could bring all nonverbal means into action. The only question that remains is, in situations in which it is not possible to convey nonverbal-nonvocal components of expression, whether the written compensation of nonverbal means is different from the oral compensation. Incidentally, the production of facial expressions and gestures does not exclusively serve communicative purposes (Herrmann & Grabowski, 1994, p. 471). We all noticed in ourselves or in other people that we act facially and with gesture during phone calls or when we write a letter — this can never be perceived by the listener or the addressee, respectively. First, the fact that we produce communicatively useless behavior supports our assumption that the auxiliary systems, which govern the co-ordination of verbal and nonverbal components of utterances, operate automatically and almost without attention and awareness. Apparently, system regulation by language production is more economical when the same programs are brought into action in every case; even if they generate components of behavior that do not help — but do not hinder either — the achievement of a goal in a given situation. It would be less economical to spend attentional resources and efforts in order to suppress one's nonverbal behavior in settings where it is useless. Second, nonverbal behavior often accompanies the process of utterance planning (i.e., the preparation of the proto-input) and is not meant to accompany the result of this process (i.e., the verbal utterance). (Try explaining to somebody over the phone how to knot a tie or how to tie a knot without using your hands before you explain the successive steps. You won't succeed!) Third, there are cases in which facial expressions and gestures have no connection with language production processes at all, but are the mere expression of internal states.

An interesting field of phenomena is written communication via electronic devices, particularly by regular users like the participants in newslists. There are several clues about the assumption that this necessarily written form of communication strongly follows oral everyday language. For example, a certain style of spelling is used that can only be understood if pronunciation is imagined ("4 2sday nite" instead of "for Tuesday night"). On the other hand, the fact that oral ways of expression are retained, although accompanying nonverbal components are not available, apparently called for the development of special characters for pragmatic purposes. For example, the sign "8-)" (a stylized smiley face, turned left through 90°) is intended to mean "take this to be kind and friendly; this is meant to be funny," whereas the sign "8-(" (a turned-left grimly face) is intended to express the writer's negative or serious attitude. The development of this form of communication, which is often used like a written telephone with quasi-online interaction of the interlocutors, offers the opportunity to investigate, based on the process as well as on the products, which characteristics and which means of expression are really connected to writing as such, and which of the hitherto recognized characteristics are merely conditioned by situative, social, and normative prescriptions for the use of writing.

The previous listing of some special characteristics of the writing process is all but exhaustive. Again, remember that it is not speaking or writing as such that determines either the function of central control, the generation and marking of the proto-input and of the input for the encoding mechanism, or the adjustment of the auxiliary systems and the encoding mechanism. Rather, the determinants of the language production process are the information about the present situation as it is represented in the speaker/writer, information about the communication partner, and information about the goals that the language producer wants to pursue. It is also the general, often schematized knowledge about the instrumentality of certain linguistic utterances, and knowledge about the rules and norms, that make certain utterances advisable and other utterances misplaced.

The next section addresses a question that is particularly salient in the context of the writing process (Klein, 1985) and one that concerns the early cognitive processes at the level of central control. The purpose of this final section is to illustrate the experimental translation of research issues in the framework of our model of language production.

In order to manage the local and global planning of utterances and their coherence, a speaker must — at first literally (Sachs, 1967), then in terms of the propositional gist (Herrmann & Grabowski, 1994, p. 332) — continuously maintain a mental discourse protocol of the already produced utterances. In writing, the producer is released from this mental load because the already written text, being a conserved trace of behavior, can serve as an external, easily available discourse store. Does this relief in favor of the cognitive resources improve or support the quality of other processes, for example, the retrieval of knowledge from memory?

Retrieval from memory and external store

In a context different from writing, we conducted experiments on the situation-specific language production processes that are involved in verbal accounts of events (Grabowski, Vorwerg, & Rummer, 1994; Rummer, Grabowski, & Vorwerg, 1995). We consistently found, as others did before, that speakers often omit certain parts of the recounted event. In this particular research, we had difficulty showing that the information thematized in the event-related accounts is in fact the result of the situation-specific selection of information to be verbalized. It was necessary to exclude the alternative explanation that the selection of information would be merely due to the incomplete or deficient cognition and/or memory of the event. For example, we presented participants — under experimental control — with a film about a theft of sunglasses at the optician's. Participants were asked to imagine that they observed the theft. Afterward, they were to give an oral account of the event in two different types of situation: to produce an eyewitness report that was addressed to a policeman; to produce an entertaining narration that was addressed to a curious neighbor. Systematic and significant differences occurred between both situations with respect to the completeness of the thematized episodes, and the thematization of inference-based information. In order to prove selection processes, participants observed the theft under identical conditions, but we asked them to write down all event-related information that they could remember. In this case, the accounts were significantly more complete compared to the previously mentioned oral conditions. (However, see Bekerian & Dennett, 1990, for contrary results.) This result was sufficient to show that the speakers in the oral situations (i.e., when reporting to a police officer and narrating to a neighbor), would potentially have had more event-related knowledge available than their utterances actually contained. We can account for this difference in terms of situation-specific selection processes. However, how can the difference between the oral accounts and the written accounts of an event be generally explained in terms of the underlying cognitive processes of language production? (Incidentally, the reported results raise the general question of optimal and appropriate methods for the diagnosis of event-related knowledge and of knowledge in general, as it is relevant with eyewitness reports or exams.)

The superiority of written accounts with respect to their completeness of thematized information, as it was found in our experiments, can be put down to several causes. These concern the relations between the (by the acquisition of knowledge) potentially available information in long-term memory, the (by retrieval from memory) actual available information in working memory, (i.e., in central control) and the information that is (by selection processes of language production) thematized in the utterance. What are the factors that determine these relations? What are the factors that are, in terms of cognitive psychology, actually responsible for the differences between writing and speaking? We assume at least the following four factors are most relevant (cf. Kellogg, 1994):

DECONTEXTUALIZATION. In the written condition, language producers' internal model of the addressee is less defined and less distinct than when they talk to a police officer or to a neighbor, respectively. Therefore, the situation is more decontexualized, which leads to the suppression of the selection processes that serve for situation-specific instrumental language production. This is not to say that writing does not contextualize at all; but the internal model of the addressee remains more pale, as it does not include momentary moods and states.

EXTERNAL STORE. We already mentioned that we assume the immediate, (i.e., literal) discourse protocol to function automatically without demanding attentional resources. (This is generally the case with the processes of the auxiliary systems.) However, language producers must maintain in working memory the propositional gist (recoded from the literal protocol) in order to ensure the global coherence of their utterances. For example, speakers must know whether they have already thematized a certain episode of the event they refer to. Therefore, a conflict exists about whether to use the limited resources of working memory for the discourse protocol, for the retrieval of information from memory, or for the initiation and control of the other processes involved in language production. With written language production, the already written passages are an external store and thus take the place of the discourse protocol. The external store possibly relieves the load on working memory. This could be of benefit to the retrieval processes. If the conflict of the use of cognitive resources is resolved by neglecting the discourse protocol in cases of oral language production, it is expected either that the produced utterances are more redundant (because some information is repeated) or that information is not thematized although it would have been available (because the producer assumes that the information has already been thematized). And, if the discourse protocol is prioritized and the retrieval processes are neglected, it is expected that the reduction of retrieval leads to utterances that contain, on the whole, less information and that show a higher amount of wrong or less accurate information.

PERIOD IN WHICH RESOURCES ARE USED. In general, the production of written utterances takes more time than the production of oral utterances. This is because more time is needed to execute grapho-motoric programs than to execute phonetic programs. Thus, the cognitive resources are used for a longer period of time when people write. This may be of benefit to all attention-consuming processes, including the retrieval of information from memory.

PACING. In spoken discourse, people are required to refrain from making too long pauses, or to fill pauses with turn-keeping signals (Sacks, Schegloff, & Jefferson, 1974). Therefore, speakers must promptly continue producing utterances if they want to keep the turn. We assumed that the habit of maintaining a certain density of language production also affects speaking in decontexualized situations due to the aforementioned fact that the costly inhibition and suppression of well-practiced processes is generally avoided. However, writing is self-paced (in cases where the addressee is not directly present). It is up to writers to interrupt encoding and the related graphomotoric activities and to use their cognitive resources exclusively for planning processes, including retrieval from memory, without spending mental energy on turn keeping and the avoidance of too long pauses.

Each of these four factors offers an explanation for the fact that knowledge retrieval is more complete in writing. The specific contributions of the four factors to the processes and results of language production can be separated by systematic experimentation. This leads to the outline of a research program that is closely related to recent concepts in general psychology (cf. Baddeley, 1986, 1992; Norman & Shallice, 1986). The program is aimed at giving detailed information about the interaction between memory, cognitive resources, consumption of attention, and the processes of oral and written language production.

If two possible values are to be assigned to each factor, 16 experimental cells emerge (2^4). These values are the situation in which language is produced is either contextualized or decontextualized, depending on whether or not a defined addressee exists; whether or not an external store is available; if the cognitive resources are either used as long as needed, or their use is restricted to the temporal progression of the execution of speaking or writing, respectively; and if language production is either self-paced or paced by external forces (e.g. by the rules of turn taking and turn keeping).

In our first experiments on this issue, we investigated the external store and the amount of time that can be spent on the access to long-term memory. For example, writing with invisible ink preserves all characteristics of writing except the availability of an external store for the discourse protocol; dictating — and stopping the tape when needed — differs from writing with invisible ink only with respect to the basic habits of oral and written language production (i.e., pacing). We found systematic and significant effects on the number of repeated information, on the lengths of the utterances, on the use of macro-propositions that condense information, on the specification of information, and on the number of errors based on either wrong inferences or bad memory access. These results led to the conclusion that the differences between written and oral products of language production are much more based on the differences in the temporal characteristics of the use of cognitive resources than based on the fact that writing, but not speaking, offers an external store for the discourse protocol.

Conclusions

Our position is intended to be a plea for the intensification of pure research on the production of written language, employing the theoretical and experimental means of general psychology. As regards the technological and application-related issues of developmental and educational psychology, we only referred to the aspect of the retrieval of potentially available information in memory being more or less complete. We did not discuss other important issues such as the teaching and acquisition of writing strategies, the improvement of the quality of texts (whatever "quality" is defined to be), or creative writing. However, detailed insight into the individual cognitive processes of writing and into their determining factors will not only increase our general knowledge. It will also be helpful for the use of measures in order to improve writing-related skills, and for the problem of how to use these measures most effectively and at the most suitable points of the writing process and its development. For example, instructional measures should be taken in consideration of the automatized regulation mechanisms of the language production system; and they should be taken at points where not many other things put load on the resources of working memory. Furthermore, there are obvious implications for the optimal diagnosis of knowledge, that is, where maximum completeness of the information available in memory is required, whether before the court or in education.

Acknowledgments

Large parts of these ideas were developed while I was a visiting researcher at Princeton University, supported by a grant from the German Science Foundation (DFG). I am grateful to George Miller and Christiane Fellbaum for their hospitality. Ralf Rummer helped to develop and improve theory and experimentation. Jim Grimes skillfully edited my German English.

— 5 —
WORKING MEMORY CONSTRAINTS ON WRITING QUALITY AND FLUENCY

Sarah Ransdell
Florida Atlantic University

C. Michael Levy
University of Florida

Expressing one's thoughts in writing is often a dreaded and onerous task. Other times it can be pure joy — fluent, fluid, and seemingly effortless. Most often, however, writing is very demanding, and relative to speaking, a process that requires extensive self-regulation and attentional control (see also Grabowski, chapter 4, and Kellogg, chapter 3 in this volume). Part of the reason for the relative difficulty of writing is that it requires that a number of subprocesses be simultaneously managed. Writers must change ideas into text, repair organization and mechanics, and monitor their success — all while trying to formulate a coherent message. Working memory capacity limits in multitask situations like this implicate the central executive component of Baddeley and Hitch's model (1974). The central executive has limited resources that coordinate task performance through the selection, facilitation, and control of subprocesses. How the central executive contributes to successful and fluent writing may also help us understand the nature and timing of these various subprocesses.

We review in this chapter some recent evidence that the quality and fluency of one's writing can be constrained by individual differences in working memory. *Writing quality* is defined by the Six-Subgroup Quality Scale (SSQS, explained in Appendix 5.1), which is a holistic quality score based on reliable ratings of 13 dimensions of writing success. Initial research in this area suggests that working memory contributions to writing quality are complex and mediated by reading comprehension ability (Kellogg, chapter 3 in this volume; Madigan, Johnson, & Linton, 1994; McCutchen, Covill, Hoyne, & Mildes, 1994). Researchers continue to employ a variety of different complex span measures and often arrive at somewhat different conclusions regarding working memory contributions to writing quality. Writing fluency, on the other hand, is much more consistently related to working memory capacity and is positively correlated with writing quality. As we discuss later, those with greater working memory capacity as assessed by complex span measures (reading, speaking, writing span) are more likely to generate words fluently in an essay writing task (Ransdell & Levy, 1995a).

Reading ability also plays a fundamental role in Hayes' new model of writing and is likely to be intimately tied to writing ability (Hayes, chapter 1 in this volume). In Hayes' model, evaluative reading is accompanied by problem solving and language generation as the three main subprocesses of a writing task. Reading comprehension has already been extensively linked to individual differences in working memory capacity (i.e., Daneman & Carpenter, 1980). It is perhaps no coincidence that reading comprehension provides an easily obtained and reliable measure of success and has been thoroughly tested with regard to working memory constraints. The assessment of writing quality has proven in a more difficult measure to validate in laboratory research, especially for those viewing such research from a pedagogical perspective (i.e., Cox, 1990; White, 1994). The chapter thus begins with the topic of assessment including a description of the quality rating procedure used in our research, the SSQS. Assessment issues are followed by a review of the relation between reading comprehension and reading span, a working memory predictor of reading comprehension. The chapter continues with the introduction of a writing span measure for predicting writing quality and writing fluency and concludes with future directions for writing research.

The assessment of writing

Writing quality is a very complex set of measures resulting from a variety of cognitive processes. In fact, some readers of this volume may believe writing to be an art that defies scientific analysis. As this section shows, writing quality can be reliably assessed and studied in the laboratory in a meaningful and productive way. Assessment is related to the question "Why do we know so much less about writing than we do reading?" Reading comprehension has a much longer history of research and is relatively easy to assess by accuracy measurements. The question "Has one comprehended this prose?" has been a much clearer question that "Has one written good prose?" Most researchers agree that assessing writing is a formidable task and yet one of the most important considerations for the field. This chapter deals with assessment because it is paramount to understanding working memory constraints on writing. Assessment is also important for ecological validity. Writing research should provide teachers as well as researchers with some knowledge of the cognitive factors that promote high quality writing.

Two reliable measures of writing performance, writing fluency and writing quality have been shown to be partially explained by individual differences in working memory capacity (Ransdell & Levy, 1995a). Writing fluency is operationally defined as the number of words created per minute controlling for typing speed (Madigan, Holt, & Blackwell, 1993; Ransdell, 1995a). Key-capture programs make fluency a readily available assessment of word processed writing (Ransdell, 1990). As mentioned earlier, we have recently discovered that writing fluency is directly associated with higher working memory capacity and better quality writing (Ransdell & Levy, 1995a). Furthermore, across two experiments, the relationship between writing fluency and working memory was consistently stronger than the relationship between writing quality and working memory. The irrelevant speech effect occurs when working memory is impaired in the presence of human speech, even if it is to be ignored (Gathercole & Baddeley, 1993). In our research, listening to irrelevant speech while writing slowed fluency indicating working memory involvement, but did not significantly decrease writing quality. Apparently, the timing made possible by increased working memory capacity affects translating fluency more directly than it does the quality of the written product. The section on writing span later in the chapter will develop more fully the issue of specific working memory contributions to quality and fluency. But first, we consider the nature of writing quality. The next section describes our quality scale and compares it to another widely-used measure, the essay sort procedure developed by Madigan, Johnson and Linton (see chapter 15 in this volume).

The SSQS, our writing quality measure, is an analytic composite score taken from 13 ratings by two independent judges. Appendix 5.1 provides a description of the six subgroups and the specific values to be found in writing samples for each score on a 5-point scale. Typical writing assignments are expository writing about topics for which most college students have knowledgeable opinions (i.e., qualities of a good professor, good undergraduate course, or good boyfriend/girlfriend). Writers compose essays as if they are writing for a graded school assignment. The measure provides scores for word choice and arrangement, technical quality, engagement in content, purpose/audience/tone, organization and development, and style (Levy & Ransdell, 1995; Ransdell, 1990; Ransdell & Levy, 1995a & 1995b). The SSQS was adapted from a university-level English placement exam and has proven both reliable and discriminating with college-level samples (typical interrater r's are in the .80s and .90s).

The basic procedure is as follows: Quality raters first participate in group discussions of the scale and study examples in a sample set of essays. Then raters read all the essays in the sample first to get an idea of the overall range in holistic quality. Next, raters provide analytical ratings by reading the essays, one at a time, for a particular dimension in the order in which they are presented on the scale. Raters make independent judgments of each dimension. The raters begin by judging whether the essay is in the top half, toward a score of 5, or the bottom half, toward a score of 1. Next, they decide whether the essay is closer to a 2 or a 4. The middle score of 3 is assigned only as a last resort. The raters then discuss all ratings different by more than two points on the 5-point scale (trained raters need discuss less than 10% of the ratings at this point). Quite high interrater reliabilities can be achieved with this procedure as average correlations between raters is .85 across all 13 dimensions (highest reliability is achieved in the Mechanics subgroup and lowest in the Style subgroup). In terms of concurrent validity, the SSQS consistently predicts Nelson-Denny reading comprehension scores accounting for up to 25% of the variance across three experiments and 139 subjects (Ransdell & Levy, 1995a). The scale also reliably discriminates between basic and advanced writers (Ransdell & Levy, 1995b).

The internal structure of the SSQS Scale is cohesive. Overall quality, the 6 subgroup quality dimensions, and Nelson-Denny reading comprehension scores (Nelson & Denny, 1993) are represented in Table 5.1. In Ransdell and Levy (1995a), overall quality correlated most highly with the subgroup Engagement in Content (r = .73), Organization (.74), Style (.85), and Mechanics (.85). Reading comprehension was significantly correlated with Organization

(.34) and Mechanics (.35). A principal components factor analysis indicates that quality measured in this way can be considered a unitary dimension and that, on average across three experiments, 55% of the variance in quality scores can be accounted for by a single factor which we named *Six-Subgroup Quality*. Several researchers have found only a moderate relationship between writing quality and fluency measures (e.g., Kellogg, 1994; Madigan, Johnson & Linton, 1994). But again, researchers have used different quality and fluency metrics. And as Kellogg points out in chapter 3 of this volume, quality is not directly dependent on processing rates. Other researchers have not found a link between reading span and writing quality. The essay sorting procedure devised by Madigan et al. involves a holistic rating based on placing essays in quintiles from poor to good. Johnson, Linton, and Madigan (1994) found that students whose decisions about writing quality matched those of their instructors received higher ratings on their own writing. Madigan et al. found a significant correlation between this essay sorting procedure and reading span. A recent study by Ransdell and Levy (1995a), however, found neither overall quality nor any subgroup quality dimension to be related reliably to reading or speaking span measures. In a later section of this chapter we will discuss a writing span measure that does predict quality.

Table 5.1
Intercorrelations among overall Six-Subgroup Quality, each subgroup quality dimension, and reading comprehension in Experiment 1, Ransdell and Levy (1995a)

Scales	2	3	4	5	6	7	8
1. Overall quality	.73	.48	.40	.74	.85	.85	.32
2. Engagement in content		.27	.05	.48	.76	.52	.11
3. Purpose and audience			.25	.56	.32	.49	.01
4. Word choice				.23	.35	.47	.13
5. Organization					.58	.65	.34
6. Style						.73	.22
7. Mechanics							.37
8. Reading comprehension							

   The essays written by subjects in Experiment 2 of Ransdell and Levy (1995a) were also scored using the Madigan et al. essay sort procedure. The correlation between essay sort quality scores and our 13-point scale was $r = .25$, with interrater reliability averaging .65. Essay sort quality accounted for less than 1% of the variance in our measure of writing span. Our quality measures accounted for about 8% of the variance in writing span. The Six-Subgroup Quality score correlated .51 with reading comprehension scores and the essay sort, .13. It is possible that our 13-dimension scale taps a more general verbal ability and that the Madigan et al. scale, organizational skills specifically (Madigan, personal communication). Only subsequent research can untangle this interesting quandary. We do know that essay sort quality is most related to subgroups Style ($r = .24$) and Word Choice ($r = .21$) in the SSQS. It is also clear from this comparison that more attention should be placed on content validity in writing quality research. The next section highlights the established link between reading span and reading comprehension. Perhaps the bright light emanating from research on reading and working memory will cast a clarifying glow on our understanding of writing performance.

Reading comprehension and reading span

One of the main premises of this chapter is that working memory plays a very important role in language production. It is well documented that it does so in language comprehension. Written language production requires the constant monitoring of variety of complex subtasks, including problem solving, language generation, and evaluative reading (Hayes, chapter 1 in this volume; Hayes & Flower, 1980). Despite this obvious role of central executive resources in working memory, research has only just begun. Part of the logic of our approach to advancing the field is to compare working memory constraints on reading comprehension to constraints on writing performance.

The storage of information for temporary use was first conceived of as short-term memory and was measured by simple spans like digit or word span (Miller, 1956). The problem with simple spans was that they did not predict complex behaviors like reading. The key difference between simple and complex span is that complex span involves both a storage and processing component, whereas simple spans, like digit, involve only storage. This later reconceptualization viewed working memory as a multicomponent system for both storage and processing of verbal and visuo-spatial tasks (Baddeley & Hitch, 1974; Gathercole & Baddeley, 1993). In fact, Daneman and Tardif (1987) argued that tradeoffs between storage and processing are a critical factor when predicting working memory and language relations. Ransdell and Levy (1995a) reported that writers with high reading comprehension ability are better able to impose advantageous strategies focusing on storage or on processing during a writing span test than are those with low reading ability. In this case, as in many others, high reading comprehension affords greater strategic flexibility (see also Gernsbacher & Faust, 1991). We also found that those with higher reading comprehension skill remembered more words when asked to focus on memory and wrote more complex sentences when asked to focus on writing. The writing span task proved to be much more difficult than either the reading or speaking span measures on which it was based. Confronted with increased difficulty, some participants focused on memory, others on writing sentences. The resulting span measure reflected this strategic confusion, and did not predict any behaviors reliably. This writing span measure and what it predicts are discussed in more detail later.

The study of individual differences in working memory benefited greatly from the creation of a complex span called reading span, created by Daneman and Carpenter (1980). The reading span test is devised to simultaneously draw on the processing and storage resources of working memory specifically during reading. Participants read aloud increasingly larger sets of unrelated sentences. At the end of each set, they recall as many of the last words in each sentence as possible. Daneman and Green (1986) also created a speaking span test measured by individuals producing rather than simply comprehending the sentences. Reading and speaking span require similar storage tasks, but different processing tasks, reading comprehension and speech production, respectively.

Many studies have shown that these measures of working memory capacity predict differences in reading comprehension (Daneman & Carpenter, 1980; Daneman & Green, 1986; Just & Carpenter, 1992; Masson & Miller, 1983; Palmer, MacLeod, Hunt, & Davidson, 1985). Reading span is correlated not only with reading comprehension, but with fact retrieval and pronomial reference skill (Daneman & Green, 1986), the ability to draw inferences from text (Masson & Miller, 1983), lexical decision and Posner name matching times (Baddeley, Logie, Nimmo-Smith, & Brereton, 1985), syntactic processing (King & Just, 1991) and the resolution of lexical ambiguity (Miyake, Just, & Carpenter, 1994). Comparing reading span to reading comprehension and other language behaviors also addresses the issue of generality in working memory constraints. Engle, Cantor, and Carullo (1992) are among those researchers favoring a general capacity explanation of working memory constraints on comprehension. We seek to extend this explanation to language production. Ransdell and Levy (1995a) suggested that working memory capacity is affected by strategy efficiency. We found that reading comprehension is correlated with reading, speaking, and writing span suggesting some generality of working memory contributions to language tasks but tradeoffs between storage and processing were important qualifiers to such relations.

The following section highlights our recent results regarding writing span and writing performance relations. We reasoned that if the efficiency of the processing component during a span measure is important, then a writing span measure will best predict writing fluency and writing quality.

Writing performance and writing span

Hayes and Flower (1980), as well as more recent models of working memory and writing (e.g., Kellogg, chapter 3 in this volume) have proposed that individual differences in writing performance will be related to the ability to manage the simultaneous constraints of planning, generating text, reviewing, and revising already written text. It is therefore likely that a complex problem-solving task like writing will depend a great deal on the ability to maximize working memory capacity. There is also some evidence that writing performance is related to working memory through writing fluency rather than through writing quality performance directly (Ransdell & Levy, 1995a). The next section focuses on the importance of tradeoffs between storage and processing during span measures and their relation to writing fluency.

Writing span affords two measures of performance, *percent of words recalled* and *mean sentence length*. When the required strategy is remembering as many words as possible at the cost of generating "short and dull" sentences, memory performance during writing span predicts reading comprehension at least as well as speaking span does (Ransdell & Levy, 1995a). Conversely, when the required strategy is producing the best possible sentences at the cost of remembering words, sentence length in writing span measures predicts both reading comprehension and writing quality. McCutchen, Covill, Hoyne, and Mildes (1994) also found that reading span predicts writing quality when a semantic task is emphasized. Reading span predicted writing quality when sentences were semantically related in each set — that is, presented in story format — but not when the sentences were unrelated to each other. Both of these findings suggest that attention to written language production during a span measure makes that measure more likely to predict writing performance.

As discussed earlier, writing span also consistently predicts writing fluency. We have found stronger relations between writing span and fluency than span and quality. Those subjects who write more quickly, controlling for typing speed, also tend to create more successful essays (Ransdell & Levy, 1995a). It is likely that working memory contributes to writing quality by way of sentence generation processes that in turn influence the ability to produce high quality documents. Power (1985) found that subjects who generated spoken sentences while holding a digit load in working memory actually speeded their production with correspondingly poorer quality sentences created. Jeffery and Underwood (1995) replicated this speeded response under a 6-digit load during a written sentence generation task (writing sentences from grids of words). They determined that if semantic processing is required during a language task, as in generating meaningful sentences, then working memory contributions to the task, as measured by a digit load, speed production. Jeffery and Underwood compared sentence creation to sentence dictation, the latter being relatively devoid of semantic processing. They found that when no semantic processing was required, digit preload slowed sentence production.

In contrast to increasing production fluency, Baddeley and Hitch (1974) found that a 6-digit preload, which is "at capacity" for most individuals, caused subjects to slow recall and reasoning performance. A 0- or 3-digit preload, which presumably does not require central executive resources because it is below the capacity constraints of the system, does not impair such performance. Gathercole and Baddeley (1993) reviewed several speech production studies and concluded that the central executive component of working memory is therefore involved in planning the conceptual content of speech. On the basis of these previous results, it is likely that the central executive plays a major role during written language production as well. That role is critically dependent on whether the processing task involves meaningful semantic processing, especially that required of sentence generation processes.

Our results thus far support a general system with unitary capacity. Capacity varies as a function of how efficient an individual is at the specific processes demanded by the task to which working memory is applied. Working memory constraints on language tasks require the same general working memory capacity, but different resource allocations are required given the different demands of reading, speech perception, speaking and writing (Daneman & Carpenter, 1986; Just & Carpenter, 1992). In addition to the role of the central executive demanded by such a focus on efficient strategy use, it is also likely that the phonological articulatory loop and visuo-spatial sketchpad slave systems of Baddeley's working memory model play some role in writing performance. Studies of the contributions of these support systems are presently underway.

Conclusions

Several conclusions can be drawn from recent work on working memory constraints on writing quality and fluency. First, at least within the language domain, working memory constraints will vary as a function of how efficient one is in allocating resources to reading, speaking, and writing. Complex span measures can provide an independent assessment of the likelihood of such efficiency. There is some evidence that writing span is the best predictor of working memory efficiency during realistic writing tasks. Second, the relation between reading and writing ability is complex and more experimental studies are needed (Cox, 1990). We found that reading span and writing quality together account for over 30% of the variance in reading comprehension scores (Ransdell & Levy, 1995a). Other studies have found such links between reading and writing skill. Moravcsik and Kintsch (1993) manipulated writing quality by creating very poorly or very well-written texts and determined that the resulting quality had an effect on reading comprehension independent of domain knowledge, one of the strongest determinants of comprehension ability. This suggest that one's writing skill contributes directly to one's reading comprehension skill and that working memory efficiency may be one of the individual difference variables linking the two language behaviors. Schewe and Froese (1987) found that evidence of a story grammar in writing samples and reading comprehension ability were significantly correlated. It is clear that readers and writers both must construct meaning from text, however, more research is needed to determine how working memory capacity or other factors mediate comprehension and production processes.

One of the most pervasive findings of our research is that working memory contributions to reading comprehension and writing quality and fluency are influenced by strategy efficiency. We found that under a processing focus, writing span predicts writing quality better than under a storage focus. In other words, those who write longer sentences when asked for a processing strategy also write better quality essays. Conversely, those who remember more words when asked for a storage strategy, generate words more quickly. A complex span measure must be considered in the context of its requirements. For example, the writing span task is a very difficult one for most subjects such that if they are not given explicit strategy requirements, the span measure is not reliable. When writers are asked to write the best and longest sentences they can at the cost of remembering fewer words they are performing a task much like that when they are writing an essay. When writers are asked to write short sentences and mainly just remember the words, they are not writing in the same context as when they write normally.

Finally, the effects of secondary tasks during writing are clearly mediated by individual differences in writing span and reading comprehension. The relation between writing fluency and writing span depends on capacity allocations based on processing versus storage tradeoffs. Higher reading comprehension and writing ability afford greater processing flexibility. Flexibility is most easily seen in tradeoff situations. Research therefore needs to focus on experiments that view performance under varying strategic conditions. Perhaps digit span tasks that focus entirely on memory do not predict complex language behavior because there is no possibility of a process-storage tradeoff. Writing research is beginning to glow with the light of new evidence linking central executive flexibility and efficiency to successful writing quality. That writing fluency is even more closely linked to such efficiency demands that future research focus on the temporal patterns of idea generation and the monitoring of organization and mechanics. This will allow us to determine strategies that successful writers employ to maximize their resources and the success of their writing.

Acknowledgments

Preparation of this chapter was supported in part by a grant from Florida Atlantic University, Division of Sponsored Research and a grant from the Norman Shulevitz Foundation. Thanks to Ronald Kellogg and Robert Madigan for their thoughtful comments on earlier drafts of this chapter.

Appendix 5.1
QUALITY RATING GUIDELINES

Subgroup 1 — Words: Choice and Arrangement

1. Readable vs. Awkward

This is a measure of how well the reader can derive meaning from the sentence. Essays should be read aloud for this point only. (NOTE: pausing to derive meaning from the sentence should only be considered when it is attributable to the essay and not the rater.)

> 5 = When read aloud, all sentence meanings were crystal clear the first time. It is not necessary to pause and think.
> 4 = When read aloud, all sentence meanings are clear the first time. Some pausing to think is needed.
> 2 = When read aloud, more than one sentence needs to be repeated to derive meaning. The writer's intent/idea is ambiguous.
> 1 = After repeating, writer's intent is still unknown.

Subgroup 2 — Technical Quality: Mechanics

The three technical ratings (tenses, grammar and spelling) will be more quantitative than qualitative in nature than the remaining. In rating these points, a predetermined number of errors should define "many" and "few" based on the average length of the essay.

2. Tenses
> 5 = All tenses correctly used.
> 4 = Most tenses correctly used.
> 2 = Most tenses incorrectly used.
> 1 = Consistent tense errors throughout.

3. Grammar
> 5 = Almost no grammatical errors.
> 4 = Few grammatical errors.
> 2 = Many grammatical errors.
> 1 = Little evidence of grammatical knowledge. Very poor grammar throughout.

4. Spelling
Incorrect hyphenation within words or making one word into two (i.e.,"class room," rather than "classroom") are considered spelling errors, not grammatical errors. Obvious typos are not to be considered misspelled words. For example, "misspelled words." Additionally, incorrectly spelled words can be attributed to typing errors if they are correctly spelled in another part of the essay.

> 5 = No misspelled words.
> 4 = One misspelled word.
> 2 = Two or more misspelled words.
> 1 = Two or more misspelled words with some of them being commonly used words (elementary school level).

Subgroup 3 — Content of Essay

The next two scales are an evaluation of the writer's global attitude with regard to the assigned topic.

5. Engaged vs. Uninvolved
> 5 = Extremely serious or passionate and very engaged with the subject at hand; formal and not redundant. No use of inappropriate jokes.
>
> 4 = Not quite as engaged or passionate as a 5 rating, while remaining formal and not redundant; serious and almost no use of inappropriate jokes.
>
> 2 = Some inappropriate use of jokes and not very serious; casual and unengaged.
>
> 1 = Many inappropriate uses of jokes and a sense of not really caring about the topic. Very redundant, casual and uninvolved.

6. Alternative Points vs. Egocentric
Does the writer ever acknowledge the existence of anyone other than him or herself? When a writer refers to his or her argument as "my opinion," he or she thereby acknowledges that other points of view exist, even though other viewpoints may never actually be discussed in the essay.
> 5 = Consistent acknowledgment and discussion of other points of view.
>
> 4 = Some acknowledgment and discussion of other points of view.
>
> 2 = Few acknowledgments and almost no discussion of other points of view. Very vehement and closed-minded.
>
> 1 = Almost no acknowledgments and a lack of discussion of other points of view. Very vehement and closed-minded.

Subgroup 4 — Purpose/Audience/Tone

7. Purpose Clear vs. Unclear
A clear and definite statement of purpose with elaboration would be rated high. A stated purpose for writing is usually evident by the end of the first paragraph.
> 5 = There is definite statement of purpose, and at least 75% of body revolves around the thesis.
>
> 4 = When 50 to 75% of body revolves around the statement of purpose.
>
> 2 = There is no statement of purpose, but essay has coherence.
>
> 1 = There is no statement of purpose, and essay is sporadic.

8. Language and Tone Appropriate/Consistency
Depending on the topic, raters must decide if they are seeking appropriate language and/or looking for consistency throughout the essay with regard to language and tone). Examples of informal words include "a lot" and "kind of." Clichés and second person are also inappropriate.
> 5 = Respectful, formal and no sarcasm. Nearly total consistency.

4 = Respectful and formal containing almost no sarcasm or double meanings. Almost no inconsistencies.

2 = Containing some sarcasm or jokes; casual; 50% of essay does not use the same language and/or tone as the other 50%.

1 = Very casual bordering on disrespectful, sarcastic and/or containing jokes. Essay is totally disconnected throughout.

Subgroup 5 — Organization and Development

9. Support and Elaboration

This point quantitatively measures the number of arguments and how well they are presented. First, establish how many arguments constitute "few" and "many." The degree of elaboration will differentiate between a rating of 4 and 1 and a rating of 5 and 2. Marking each reason as you read the essay is helpful.

5 = Many different reasons and at least 65% are elaborated.

4 = Few reasons and at least 65% are elaborated.

2 = Many reasons and less than 65% are elaborated.

1 = Few reasons and less than 65% are elaborated.

10. Sense of Completeness

5 = All thoughts or ideas tied together by one or more conclusions.

4 = Most thoughts or ideas tied into a conclusion.

2 = No general conclusion, but thoughts have closure.

1 = No conclusions.

11. Paragraphing

5 = Sufficient use of paragraphs between thoughts. Paragraphs contain an opening sentence and some elaboration. They should end with a sentence that leads smoothly into the next paragraph.

4 = Sufficient use of paragraphs between thoughts. Paragraphs contain opening sentence and some elaboration. Choppy transitions between paragraphs.

2 = Insufficient us of paragraphs. Only 1 or 2 paragraphs used when 5 or 6 are needed or excessive use of paragraphing. Almost no use of opening sentences. Choppy transitions.

1 = No paragraphing is used or paragraphing is arbitrary.

Subgroup 6 — Style

Scales 12 and 13 should be assessed assuming the writer possesses a college level use of English.

12. Sentence Structure and Conciseness

5 = Almost no run-on sentences or wasted words. Clear and to the point.

4 = Almost no run-on sentences, few wasted words.

2 = Redundant and immature. Not clear or concise.

1 = Many wasted words and many run-on sentences. Immature. Very slow to read.

13. Daring versus Safe
Be careful not to let opinion enter here.

5 = Unique ideas and very mature, creative, extensive use of the English language.

4 = Unique ideas or very mature, creative, extensive use of English language.

2 = No new thoughts and moderate use of English.

1 = No new thoughts and/or very simple English with a limited vocabulary.

— 6 —

THE DYNAMICS OF COMPOSING — AN AGENDA FOR RESEARCH INTO AN INTERACTIVE COMPENSATORY MODEL OF WRITING: MANY QUESTIONS, SOME ANSWERS

Gert Rijlaarsdam
University of Amsterdam

Huub van den Bergh
Utrecht University

One of the features of a writing process is the continuing changing task situation. The amount of available information changes as the text produced so far increases. "the recursive nature of the writing process observed in studies in planning and revision allows, *and in fact calls for*, re-representation" (Carey & Flower, 1989, p. 6; italics added). Writers might adapt to changes in task situations and changes in processes and strategies (cf. Snow, 1980; Snow & Yalow, 1982), which means that some cognitive activities might be dominant during certain moments of writing, while they are not in other moments. Task adaptations are essential for problem-solving processes in general and for writing in particular, because of the developing text, and in some task situations the changing sources for writing.

Task adaptations during writing or re-representations are not observable directly but are to be inferred from the writing behavior: changes in the dominance of cognitive activities in the writing process so far. These changes in the writing process reflect differences in the changing task situation. Because of the impossibility to observe mental representations of task situations, we propose to indicate changing task situations by the variable time. One feature of task adaptations is time. Assuming that task adaptations happen all the time, they can be described by the amount of time elapsed from the start of the writing process. So we propose to consider task adaptations considered as functions of the time variable in writing process. Time is so to say a proxy-variable: It is an (observable) indicator of another conceptual variable, the changing task situation.

Time as a variable in writing has not been studied very thoroughly. Bridwell (1980), Monahan (1982), Kennedy (1985) and Kellogg (1989) demonstrated that skilled and unskilled writers not only differ in the frequencies of

107

time-dependent differences in writing processes and the resulting text quality (see Levy & Ransdell, chapter 8 in this volume).

In this chapter we propose a research agenda for a new generation of writing process studies in which time is a key variable. We demonstrate how some of the questions can be answered, using data from original research. We do not provide statistical details on the procedures; they are located in van den Bergh and Rijlaarsdam (chapter 11 in this volume).

Time as a key variable in writing process studies: A basic model

Flexibility as a key-feature

If we agree on the dynamic character of the writing process, then we assume a probabilistic parameter-setting model underlying writing process theory. The Hayes and Flower model (1981) is basically a heuristic model, which supports the search for types of cognitive activities playing a role in writing and for the possible interactions between the activities distinguished. Although not explicitly, the Hayes and Flower model allows that all cognitive activities can facilitate or hinder the functioning of each other. We begin with an explicit statement that our model is completely free of restrictions of relations among cognitive activities. Any cognitive activity can precede or follow any other cognitive activity. Everything is related to everything. Descriptive research and explanatory hypothesis-testing research must be carried out in order to define restrictions, related to task and subject characteristics.

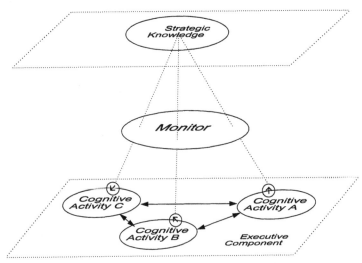

Figure 6.1. Dynamics of composing: A probabilistic model of writing processes.

Components of our model are an executive module, containing all cognitive activities involved with the execution of writing processes, a management module including the monitor and several domains of knowledge, and storing cognitive information involved in language processing as linguistic, pragmalinguistic, textual and socio-cultural domains of knowledge. Crucial writing process information is stored in the strategic domain (Oostdam & Rijlaarsdam, 1995), which contains information about the distinguished cognitive activities and their functional relations. This domain of strategic knowledge contains cognitive strategies. The smallest unit of strategy coincides with a type of cognitive activity — structuring or generating or evaluating. A cognitive strategy contains condensed information on conditions or circumstances in which the activity will be exploited. We call this information *parameter settings*, which take the form of "if-then" statements such as "If the writing task has to be fulfilled in 1-1/2 hours, and only 20 minutes are left, starting to copy the draft instead of rewriting the draft will the only successful activity." A cognitive strategy is the "memory" of a cognitive activity, which is based on different types of learning activities: experiences of executive processes (residuals of trial-and-error practices), explicit instruction, or self-construction.

Parameter settings are probabilistic information about the probability of occurrence of a cognitive activity given the context of occurrence: the preceding activities and the initial and developing task features. This kind of contextual information is fluent, because the writing process is characterized by a changing task situation. So the probabilistic information of the occurrence of a cognitive activity and the relation with preceding and following activities is allowed to change according the time during the writing process. At least two types of parameter settings can be distinguished. Within writers parameter settings can differ as a result of writing task or writing assignment features. In that case, a writer will show different parameter settings according to different assignments. Within writers, parameter settings can differ too as a result of the changing situation during writing within an assignment. In that case, parameter settings differ as a result of writing time. So writers can be characterized by the variety of approaches (parameter settings) related to different tasks and by the way they change the parameter settings during the writing process. Of course, interactions between assignments and within tasks differences should be allowed. This means that writers may differ in the way they change the parameter settings during the execution of the same task. So between writers, both types of parameter settings can differ. We return to this point later.

If we try to visualize this probabilistic model, we may reproduce the strategic information by a meter, which indicates the probability of occurrence, given the probability of occurrence of other activities. Values on these meters vary from 0 to 1. A value of 1 means that the probability of occurrence, given the probabilities of occurrence of other activities, is 100%. We study the differences in values on the meter, related to the moment in the writing process and to the type of writing task. Note that these kinds of models are already used to describe economic systems and eco-systems. All variations are allowed, just to discover which variables account the most for differences in output or text produced. Theories have to be developed, that can be tested by putting hypotheses forward which predict writing behavior under certain circumstances in terms of restrictions to the parameter settings.

Seven implications for writing process research

1. Concerning the structure of the model, assume that in general, the probabilities during the writing process change: The configuration of the parameter setting changes during the execution of the writing task. Some cognitive activities have a higher probability of occurrence than others in the beginning of task execution. Reading the task, for instance, and reading the sources in the documentation will have a higher probability of occurrence in the beginning of the writing process than at the end. Writing process research is trying to find general patterns in differences between probabilities related to changing task situations indicated by writing time elapsed.

2. Concerning strategic competence, writers may differ with regard to the default of the parameter setting: the ordinary way they accomplish writing tasks. Some writers are accustomed to stress on planning activities in the first part of the process, then on formulating in the second episode of writing, and then on reviewing and revising and editing. Others stress saying as much as possible on the topic, trying to find their focus. They are writing for finding a meaning and will redraft the paper then completely. These two types of writers are to be identifiable by their default settings of the probabilities of occurrence. For instance, the first type will show a setting with a high probability of generating and structuring activities in the beginning of the process, while the second type will show a setting with high probabilities of generating in the beginning and low probabilities of structuring.

3. Writers will differ on the complexity of the parameter settings to the extent that they adapt their configurations during the task execution to the changing situation. In more operational terms, the between-writers variance will vary from time to time, and will prove to be time dependent. That is, some writers will adhere to their initial default setting, but others will change the configuration from time to time. Therefore, the distribution of process probabilities at different moments in the task execution should be modeled explicitly.

4. Concerning the dependencies of cognitive activities, one should take into account that cognitive activities can serve different purposes, each related to the moment in the process. The relation between cognitive activities may change as a function of time. Sometimes reading of text written so far functions as input for evaluative activities on behalf of revising, sometimes as input for generating activities. The probability that one or another functional relation will perform differs as a function of time. Reading as input for revising has a higher probability at the end of the process, reading as input for generating a higher probability earlier in the process (Breetvelt, van den Bergh & Rijlaarsdam, 1995).

5. Concerning contextual factors, writers will differ in the degree and the way they adapt their default settings to task conditions: goal or purpose, audience, writing medium, text type. See for instance van Waes (1991) who found that some writers did not show different writing profiles when using pen and paper or computers, and others clearly did show differences. In fact, one studies the extent into writers are sensible to assignment features: the representation of the task. This theme can also be applied to the case of good

and weak novices. Representation of the assignment makes a difference between what we call *good novices* and *weak novices* (Elshout, 1994; Rijlaarsdam, 1993a; Torrance, 1996). Weak novices represent the writing task as a task to execute. They write and maybe observe the writing process in the light of the assignment. In the best case, their criterion for evaluation will be whether the assignment is accomplished. Good novices represent the assignment as a writing task *and* as a learning-to-write task (Couzijn & Rijlaarsdam, 1996; Oostdam & Rijlaarsdam, 1995; Rijlaarsdam, 1993a). In principle, every task execution can be the object of learning. Every writing assignment can be utilized as a learning experience. When the writer represents the assignment not only as a writing assignment but also as a learning-to-write assignment, then the monitor observes the task execution from both perspectives. The monitor offers the results of the execution of the learning task to the strategic competence. Although good and weak novices cannot be identified when regular tasks are presented, good novices can be identified because they are able to cope with a new, demanding task, and to keep up performance rather well.

6. Concerning the relation between writing processes and resulting text, it seems reasonable to assume that some differences between writers in their probability settings have a greater impact on text quality than others. So there is *free variation* and *effective variation*. For instance, one may hypothesize that a setting allowing the writer to edit all along the process, compared with a setting that leaves editing the most at the end of the process, will affect the text quality less than the same difference in structuring activities. For when structuring is postponed to the end of the process, it will be too late to relate generated ideas to each other.

But not only the parameter setting of the start of the process should be studied in relation to text quality. The key variable, time, should be included in this reasoning. The differences in the changes writers make during writing in the parameter settings will co-vary with text quality. If one sticks to the initial setting while the task situation cries for changes, but the writer is not aware of the changes in task situation and/or is not able to change, the quality of the text will be adversely affected. So in writing process research, our challenge is to discover the differences in parameter setting during the writing process that account for the most to the variance in text quality.

7. Concerning the explanation of differences between writers (default setting, adaptations during task execution, relations between processes and text quality, etc.), one may assume that differences in cognitive skill will contribute. The proportions of cognitive activities, and the distribution over the process, will be affected by the quality of execution of an activity, or the level of cognitive skill. A writer with a high level of divergent thinking will generate qualitatively differently from a writer with a low level of divergent thinking. The quality of an activity as generating, structuring, or reading the task will have consequences on the probability of occurrence of other cognitive activities. For instance, whereas writers in the beginning of the process perform activities such as reading the writing task to an equal extent, differences between writers may show up later in the process. Good readers will return with a less higher probability to this activity than less able readers.

Whether these differences in cognitive skill and differences in writing processes will be related to text quality depends on the compensatory effect of executing different processes. The fact that one writer returns more times to the assignment during the writing process, as a consequence of a low ability to read, may be *compensatory* compared to the well able reader, who analyzed and synthesized the gist nearly at once. If the writer compensates sufficiently, then the difference in process will not vary with text quality. Hence, writing is an interactive, compensatory process.

The essence of our approach is the attention paid to time as an important variable in writing process research, because time is inherent in the concept of process. Time is a key variable in our model: The configuration of probabilities varies with time, and the variance between writers varies with time. Note that the notion of probability of occurrence or configuration or parameter setting is strongly related to the notion of monitor in the Hayes and Flower model. Hayes and Flower (1981) described four "default settings" of the monitor, more or less to be interpreted as "writing process plans." We prefer to make a distinction between the strategic competence, which stores configurations, and the monitor, which is an instrument, relating executive processes with competencies. The monitor observes the execution of cognitive activities in order to relate the output of the activity to the representation of the assignment. The functioning of the monitor and the quality of the representation of the assignment is crucial for the parameter setting and the way the probability of occurrence is changing while the process progress.

Central questions in writing process research

This section offers a coherent set of research questions that promote the study of the dynamics of composing. We distinguish three sets of questions. The first set is labeled *Descriptive Research on Writing Processes*. This set concerns issues on cognitive activities as independent factors (univariate questions) and correlated factors (multivariate questions) in the writing process. Every question may be applied to a various number of cognitive activities. The second set is labeled *Descriptive Research on Writing Processes and Text Quality*. If we obtain some insights on differences between writing processes of different writers and/or associated with different tasks, it will be useful to know which differences in the processes are associated with differences in text quality, as an output measure of the writing process. The third set of questions is called *Explanatory Research in Writing Processes*. Knowing that writing processes of different writers are different is one thing, but explaining them is another. We propose to include in designs of writing process studies measures of cognitive skill, which will explain differences in writing processes, differences in text quality, as well as differences in the relation between processes and text quality.

We present our proposal for a research program on the following pages in Tables 6.1a, 6.1b, and 6.1c.

Table 6.1a

Descriptive research on writing processes

Univariate Questions Research on cognitive activities	Multivariate Questions Research on the temporal organization of cognitive activities
1. General Probabilistic Model of Cognitive Activities in Writing	1. General Multivariate Probabilistic Model of Cognitive Activities in Writing
What is the general pattern of cognitive activities during the writing process?	What is the overall structure of the temporal organization of cognitive activities? Which cognitive activities dominate writing at which moments of the process? For instance, which cognitive activities dominate at the start? Which changes describe the general pattern of temporal organization?
Or, in terms of a probabilistic model:	
Q1. What is the probability of occurrence of a cognitive activity during the writing process?	Q1. Which changes in dominance of cognitive activities during the writing process can be described?
The answer gives a general (mean) impression of the changes in the probabilities of occurrence of a cognitive activity as a consequence of changing task situations, indicated by writing time elapsed from the start of the writing process.	The answer gives a general impression of the temporal organization of cognitive activities: the changes in dominance of cognitive activities as a consequence of changing task situations, indicated by writing time elapsed from the start of the writing process.

2. Individual differences.

The general (mean) parameter-setting configuration is an abstraction. The mean writer does not exist. So, we are more interested in the individual changes in occurrence of a cognitive activity. Individuals may differ in two respects: with regard to the probability that a cognitive activity occurs and with regard to the moment they are inclined to undertake this cognitive activity.

Univariate	Multivariate
The first issue is about the description of the probabilities of occurrence during a writing process: the extent to which a writer exploits a cognitive activity and the changes during writing.	The cognitive activities should be studied in relation to each other. One may assume that individuals differ with respect to the temporal organization of the writing process. The patterns of dominance will differ between individuals.
Q2a. Intraindividual differences: How and when do the probabilities of occurrence of a cognitive activity change during the writing process?	Q2a. Intraindividual differences: To what extent do temporal organizations differ due the changing task situation, indicated by the writing process time elapsed from the start of writing?
The answer will give a "developmental" or "growth" curve per subject, showing that the probability of occurrence of a cognitive activity changes as a function of the changing task situation, indicated by time. Assume that these developmental curves (see Q2A) differ between subjects. We expect that variances between subjects vary with time.	The answer will give a picture of the temporal organization per subject, showing that the temporal organization of the cognitive activities involved changes as a result of changing task situations, indicated by time elapsed from the start of writing.

Q2b. Intersubject differences: To what extent do the intraindividual differences of parameter settings of a cognitive activity during the writing process differ between subjects?

The answer will sketch different developmental curves for different subjects. The individual curves cover the variability, obscured by the general curve generated by Q1.

Q2b. Intersubject differences: To what extent do these patterns of temporal organization (see Q2A) differ between subjects? Or, to what extent do the differences in temporal organization due changing task situations, indicated by time from the start of writing?

The answer will sketch different pictures of temporal organization for different subjects. The individual patterns cover the variability, obscured by the general curve generated by Q1.

The combination of (at least two) cognitive activities could attribute more to our understanding of the writing process then would be possible from each in isolation, if interdependency in parameter settings or correlations are accounted for (the multivariate model). To what extent do different pairs of cognitive activities covary? The multivariate model of the probabilistic model should also take in account that patterns of mutual dependencies between cognitive activities can vary as a consequence of changing task situations: The function of one activity for another can change at a given phase in the writing process. So the question is whether relations between cognitive activities are stable or change during the task execution: change as a function of time as proxy-variable of context.

Q2c. To what extent do covariations between pairs of cognitive activities vary as a function of time?

3. Generalizability.
In studies on writing ability, the tradition was to consider different occasions of writing as repeated measures of the same construct, (i.e. writing see Coffman, 1966; Godschalk & Swineford, 1966; Quellmalz, Cappel, & Chou, 1982). Without exception, low correlations were found between essay scores (Conry & Jerolsky, 1980; Johnson & Mazzeo, 1995; van den Bergh, 1988). But note that none of the studies included repeated measurements in the true sense of the word. So the task or assignment effects that were found were not pure: variance to be attributed to instability, appearing from the correlation between twice the same task, was not disengaged.

Currently, the trend is to consider different writing assignments as operationalizations of (partly) different constructs. If this position holds, then different assignments will elicit different developmental curves, depicting differences in probabilities of occurrence of a cognitive activity, due to the moment in the writing process. In other words: different assignments ask for different parameter settings of probabilities of occurrences.

It is remarkable that until now, most studies on writing processes just tap one process per subject (but see, for exceptions Levy & Ransdell, chapter 8 in this volume, and Cumming, 1989). For generalizalibilty, research on *stability* and assignment effects is a necessary part of the research agenda. It is necessary to know which part of the variability of subjects is due to instability, and which part can be attributed to assignment features. It is very interesting to study the differences between writers in the extent and way they adapt to assignments. One of the interesting issues is the difference with this respect between weak and good novices. Some novices are called weak, others are called good novices, because the latter perceive and use the new writing assignment as a learning task: They learn while writing, whereas others just try to reach the end of the task. And it is possible, that some writers have more than one route available to solve the problem of the writing assignment, and others stick to one routine, regardless the assignment. The learning of this latter group will be slower.

Stability and generalizabilty should be key words in the research agenda on writing processes. One of the implications proposed involves collecting real repeated measures for writing processes and text quality, data elicited by one and the same task, submitted at least twice to the same subjects. This research design has, to our knowledge, never been implemented with written products and/or with writing processes.

Q3A Stability
This issue concerns the stability of differences in parameter settings of a cognitive activity during the writing process (Q2a) when assignments do not differ.

To which extent do individual developmental curves of a cognitive activity differ when repeated measurements (same assignments) are elicited?

Q3a Stability
Are the differences in temporal organization of cognitive activities stable when assignments do not differ?

Q3B. Assignment adaptation
How do writers differ in making adaptations of parameter settings of a cognitive activity allocating assignment features, the writing medium, and other relevant circumstances?

Q3B. Assignment adaption
How do writers differ in making adaptations to the temporal organization of cognitive activities allocating assignment features, the writing medium and other relevant circumstances?

A special case in this respect is the case of "good" and "weak" novices. In what respect do these groups differ when confronted with a unusual, difficult assignment? Or, how do "good" novices change their "default" parameter setting in order to prevent performance loss when engaged in a demanding task situation?

Table 6.1b
Descriptive research on writing processes and text quality

Describing writing processes in general, and differences between and within writers is one part of the writing process research. Relating these processes to their effectiveness is another. Writing process research was devoted to reveal differences between experts and novices. We argue for a less dichotomous distinction, because writing proficiency is a continuous variable. We propose research that uses the resulting text quality of the writing process under study as a proxy-variable or indicator of effectiveness. Note that a causal relationship between writing process and text quality is never indicated, because the relationship is reciprocal.

The research questions are not split into two categories, as we did above, because our research questions are multivariate in nature.

Q4a. To which extent do differences between writers in probabilities of occurrence of a cognitive activity (see Q2b) covary with text quality?

Q4b. To which extent do differences in temporal organization between writers covary with text quality?

Q4c. To which extent do differences in probabilities of occurrence of a cognitive activity, within writers, between assignments (see Q3b) covary with text quality?

Table 6.2c

Explanatory research on effective writing processes. Explanatory variable: Cognitive skills

Until now, no efforts were made to explain differences between writing processes and different relations between writing processes and text quality. But is seems logical that the quality of task execution and differences in the quality of task execution has an effect on the writing process as such. Therefore, we include the quality of the execution of the distinguished cognitive activities in the research agenda, here referred to as cognitive skill.

Q5a. To what extent are differences in intrawriter configurations (see Q2a) and/or interwriter variability (Q2b) in developmental curves explained by variability in cognitive skill?

Q5b. To what extent differences in intra-writer configurations of temporal organization (see Q2a) and/or inter-writer variability in temporal organizations can be explained by variability in cognitive skills?

Q5c. To what extent are differences in stability (Q3a) explained by variability in cognitive skill?

Q5d. To what extent are differences in assignment adaptations (Q3b) explained by variability in cognitive skill?

Q5e. To what extent are differences in stability (Q3a) in temporal organizations explained by variability in cognitive skill?

Q5f. To what extent are differences in temporal organizations as a consequence of assignment features (Q3b) explained by variability in cognitive skills?

Q5g. To what extent do differences in cognitive skills covary with text quality?

Q5h. To what extent are covariances between temporal organization and text quality explained by cognitive skills?

Q5i. To what extent do covariances between parameter settings or changes of occurrence of a cognitive activity and related cognitive skills vary with resulting text quality?

Some answers: Four demonstrations

A fundamental question asks which cognitive activities constitute the writing process. The original Hayes and Flower (1980) model and the revised model (chapter 1 in this volume) are to be considered as heuristic tools, indicating the categories of actions derived from thinking-aloud protocols and problem-solving theories. Empirical research according to the expert-novice paradigm confirmed the categories of actions, because experts and novices appeared to differ in the frequency of occurrence of the distinguished actions. This is a very first step in process research. The limitation of the answer is clear. It is a one-dimensional answer, because one considers every occurrence of an activity as a representation of the same phenomenon, without reckoning the context of occurrence. It is questionable whether a one-to-one relation between observation and function can be postulated. That is, observing a reading activity is one thing, determining the function is another, and can only be done if the context of the activity is taken into account. Our model provides for the possibility that each activity can serve several functions, dependent on the role the activity plays in a specific context. A rough indicator for context of a cognitive activity is the moment of occurrence, reckoned from the start of the writing process. In the demonstrations of the proposed research agenda the proxy-variable time is the key feature.

In the following sections we describe research strategies for answering some of the questions from the proposed research agenda. For details on the analyses, refer to chapter 11 in this volume.

Research materials

The data for our demonstrations come from a study carried out by Breetvelt (1991), in which relations were studied between writing processes and the quality of the text. Subjects were pupils, about 15 years old, from several schools and several classes of lower, middle, and higher streams of secondary education. Each of them wrote two persuasive documented essays under composing-aloud conditions. The documentation was included in the task in a separate booklet and consisted of quotations from magazines, newspapers, and books. The protocol fragments were classified according to distinctions made by the Flower and Hayes (1980) model: reading the assignment and documentation, goal setting, generating, structuring, formulating, re-reading the text written so far, evaluating, and revising. Breetvelt added categories of metacognitive activities, such as self-instructing and commenting on assignment. Self-instructing could be coded for each activity. So she could distinguish between, for instance, "Structuring" and "Self-instruction to structuring." Every category consisted of several subclasses. This classification scheme was a reliable instrument (Rijlaarsdam, 1986); the intercoder reliability was .76 (Cohen's Kappa).

The writing products or texts were evaluated by four trained and experienced raters who used analytical schemes, supplemented with essay scales for each of the four distinguished aspect of texts: goal-orientation or focus and development, organization, reader-orientation, and style. The scores of those aspects were totaled per essay. Stability of scoring was .90. The reliability of the total score was .93. The time variable is included by adding to each process code the time elapsed from the start of the process in seconds.

We restrict this demonstration to one assignment, and to one cognitive activity and its metacognitive counterpart: "structuring" and "self-instructing to structuring." There were 22 cases with complete data. For other analyses, see Breetvelt, van den Bergh and Rijlaarsdam (1994) for the writing process in general, to van den Bergh, Rijlaarsdam and Breetvelt (1994) for revision processes, to Breetvelt, van den Bergh and Rijlaarsdam (1996) for reading and generating, and van den Bergh, Rijlaarsdam and Breetvelt (1992) for goal setting.

Demonstration 1: General pattern

What is the general description of the probability of occurrence during the writing process of structuring and self-instruction to structuring?

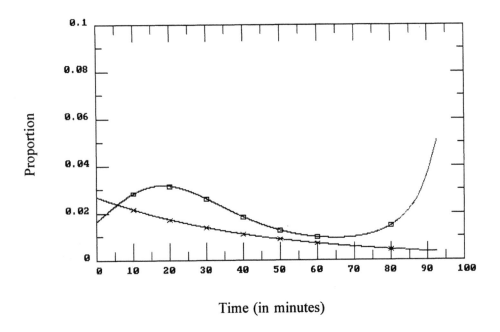

Time (in minutes)

Figure 6.2. General pattern of probabilities of structuring (squares) and metastructuring (asterisks).

In Figure 6.2 the univariate modeled developmental curves for structuring and metastructuring are depicted. The X-axis plots time in minutes and the Y-axis plots the probability value. The general pattern for structuring shows that from the start of the process the probability of occurrences of structuring increases, with a peak at about 20 minutes of writing time, after which the probability of occurrence decreases, with the lowest point about 70 minutes from the start. Then, the probability of occurrence increases strongly.

For metastructuring, the general pattern is simpler. The probability of an occurrence is slowly, not linear decreasing as a function of time. Related to structuring, the probability of occurrence is always except at the very beginning of the process. This indicates that during the first 10 minutes, in general, the chance of meta-activities occurring is larger than the chance of cognitive activities.

Demonstration 2 : Interindividual curves

Which intra- and interindividual differences in probabilities of occurrence of structuring and metastructuring exist? When writing researchers claim that novices run other writing processes than experts, more generally they refer to the existence of differences between writers. In theory, those differences can be based on one of the following three types of data (or a combination):

1. The differences are expressed by differences in absolute frequencies (time-on-task) while all other features of the writing process are equal. In other words, experts just work longer on the task and through that they perform more activities, but in the same proportion as novices.

2. The differences are expressed by differences in the relative contribution of cognitive activities. The amount of cognitive activities is the same, the time on task is the same, the only difference is that other cognitive activities dominate. For instance, the proportion of self-instructing to structure of one group is the proportion of structuring of the other group, whereas the ratios of structuring and metastructuring in the two groups are the opposite of each other. So the structure of the processes is equal, but dominances differ.

3. The differences are expressed in the distribution of the frequencies across the process while the amount of time and the frequencies of cognitive activities are equal. Whereas experts perform the activity of structuring in the same amount as novices, they structure in a rather constant level of frequency during the process, while novices structure practically the same amount, but solely in the beginning of the process.

As we proposed in our model, we prefer the less restrictive model to describe individual differences: frequencies may differ, time-on-task may differ, and the distribution of activities across the process may differ. So our second demonstration refers to inter- and inter-individual differences. Figures 6.3a and 6.3b depict the individual developmental curves.

The figures show clearly differences of probabilities within writers and differences between writers. These differences appear not only at the start — some writers start at the beginning with structuring and keep some time on a rather high level of probability, although others start on a much lower level — but also according to other parameters of the curves like the extent to which the probability of occurrence increases and decreases. The most important consequence we can draw is that the variance between writers varies according to time. Not only the parameter setting differs from writer to writer, but these differences vary per moment of the process.

For structuring, for instance, we observe large differences in the beginning, a general tendency to increase the probability of structuring in the first episode, and then a general tendency to decrease, although the steepness of decreasing differs between writers. Then, at the last episode of writing, a general tendency to decrease can be observed, with one very typical observation of a very steep increase. On every moment of writing, the variance between writers is different. In addition, many writers start low, and stay low, but some others vary considerably during writing.

The structure of the developmental curves of metastructuring is different from structuring. Most writers do not vary much during writing: that is, the intrawriter variance is small. They start roughly on some level of probability, then the probabilities are lowered a bit, some with a steeper decrease than others. But some writers, in fact two of them, show a completely other picture. The probabilities on metastructuring are increasing very strongly.

Strong interwriter differences seem to exist with regard to their intra-writer developmental curves of structuring and metastructuring. The next section addresses whether these differences covary with text quality. But first, we have to determine what the relationship is between structuring and metastructuring. Thus, we next introduce the multivariate model.

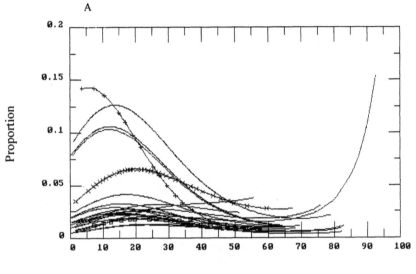

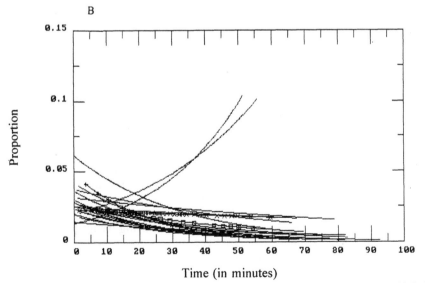

Figures 6.3a and b. Individual patterns of probabilities of structuring (6.3a) and metastructuring (6.3b).

Demonstration 3: Relations between cognitive activities

Until now, we looked at both cognitive activities as if they were independent variables, which is rather unlikely, especially when the cognitive and its metacognitive counterpart are involved. In general, the succession of activities is unlikely to be random. We assumed that activities (or a series of activities) relate to each other as in a means-end relation. Also, the time dimension issue should be added: To what extent is the relation between two cognitive activities a function of process time? Do the relations change according as the process progresses?

So a subsidiary question in the research into writing processes should be on the interrelation between the distinguished cognitive activities, especially the relation between metacognition and cognitive activities. What is the functional span of metacognitive activities? To plan to structure, but not engage in not structuring at all for some reason, and to plan to structure followed by structuring should have different outcomes.

We estimated the covariance between time and the correlation between structuring and metastructuring. Figure 6.4 shows that the correlation between both activities varies. After a very short time the relation becomes stronger, and then, after peaking, plateaus at a high level (.70) about 45 minutes from the beginning of the writing session.

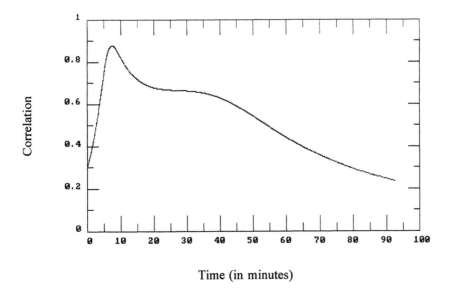

Time (in minutes)

Figure 6.4. Relation between writing process time and the correlation between structuring and metastructuring.

These changing relations between the probability of occurrences of structuring and metastructuring could indicate a change in relation. It is most interpretable that metastructuring sets on structuring: A metacognitive action triggers a cognitive action. In general, this interpretation seems to hold for metastructuring and structuring, but stronger in some episodes of writing than in others. Recall that we scored metastructuring only as forward planning. Thus, it seems in the beginning that the proportion of actions of metastructuring balanced the proportion of actions of structuring. Later, structuring became less dependent from metastructuring, although a rather strong relation was indicated. It could be that the span of metacognition became larger. In the first half of the process, some structuring acts are accompanied by metastructuring acts, but in the second half differences in the probability setting between writers occur more and more.

Now what type of temporal organization is related to text quality? What type of organization is successful?

Demonstration 4: Relations between patterns and text quality

The observation that obviously interindividual differences exist in the distribution of cognitive activities over the writing process gives us the opportunity to determine which differences in the process correlate with text quality at any moment of the process. Because the differences between the curves are a function of the time variable, the covariance between intra-individual curves and text quality varies too, and therefore we can plot the relation between probabilities of occurrences and text quality dynamically, as in Figures 6.5a and 6.5b.

Figure 6.5a shows that the relation between probabilities of occurrences and text quality varies, and even changes from positive to negative for Structuring. At the start of the writing process, for both cognitive activities, a positive, and for structuring, even a very strong positive correlation with text quality is observed. Note that the correlation between structuring and text quality is almost unity at the beginning, which indicates that structuring obviously is correlated strongly with other cognitive activities.

After some time, the correlation decreases to zero (metastructuring after 10 minutes) and to the negative (structuring after 60 minutes). So writers with a parameter setting with high probabilities of structuring at the beginning have a relatively good chance to deliver a relatively good text. Writers who structure after the midpoint of the process relatively often (compare Figure 6.3a) deliver a text with a low quality score. The probability of metastructuring does not seem to play a role in relation to text quality.

Note that both activities are interpreted as independent. This distorts the interpretation, because we observed a time-dependent, positive relation between those activities (Figure 6.4). If we want to estimate the pure relation between probability of occurrence and text quality, we have to apply the multivariate model of writing processes. In Figure 6.5b the correlations are plotted based on the multivariate model. It is shown that the correlation between metastructuring and text quality do not change, as compared with Figure 6.5a. But the correlation between structuring and text quality did change as a result of the purification.

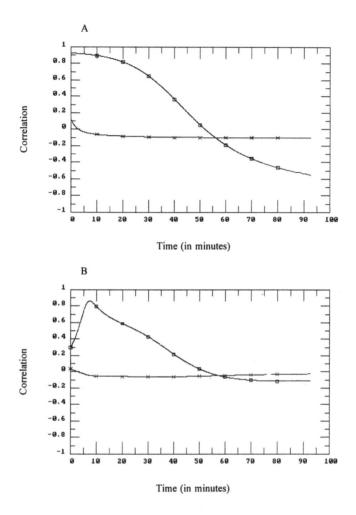

Figures 6.5a and 6.5b. Relation between writing process time and the correlation between text quality and structuring (6.5a) and metastructuring (6.5b).

It seems that in the initial phase of the writing process, something interesting is happening, as compared to Figure 6.5a. Although the correlation between structuring and text quality is positive at the start (.3), it is not that high as in Figure 6.5b. Then the correlation increases until the maximum has been reached about 10 minutes after the start. That implies that writers with an increase in the probability of the occurrence of structuring during the first 10 minutes write better texts then those who did not. Another difference due to the purification is the effect of structuring after three quarters of an hour. According to Figure 6.5a, we would conclude that the higher the level of probability of structuring in the second part of the process the lower the text quality. But Figure 6.5b suggests that the proportion of structuring does not affect the text quality at all.

A prescriptive statement based on Figure 6.5a, says that it is unwise to structure in the last phase of writing. Based on Figure 6.5a: Do not start at once with structuring, but start rather soon after the beginning, and keep that level during the first half of an hour. If you need to structure after two thirds of the writing time, then do, but if you do not need to structure, do not structure. If you do think structuring is not necessary, forget about it, because it seems not to affect text quality in that phase.

Conclusions

In this chapter we argued and demonstrated that time is a very important factor in describing writing processes on several levels: a generalized process (the "mean"), the interindividual variances, and the interindividual variances. Studying writing processes should be interpreted as minilongitudinal studies. In that case, more specific relations can be obtained between differences in writing processes and text quality because the relation between text quality and the probability of occurrence of cognitive activities seemed to be time dependent. Without the inclusion of time, the writing process is robbed of its dynamic features. Including time not only leads to more questions, but also elaborates our theory on writing. The relations between cognitive activities, for one thing, can only be studied by including the time variable. This enhances our view on the dependencies, on means-ends relations, between cognitive activities, and shows that one cognitive activity can serve different functions.

We proposed a research agenda of writing process studies, in which time is a key variable. It indicates that including the quality of the execution of cognitive activities, referred to as cognitive skill, will give new perspectives on the relationship between process and product. Unfortunately, we could not demonstrate the impact of this variable on the explanation of differences because no data are available about this variable yet. But now, a first attempt is underway (van der Hoeven, 1996).

The last point is the exchange of the expert-novice paradigm for the weak-good novice paradigm. Good novices are able to reduce the normally expected performance loss when executing new tasks or regular tasks under difficult (cognitive load) conditions (Rijlaarsdam, 1993b, p. 252). Some students succeed in tasks they have not previously performed, which call for acquired skills (writing situation that makes new demands on their behavior, a type of text with which they are unfamiliar, or writing in a second or foreign language in which they are only moderately competent) and means they have to approach fairly closely the limit of their competence, which has been determined in other writing tasks. Such pupils are evidently capable of employing their available skills in a productive way, whereas other pupils of a comparable level of competence are unable to succeed in the same assignment. This component of transfer should be carefully examined because it is a form of autonomous learning. If this component exists, and it can be described, maybe the learning strategies "good novices" exploit can be taught. The theoretical and statistical models (see van den Bergh and Rijlaarsdam, chapter 11 in this volume) we propose offer possibilities for this kind of studies. The statistical method of multilevel analyses enables a description of individual writing processes rather precise, and allows, in combination with the proposed basic model, testing hypotheses on writing behavior.

— 7 —

AN ACCOUNT OF WRITING
AS CREATIVE DESIGN

Mike Sharples
University of Sussex

This chapter attempts to answer the question *How do we write?* by looking beyond writing as a problem-solving process to consider the writer as a creative thinker and a designer of text. The aim is to take a step toward a general account of the processes of writing, and to resolve some of the seeming contradictions in studies of writers, such as:
• Writing is a demanding cognitive activity, yet some people appear to write without great effort.
• Most writing involves deliberate planning, but also makes use of chance discovery.
• Writing is analytic, requiring evaluation and problem solving, yet it is also a synthetic, productive process.
• A writer needs to accept the constraint of goals, plans, and schemas, but creative writing requires the breaking of constraint.
• Writing is primarily a cognitive activity, but it cannot be performed without physical tools and resources.
I shall call on theories of cognition and creativity by Boden (1990; 1994a), Gelernter (1994), and Karmiloff-Smith (1990), as well as descriptions of how designers think by Lawson (1990) and others. These form the basis of an account of writing as creative design.

The central part of the account is that writing is an open-ended design process, mediated by tools and resources. The way that a writer generates new material, and also manages the proliferation of possible next actions, is by imposing appropriate constraint. The constraints come from a combination of the given task, external resources, and the writer's knowledge and experience. Implicit constraints guide the writing process, and a writer re-represents some of these as explicit conceptual spaces.

Creativity in writing occurs through a mutually promotive cycle of engagement and reflection, both guided by constraint. A session of engaged "knowledge telling" generates written material for consideration. Reflection involves reviewing and interpreting the material as a source for contemplation. Contemplation generates new ideas, which are explored and transformed, producing plans and constraints that drive a further period of engaged writing. This basic creative mechanism supports a variety of writing strategies, depending on the timing and relative emphasis given to reviewing, contemplation, planning, and engagement.

Writing as design emphasizes the writer as a user of tools and a creator of cognitive artifacts. A writer is a thinker in a self-constructed environment that affords, constrains, and mediates the writing process. Writing as design emphasizes the use of a primary generator (a "guiding idea") in inspiring and guiding the entire task. As a writer's thoughts become externalized in sketches, notes, drafts, and annotations, so these designs become source material for the iterative process of interpretation, contemplation, and re-drafting.

Writing is not an isolated mental activity, but is closely linked to other creative design tasks such as drawing and music composition. The skill develops spontaneously from oral language production through a general cognitive mechanism whereby a thinker re-represents knowledge that was embedded in automated processes into an explicit form.

Although the account is far from complete, it can form a bridge between the more detailed cognitive models of a writer as thinker and the broader theories of writing in a sociocultural setting.

Writing and creativity

All writing is novel in that it generates phrases and sentences that have never been composed before. Most writing is appropriate, fitting the demands of the task and audience. And some writing displays such radical originality that we call it creative. A general account of the writing process needs to distinguish between novelty, appropriateness and creativity, and to go some way toward describing the psychological mechanisms underlying creative writing.

Boden (1990; 1994a), in her analysis of cognition and creativity, started by separating out the great historic acts of creativity (H-creativity) from psychological creativity (P-creativity): "A valuable idea is P-creative if the person in whose mind it arises could not have had it before. By contrast, a valuable idea is H-creative if it is P-creative *and* no one else, in all human history, has ever had it before." (Boden, 1994b, p. 76.)

It follows from this definition that there can be no solely psychological explanation of H-creativity. It can only be analyzed by reference to the society and culture in which its creator lived. But H-creative ideas are, by definition, also P-creative, and P-creativity is amenable to a psychological explanation. So, in this account of the psychology of writing, we restrict ourselves to P-creativity as a mental phenomenon and leave H-creativity to the biographers and literary critics.

Constraints and conceptual spaces

What is it that distinguishes P-creativity from novelty? The sentence "A pink rainbow flooded into my cup of steaming coffee" is certainly novel, but does it qualify as P-creative? To answer that question, we need to look at the structures and constraints within which language is produced. Language, as a system, is generative in that people who follow the rules of grammar are able to produce well-formed sentences, many of which have never been uttered before. By selecting the grammatical structures that form sentences and slotting in words with the correct parts of speech one can generate sentence after sentence of the kind already given. The prose may be novel and grammatically correct, but it would also be mostly nonsensical and certainly would be inappropriate to any writing task. So as well as being novel, writing must also be appropriate to the task and to the audience, otherwise it degenerates into a ramble of nonsense.

Individuals arrive at appropriateness by imposing constraint. This is key to an understanding of creativity in language. The generative system of grammar provides a framework for the production of language, and onto this framework a writer imposes schemas of knowledge and rhetorical structures, appropriate to the task and audience. These constrain the generative system to form what Boden described as a "conceptual space." The dimensions of a conceptual space are "the organizing principles that unify and give structure to a given domain of thinking" (Boden, 1994a, p. 79). A conceptual space eases the mental burden of writing by limiting the scope of search through long-term memory to those concepts and schemas appropriate to the task. Thus, a conceptual space can be restrictive, invoking a flow of conventional, predictable ideas. But it also provides the source material for creativity.

The paradox is that constraint enables creativity. By constraining the generative system into an appropriate conceptual space, a writer gains a conceptual structure that can be systematically explored and transformed. A conceptual space can be explored by testing the bounds of the existing constraints. For example, Sterne in *Tristram Shandy* mocks the conventions of narrative form through exuberant digressions; Shakespeare takes the language of officialdom to the extreme in the pompous pronouncements of Malvolio; and Dickens (cited in Boden, 1994a, p. 79) pushes at the boundaries of the English adjectival phrase by piling on adjectives to describe Scrooge as "a squeezing, wrenching, grasping, scraping, clutching, covetous old sinner."

Conceptual spaces can also be given a slight modification or a wholesale transformation. Creative thinking involves, in part, calling on general-purpose processes and applying them to conceptual spaces (see Perkins & Salomon, 1989, for a discussion of general and specialized methods of problem solving). The psychiatrist Albert Rothenberg (1976) carried out numerous interviews with creative people and found evidence for general creative processes, such as "Janusian thinking" (the "simultaneous conceptualization of opposites") and "homospatial thinking" (actively conceiving two or more discrete entities occupying the same space). The experimental language of James Joyce, Walt Whitman's abandonment of the ordinary rules of prosody, and Ted Nelson's development of hypertext with its multiplicity of paths and readings, are some notable examples of the transformation of literary structure. Lesser minds are still able to perform conceptual transformations during everyday problem solving by applying general operators such as "consider the negative," "remove a particular constraint," "substitute one structure for another," and "reconsider from a different viewpoint." The hard part is, first, to become aware of our own conceptual spaces, and, second, to see how to transform mental structures we are accustomed to taking for granted.

In short, we can distinguish creativity from novelty in that creativity involves setting appropriate constraints to form a conceptual space that is relevant to the writer's purpose, bringing aspects of that conceptual space into conscious awareness, and then deliberately exploring and transforming it to create an original and valuable product. Of course, not all explorations and transformations will be valuable, and very few will lead to a great work of literature. But this does appear to be one technique used by experienced writers, as is shown in the following verbal protocol from an experienced writer who has been asked to write a short story on "A Night at Luigi's":

> Now let's say Luigi runs the restaurant and, er, he wants to create an image of, er, good image, so he wants the customers, he wants them to come back, he wants them to talk about Luigi's, so how would he do that, OK. Now let's say somebody orders wine and, er, he tastes it. OK. So, if the wine's not good they send it back. So that's no story in there. But there is a story if the wine is good and it goes back. Would be even more of a study, story, if Luigi tastes it himself and takes it back. OK. I think we've got a story. (Sharples, 1985, p. 24)

The writer begins by setting a general goal (Luigi the restaurant owner wants to create a good image) invoking a restaurant schema. The schema covers a set of conventional activities that might be performed in a restaurant: order wine; waiter brings wine to the table; customer tastes the wine; if wine is bad then customer sends it back; otherwise customer drinks wine. The writer chooses a part of the schema (ordering wine) and considers the condition ("if the wine's not good they send it back"). Realizing that this would not make an interesting story, he tries a negation operator ("if the wine is good and it goes back"), and then a substitution ("Luigi tastes it himself and takes it back"). He ends up with a plot (which he later turns into a draft story) about a restaurant owner who impresses his customers by publicly tasting and rejecting his own wine.

Some successful writers have developed the transformation of entire story spaces into a lucrative craft. Eco (1982) wrote a penetrating essay called *The Narrative Structure in Fleming*. He showed that Fleming's James Bond novels are built around a series of contrasts between characters and values, such as Bond–M, Bond–Villain, Villain–woman, love–death, luxury–discomfort, loyalty–disloyalty. He set out 14 of these "oppositions" which, Eco suggested, include all of Fleming's narrative ideas. For example, in the contrast between Bond and his boss "M" there is a "dominated-dominant relationship which characterizes from the beginning the limits and possibilities of the character of Bond and sets events moving" (Eco, 1982, p. 245). The plots of all the Bond novels can be seen as games with the "'oppositions" as opposing pieces, governed by fixed rules and moves. The invariable scheme of moves is as follows:

A. M moves and gives a task to Bond.

B. The Villain moves and appears to Bond (perhaps in alternative forms).

C. Bond moves and gives a first check to the Villain or the Villain gives a first check to Bond.

D. Woman moves and shows herself to Bond.

E. Bond consumes Woman: possesses her or begins her seduction.

F. The Villain captures Bond (with or without Woman).

G. The Villain tortures Bond (with or without Woman).

H. Bond conquers the Villain (kills him, or kills his representative or helps at their killing).

I. Bond convalescing enjoys Woman, whom he then loses.

Although the scheme is fixed, in the sense that all the elements are always present in every novel, the order may change. In *Dr. No* the order is A B C D E F G H I , but for *Goldfinger* it is B C D E A C D F G D H E H I.

As Eco concluded, it is clear how the James Bond novels have attained such a wide success. They translate the purity and order of epic stories into current terms, and transform a network of elementary associations into new but familiar patterns.

> In the novels of Fleming the scheme follows the same chain of events and has the same characters, and it is always known from the beginning who is the culprit, and also his characteristics and plans. The reader's pleasure consists of finding himself immersed in a game of which he knows the pieces and the rules — and perhaps the outcome — drawing pleasure simply from following the minimal variations by which the victor realizes his objective. (Eco, 1982, p. 259)

Fleming clearly understood how to create and transform plot structures and exercised this skill for all its considerable worth.

Representational redescription

Before moving on to the processes of writing, we need to make an important distinction between regular activity and explicit knowledge. A regular, grammatically correct language can be produced without being able to recite the rules of grammar. But to explore and transform conceptual spaces we must call up constraints and schemas as explicit entities, and work on them in a deliberate fashion. This requires an ability to recast the regularity of implicit language production as explicit mental structures.

Karmiloff-Smith's (1990) theory of "representational redescription" states that as a natural part of skill development we become able spontaneously to re-represent knowledge that was previously embedded in effective procedures. Young children can create a simple story by recalling some episode from the past or by summoning up a train of ideas governed by implicit schemas and constraints. But only when they develop cognitive awareness are they able to re-represent such an episode in a form that allows them to insert new events, or alter it to provide a new conclusion.

In more general terms, the mind exploits knowledge it has already stored (both innate and acquired) by re-representing tacit procedures as explicit structures. Representational redescription provides us with the means to reflect on experience. It allows us to review an activity, re-cast it as a mental schema, and use this to probe long-term memory, recall related schemas, integrate the new knowledge with the old, and explore and transform it.

The transition from tacit knowledge to deliberate cognition is not easy. Although re-representing tacit knowledge is a natural part of skill development, even in adults it is muddled and incomplete. Reflective understanding alone may be inadequate to drive the writing process: Bringing tacit knowledge into conscious awareness is no guarantee of being able to understand or control it. We have no everyday vocabulary to describe our mental processes to ourselves. The increased mental burden of trying to reflect on one's own thinking can cause cognitive overload and this, combined with the attempt to work on incomplete schemas, can lead to a drop in the general quality of writing. It is at this point that learners need help to develop a coherent mental framework of plans, operators, genres, and text types that can guide the process of knowledge integration and transformation.

The component processes of creative writing

The exploration and transformation of conceptual spaces is part of the process of writing, but by no means all of it. Very little of everyday writing qualifies as P-creative by Boden's definition. Boden's analysis of creativity helps to explain creativity in writing, but it leaves open the more general issue of how a writer goes about the everyday business of composing novel, appropriate, and sometimes creative prose.

A writing task starts with a given set of constraints. These may be external, such as an essay topic, previously written material, or a set of publisher's guidelines. They may also come from within the writer, as the schemas, interrelated concepts, genres, and knowledge of language that form a writer's conceptual spaces. The task is also constrained by the tools a writer employs and by the context in which the writing occurs. These constraints act together to channel mental resources and to frame the activity of writing.

Scardamalia and Bereiter (1987) describe two fundamental processes of writing, which they termed *knowledge telling* and *knowledge transforming*. Knowledge telling is where the writer creates ideas by a process of association. One idea is generated that contains aspects or features that prompt another idea to be recalled, and so on along a chain of conceptual relations. When this is carried out as a purely mental activity, then we call it *daydreaming* or *free associating*. But it is also an effective way of writing. Each concept is translated into words that are set down on paper and these act as an immediate prompt for further association and writing. In children, this appears in text as a "what next" sequence of propositions, linked by simple "and" or "but" connections:

> one day in the street a sale was on and a little girl was gow-
> ing to school and hur mum said take this dinner munny but
> she knew that it was to much and she spent sume of it. wen

*she got to school the teacher said where have you been the
girl said nowhere sorry. at home time she took the toy rabbit
home and her mum said go to bed. The End.* (Story written by
7-year-old child.)

In adults, knowledge telling can range from a loosely controlled "stream
of consciousness," to the seemingly controlled but effortless writing of some
experienced novelists. Aldous Huxley (cited in Chandler, 1991) revealed,
"The thing develops as I write." And Amy Lowell (cited in Ghiselin, 1954, p.
112) remarked that "Suddenly words are there, and there with an imperious
insistence which brooks no delay. They must be written down immediately."
Success comes from the way in which the knowledge telling is guided by
constraint. A successful writer is able to invoke just the right schemas and
text structures to create an appropriate "story world" in which the knowledge
telling can be performed. Knowledge telling is particularly suited to narrative
fiction writing, where the writer retells an event or creates a scene and allows
imagined characters to act it out.

Knowledge transforming appears to be similar to Boden's description of
the processes governing P-creativity. The writer forms initial states of knowledge appropriate to the task. These constrain and drive the writing. During
drafting the writer monitors the text in relation to the constraints and, if they
diverge, revises the text or the plans to keep them in harmony. Scardamalia
and Bereiter characterized knowledge transforming as an interaction between
two problem spaces — content and rhetoric — with the content space being
the writer's beliefs about the writing topic and the rhetorical space containing
the writer's knowledge about the text and writing goals. But there seems to
be no good reason to stop at two knowledge spaces. In general, a writer as
thinker will be working with multiple overlapping areas of knowledge, drawing analogies between related concepts in different spaces and using problems encountered in one knowledge space as goals to be achieved in another.

High and low focus thinking

Having set out the two component processes of knowledge telling and
knowledge transformation, the next question asks how these processes fit
together. To understand this, we need to go back to more general theories of
creativity.

In an analysis of creative thought, Gelernter (1994) offered the notion of
a spectrum of cognitive activity, from *high focus thinking* where ideas are
constructed and manipulated, to *low focus thinking* characteristic of day-
dreams, where whole episodes from memory are blended and linked together
by a common flow of emotion. Rather than seeing these as two separate
modes of thought, he suggested that they form a continuous spectrum so
that a person might come out of a daydream of low focus thought into a more
controlled bout of analytic thought, abstracting common features from the
memories to produce new mental concepts. To substantiate his claims,
Gelernter summoned up quotations from the Romantic poets, Freud's (1976)

accounts of dream-thought (although, inexplicably, he did not refer to Freud's only direct account of the creative process) and passages from the Scriptures, in an attempt to show a connection between creative daydreaming, childhood memories, and ancient thought.

There are problems with the details of Gelernter's theory. He proposed that low focus thought consists of memories bound together by shared emotion. But a sound (remembered or external), a color, an object, or a word can also be the link between one dreamlike episode and the next. Dream thoughts may often evoke emotions, they may also be influenced by emotions, but there is no good evidence that emotion is the indispensable force that binds the creative imagination. Gelernter also claimed that low focus, affect-linked thinking provides the solution to "the most significant unsolved problem of cognition" — that of analogical thinking and creativity. Creativity, Gelernter claimed, boils down to the discovery of new analogies that occur when one thought sparks off another one related to it only by a deep bond of emotion. But this is at odds with Boden's account of creativity arising from deliberate mental explorations and transformations.

We can reconcile these claims by proposing that high and low focus thinking both contribute to creativity. One way in which they can combine is through the deliberate re-creation of emotional experience in the mind, until it wells up and drives composition. Wordsworth described this process as "emotion recollected in tranquillity:"

> The emotion is contemplated till, by a species of reaction, the tranquillity gradually disappears, and an emotion, kindred to that which was before the subject of contemplation, is gradually produced, and does itself actually exist in the mind. In this mood successful composition generally begins, and in a mood similar to this it is carried on. (Wordsworth, cited in Owen & Smyser, 1974, p. 148)

The emotion appears to act as both a generator and a filter of thought, prompting and combining ideas that have, in the past, been associated with that same mood.

Where Gelernter's theory is most useful — at least to an understanding of writing — is in seeing low and high focus thinking as being parts of a continuous spectrum of cognition. When a person sits back and thinks, there is no barrier between the free association of ideas and the controlled transformation of mental spaces or the solving of problems. Indeed, all these aspects of thought combine and support each other, with contemplation summoning up emotion, and ideas generated by dreamlike thinking becoming the raw material for deliberate analysis. Freud (1976, p. 48) captured this process by describing creative writers as those who mold their own wish-fulfilling fantasies into a form that is pleasing and attractive to others. If low and high focus thinking are directed toward producing text, then they become the processes of knowledge telling and knowledge transforming.

The externalization of cognition

Even cognitively mature writers can find it difficult to mold fantasy into attractive prose, as the following protocol of an inexpert adult writer shows:

Well I first thought of a basic structure in my head. Going to a restaurant. Getting some food. Food leading to some sort of problem, ending in mayhem, was the basic structure. Right at the beginning. But then there was how to get from step to step, as we went along (Sharples, 1985, p. 26).

Although he was aware that he should structure his writing, his knowledge of story schemas and how to explore and transform them was inadequate to drive the production of text.

Expert writers can call on a large stock of remembered plans and schemas, built up through a long apprenticeship in the craft of writing. But an inexpert writer has less of this precompiled knowledge and so must construct plans to order, calling on everyday experience and guided by a general knowledge of how to design artifacts, transform mental structures, and solve problems. Even an accomplished writer sometimes needs to call on these general methods if faced with a new type of rhetorical demand.

One way to overcome the difficulties of performing such complex knowledge manipulation in the head is to capture ideas on paper (or some other external medium such as a computer screen) in the form of external representations that stand for mental structures. So long as ideas, plans, and drafts are locked inside a writer's head, then modifying and developing them will overload the writer's short-term memory. By putting them down on paper (or some other suitable medium) the writer is able to explore different ways of structuring the content and to apply systematic transformations, such as prioritizing items, reversing the order, or clustering together related items. Writing creates external representations and the external representations condition the writing process.

Cognition is not simply expressed or amplified through the use of external representations, but rather the nature of thought is determined by the mind's dialectical interaction with the world as constructed by human beings (Kuutti, 1991; Wood, 1992). Notes, sketches, outlines, tables, topic lists, concept maps, and argument structures are both representations of mental content and things in themselves, new stimuli dissociated from the moment of their production and available for reinterpretation. To take our account further, we need to look beyond the writer as a disembodied mind and consider the role that the external environment plays in mediating cognition by considering writing as design.

Writing as design

There are striking similarities between studies of cognition in design and the cognitive theories of creativity in writing discussed in the previous section. For example, Lawson's (1990) influential book on how designers think contains a chapter on creative thinking and he based his model of the design process around the creation and manipulation of appropriate constraints. But rather than concentrating on the similarities between theories of design and theories of creativity, it is necessary to look at some aspects of design that might help to extend our understanding of writing. Lawson (1990, pp. 90 - 93) described the following properties of design problems and processes, all of which apply to writing.

Design problems are open-ended and cannot be fully specified. They are not like the classic problems studied by cognitive psychologists, such as chess or the Tower of Hanoi, with a fixed set of goals and a sequence of steps each of which can be evaluated in terms of its nearness to a goal. The number of actions that a designer might take at any stage is uncountably large, and there is no simple function to evaluate each step in the process.

The design process is endless. A designer is faced with an inexhaustible number of possible solutions, and the end of the design process is a matter of judgment. It follows that a designer is rarely pleased with the product, but stops when it no longer seems worth the effort of trying to improve its quality, or when halted by some external factor such as running out of time or resources.

There is no infallibly correct process of design. There are many different and equally successful approaches, and good designers are able to control and vary their strategies according to the task.

The process involves finding as well as solving problems. The design process does not consist of a neat sequence of stages leading up to a finished product, and much of a designer's time is spent in identifying and refining the problem. "It is central to modern thinking about design that problems and solutions are seen as emerging together rather than one following logically upon the other" (Lawson, 1990, p. 91). This rejection of stage models in favor of a more integrative analysis mirrors the development of research in writing, beginning with the insight of Flower and Hayes that "the act of writing is best described as the act of juggling a number of simultaneous constraints. This is in contrast to seeing it as a series of discrete stages or steps that add up to a finished product" (Flower & Hayes, 1980, p. 31).

Design inevitably involves subjective value judgment. A designer asks questions that are value-laden and produces products that can only be judged by a subjective assessment of quality.

Design is a prescriptive activity. Unlike the process of scientific discovery, where the aim is to describe the world, design is concerned with what might, could, and should be. It prescribes and creates the future, and so demands both ethical and moral scrutiny.

Designers work in the context of a need for action. Design is a process that will result in some change to the environment. The environmental impact of writing is less obvious than in engineering or architecture, because writing changes the landscape of thought. We can easily produce cases (such as *The Communist Manifesto*) where texts have incited great actions, but this hides the fact that all writing performs speech acts (such as informing or persuading), and all writing can act as the inspiration and source material for further writing activity.

Now having established writing as a design activity, at least in so far as it fits the essential properties of design as given by Lawson, we look at aspects of how designers work that might contribute to our understanding of how people write. The three aspects that are most useful to our analysis are: primary generators, the fusion of analysis and synthesis, and the use of tools and external representations.

Primary generators

A *primary generator* is some powerful but easily stated idea that a designer summons up early in the task to prompt and guide the activity. The term is attributed to Darke (1978), who interviewed British architects about their intentions when designing local authority housing. She found that the architects tended to latch on to a relatively simple idea very early in the design process. That idea narrowed down the space of possible solutions and acted as a framework around which to create the design.

Accomplished novelists, when describing what initiated their writing, often talk in terms of primary generators:

> *With me a story usually begins with a single idea or memory or mental picture. The writing of the story is simply a matter of working up to that moment, to explain why it happened or what caused it to follow.* (Faulkner, cited in Plimpton, 1958, p. 121)

> *I had an idea of what I wanted to do, but there was something missing and I was not sure what it was until one day I discovered the right tone — the tone that I eventually used in* One Hundred Years of Solitude. *It was based on the way my grandmother used to tell her stories. She told things that sounded supernatural and fantastic, but she told them with complete naturalness. When I finally discovered the tone I had to use, I sat down for eighteen months and worked every day.* (Garcia Marquez, cited in Plimpton, 1985, p. 323)

For academic writers, a primary generator may come in the form of a research question or an organizing schema (such as a thesis proposal). These early ideas can influence the entire writing process and in academic writing are sometimes stated explicitly in the introduction to the text.

However, designers can also gain insight into the problem as the design progresses and this may lead them to reject or modify the primary generator. A primary generator can cause great difficulties if it presents an insuperable hurdle, but if the designer succeeds in overcoming such difficulties and the original ideas were good, we are quite likely to recognize this as an act of great creativity (Lawson, 1990, p. 36).

The fusion of analysis and synthesis

In an experiment with experienced designers, Eastman (1970) set the task of redesigning a bathroom. He recorded what the designers did and how they described what they were doing. These protocols showed no meaningful division between analysis and synthesis, but rather that designers learned about the problem through a series of trial solutions (Lawson, 1990, p. 33).

In other areas, such as software design, it is recognized that design is an iterative process, with the intermediate products acting as generators of new ideas.

> One thing we always experience during design is a need to shift constantly between two kinds of design activity, analysis and synthesis. During analysis we test the design to determine whether it is meeting our targets for usability and software quality. During synthesis we shape the design, drawing on fresh ideas and on solutions to similar problems that have worked well in the past. (Newman & Lamming, 1995, authors' emphasis.)

Iteration is also a fundamental part of the model of writing developed by Hayes and Flower (1980), where the synthetic process of translating ideas into prose is interrupted by the analytic process of editing, which may in turn lead the writer into a new sequence of planning, translating, and reviewing.

Tools, external representations, media and resources

A cognitive model of writing is concerned primarily with the writer as a thinker and problem solver. It does not address such questions as: What purposes are served by written notes, plans, and outlines? Why do writers prefer one tool over another? Which types of media are suited to which writing tasks? An account of writing as design takes a broader view. A designer is a thinker who works within a carefully constructed material world, surrounded by books, files, notes, drafts and drafting tools. The designer, the artifacts, and the setting form a rich inter-operative system. Each artifact conditions the activity, assisting certain operations while restricting others, and an analysis of a writer's use of tools, external representations, media and resources plays an important part in an understanding of writing as design. Writing *tools* include pencils, pens, erasers, computers, and dictating machines. They create, erase or modify marks on *media*, such as sheets of paper, file cards, computer displays, and audiotapes. The marks act as signifiers, to form an interrelated system of *external representations* that can convey meaning to the writer and others. A writer also calls on external *resources* such as databases, reference books, and colleagues for information and support.

Tools

The skills of design are learned not in the abstract, but through the con-tinued use of a system of tools. Tools have intrinsic properties, such as size and portability, but their qualities as components of design are not inherent in their structure, they only arise through usage. A pencil is a pencil not be-cause it is a stick of graphite surrounded by a sheath of wood, but because it can be employed as a particular type of writing implement. When an individ-ual writes with a pencil it is no longer a separate object but a conduit for ideas. Observers of a writer may reflect on the properties of the pencil and how the writer holds it, but for the person engaged in the flow of writing it does not exist as a distinct entity. Its "pencilness" only becomes apparent if there is a breakdown in the writing activity, for example, if the point snaps.

Thus, the properties of a tool only become apparent to its user when the tool ceases to be an extension of the self, in the event of some breakdown in its action. This insight is due to Heidegger, and its relation to design is dis-cussed by Winograd and Flores (1986). The most immediate implication is that we need to consider not only the intrinsic properties of tools, but also how a tool is experienced by its user, and how its structure is revealed through breakdown.

A writer's choice of tool is not just a matter of selecting the best imple-ment to perform a particular task, but is an expression of an apprenticeship and an approach to the craft. Some writers report having strong, even ritual-istic preferences for particular tools. Steinbeck revealed, "For years I have looked for the perfect pencil. I have found very good ones, but never the per-fect one. And all the time it was not the pencils but me. A pencil that is right some days is no good another day" (cited in Chandler, 1995, p. 136).

A discussion of the resonances (such as Freud's depiction of writing as "making a liquid flow out of a tube onto a piece of white paper") and the aesthetic appeal of writing tools is beyond the scope of this chapter, but for a rich account of the phenomenology of writing see Chandler (1995).

Tools become apparent to their users when there is a breakdown in nor-mal activity. When the point of a pencil snaps, the writer turns from tran-scribing ideas as text to considering the construction of the pencil and how to repair it. In this case, the repair is simple and there is no need to delve into the chemical composition of graphite or the structural properties of wood. But when writing by computer breaks down a writer is confronted with a series of interlocking "system images." A system image (Norman, 1986) is the guiding metaphor that a computer system shows to the user. Depending on the type of breakdown, a word processing program may present different, possibly conflicting, system images: the electronic typewriter, the filing sys-tem, the desktop. Some breakdowns display layers of embedded systems, down to the level of the computer operating system.

Dealing with breakdowns of all kinds is an integral part of the writing process and one aim of recent research in writing has been to look beyond the untroubled flow of words. The contribution of the cognitive approach has been to portray the writer as a problem solver, coping with the need to satisfy rhetorical demands, retrieve appropriate material from memory, and juggle multiple constraints. Sometimes these become unsatisfiable or overwhelming, leading to coping strategies or writer's block. Writing as design shows the writer as a user of tools. These support the writing process by providing a means to express plans and ideas as they occur, but the tools themselves may be contexts for other types of cognition and action, from displacement activities to breakdowns in which the tool rather than the writing becomes the focus of attention.

External representations

External representations serve multiple purposes. First, they act as an external memory, so that ideas, intentions, and plans can be kept for future reference and not forgotten. For example, a writer can glance at a list of previously written topics to recall ideas and to see whether the text is heading in the intended direction. One of the writers studied by O'Malley (1988) annotated her draft text with terse reminders (such as asterisks) to indicate parts that were incomplete or needed revision.

Second, they act as a mediation between different people, and between designers and themselves at another point in time. By sketching out a complex idea as a diagram it is possible to gain an overview of a complex set of relations and to present it in a compact form. A simple ad-hoc sketch can indicate intentions that are too fluid to express easily in words. In his studies of pairs of collaborating authors, Wood (1992) described how one author drew a large funnel shape to represent the overall structure of the paper, and later both writers referred to places in this shape when talking about parts of the paper.

Third, external representations are a means of capturing intermediate products in a form that is intermediate between mental schemas and a finished text. Notes Networks (Sharples, Clutterbuck, & Goodlet, 1994; Trigg & Suchman, 1989) and Mind Maps (Buzan, 1989) are intended as "intermediate representations" allowing a writer to visualize associations between mental concepts before committing them to text. Similarly, by setting down a plan as a table, a writer can gain an overview of the relations between items, and can check that all the relevant dimensions have been explored.

An external representation is a fixed point in the design process, indicating both previous cognition and the form of the product under design.

Media

The media on which external representations are formed have their own intrinsic properties, resonances and breakdowns. For example, a word processor with a standard 20- to 24-line display makes it difficult to gain an overview of a long document or a good "sense of the text" (Eklundh, 1992; Haas & Hayes, 1986). A full analysis of writing media would follow much the same path as a study of tools. But the essential function of a writing medium is to be a carrier of signs and one way to understand the influence of media on the writing process is to consider the relationships between media and external representations (Sharples & Pemberton, 1992). We have mapped five common writing media — computer screen, sheets of paper, file cards, dictating machine, sticky notelets, white board — against generally beneficial properties of external representations:

- *Entire document*. An entire document of medium length can be held on the medium.
- *Usable in end product*. The material can be used directly in the final document, without the need for transcribing or rewriting.
- *Portable*. The material is easy to carry around.
- *Overview*. The writer can rapidly gain an overview of a large document
- *Allows reordering*. The items can be easily reordered.
- *Allows nonlinear organization*. Items can be grouped spatially, or by means of explicit links, into networks, tree structures, tables, etc.
- *Permanent*. The material can be kept permanently available, for reuse in other documents.
- *Allows annotations*. The items can be annotated with memo notes, highlights, and so on.
- *Indexable*. Items can be accessed rapidly by means of an index created on the same medium.
- *Re-representable*. One type of representational structure can be transformed automatically into another type, for example, a document can be presented as an outline.

Table 7.1 sets out the properties of a number of different media according to their normal usage (whiteboards, for example, could be made portable, but normally are not). No medium has all the desirable properties. Sheets of paper, file cards, and the computer screen all score well, with sheets of paper offering the benefit of rich annotation, file cards supporting nonlinear organizations, and the computer giving the ability to change representations. The limitations of the computer are all surmountable and new computer systems are being developed that provide portability, nonlinear organization, annotation, and overviews of text.

But even if a computer can offer the facilities of other media, even if it permits input by handwriting, it still provides the writer with a different experience, and a different set of breakdowns, than a pen and paper or a white board.

Resources

External resources form part of the wider world of work in which a designer is embedded. When resources are both appropriate and ready to hand then they become absorbed into the design process. An online thesaurus, for example, is just another part of a writer's toolkit. But if they are separated, physically or by function, from the main task, then work with the resources is interleaved with design. So design becomes one activity within a complex working environment.

The writing environment is changing rapidly, as the physical and social resources of the writer are being drawn into the computer. A journalist can now browse the Internet for leads, search online databases for source material, and conduct interviews by e-mail. New technology offers a wealth of resources on the desktop. It can also fracture social contact and confine research to a self-referential infosphere. Instead of muddying his boots, the modern Wordsworth need only call up a CDROM of the "Lakeland experience." For a survey of the changing environment of writing, see Sharples and van der Geest (1996).

Table 7.1
Media and their properties

	Computer screen	Sheets of paper	File cards	Dicta-phone	Stickey notelets	White board
Entire document	✓	✓	?	✓		
Usable in end product	✓	?				
Portable	?	✓	✓	✓	✓	
Overview	?	✓	?			✓
Reordering	✓	?	✓		✓	✓
Nonlinear organization	?	?	✓		✓	✓
Permanent	✓	✓	✓	✓	?	
Annotations	?	✓	✓		✓	✓
Indexable	✓	✓	✓	?		
Re-representable	✓					

In summary, writing as design emphasizes the writer as a user of tools and a creator of cognitive artifacts. A writer is a thinker in a self-constructed environment that affords, constraints, and mediates the writing process. Writing as design emphasizes the use of a primary generator in inspiring and guiding the entire task. As a writer's thoughts are externalized in sketches, notes, drafts, and annotations, these designs become grist for an iterative process of interpretation and re-drafting.

A theory of writing as creative design

The previous sections have re-conceptualized writing as a process that combines creativity and design. This section weaves together these two strands into a single fabric.

A writing episode starts not with a single goal, but with a set of external and internal constraints. These come as some combination of a set task or genre (such as a college essay), a collection of resources (for example information on company performance to be pulled together into a business report), aspects of the writer's knowledge and experience, and a primary generator (or "guiding idea"). A primary generator is particularly important to imaginative writing as it provides a mental construct around which to form the text. When novelists describe the inspiration for their writing in terms of such a construct, it can seem as though they had thought out the entire text in advance. But the skill of a great writer is to create a generator that is manageable enough to be realized in the mind, yet sufficiently powerful to spawn the entire text.

As the writing progresses, constraints provide the tacit knowledge to guide the writing process. The writer may re-represent some of them in a more explicit form, as a conceptual space to be explored and transformed. The movement between engaged writing, guided by tacit constraint, and more deliberate reflection forms the cognitive engine of writing shown in Figure 7.1.

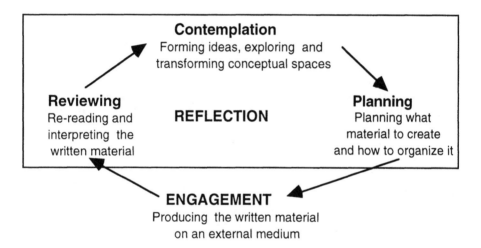

Figure 7.1. The cycle of engagement and reflection.

Engagement

An engaged writer devotes full attention to creating a chain of associated ideas and turning them into text (as notes or fully fleshed-out prose). Working memory is entirely devoted to the task, and the only other deliberative mental activity that the writer can perform while engaged in text creation is to speak the words out loud. We think *with* the writing when we are producing text, but we cannot think *about* the writing (or about anything else) until we pause. In the terms used by Karmiloff-Smith (1990), a writer cannot simultaneously enact a writing procedure and re-represent it. In order to reflect on the text it is necessary to stop writing, and the result is that periods of engaged knowledge telling are interleaved with periods of reflection.

Reflection

Reflection is an amalgam of mental processes. It interacts with engaged writing through the activities of reviewing, contemplation, and planning. Reviewing involves reading the written material while carrying out minor edits. Through a process of interpretation the writer re-represents the procedures enacted during composing as explicit knowledge that can then be integrated with an existing conceptual space.

This leads to contemplation. Contemplation may involve the high focus thinking of deliberate knowledge exploration and transformation of conceptual spaces. Or, it may involve low focus thinking: calling up trains of associated and analogous thoughts, linked by some common emotion, theme or experience. Planning takes the results of contemplation as the source for creation of plans and intentions to guide a further period of engaged writing.

Writing as a creative mental process consists of a regular movement between engagement and reflection. An engaged writer is devoting full attention to the task of creating text (whether it be notes or fully fleshed-out prose). Reflection consists of "sitting back" and reviewing all or part of the written material, conjuring up memories, generating ideas by association, forming and transforming ideas, and planning what new material to create and how to organize it.

It is usually engagement in the production of text that is described as being creative, "It is the act of writing that produces discoveries" (Mandel, 1978). But Boden argued that creativity arises also from the reflective exploration and transformation of conceptual spaces, and Gelernter proposed that it wells up from a process of analogical association. The suggestion here is that it is the entire cycle of engagement and reflection that pushes composition forward, with engagement providing new material for consideration, and reflection offering a reinterpretation of the material and new plans to be enacted.

The cycle of engagement and reflection sets up distinctive rhythms that characterize the processes of writing. The period of these rhythms may be short, as when a writer looks back over each sentence as it is written, or long, when a writer re-reads an entire piece of writing and plans a major revision. At the most general level, the writing process can be described in terms of how these rhythms are affected by the writer's approach to the task, the tools a writer employs, and the types of representation on which they operate. According to Ihde (1979, p.), "The rhythm of the pen is slow and enhances the deliberation time which goes into writing, Contrarily, the typewriter composer, if the rhythm of the instrument is to be maintained, finds almost as soon as the thought occurs it appears on the paper."

In a statistical study of the writing process, van Waes (1992) used cluster analysis techniques to uncover profiles of writing. He first selected 12 variables to describe the writing process. These included share of revisions in the first phase of the task, total number of revisions, duration of initial planning (seconds), and degree of recursivity (in terms of formulating followed by revision). He then set 40 people the task of writing two short reports (some on a computer and some using pencil and paper) and used video observation combined with automatic logging of the computer keystrokes to compile a record of each writing episode in terms of the 12 variables. He found five basic clusters, or profiles, of activity. These types of writing activity are described here using the labels given by van Waes, but they have been cast in terms of the cycle of engagement and reflection.

PROFILE 1: INITIAL PLANNERS. This process is characterized by an initial phase of reflective planning, followed by drafting and a relatively small number of revisions to the text. This is typical of a preplanning approach to writing, with the engaged writing driven by a tight set of constraints.

PROFILE 2: AVERAGE WRITERS. This can be seen as a middle way, with average values for each of the variables.

PROFILE 3: FRAGMENTARY FIRST-PHASE WRITERS. Initial planning is brief. There are a large number of revisions concentrated in the first phase of the writing process. It can be seen as a rapid cycle of engagement and reflection, with the writer making continual adjustments to keep constraints and text in harmony.

PROFILE 4: SECOND-PHASE WRITERS. The writers do some initial planning and then, once they have started drafting, pause infrequently for long periods. Revision is concentrated in the later phase of writing, with attention given to changes above word level. This can be seen as a longer cycle of reflection and engagement, with the writer creating a loose set of constraints to guide a session of engaged writing, followed by a period of major readjustment.

PROFILE 5: NON-STOP WRITERS. These writers spend little time on initial planning. They revise least and pause less often than the other groups. These are writers who appear able to engage with the text for long periods, without stopping for reflection.

The profiles found by van Waes give an indication of how differences in approach to engagement and reflection produce different types of observed writing activity. For a more detailed analysis that includes the writer's disposition, the text type and the type of representation, see Sharples (1994).

Validating the account

How can we judge the worth of the account of writing as creative design presented in this chapter? There are a number of ways in which it can be validated and applied, and this section does no more than suggest some possible approaches.

First, the account is testable. The verbal protocols and self-reports of writers can be studied for evidence of primary generators and of the types of creative thinking proposed by Boden and Gelernter. Studies of children, inexperienced adult writers and experts (similar to studies by Karmiloff-Smith of drawing ability) can be carried out to investigate whether their writing abilities conform to the account of representational redescription (see, for example, Bereiter & Scardamalia, 1987; Sharples, 1985). It is also possible to look for similarities between writing and other design tasks by comparing the use of tools, media and external representations. Studies of this type include Wood (1993) and Medway (1996).

Second, the account can be matched against other general theories of writing. The description by Scardamalia and Bereiter (1987) of the knowledge-telling and knowledge-transforming processes of writing matches Gelernter's distinction between high and low focus thinking, with knowledge transforming corresponding to Boden's (1994a) analysis of creativity occurring through the mapping, exploration and transformation of conceptual spaces. The account extends the cognitive model of writing proposed by Hayes and Flower (1980; chapter 1 in this volume) while proposing a different emphasis. It shares with Hayes and Flower a stress on the setting and manipulation of constraint and on writing as an iterative process, with intermediate products acting as a prompt for new ideas. The component processes are similar, but with the addition of contemplation as an activity separate from planning. It gives more stress than Hayes and Flower to the essentially cyclical nature of the writing activity, with the process of review and interpretation providing an explicit rerepresentation of enacted procedures, leading to contemplation, planning and re-engagement. But the emphasis of this account is not on writing as problem solving but writing as design, with the task environment not just influencing performance, but mediating and extending cognition. The account relates writing to other productive, creative activities, and to the writer's physical and social environment. It is much closer to the new model of cognition and affect in writing set out by Hayes in this volume, which incorporates visual-spatial representations and replaces revision by text interpretation and planning by reflection.

Third, the account resolves the apparent contradictions set out at the start of the chapter:

• *Writing is a demanding cognitive activity, yet some people appear to write without great effort.* Writing involves both engagement (the direct recording of conceptual associations) and reflection (the deliberate and cognitively demanding process of re-representing embedded processes and exploring cognitive structures). An engaged writer who has created an appropriate context and constraints can be carried along by the flow of mental association, without deliberative effort.

• *Most writing involves deliberate planning, but also makes use of chance discovery.* The products of engaged writing become source material to inspire and constrain deliberate planning.

• *Writing is analytic, requiring evaluation and problem solving, yet it is also a synthetic, productive process.* Analysis and synthesis are not in opposition, but form part of the productive cycle.

• *A writer needs to accept the constraint of goals, plans, and schemas, but creative writing requires the breaking of constraint.* Constraints serve a dual purpose: They act as a tacit generative framework, but an experienced writer is also able to represent constraints as explicit structures and can apply general-purpose procedures to explore and transform them. This transformation breaks out of the original framework, and in so doing creates a different conceptual space and set of constraints.

• *Writing is primarily a cognitive activity, but it cannot be performed without physical tools and resources.* It is not possible to write a long piece entirely in the head, because of the limitations of short-term memory. A writer needs to record the intermediate products and this act of recording requires tools, which both assist and restrict the process.

Last, it can inform the practice of writers, writing instructors, and the designers of new writing technology. Because it relates writing to design, the account can apply to new activities that combine writing with other types of design (e.g., the design of online documentation, help systems, and hypermedia). It suggests that general theories of creativity and studies of design might be of value to teachers of writing. For example, writers might be taught ways to re-represent their implicit schemas and constraints as explicit knowledge that can be shared and discussed with a teacher. They might also be helped to develop general-purpose operators and techniques for the exploration and transformation of conceptual spaces.

Earlier versions of this account of writing have provided requirements for a new computer writing environment (Sharples, Goodlet, & Pemberton, 1992). The Writer's Assistant is designed for people who create complex documents as part of their professional lives. One aim of the system is to support cognition by providing the writer with explicit text structures, constraints, and external representations (such as notes networks and document structures), all of which can be viewed, altered, and transformed.

Conclusions

The account of writing as creative design complements and extends previous models of writing as problem solving, providing an analysis of how creativity occurs, and of the relation between writers and their environment.

Writing is certainly a cognitive activity — it involves setting goals, planning, and organizing ideas. But it does not fit the mold of traditional problem solving activities. The writer is always faced with an uncountably large set of choices, with no simple means to evaluate each possible action. There is no set search space, and the problem must be generated as it is being solved. Writing is creative and, like other creative activities, has no simple goal. It involves the exploration of experience through reflection, or in the more elevated words of Wordsworth, "passion recollected in tranquillity." Writing also has much in common with the practices of architects, composers, engineering designers, and graphic designers. A writer as designer is dependent on tools and resources and is embedded in a community of practice, following guidelines of style and structure, and building on the work of others. Lastly, writing is developmental, and Karmiloff-Smith's theory of representational redescription provides a means to understand the development of writing abilities and the acquisition of new skills.

The account given here is still far from complete. It does not cover motivation or writers' habits. It does not reach the level of detailed cognitive processing provided by the accounts of Hayes and Flower or Scardamalia and Bereiter. It has little to say about individual approaches to writing, or specific techniques such as brainstorming or outlining that a writer can employ. It needs to say more about types of representation and about interactions between cognition and the external world. And it only covers single person writing, yet more and more writing is done in collaboration. But, despite the limitations, it offers the basis for a greater understanding of writing and, by calling on studies of creativity and design, it situates writing within in a wider spectrum of mental and physical activities.

Acknowledgments

I would like to thank Steve Graham, Michael Levy, Iris Levin, Rafael Perez y Perez, and Mark Torrance for providing valuable comments on drafts of this chapter.

Analytic Tools and Techniques

— 8 —
WRITING SIGNATURES

C. Michael Levy
University of Florida

Sarah E. Ransdell
Florida Atlantic University

If random samples of prose by James Joyce, Agatha Christie, and J. D. Salinger were examined by even modestly sophisticated readers, there would almost certainly be substantial agreement that the passages were not created by the same writer. In fact, many stylistic features could be identified to support the differentiations among the writers. These differentiations signal differences in the style of the writers' *products*.

From a psychological perspective, however, it is much more interesting to inquire about differences in the composing *process* that may be manifest by an individual writer. To study the composing process itself requires access to living writers, of course, and appropriate tools for collecting and presenting information gathered during writing sessions. It has taken several years to develop such tools and assemble information in multiple ways in an effort to characterize, objectively and quantitatively, what distinguishes writers from one another in terms of what they *do* when they write. As we will describe in this chapter, the composing process of writers differ in ways that are often stable across time, across writing topic, across writing genre and within writing sessions. They are generally so characteristic of an individual that we have labeled them *writing signatures*.

This did not begin as a quest for writing invariances; their discovery was serendipitous. Understanding how we discovered them requires an appreciation of our research environment and protocol.

The research context

We were in the midst of a series of studies that required people to compose documents of various sorts on word processors in our laboratories. One particular, large-scale effort sought to determine the time course and effort involved in planning, generating text, reviewing, and revising both within and across many writing sessions.

The experimental setup for this project is illustrated in Figure 8.1. We recorded on videotape every keystroke the writers made using an off-the-shelf commercial device that simultaneously displayed the appropriate information on the writer's monitor and transformed it to a broadcast-quality signal suitable for recording. This obviated the need for a videocamera in the room, which had the potential of being intrusive (at least initially), and would have presented difficult problems in synchronizing with the video refresh rates (necessary to eliminate "scrolling" of the images on the tape recordings). Reviewing these tapes later, it was possible to unambiguously determine from the writers' behavior whether they were generating new text or revising previously written text. Determining when writers were planning future text or reviewing text already generated was problematic from the video record alone, because both writing processes are associated with pauses.

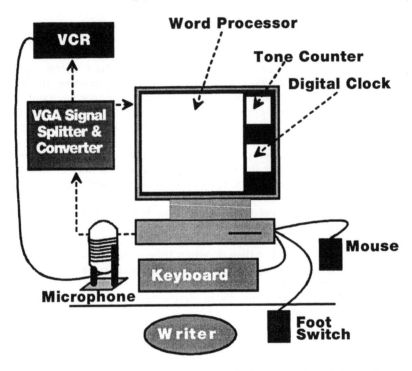

Figure 8.1. A schematic representation of the experimental environment. (Adapted from Levy and Ransdell, 1994. Reprinted with permission.)

Disambiguating planning and reviewing activities required an additional tool; the one adopted was the *concurrent verbal protocol* (see Bereiter, Burtis, & Scardamalia, 1988; Bereiter & Scardamalia, 1987; Ericsson & Simon, 1993; Hayes & Flower, 1980, 1983). The contents of verbal protocols provide a rich description of the subprocesses writers use when they compose. Hayes and Flower (1983) argued that verbal protocols provide direct information about the major writing processes through a working memory monitoring system. Information maintained within working memory drives the contents of one's written and verbal protocols, as well as how one manages the constraints of writing subprocesses.

We asked participants to continuously provide concurrent verbal protocols as they wrote after several weeks of practice writing in the laboratory. Great care was taken to ensure that writers understood that in generating and they were not to introspect or attempt to justify what or how they were writing.[1]

We measured the mental effort writers devoted to each subprocess by recording the latency of the writers' depression of a footswitch whenever they heard the computer sound a tone. Similar secondary, interference tasks have been used in other process-oriented research in writing (Kellogg, 1988; Kellogg & Mueller, 1993). In each writing session, the tone occurred randomly about every 30 seconds.

Ten undergraduates volunteered for a 10-week writing initiative, during which they composed once a week under standardized conditions for 40 minutes at a time. These volunteers were accomplished in the use of a word processor and were eager to participate because they enjoyed writing, wrote often, and considered themselves to be fairly successful writers. We attempted to maintain their initial enthusiasm by promising a $100 award to the individual who wrote a document judged by independent raters as exhibiting the best overall quality.

The writers were assigned a new title for their compositions each week, immediately after their baseline response times to the tones were collected. The topics were open-ended and designed to enable writers to approach the subject from any of several different perspectives. Some examples include, "The Greatest High of All," "Perfect Job," and "That Sense of Humor." The writers were challenged to create documents that would be appropriate for submission to the editor of a sophisticated national publication, such as *The New Yorker* magazine. They were free to use whatever genre they felt appropriate.

Scoring the protocols

It was our intention at the outset to codify the composition process using the finest possible temporal resolution. We ultimately demonstrated through reliability estimates that 1-second intervals were acceptable for scoring. At this resolution, there were 240,000 writing epochs to analyze.

The analysis began with the training of 12 student assistants in the use of EventLog (Henderson, 1989) to score sample videotapes until they reached satisfactory agreement with reference standards. EventLog is a computer program that enables a DOS-based PC to emulate an n-channel event recorder. That is, whenever a key such as "T" (representing "text generating") was depressed, a *virtual* pen moved from its baseline, returning only when the rater released the "T" key. Any combination of keyboard keys can be defined to represent observable events, and, in theory, any number of keys can be simultaneously depressed.

We were particularly interested in mapping behavioral sequences of writing and pausing into four underlying cognitive processes: planning,

---

[1] Our use of verbal protocols here is nontraditional in that we did not need to transcribe them to use them effectively.

We were particularly interested in mapping behavioral sequences of writing and pausing into four underlying cognitive processes: planning, translating (which we called text generating), reviewing and revising. We accomplished this mapping by first coding each second of the records according to the behavior that was occurring.

In scoring the replay of the writing itself, after muting the audio track, judges indicated the points when typing, pausing, deletions and insertions started and stopped. When judges listened to the audio track, they indicated when the writers were obviously planning what they were about to write next, and when they were re-reading aloud what they had already written. Different judges were involved in the scoring of the audio and visual tracks of the tapes, and each tape was scored by at least four judges.

EventLog reported the clock time of each key press and the duration, accurate to 1 millisecond, that the key was held down. Because the judges' own reaction times were clearly a component to be reckoned with, we rounded their responses to the nearest whole second.

For example, Figure 8.2 shows a representation of the EventLog output from two judges who scored the visual and auditory events that occurred during a particular time period. The horizontal marks represent the EventLog "virtual ink" tracings as keys were pressed and released by the judges to signal the onset and offset of particular behaviors. The behaviors that the judges monitored are shown in Table 8.1.

Table 8.1
Behaviors scored on visual and auditory tracks of the videotapes

Behaviors coded from visual track	Behaviors coded from auditory track
Typing	Writer questions experimenter
Deleting	Experimenter replies
Pausing within a word	Planning future topic content
Pausing within a clause or sentence	Rereading text written
	Evaluating one's own writing
Pausing within a paragraph	Writing content
General pausing or between paragraphs	Speaking and writing the same text
	Commenting on difficulty of the task
Any movement in text	Asides
Starting new paragraph	Prompts to speak
Superficial changes	Other speech sounds
Meaningful changes	Pausing
Question last behavior coded	Tone sounds
Disregard last behavior coded	Other nonspeech sounds
	Question last behavior coded
	Disregard last behavior coded

Next, we had to determine that our raters were reliable. We defined rules for our computer program, AGREE (Levy & Ransdell, 1994) to combine the decisions of judges who scored the visual records. We operationalized the rules to combine the separate behavioral scoring records into a single record for each session that indicated on a second-by-second basis, in what writing process the writer was engaged.

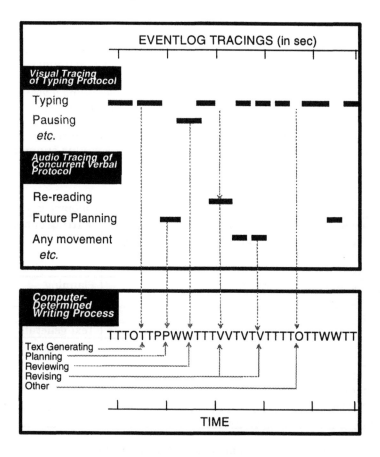

Figure 8.2. A representation of the EventLog output from the audio and visual tracings and a depiction of how the behaviors were coded.

Determining interjudge agreement was straightforward. We devised a computer program to do simulate to what individuals do themselves when they compare any two tracings, noting the degree of overlap between them. Two things were clear in these data. For a substantial amount of the time, the judges agreed that the same activity was occurring. But there were segments when one judge pressed or released a key before the other judge did and segments where the judges pressed entirely different keys to score the same events. To quantify the degree of agreement between the judges, we simply divided the 40-minute writing session into 2,400 discrete 1-second episodes, and counted the number of times the judges agreed with one another. Such indices of agreement produced values of 90% or more.

Interrater reliabilites associated with the scoring of visual records ranged from $r = .83$ for pausing to $r = .95$ for paragraphing. For the audio records, the correlation coefficients were all .90 or greater.

Once the visual and auditory tracks from the videotape were coded in EventLog files, we combined the judges' decisions about when each writing behavior began and ended. Because disagreements between judges occurred so infrequently, we determined that a little variance would be added to the data if a computer program resolved disagreement by tossing a virtual coin to determine which judge was correct in a specific 1-second episode.

Arguably, the most controversial aspect of this research are our rules for combining the behaviors scored from the visual and audio tracks. Table 8.2 summarizes these rules, which assume that only one writing subprocess can occur at any time.

Table 8.2
Combinational response patterns for determining writing subprocesses

Responses from writing protocol scored from visual track	Responses from verbal protocol scored from audio and visual tracks	Writing subprocess
Pausing or starting new paragraph	Not re-reading	Planning
Anything	Future planning	Planning
Typing	Anything	Text generating
Deleting, making meaningful or nonmeaningful changes, or any cursor movement	Anything	Revising
Pausing	Re-reading	Reviewing

There will probably be no argument that when the visual track indicated the writer was typing, it would be reasonable to declare that text generating was in progress, regardless of whatever might be occurring on the auditory track. This is the general rule that used to define text generating, and there was only one exception to it, as indicated later.

If, in contrast, a writer stopped typing and the auditory track indicated that he or she was re-reading or critiquing, we declared that reviewing was in progress. Alternatively, if the visual record showed the writer deleting text, moving the cursor, or making any meaningful or nonmeaningful change to the text, we defined that as indicative of the revising process. This leaves the planning process to explain.

Planning was defined to occur in several different ways. One of these was indicated by the writer's talk-aloud protocol exhibiting future planning (e.g., *I think what I want to do next is...*), regardless of what was occurring on the visual track. So even if the writer was typing, if the audio track indicated that the writer was planning for the future at the same time, our scoring rules demanded that the episode be scored as planning rather than text generating. Planning was also defined as occurring whenever the writer paused and was not re-reading or started a new paragraph and was not re-reading.

One of the important characteristics of these keystroke analyses is that second-by-second scores for the audio and visual tracks are on computer disc, so anyone who wants to combine them differently merely needs to re-write the combinatorial rules and rerun the program.

Finally, the documents produced by each writer were uniformly printed, combined with those of all other writers, sequenced in a random order, and presented to a pair of judges who provided blind ratings. Each judge used a tool developed in holistic quality assessment as part of university English placement examinations (Nees-Hatlen, 1989) to score the documents on 13 dimensions of writing quality. Some of these included content, purpose, style, word choice, organization, and mechanics. Judges scored all documents on one dimension before addressing the next dimension. Interrater reliability across all dimensions and documents was .90. The quality score assigned to a document was the sum of the 13 ratings for the two judges.

Some basic results

One of the most striking things to emerge from the primary analyses of our data (more fully described in Levy & Ransdell, 1995) was the remarkable consistency of writers in how they allocated time to planning, text generating, revising, and reviewing across weeks of composing. For example, the correlations between the number of seconds spent planning between all pairs of adjacent weeks varied between .6 and .7; for text generating, the corresponding values were about .8. Writers devoted comparatively little time to revising and reviewing (generally less than 10%), and their patterns of revising and reviewing times were less consistent from week to week. The adjacent-week correlations were typically less than .1 for these processes.

The pattern of intrawriter consistency increased strikingly when multiple correlations were examined. For example, the multiple Rs predicting the time spent on any of the four writing processes on Week 10 revealed that from 80–95% of the variance was accounted for by the times allocated during the prior five weeks. Such patterns of consistent allocation of time led us to search for ways to depict better the relations among writing processes over time both between and within composing sessions. The obvious place to start was with an examination of the individual epochs of planning, text generating, revising, and reviewing.

Composing epochs were defined by the onset and offset of a writing process as determined by the computer program that combined the rater's EventLog scores from the visual and auditory tracings. Epochs determined in this way were surprisingly brief. Because their temporal distributions were skewed, we studied the median epoch durations. Text generating epochs thus averaged about 7.5 seconds, and were reliably longer than epochs devoted to planning, reviewing, and revising, which were about 2.5 seconds long each, $F(3,78) = 82.73$, $MSE = 4.42$, $p < .001$. We also noted that writers produced 46 planning and 37 text generating epochs in a typical session, but only 15 reviewing and 21 revising epochs, $F(3,78) = 81.17$, $MSE = 266.8$, $p < .001$. Even though fewer text generating than planning epochs occurred, because of the clear differences in average epoch duration, significantly more time overall was spent generating text than to any other process.

Transition probability matrices

When the duration of epochs is ignored, the shifts writers made from one writing process to another can be analyzed by studying tables of transition probabilities. Values in the probability matrices result from dividing the number of occasions on which a writer shifted from one writing process to another by the total number of writing epochs within a specified time period. We used 10-minute blocks of time here in order to have at least 100 epochs represented within any single matrix.

These matrices are independent of the absolute frequencies of occurrence of writing processes. Suppose, for example, that during the first 10-minute block, Writer A shifted from planning to text generating 55 times, and from text generating back to planning 39 times. If this writer exhibited a total of 105 writing epochs of at least 1-second duration, then the transition probability for planning→text generating would be .53 (55/105), and for text generating→planning it would be .37 (39/105). For comparison, consider Writer B, who provided 210 epochs within a 10-minute period, which included 110 planning→text generating and 78 text generating→planning epochs. The transition probabilities for Writers A and B are identical during this block of time, despite the fact that Writer B exhibited twice as many epochs.

Matrices containing all possible shifts among all possible combinations of writing processes appeared to offer a means to capture the recursiveness of writing. Figure 8.3 shows the transition probability matrices of two writers during their four 10-minute time blocks of writing during Weeks 5 and 10, the first and last weeks involving concurrent verbal protocols in this study. The top left matrix displays the transition probabilities for Writer 1 during the first 10 minutes on Week 5. The remaining matrices on the left contain the matrices that correspond to successive 10-minute writing blocks during that week. The next column of matrices reveals the pattern exhibited by the same writer on Week 10 for the same time periods.

The gray-scale coloring in the cells varies between white (representing probabilities less than .05) and black (representing probabilities greater than .40). The top row illustrates the probability of the writer shifting from planning to text generating, reviewing, or revising. The leftmost column illustrates the probability of the writer shifting from text generating, reviewing, or revising to planning. The diagonal cells are undefined.

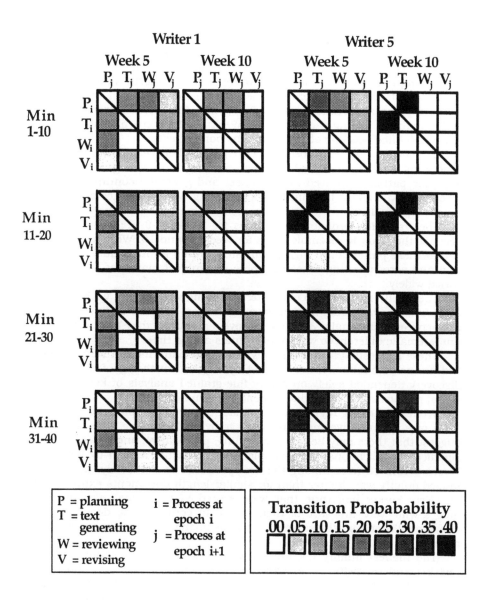

Figure 8.3. Transition probability matrices for two writers' composing sessions during Weeks 5 and 10. (Adapted from Levy and Ransdell, 1995. Reprinted with permission.)

During the first 10-minute block on Week 5, Writer 1 shifted between planning to each of the other three writing processes (reflected in the top row of the matrix) and from each of these other writing processes back to planning (as reflected in the left column) at about the same rates. During the succeeding time periods, this writer moved back and forth among all writing processes at comparable probabilities. This general pattern of widely distributed process allocation also characterized this writer's transition probability matrices during each period of Week 10. The general gestalt that this writer exhibited was one characterized by homogeneity.

In contrast, Writer 5 oscillated frequently between planning and text generating, and rarely shifted between reviewing and revising or text generating. This pattern appeared at the outset and generally continued for all of Week 5 as well as all 10-minute blocks during Week 10. Once again, homogeneity was evident.

The transition probability matrices for Weeks 6-9 are not shown here because they closely resemble those for Weeks 5 and 10. What is remarkable is that these patterns are highly consistent within an individual writing session and across writing sessions where the subject matter of the document varied widely.

These patterns seem so characteristic of individuals that we have termed them *writing signatures*. Like cursive signatures, they are distinctively different between individuals. And like cursive signatures, they exhibit small and unsystematic differences within individuals across time.

These interesting and potentially important patterns that we have identified are neither inherent nor implied by any known theory of writing. Their discovery depended solely on a very fine-grained analysis of keystrokes and verbal protocols that yielded a tremendous volume of data.

What do they signify? Beyond the fact that they are pictorial representations of a quantitative measure of an individual's writing style, these data suggest that there may be other intriguing, provocative, and potentially more significant implications. For example, the documents written by Writer 1 on Weeks 5 and 10 were among the best-produced in this study. In fact, their judged quality was greater than for similar-length documents extracted from *The New Yorker* magazine that were scored in the same sessions by the judges who were unaware of their origin. In contrast, the documents produced by Writer 5 on the same weeks were among the worst in overall quality rating.

The highest quality documents were associated with about 40% more revising and reviewing time than the lowest quality products, 209 vs. 156 sec, $F (1,29) = 5.54$, MSE = 8.5, $p < .03$. Because the average epoch duration for the writing processes was nearly the same for those quality groupings, and because the total writing time was constant for all sessions, the relatively homogenous pattern of transition probabilities exhibited by Writer 1 may simply be a by-product of a greater number of revising epochs. One way to partial out the differential contributions of these factors would be to systematically vary the time allowed for each composition; with more or less writing time, there would be greater or lesser numbers of writing epochs. It is not clear whether quality scores would shift in proportion to the total number of such epochs or whether they would be determined better by the percentage of revising to the total number of epochs.

These observations are offered with appropriate caution because they are based upon the results of only one investigation, and no precedent for them has been found elsewhere in the literature. Although replications and extensions of this investigation will be forthcoming, they will be slow in coming. After all, each of the 16 transition probability matrices in Figure 8.3 was derived from the coding of 2,400 data elements (600 seconds by at least four judges, two of each for the visual/written and the concurrent verbal protocols).

If these observations are supported by replication, then some important education and training issues come to mind. For example, if certain patterns of transition probabilities are reliably associated with high quality documents and others with low quality work as we suggest here, it would be important to know whether this relation is causal or merely correlational. If it is causal, then possibly with a sufficiently clever methodology, it should be feasible to intervene in the writing process, nurture the appropriate pattern, and thereby enhance the quality of the finished work. If such pattern training then shows positive transfer to other writing contexts, writing instructors will have a valuable new tool to use.

One major stumbling block to these replications is the matter of the measurement of quality itself. There are two different, but complementary, approaches to measuring the quality of a document – holistic and analytic – and there are virtually no benchmarks against which to make comparisons across laboratories even when the same basic approach is used. The absolute score assigned to a document may more likely depend on the other documents that a judge has recently read rather than the universe of all possible documents of the same genre. So, within any particular study, the quality scores may be best understood as relative versus absolute measures. It would be extremely useful to have an archived ensemble of reference documents available to the research community that represented critical points along the quality continuum. Such reference standards would be an important step toward facilitating comparisons of research results across laboratories.

Virtues of keystroke analysis

Keystroke capturing implies that important aspects of a writing session are captured on some medium for later use. Archiving of writing so that it can be studied over time within a lab also means that writing episodes can be studied in labs around the globe where the underlying assumptions behind the data analyses are very different. Because those in the writing community come from diverse backgrounds, it is natural to have different perspectives when studying the subject. When those differences are coupled with unique methodologies used in various laboratories, there is a situation where the prospect of finding support for other's work is rather small.

It does not have to be this way, of course. The researchers who collect keystroke data already have the technology in place to archive their raw protocols so that they can be studied and possibly reanalyzed by others. A central repository would be useful, and as long as data can be digitized, it can be distributed globally quickly and efficiently using the Internet.

Conclusions

The work described in this chapter has clearly derived from the model of writing put forth by Hayes and Flower almost 15 years ago. Despite the enhancements to this model in the first two chapters of this book, it remains one firmly tied to the assumption of a central executive. The original Hayes and Flower model appeared at a time when most mainframe computers had a single central processor, and implementations of distributed processing were far into the future.

But the future is now. Now our mainframes and many of our desktop computers have multiprocessors. Client–server relationships among computers are commonplace. Highly distributed processing seems to be a new focus in the computer sciences, and connectionist models seem to be driving a Kuhnian paradigm shift in some areas of cognitive psychology.

Other aspects of data collected using our current research methodology (see Levy & Ransdell, 1995) speak to the need to begin thinking of writing as a series of subprocesses that can take place concurrently with other cognitive processing and (possibly) with other writing subprocesses. If future research can provide evidence that some of these processes can occur simultaneously and independently of one another, then the metaphors of single executives (programs) borrowed from other disciplines may become less useful and it will be necessary to seek other metaphors.

It is generally accepted that data help shape theories, and research methods limit data. So an understanding of a process as complex as writing is determined at least as much by our methods as our data. Perhaps we are still more or less stuck in a single processor mode of theorizing about writing because our methods have limited our data to whatever can be obtained from a person's hand or mouth. Most people write or type only one character at a time and they speak only one word at a time.

But there is ample evidence that people can process distributively (see, for example, Clark, 1989; Besner & Humphreys, 1990; McClelland & Rumelhart, 1988; Morris, 1989). If people can engage in multiple writing processes simultaneously, then perhaps only the most dominant or salient may be manifest in overt behavior at any one moment. Using the methodology described in this chapter, for example, for a few moments a writer may seem from their overt behavior to be reviewing or revising or planning, and the next moment they may be generating text.

Our data indicate that the time writers devote to any one of these writing processes before going on to another writing process is very small, typically 2 to 5 seconds. But recall that our scoring rules were derived in such a way that one — and only one — process could be said to be occurring in any single 1-second scoring period. Thus, despite substantial evidence from other quarters that distributed processing of information is occurring, our methods may be predisposing us into believing that writers can only plan or generate text or review or revise at any one moment.

Our methods may cause us to interpret recursiveness in overt behavior as indicative of recursiveness in cognitive processing. It is still much too early to tell whether overt recursiveness is a veridical representation of internal recursiveness or whether it is an illusion based on our methodologies. Building — or building up to — processing models that derive from wholly different assumptions about the nature of cognitive processing may be an approach that many researchers take during the next decade.

Acknowledgments

We thank the trustees of the Norman Shulevitz Foundation for their support of our research. The chapter benefited substantially from the constructive suggestions kindly offered by Dick Hayes, Ron Kellogg, Pam Marek, Joseph Lea, Kerstin Eklundh, and Gert Rijlaarsdam.

— 9 —
A COMPUTER TOOL AND FRAMEWORK FOR ANALYZING ONLINE REVISIONS

Kerstin Severinson Eklundh & Py Kollberg
Royal Institute of Technology, Sweden

The use of computers has implied substantial changes for both writers and writing researchers with regard to revision processes. The revising opportunities offered by computers give room for a more flexible organization of the writing process, allowing writers to work recursively and to explore their topic through reconsidering what has been written. Moreover, researchers can use computers as observation and analysis tools, which has implied improved opportunities to study revision as a process.

We present a new method, *S-notation*, for tracing a writer's changes to a text while composing at the computer. The method facilitates the study of revision as an online process, by following writers' continuous reshaping of the written text. It gives a complete history of the changes that occur in a text during a writing session, and may therefore be of use as a tool not only by researchers but also by teachers and by writers themselves.

We will subsequently discuss some methodological problems that have arisen when using this tracing method to analyze online writing sessions. Some of the problems are primarily associated with the computer as a writing medium, whereas others are inherent to any revision analysis, but are made explicit when attempting to apply an automatic analysis tool. These problems raise general issues about the relation between description and interpretation in an account of writers' activities.

Research on revision

The study of revision has been an important part of writing research throughout the last decades. Along with gradually evolving theoretical perspectives, a number of empirical studies have been carried out, mostly addressing pedagogical issues on the value of revising. The issues studied have included how writers' revision strategies are influenced by their writing experience, by the nature of the writing task, and by the writing medium. A central concern has been how to define a useful taxonomy of revisions which could guide studies of revision and help explain the role of revision in the development of writing competence (Bridwell, 1980; Faigley & Witte, 1981).

Early studies on revision emanated from a largely product-oriented view of writing. During the 1980's, as researchers began to orient themselves more to the cognitive aspects of writing, their interest focused more on the process of revising. Whereas previously revision was seen only as a means of improving the quality of a text, a new paradigm of revising studies developed that attended to the nature of writers' struggles and strategies while attempting to reach an acceptable solution to a rhetorical problem.

Flower and Hayes' (1981) cognitive model of writing included evaluation and revision as parts of a reviewing component. Reviewing could occur either as a planned action (e.g. as a result of the writer's conscious decision to reread the text), or outside of the plan, in response to the discovery of some problem in the management of the task constraints. According to a later refinement of this model, the revision process contains three stages: detection of an incongruence between the writer's intentions and the state of the text produced; diagnosis of the nature of the incongruence; and formation of a strategy for repairing or removing the state of incongruence, leading to a successful revision (Flower, Hayes, Carey, Schriver, & Stratman, 1986).

In Hayes (chapter 1 in this volume), the cognitive perspective of writing has been broadened to include social and motivational aspects. Compared to the previous process model, reading is given a more prominent role. Revision is described as a result of a general process of text interpretation, guided by specialized "task schemas" that incorporate knowledge, such as goals for improvement of the text, knowledge about specific revision activities, and criteria for the quality of texts.

The cognitive tradition of writing research has implied a recognition of the fact that writers review not only completed sentences, but also unwritten or partly written text. In other words, evaluation as well as revision may occur before ideas have been clearly manifested in text. Witte (1985), in a critical discussion of the development of revision research, suggested that writers develop a mental "pre-text" during planning that is gradually reshaped during the composition process. According to this view, a strict focus on the writer's external revisions (or "retranscriptions" in Witte's terms) cannot yield a coherent picture of a writer's overall revising activity. Furthermore, recent research has shown evidence that the writer's total amount of revisions is not correlated with the quality of the written text (Ransdell & Levy, 1994), and that it may rather be the act of evaluation that has a positive influence on text quality (Breetvelt, van den Bergh, & Rijlaarsdam, 1994).

Although the view of revision as including both ideas and text is generally accepted, many researchers have continued to view writers' actual changes to the written text as a "window" onto their cognitive processes. Matsuhashi (1987) used the videotaped writing activity of a high school student to explore the nature of the constraints imposed on a writer during real-time text production. Writing was described as "shaping at the point of inscription," analogously to the production of spoken language. According to Matsuhashi, revision has a central role in this process: "It is the very potential for revision that allows the process to move forward efficiently. Without the option to revise — to evaluate the evolving plan and the text — progress in producing any but the most facile, rote texts would grind to a halt" (p. 201).

To revise, according to Matsuhashi, is a strategy for reducing complexity during writing because it allows the writer to "shift focal attention to an evaluation mode, revising the plan for the text and perhaps by altering the text itself" (p. 202). Less experienced writers may find it difficult to use revision as a means for successful reconstruction of the task, because they are easily overwhelmed by the low-level problems of real-time text production. This is supported by findings (see, for example, Bridwell, 1980; Ransdell & Levy, 1994) to the effect that inexperienced writers make more surface-level revisions while revising less on the higher levels of the text.

Online revision as an object of study

Matsuhashi's study yielded a complex picture of a writer's concerns during the process of writing that could not have emerged from static accounts of revisions. Generally, online revision can reveal important information about writers' shifts of attention and successive decisions during the writing process. However, the study of online revision also raises specific methodological issues with respect to the observation, description, and analysis of revisions.

To *observe* composition online requires methods that capture the writer's successive changes in the context of the entire writing activity. Early studies of revising used writers' marked-up drafts to study "in-process" revision (Bridwell, 1980), but this obviously leaves most of the process-oriented aspects aside. Matsuhashi (1982, 1987) used videorecording to explore writers' pausing and revising behavior in her case studies of handwritten composition, taking into account the writer's movements and the interruptions in the flow of the pen on the paper.

As more and more writers use a word processor, keystroke-recording (logging) has become an established method for capturing data about revision. Although the method is used in many forms, it usually involves continuous registration of the writer's keystrokes and pauses as well as a replay facility. The method has been used for studying isolated pause and revision variables as well as comprehensive strategies and profiles of writing (see, e.g., Bridwell-Bowles, Johnson, & Brehe, 1987; Lutz, 1987; Ransdell & Levy, 1994; Severinson Eklundh, 1990; van Waes, 1991). In comparison with other ways of studying online revision, keystroke recording is reliable and facilitates the collection of large bodies of data. Since it gives only indirect information with respect to the writer's mental processes, it should be used as a complement to other methods. Levy and Ransdell (1994 and chapter 8 in this volume) combined think-aloud protocols with a continuous video registration of writers' activities at the computer to study their shifts between processes, allowing the identification of individual "signatures" of writing.

Apart from capturing the data, the study of online revision is associated with specific problems in the *description* and *interpretation* of data. Whereas static accounts of revisions are enabled by comparisons between drafts, writers' actions online are often problematic to interpret due to the fact that they concern a partially incomplete text. Often, it is not even clear how to describe a revision in an unambiguous way. The use of computers for writing has made the problems of description even more prominent, because it has given rise to a wider and different revising pattern, influenced by the properties of word processors. For example, as we discuss later, the variety of movements possible in the text, and their representation in a keystroke record, partly depend on the scrolling and cursor-positioning characteristics given by the word processor.

Yet another type of problems concerns the *classification* of online revisions. Placing an online revision in a static category is often difficult, and does not reveal much about the process leading to the revision. This holds not only when the revision applies to half-written text. According to Matsuhashi (1987), the taxonomies that have traditionally been used to classify revisions have sometimes obscured rather than clarified what goes on in real-time revision. As an example, she examined the substitution of the word "conversely" for "and" on the part of one of her writing subjects. By simply classifying this as a low-level (word) revision, she argued, one misses the fact that this change addresses a high-level conceptual relation in the text. It is also important, Matsuhashi pointed out, to know when the writer actually makes a revision in order to understand its significance — for example, if this revision was made immediately after writing the word "and," or if it was made later, perhaps when other aspects of the task had triggered a discovery of logical relations in the text.

The role of the writing medium

The problems involved in analyzing online revisions are partly dependent on the writing medium. This fact may seem obvious, but has often been ignored in previous discussions of revision. The medium restricts both the actions that writers can take to alter their texts, and the methods available for the researcher to observe this process.

When writers use a pen and paper, making revisions is comparatively cumbersome and may require rewriting. Continuous observation requires following the flow of the pen on the paper, and registering the writer's actions whenever this flow is interrupted (Matsuhashi, 1982). Writers must usually be instructed to mark revisions in a way that facilitates for the researcher to identify them in the records.

Writing with a computer, on the other hand, facilitates both writing and revising, but requires both knowledge of word processing and proficiency in handling a keyboard. Computer-assisted writers tend to compose and revise online to an ever increasing extent (see e.g. Severinson Eklundh & Sjöholm, 1992), a process that can be followed by collecting records of writers' keystrokes. Altogether, the increased use of computers for writing emphasizes the need for better-developed procedures for analyzing online revisions.

A computer-generated notation for revisions

In connection with her case studies, Matsuhashi (1987) outlined a research methodology that allowed for the recognition of the nature of each revision within the context of the entire composition process. She also presented a formalism for documenting writers' revisions as they occurred in the text, taking account both of the nature of a revision and the point at which it was performed. The system was used for manual annotation of the handwritten records, in which researchers could add their own comments and interpretations.

The work that we describe later emanated from the need for capturing revisions made in a word processor as writers compose. By recording writers' keystrokes, one has a rich opportunity to follow the successive episodes of writing, revising, and pausing as writers compose in a word processor. However, keystroke records also pose a range of problems for the researcher, in particular with regard to the identification of revisions. The records are chronologically ordered, and it is usually coupled with significant work to identify revisions clearly (see, e.g., Severinson Eklundh, 1990). Often, replay on a second-by-second basis is required to find out the effect of a revision or its place in the text. Moreover, the records used depend on the word processor used, and do not lend themselves to comparison between different computer environments (Severinson Eklundh & Kollberg, 1995).

Against the background of these problems, and inspired by the work of Matsuhashi, we have developed a method and a notation (S-notation) for capturing and describing online revisions made on a computer. The notation is generated automatically from a keystroke record, using an intermediate representation that is independent of the text editor or word processor used. This notation implies a step forward of the study of online revision both by allowing an automatic registration of revisions, and by providing a language for describing them in an unambiguous way. The methodological problems associated with studying revision can therefore be discussed more easily.

The characteristics of S-notation

S-notation represents a writing session is in such a way that revisions appear explicitly in the text produced. For each revision, a *break* (interruption) also appears at the position of the action preceding the revision.

Figure 9.1 shows an example of a writing session with S-notation. After writing the first sentence, the writer inserts the word "short" between "a" and "text". After the second sentence, the word "probably" is deleted. Immediately after this change, the word "somewhat" is also deleted. In the final sentence, the words "I am" are deleted immediately after they are written.

The visual appearance of the notation was partly inspired by the annotation system developed by Matsuhashi (1987). Two major differences between the systems should be emphasized:

Whereas Matsuhashi's notation was designed for manual transcription of writers' changes in a text, S-notation is computer-generated. It is derived automatically from a keystroke record of the writing session, using a set of rules interpreting all text editing actions as an insertion or a deletion. These rules were originally developed by Kollberg (1995). The intricate rule system reflects many problems in finding a natural and unambiguous representation of text editing actions on a computer. The development of the rules, therefore, is an ongoing process that must be tightly interleaved with the analysis of empirical data.

Example of a writing session with S-notation:

I am writing a { short}[1] text.‖[1] It will [probably][2]‖[3] be revised [somewhat][3] later.‖[2] Now [I am‖[4]][4] it is finished.

The text produced in this example reads as follows:

I am writing a short text. It will be revised later. Now it is finished.

The S-notation uses the following symbols:

‖	The break (interruption) with sequential number i
{inserted text}[i]	An insertion following break #i
[deleted text][i]	A deletion following break #i

When needed for the sake of clarity, the index is shown both at the beginning and at the end of a revision. To emphasize the range of revisions further, there is an option in Trace-it to present insertions as underlined text, and deletions in italics.

Figure 9.1. Overview of the principles for S-notation.

In Matsuhashi's notation, several text changes could be treated as belonging to "the same" revision and assigned the same sequential number. When attempting to represent revisions in this way, one often encounters problems because it entails an interpretation of relatedness in the data that is difficult to establish with accuracy. In contrast to such a description of revisions, and as a necessary requirement for a computer implementation, S-notation represents all editing actions in a neutral way, as an independent insertion or deletion (henceforth *elementary* revisions). This amounts to a lower level of description, which is based only on the writer's overt actions in manipulating the text. We will later outline how more complex categories of revision, as well as comprehensive revising episodes and patterns, could be described as a combination of such elementary revisions. The latter step entails a second level of analysis, involving an interpretation of writers' actions that may need to be supported by information from other sources such as verbal reports from the writer.

Appendix 9.1 describes the basic principles and rules for the S-notation. In Kollberg (1995), a range of special cases as well as the technical aspects of the S-notation are presented in more detail.

An interactive tool for tracing revisions

The S-notation has been incorporated into an interactive program, Trace-it, designed to support the analysis of writing sessions. In one window on the screen, it presents the writing session with all revisions displayed directly in the text (see Figure 9.2). The user can "navigate" in the writing session by pointing and clicking on the revisions, or by following the order in which the writer performed them. It is also possible to remove or "execute" a revision to suppress either just the revision itself, or both the revision and the action preceding it from the record.

Figure 9.2. Screen presentation in Trace-it.

In another window, the written text is simultaneously displayed. The user can choose to play back the session one revision at a time, forward or backward. A list of all revisions in the session can be obtained, displaying their size, range, and distance from the point of inscription or from the previous action. A summary of all revisions can also be generated (see Table 9.1), specifying the number of revisions on different linguistic levels (character, word, phrase, sentence, paragraph, and text).

The input to Trace-it is a logfile in a special format called MID. This format is simple and general, and could be generated by any screen editor. It consists of a list of elementary operations (moves, insertions and deletions) in their order of appearance during the writing session, including a time stamp for each event.

In our own studies, Trace-it has been used in combination with JEdit, a word processor for the Macintosh which was designed for composition studies. JEdit generates a logfile which can be converted into MID-format, and thus constitutes an environment for testing S-notation in actual practice. Appendix 9.2 shows an excerpt from a keystroke logfile using JEdit, and a corresponding part of the session in S-notation.[1] In Appendix 9.3, JEdit's conventions for presenting text editing actions in a logfile are summarized.

A more extensive description of the Trace-it program is given in Severinson Eklundh & Kollberg (1995) and Nilsson (1993).

Table 9.1
Summary of revisions made in the session "My way to work"

Level	Type of revisions		
	Immediate	**Distant**	**Total**
Character	34	8	42
Word	15	10	25
Phrase	21	8	29
Sentence	0	0	0
Paragraph	0	0	0
Text	0	0	0
All	70	26	96

Inserted characters:	309	
Deleted characters:	651	
Typed characters:	4027	

Implications of S-notation and Trace-it

One of the most important aspects of S-notation is that it provides a general, system-independent language for describing revisions performed on a text. Previously, it has been a problem to describe online revisions in an unambiguous way, e.g. changes made at the point of inscription and revisions made to parts of the text that are later deleted (see, e.g., Williamson & Pence, 1989). The S-notation record shows the complete text written by the writer, including all revisions as they appeared in the text. This means that any part of the text can be searched for in the record, whether or not it remains in the final version.

The interactive session analysis supported by the Trace-it program has many applications. Writing researchers who collect data by keystroke recording can save considerable time in using this tool for the identification and analysis of revisions, as well as for exploring comprehensive revising pat-

---

[1] In general, excerpts from S-notation records do not match the corresponding keystroke records exactly, since the former is presented in the order of the resulting text, whereas the latter is presented in chronological order. In this case, however, the sequence of these presentations coincided due to a largely linear writing mode.

terns. Whereas many studies so far have used playback of ordinary, chronological keystroke files to identify and code revisions — a process that is time consuming and error prone — the access to a text-based, computer-generated notation for all online revisions is a step toward a more exact and reliable procedure in this respect.

For researchers who study text-editing systems, these tools may also have far-reaching implications. Because the MID format is independent of the text editor and computer system used, S-notation can be used to compare editing patterns of users in different computer environments.

Finally, Trace-it has a potential application as a history tool for writers. In many situations, it may be of interest for writers to save and store all previous text formulations and revisions made during a session, perhaps to be able to reconsider them later. This kind of application, which is relevant for both individual and collaborating writers, can already be explored with the current version of the tool, although a more complete integration with the writing environment would be an improvement in this context, allowing for instant access to the history records.

A study of revision and linearity in computer-assisted writing tasks

The tools already described have recently been used to study revisions in a writing experiment, involving a group of student writers, each of whom performed four writing tasks. The purpose of the study was to investigate how different properties of a writing task may influence writing strategies with a computer. Because most previous studies of computer-assisted composition had only included one type of task, it was hypothesized that the uniformity of task selection could account for some of the results in those studies, especially the tendency for low-level, local revision as the most dominant revising strategy (cf. Lutz, 1987; van Waes, 1991).

The experiment included the following tasks, chosen to represent different levels of complexity with respect to the demands for restructuring and integrating knowledge about a topic:

REPORTING. The subjects were asked to describe their way to work or school during a typical morning to an audience of colleagues or fellow students.

SUMMARIZING AND STRUCTURING. The subjects were shown a 20-minute film illustrating how to avoid back strain during house repair and construction work. The task was to summarize the main content of the film in a short, well-structured instruction text that might be put on a notice board or circulated in a workplace.

COMPARISON. The subjects were given two different college newspapers, and were instructed to compare them with regard to both form and content. The proposed audience was a committee meeting to discuss student newspapers.

ARGUMENTATIVE. The subjects were given a short reading material about traffic problems. The task was to write an argumentative text about the city traffic in Stockholm, intended to appear in the readers' debate column in a daily newspaper.

In Severinson Eklundh (1994), these data were used to study the linearity of text production for five of the writers. The underlying assumption was that linearity (the order in which the text is produced, compared to the order of its final presentation) can be expected to reflect cognitive aspects of the task, such as the need for planning and the recursivity of the writing process. A concept of linearity was used that could be assessed from S-notation records, using a combination of the variables *range, distance,* and *frequency* of elementary revisions. This implied that a writing session was considered nonlinear only when there were many large revisions made at a distance from the point of inscription.

The results suggested that the nature of the task influences the linearity of text production as well as the general pattern of revising. In particular, the broad category of knowledge-forming tasks — tasks that require integration and transformation of knowledge structures in addition to reporting existing knowledge (represented by Task 2, 3, and 4) — all resulted in less linear text production than a reporting task (Task 1). However, the patterns that emerged were complex, and there were great individual variations among the writers. These findings in turn suggested a need for better-developed procedures for describing comprehensive writing strategies and profiles.

Later, we will use the experiences gathered from this study as a basis for discussing some methodological issues in the analysis of online revisions. Excerpts from an adult, English-speaking writer's session when performing the reporting task (*"My way to work"*) will be used as illustration. The subsequent discussion is aimed at clarifying which aspects of revising can be supported by a computer-based analysis, and how S-notation can fit into a larger framework for describing and interpreting writers' actions.

Problems in the description of online revisions

The description and classification of immediate revisions

During an online composing session, a writer frequently deletes something just written, and then continues writing. Sometimes several such revisions are made in a sequence, as the writer hesitates about what to write. These immediate revisions often pose a problem for the researcher, because the writer's intentions may be difficult to interpret. This includes both the problem of how to identify the boundaries of a revision, and how to classify it, especially if it concerns a sentence not yet completed.

Figure 9.3 shows different examples of immediate revisions, taken from the session *"My way to work."* In Example 3:1 the writer deletes the "P" just written, and goes on with *"Out the door I make a right, and then..."* How should this revision be described? Is it fair to say that the letter "P" was substituted by an "O," implying a character-level change? This may be the case if the writer simply struck the wrong key. Or, is the P perhaps substituted by the whole following phrase or sentence? Evidently, there is no way of knowing (in the absence of other data than the computer record) what the writer actually intended to write, and therefore there is no satisfactory way of classifying this revision as a substitution.

(3:1)	[P⟦⟧₃] ³ Out the door I make a right, and then almost
(3:2)	this morning [the thought of ⟦⟧₉] ⁹′ s choice of a warm, dry bus or a [muddy⟦⟧₁₀] ¹⁰ snowy, muddy walk
(3:3)	I hate being bored[. When the ⟦⟧₆₈] ⁶⁸, even for 10 minutes. When the train comes
(3:4)	waiting, or if [i shou⟦⟧₇] ⁷ I should just walk.
(3:5)	As [d⟦⟧₂₇] ²⁷ we stream into the subway station

Figure 9.3. Immediate revisions from the session "My way to work."

Few researchers have explicitly discussed the problems involved in the analysis of immediate revisions. Such changes abound in computer-assisted composition, reflecting the ease of changing the text in the computer and trying out different formulations (see Severinson Eklundh, 1990, 1994; van Waes, 1991). An illustration is that in the reporting task of our experiment, the rate of immediate revisions was 77.5%; if character-level revisions were excluded, the rate was 60%. As Table 9.1 shows, the writer of "My way to work" performed in all 96 revisions, 70 (73%) of which were immediate revisions. Williamson and Pence (1989) found a recurring pattern of immediate revisions to be characteristic of a specific writing profile at the computer, the "recursive reviser" (see also Severinson Eklundh, 1994).

A pattern of repeated immediate revisions may also occur in handwritten composing sessions. Bridwell (1980), in her study of 12th-grade writers, referred to it as "stuttering in writing:"

> Many students would write a word on the page, delete it, add it again, substitute a similar word, and so on, almost as a recurring lament, 'I know what I want to say, but I don't know how to say it' were revealing itself in the revising process (p. 211).

In S-notation, which is neutral with respect to writers' intentions, an immediate revision is simply described as a deletion with distance zero, placed directly in its context within the text (see the examples in Figure 9.3). This has the advantage of giving the same formal description to any change of this type, regardless of any interpretation of the writer's intentions. However, it also means that there must be other stages of analysis following the S-notation analysis, in which the researcher attempts to interpret the writer's behavior.

Substitutions within existing text

Substitutions are a part of most of the revision taxonomies used in the literature. To make a substitution is usually taken to mean replacement of a linguistic unit by an alternative form (Bridwell, 1980). If the units are not equal in range, the terms *distribution* ("material in one text segment is passed into more than one segment"; Faigley & Witte, 1981) and *consolidation* (several segments are passed into one) are sometimes used.

In S-notation, a substitution within already written text is rendered as two revisions, a deletion and an insertion (see Figure 9.4, Example 4:1). This description is a natural consequence of the neutral character of the notation, and reflects the fact that the temporal adjacency of a deletion and an insertion does not guarantee that they constitute a substitution in a rhetorical sense. It is also compatible with the fact that immediate substitutions are rendered simply as a deletion followed by new text (see the previous section).

```
(4:1)   As we stream into the subway station there are
        [ usually] 34[] 35{ often} 34 masses of people streaming out
        from a recently-arrived train, which often means a
        wait for me until the next train comes along.[] 34

(4:2)   [ O] 14[]15{ Even though I am living in Stockholm, o} 15ften
        the language of all the conversations is English
```

Figure 9.4. Two examples of replacements from "My way to work."

As an illustration, we may look at Example 4:2, in which a modifying clause is added in the beginning of a sentence. In order to achieve this insertion in a simple way, the writer used the word processor to replace a single character by a long string of text. This is a rather common word processing strategy, aiming at minimal work: Because the sentence should begin with a capital letter, the first letter has to be changed even if the first word is kept. In this case, the keystroke logfile showed that the writer simply selected the character "O" with the mouse, and immediately typed the string "*Even though I am living in Stockholm, o*".

Such replacement operations may be unique to computer-text editing. However, pen-and-paper revising sessions may also include adjacent revisions that are not related. Generally, there does not seem to be any formal criterion of when an item should be seen as a substitution (or distribution or consolidation) and when it is simply to be treated as a deletion followed by an insertion. Although many cases of substitutions are clear-cut in intuitive terms, this assessment is an interpretative step in the analysis of revisions, which should be made explicit as far as possible.

In the context of adding "rules" that might guide such an interpretation, the distribution of pauses in connection with revisions may prove to be a relevant factor. Furthermore, the way of performing the revisions in the word processor may be different depending on the writer's successive development of the text plan. Look at the following alternative sequences of actions for a Macintosh writer:

CASE 1. The writer selects a word by marking it with the mouse, and then immediately types another word, causing the first word to be removed.

CASE 2. The writer deletes a word, makes a long pause, and writes a new word without moving the cursor.

CASE 3. The writer deletes a word, makes a long pause, moves to another position by clicking elsewhere in the text, pauses again, goes back to the original position, and types in a new word.

All of these cases get the same description in S-notation. However, it could be argued that in Cases 2 and 3, the status of the change as a substitution should be regarded as weaker than in Case 1. In other words, pauses and movements exhibited in the keystroke logfile could be taken into account in a rule-based interpretation of writers' actions, yielding evidence for classifying a delete-insert pair as a substitution.

Movements and distance

Unlike static descriptions of revision, which look only at the result of revisions in the text, the study of online revision must take account of the writer's movements while composing. This yields information about the writer's shifts of attention throughout the composition process, and gives a context for the interpretative analysis of revisions.

Computer-recorded writing sessions offer rich opportunities for studying writers' movements, because they track the position of the cursor in the second-by-second progress of text production. In keystroke protocols, one can thus follow both the movements resulting in a revision and other, "silent" movements. In fact, the notion of movement could be interpreted in three ways: The writer shifts position and starts writing or manipulating text at the new position; the writer shifts position by changing the cursor position, but does not alter the text at the new position; and the writer changes position (e.g., scrolls through the text) without moving the cursor. (This is possible only in some word processors.)

The last two types of movement leave traces in the keystroke logfile in JEdit, but not in the S-notation, because the latter is based only on the revisions made in the evolving text. In the first case, movements can be tracked in Trace-it by examining the *distance* between writers' successive positions. The revision analysis in Trace-it, using S-notation as a basis, gives a record of the (positive or negative) distance between a break (i.e. point of interruption) and the revision that follows. If the distance is 0, the revision is termed *immediate*; otherwise it is called *distant*.

In the writing session "My way to work," there were 26 distant revisions (see Table 9.1), but only a handful of them implied a move farther away than one sentence. Figure 9.4 shows an example of a revision (number 34 in [4:1]) with distance -128 characters according to the revision analysis in Trace-it, implying a backward movement within the current sentence.

Altogether, the list of revisions and their distance in the S-notation records gives a picture of movements back and forth in the text. The only movements not included in such an account are those that do not result in a new revision. This includes the "silent" movements of Case 2 above, but also some of the movements in Case 1, namely, those involved when the writer resumes writing after completing a distant revision. The latter kind of movement is visible in the S-notation, but it is not included in the distance analysis list, because no new revision is actually started (though one is resumed) in those cases (see for example Figure 9.1, where the writer resumes writing at the position of break #1 after completing revision #1). The concept of resumed insertions reflects the hierarchical structure of revisions, and expresses the intuition the writer can be expected to eventually return to an interrupted action in the process of text production.

Lutz (1987), in a comparative study of revising with a computer and with pen and paper, examined all revisions involving a reverse or forward move in the text. She found that computer writers moved more frequently and in shorter steps than pen-and-paper writers. This is compatible with results obtained by van Waes (1991) to the effect that the computer gives a more fragmented writing process compared to pen-and-paper writing, with frequent pauses and many local revisions. Interestingly, van Waes found that when writers used a larger screen, they made more distant revisions, and the revisions were also on a higher level. The distance variable also seems to correlate with the writing task: Severinson Eklundh (1994) found, using S-notation records as data, that distant revisions were more frequent in knowledge-forming tasks than in a reporting task.

Both Lutz and van Waes measured the distance between a revision and the previous action in the number of lines between the two actions. This way of measuring distance has the disadvantage that the extent of a line depends on the character font used in the word processor. It is also difficult to compare with S-notation records in their present form, which use the number of characters to measure distance.

With respect to the cognitive significance of revisions, there is reason to distinguish between local revisions with a small distance, and larger movements in the text. A more powerful notion of distance may also reflect aspects of the discourse structure. Matsuhashi (1987) used a three-part classification of revisions with respect to distance from the revision to the point of inscription: S_i for sentence-immediate revisions (= immediate in our terms), S_d for sentence-distal revisions (revisions that are distant but yet affect only the current sentence), and T (text revision, that is, revisions more distant than the current sentence) (p. 212). The basis for her analysis was the distinction between sequential and conceptual planning, in which the sentence can be expected to be a relevant unit. In fact, in the analysis of the revisions of a high school writer, she collapsed all the revisions performed within the current sentence into one category to highlight differences between revising patterns in two different writing tasks. For some purposes, such a sentence-based criterion of distance can be expected to be more relevant than the number of characters or lines, or even a strict division into immediate and distant revisions, and it might therefore be included as an option in future versions of Trace-it.

The episodic structure and clustering of revisions

When writers revise a text, they often do so in comprehensive sequences of revisions. In some cases, such sequences appear to be the result of a single rhetorical goal; whereas in other cases, they may be related more incidentally, for example, by the fact that the writer has decided to go through the text for a round of conscious reviewing and revising. A challenging issue for research is how to describe such connected *episodes* of revisions, both structurally and with regard to their status in relation to the writer's evolving goals.

Monahan (1984), in a study of 12th-grade students' writing for different audiences, found that competent writers revised in episodes to a greater extent than basic writers. He defined an episode as a connected sequence of revisions, each revision cued by the previous one. The assessments were based on the contents of think-aloud protocols gathered from the writers.

Few other researchers have discussed the episodic nature of revisions. Williamson and Pence (1989), in a study on the effect of word processing on student writing, found that the way in which revisions were grouped in larger clusters was one of the features that distinguished individual writing styles with a computer. Based on the replay of a large number of videotaped writing sessions, they identified the following types of episodes, that is, sequences of related revisions:

1. Several, often repetitive text changes occur at one cursor location. This could occur, for example, when the writer was trying out different formulations of a sentence.

2. Embedded changes, that is, one change is performed in the course of performing another, higher level change. For example, the writer could insert a new sentence in the middle of a text, and while doing this, change a word to another word in the sentence.

3. A change in one place is related to changes in other places. For example, this occurs, according to Williamson and Pence, "when a global change requires individual changes at several cursor locations."

4. One change "seems to inspire other changes." This type of episode is derived, according to Williamson and Pence, "using the greatest degree of inference." An example was when "a student went back to add a focusing sentence in the beginning of a paragraph after adding details to the end of that paragraph." The authors suggested that the proximity in time and meaning between successive changes may allow the researcher to infer their relatedness and episodic character.

The use of S-notation has the potential of facilitating the assessment of patterns of revision significantly, because it automatically traces the sequence of revisions in a session, and also keeps track of their internal hierarchical structure (that is, revisions performed during the course of other revisions). This structure can be presented in Trace-it as a table where all revision numbers are placed according to their hierarchical relations. In addition, the structure becomes visible during stepwise replay (revision by revision) of the session, in which revisions that are temporarily interrupted are listed at the bottom of the window.[2]

---

[2] A possibility which has been discussed is to use a hierarchical numbering of revisions to emphasize their internal structure. For example, the revisions embedded in

In fact, the S-notation record of a writing session can contribute to identifying all of the structural episode types mentioned by Williamson and Pence. Type 2 is exactly the case of hierarchical embedding. Another form of relatedness inherent in the S-notation is when, after interrupting text production, the writer makes several revisions before resuming writing at the original position. This includes the "cued" revisions in the sense of Types 3 and 4. We have already touched upon the simplest case of an episode of this type, that is, the case when a delete-insert pair amounts to a planned substitution.

Finally, S-notation may also be used to find various clusters of revisions (that is, groups of revisions that satisfy a certain criterion, such as Type 1). This kind of episode is structurally less well defined, however. For example, it is probably relevant to include in Type 1 all revisions that are "reasonably close" to the point of inscription rather than only the strictly immediate revisions (that is, with distance zero). Although Trace-it does not at present include support for defining complex revision patterns or locating them in the S-notation records, this belongs to the facilities we would like to explore in future developments of the tool. Generally, it seems fruitful to use S-notation both as a language for description of revision episodes, and as a tool for exploring the various types of connection between revisions.

I lock the door to my room and go down [4] $^{92}\|_{93}$ { four} $^{93}\|_{94}$
flights ...

... to sit down and get up again. In [4] $^{94}\|_{95}$ { four} $^{95}\|_{96}$
minutes we are there and it is back up the escalator ...

... old-fashioned kind of expandable gate for a door which
[is open and] ^{96} lets you see your progress as you travel up
...

... I enter the room, turn on the computer, and another day
begins. $\|_{92}$

Analysis of revisions 92-96 as rendered by Trace-it:

Revision	Type	Level	Range	Distance (characters)
92	DEL	w	lw	-3342
93	INS	w	lw	0
94	DEL	w	lw	2117
95	INS	w	lw	0
96	DEL	f	3w	941

Figure 9.5. A connected sequence of revisions following the same break.

The revisions in the session "My way to work" did not expose much episodic structure. Figure 9.5 shows a simple example of a connected sequence

---

revision 4 would have the numbers 4.1, 4.2, and so on. The reason that this form is not used in the present version is that it makes the notation less readable.

of revisions occurring at the end of the session. The writer, after the last sentence had been terminated by a stop, made a backward move all the way to the first sentence, replacing "4" with "four." After a long reading pause of 104.9 seconds (derived from the keystroke record), she made exactly the same change at another location in the text. Finally, after pausing 47.1 seconds, she made yet another change, deleting three words that she apparently found to be unnecessary before terminating the session.

The first four elementary revisions in this sequence were apparently related, consisting of two substitutions, the second of which was evidently cued by the first. As in this case, episodes can sometimes be identified with reasonable certainty from the linguistic character of the revisions. In many other cases, however, information external to the keystroke records, such as verbal reports from the writer, will be required to support the interpretation of relatedness in temporally adjacent revisions.

Levels of text editing and revising

In previous studies, revisions have been categorized along several dimensions, one of which is *level*. This classification aims at identifying the range of the revision, or, in other words, the extent of the part of text being altered by the writer.

Looking closely at the use of this category, there is sometimes a confusion between the writers' formal operations on the text and the intended effect of those operations. Thus, for example, Bridwell (1980) distinguished between surface, lexical, phrase, clause, sentence, and multisentence revisions. Among the *surface* changes, several subcategories were introduced, such as spelling, capitalization, and punctuation, whereas the *word* level contained the categories addition, deletion, substitution, and reordering. This classification appears to be based on the assumption that writers always operate exactly on the part of the text in which they have found a dissonance to be repaired. For example, it assumes that writers do not make a word-level revision to accomplish a surface-level change (e.g., spelling or capitalization).

In our study of revisions, Trace-it and S-notation were used to perform an automatic classification of revisions according to linguistic level (character, word, phrase, sentence and paragraph), range (the length of the revised string), and distance (from the writer's previous action). The identification of level and range is formally straightforward, implying simply a count of the number of characters included in the elementary revision (insertion or deletion). However, our experiences showed that in computer-based writing, there is frequently not a direct correspondence between a text editing action and a revision. In particular, some computer writers use the word processor in such a way that they regularly delete and rewrite larger portions of text rather than just editing the part of text to be changed. Thus, among the word- and phrase-level changes made by the writer of "My way to work," about a fifth were actually revisions on lower levels, whereas some other writers in the experiment did not expose this pattern at all.

Such differences are eliminated in S-notation if they amount to the same pattern of deletions and insertions to the text, but this is not always the case. For example, in Example 3:2 in Figure 9.3, it would have been just as natural to insert the word "snowy" as to delete the word "muddy" and then type "snowy." Another frequent case is that a writer deletes several words although only one or a few characters need to be changed, as in Example 3:4.

These issues may become even more complicated when the keystroke file and pauses are taken into account. Although some deletions may actually amount to insertions of new text, this cannot generally be inferred from the S-notation alone. Example 3:3 is an example of this. From the S-notation description of this revision, one would think that the writer's plan was to insert the phrase "even for 10 minutes." However, the keystroke logfile shows that the writer arrived at this change in several steps, pausing three times before retyping the phrase "When the train comes..." (see Appendix 9.2). The pattern of keystrokes and long pauses indicates that she reconsidered the text plan several times before continuing to write.

In general, there is no simple relation between the keystrokes used by writers when revising and the effect they intend to accomplish on the text. Some word- or phrase-level revisions are concealed corrections on a lower level, as many writers find it cumbersome to use the mouse to change position within the current sentence, or to use a text-editing command. Instead, they just hit the delete key a number of times, removing enough text to accomplish the relevant change by rewriting. But during this process, they may discover new relations in the text and decide to revise their text plan, resulting in a higher level change.

Examples such as those described here give further evidence that the S-notation level should be complemented with additional levels of analysis when interpreting and classifying revisions. We will return to this issue in the last section.

Identifying typographical corrections

The examples discussed previously illustrates another problem in analyzing online revising with computers, namely, the difficulty of separating out a category of typing error corrections. Whereas such changes abound in computer-assisted writing sessions, it is usually assumed that they can be distinguished from other revisions occurring in composition tasks. Van Waes (1991), for example, mentioned that typing errors were excluded from his analysis of computer-based versus pen-and-paper revision, after reporting that they constituted roughly 30% of the total score of revisions.

Often it is more or less obvious that the writer has struck the wrong key, such as in Example 3:5. But in cases such as Example 3:1, it is not possible to make this conclusion without additional information. Perhaps even more dubious are certain changes in punctuation, for example, when writer types a period, erases it, and types a comma. There, it could just as well have been a change in sentence planning as a typographical correction, because the two relevant keys are adjacent on the keyboard.

It would seem that typographical corrections are usually character-level revisions. However, Example 3:4 is clearly also a typing error correction, but is classified as a word-level revision in Trace-it, because the writer erased a whole word to correct the error. Even if the exact nature of the change is isolated, examples like Example 3:1 show that it cannot be determined with certainty from the nature of a revision if it should be seen as the correction of a typing error. Generally, this problem should be studied in relation to pure typing and editing tasks to give statistical evidence of the frequency and variability of typing errors.

The occurrence of pauses may turn out to be a clue to a certain revision being a typing correction or not in a composing session. In the session "My way to work," 24 cases were classified by the analyst as clear cases of typing corrections. None of these revisions was preceded by a pause of more than 2 seconds (this was the threshold for pauses used in the keystroke logging program). In contrast, among the remaining 72 revisions, 57% were preceded by a pause longer than 2 seconds, and the average pause length among those revisions was 10.3 seconds.

This also seems to be an argument to include pauses as an option in the description of a writing session in S-notation. In the present version of Trace-it, pauses are not represented, although the MID file contains the relevant time information in connection with each event. One problem in connection with such an extension of the program is the fact that pauses often occur at several points during the execution of a revision. For example, a writer may make a pause, delete a word, make another pause, and delete the rest of the sentence. There is no straightforward way of describing this in relation to the S-notation without a major change of the rules (e.g., causing revisions to be split as a result of the occurrence of pauses).

Another problem in representing pauses is deciding if a certain pause should be seen as "preceding" one event or "following" the previous event (which is often taken as evidence of classifying pauses as planning or reviewing pauses, respectively). Although this problem is general and applies also to the interpretation of other data such as keystroke logfiles, it is difficult to see how pause data could be automatically included in S-notation without reaching an interpretation level rather than a purely descriptive level of analysis. However, future versions of Trace-it could support the analysis of temporal information in other ways (e.g., by displaying the start time of each revision in the list of revisions).

A multilayered model for the analysis of online revisions

As a consequence of the discussion in the previous sections, the analysis and interpretation of online revisions during a computer-based writing session should be performed in several steps, which use different levels of knowledge about the writing process. Each step yields a successively deeper understanding of the role of the revision within the task performed by the writer. Table 9.2 is an attempt to explain and illustrate these levels.

Level 1 is the pure text editing level, which describes the writer's physical actions at the computer. The input to this level may be a keystroke logfile or a video record. The data on this level can also be used to conduct studies of the writer's problems in handling the computer system.

Table 9.2
A multilayered model for revision analysis

Data	Level	Questions focuses
Verbal reports; interviews, S-notation & keystroke records	Writer's overall rhetorical goals	*How is the writer's view of the task reflected in his/her revisions?*
S-notation & keystroke records; verbal reports	Interpreted revisions and revision episodes	*Which means of revising are used by the writer to achieve a specific goal?*
S-notation records	Elementary revisions	*In which general patterns does the writer generate and change the text?*
Keystroke records	Text-editing actions	*How does the writer use the computer to shape words and sentences?*

Level 2 is the S-notation analysis, which transforms the keystroke records into a sequence of elementary revisions. This step gives a formal description of the writer's changes to the text, including their order and internal structure.

Level 3 is an account of the revisions in terms of the effect on the text that the writer intended to achieve. In other words, this step gives an interpretative description of the writer's revisions. Arriving at such a description often requires access to information outside of the computer records, such as verbal reports from the writer.

Level 4 links the revision pattern with writers' task knowledge and goals, and to their global plan for the task. This implies a more comprehensive analysis of the writers' revising strategy in the context of the whole rhetorical situation.

Generally, the analysis in this model is thought to be pursued in a bottom-up fashion, so that data from the lower levels are successively enriched and interpreted in the light of data on higher levels.

Level 3 represents the level at which most revision analysts have carried out their analyses so far. However, it seems that such categorizations have often been based on implicit assumptions, mixing description and interpretation. In order to allow for a more explicit analysis procedure, this step could preferably be built on an elementary revision analysis (e.g., as automatically yielded by S-notation), but extended to contain other sources of relevant information.

At present, there does not seem to be any generally accepted procedure for arriving at an interpretative analysis of revisions, except using the linguistic character of the changes and their context in the text. For many purposes, it seems that think-aloud protocols are necessary to get a more complete picture of writers' intentions in online revision. However, writers' retrospective accounts, if collected immediately after the composing session (cf. Greene & Higgins, 1994), may also prove to be a useful source of knowledge at this stage of the analysis. In particular, stepwise playback of revisions as allowed in Trace-it might function as a way of "stimulated recall" (DiPardo, 1994), triggering explanations that might clarify some of writers' concerns in shaping the text.

Computer support for an integrated study of online revisions

As we have shown, S-notation gives only a basic description of a writer's changes to a text. It renders all revisions in elementary form, and leaves the remaining analyses to the researcher. In particular, all work in the interpretation of writers' actions must currently be carried out outside of the system.

We have discussed the possibility of expanding the revision analysis environment to include some support for the higher levels of revision analysis. Such a system could, for example, guide the user through the sequence of elementary revisions in a session, and propose candidates for connected episodes by using the internal structure of the S-notation record. Furthermore, the program could include a coding facility that allows the user to classify the revisions (and episodes) according to a preset but flexible system of categories, allowing links to annotations or external information supporting the classification. Such information could include, for example, selected information from the keystroke logfile (including movements and pause patterns), and parts of verbal protocols and interviews.

In the present system, the classification and coding of revisions is facilitated by the fact that S-notation presents revisions directly in their textual context. However, when the writer has performed many changes in the same part of the text, the record may be quite difficult to read (illustrated by the passage in Appendix 9.2). Apart from the original keystroke record, playback of the revisions step by step is often helpful in such cases to identify the nature of each revision. Furthermore, as a basis for explicit description and coding, it would also be useful to have access to a step-by-step contextual description of each revision, showing the S-notation as it applies to the existing text at the point of performing the revision. The generation of such a "concordance" of revisions (or episodes) seems to be a useful complement to the present facilities in the revision tracking tool.

As a future extension of the S-notation environment, it is also possible to imagine a rule-based analysis of a writer's revision patterns, to be used as a diagnostic tool for various purposes. Such a system would initially learn about a writer's revising and pausing pattern, and then be used to form hypotheses about the nature of single revisions based on this knowledge. Some parts of such a system could be based on general principles. An example is a component that attempts to guess which revisions are corrections of typing errors by using information about the layout of the keyboard. Although such a component will usually not reach 100% correctness, it might be useful for some applications to be able to suppress the revisions fulfilling a certain criterion from the revision record.

Conclusions

In this chapter, we have discussed problems in analyzing online revisions, some of which have previously been neglected. We have also presented a computer-based tool developed in our laboratory, which offers both a language for describing revisions on an elementary level and an interactive environment for exploring and "navigating" in a writing session. This tool facilitates discussions of some methodological problems, and opens the way for a more rigorous treatment of revising in computer-assisted composition. However, it yields a low level of description that should be complemented with interpretative accounts to arrive at a reliable categorization of revisions.

The discussion above has shown that the computer as a writing tool generates specific methodological problems. In fact, this is a reminder that the overt realization of a revision is always to some extent an artifact of the writing medium. This has largely been ignored in both pen-and-paper-based and computer-based revision studies, as they have rarely addressed concrete problems in the description and analysis of revisions.

Some of the problems discussed have implications for the design of writing support. If word processors could help writers edit their texts in higher-level operations based on linguistic regularities of texts, the editing pattern might be closer to the intended revising level and less character-oriented. A simple example is that text editors could be programmed to "know" that a sentence must begin with a capital letter. This would make a revision such as Example 4:2 in Figure 9.4 involve only the sentence which the writer actually intended to insert, and not an additional character.

It could be argued that some of the problems discussed here should be dealt with in a theory of computer text editing rather than in composition. Evidently, some of what has been said here applies to other word processing tasks than composition. However, composition theorists cannot ignore these data, because the revision pattern occurring in pure editing tasks cannot be expected to coincide with that of composing tasks. Future studies may reveal that writers incorporate word processing knowledge with their writing process to a greater extent than has hitherto been recognized. Examples described here show that real-time composition at the computer gives rise to specific revising strategies the interpretation of which needs access to a wider range of sources than keystroke records, and whose realization is partly induced by the properties of the word processor.

Although online revisions will always remain a mystery to some extent — reflecting the fact that the writer's thoughts and plans are continuously reshaped, leaving only fragmented traces in the text — the computer may help us approach this process with greater accuracy and rigor, and therefore learn more about the real-time character of text production.

Appendix 9.1 — S-notation principles

General principles

In S-notation, a revision is either an insertion or a deletion. Each revision is associated with a break (or an interruption) at the position of the last action preceding the revision. The breaks are numbered according to the sequence of their occurrence in the writing session. Revisions are numbered according to the break that "led to" them, that is, that preceded them in the writing session.

Insertions

All text production during a session is considered as occurring as part of an insertion. The first insertion is started when the writer starts writing.

The following principles hold for the termination vs. resumption of an insertion:

1. An insertion is terminated when text is inserted or removed outside of the insertion.

2. An insertion is resumed when the writer continues writing at the end of the insertion after performing one or several revisions within the insertion.

Thus, whenever the writer does something else after a revision than resume an unterminated insertion, a new break is created.

Deletions

A deletion can occur either backwards or forwards in relation to the writer's current position in the text. The following principle holds for deletions:

3. A deletion is terminated when the writer moves the cursor in other ways than by deletion, in order to resume an insertion or start a new revision.

This principle has the consequence that two or more delete operations in the word processor can be collapsed into one revision in the S-notation.

Appendix 9.2 —
(a) Excerpt from the keyboard logfile for "My way to work"
(b) S-notation record of a passage from "My way to work"

(a) Keystroke record, generated in Jedit

```
1724.7  __There_is_quite_a_steep_<2.5>escalator_<2.3>⊠-ride_d_own_⊠⊠⊠⊠
1738.2  ⊠own_to_the_platform<7.0>,_and_this_I_enhoy_⊠⊠⊠⊠jay_⊠⊠⊠
1758.1  oy_rather_much_because_there_are_advertising_posters_<4.0>
1773.0  all_along_the_wai⊠11<3.2>_and_this_is_one_of_my_favoti⊠⊠
1785.1  rite_ways_to_praci⊠tice_my_Swedish.<8.8>⊡_and_his_is_o⊠
1804.0  translating_these<10.3>⊡s_to_practice_my_S work_on<28.9>⊡_wall_and_tran_._
1857.1  ⊡ll._transl⊠T<7.3>⊡dish.<71.7>⊡ters_all_alon⊠⊠<2.4>⊡he_wal_Tr<2.2>
1945.4  ⊡wall._Tra⊡_wall_Tr_all_the_way_down<32.3>⊡ters_along_the_⊠on<15.6>
2000.9  ⊡dish.<87.6>⊡wn.__Translating_the...y_favorite_ways_to_w⊠⊠⊠⊠
2094.6  _which_give_me_a_chance<7.3>⊡dish._<5.4>usual⊠⊠⊠⊠⊠
2145.7  Usually_I_don't_have_to_wait_more_than_10_minutes_<2.9>if_<5.5>I_am_
2165.0  <16.9>⊠⊠⊠⊠⊠⊠⊠⊠for_a_train<2.7>_at_this_hour_of_the_<3.7>day
2194.2  <9.6>,_but_I_always_bring_<13.0>a_book_to_read_in_my_bag<11.7>_-_I_hate_
2239.6  <2.4>being_bored.<7.7>_When_the_<9.1>⊠⊠⊠⊠⊠⊠⊠⊠<5.3>⊠
2269.3  <6.2>⊠,_even_for_10_minutes.<16.2>__When_the_train_comes_I_<8.8>
2310.0  step_in_but_do_not_take_a_seat.__I_am_only_going_one_stop<9.3>_and_<3.7>
```

(b) S-notation passage, covering approximately the interval represented above in (a).

```
There is quite a steep escalator45[ ‖45]45-ride d46[ own ‖46]46own to the
platform, and this I en47[hoy ‖47]47j48[ay ‖48]48oy rather much because there
are advertising posters60[ all]60‖61 62[along]62‖63{on}63‖64 the
wa49[i‖49]4911‖56[ and]56‖57 61[ all the way down]61‖62 64[57{. )57‖58
52[this]52‖53 53{58[t]58‖59 59{T}59‖60ranslating these}53‖54 is one of my
favo50[til‖50]50rite ways]64‖65 65{ which give me a chance}65 to
54[prac51[i‖51]51tice]54‖55 55{work on}55‖56 my Swedish.‖52  66[usual‖66]66Usually
I don't have to wait more than 10 minutes 67[if I am ‖67]67for a train at this
hour of the day, but I always bring a book to read in my bag - I hate being
bored68[. When the ‖68]68, even for 10 minutes. When the train comes I step
in but do not take a seat. I am only going one stop and
```

Appendix 9.3 — Explanation of logfile conventions in Jedit

Pauses

<7.7>

Pauses are shown as a number within angle brackets. The minimum length for a pause to be shown is two seconds.

Typing events

As_we_stream_into_the_subway_station,_there_are_usually

Typing by the writer is represented in the logfile as text in the Courier typeface. All spaces are shown as underscores, and line breaks are shown as paragraph markers. The typing events are sometimes split into two when they do not fit on one line in the logfile.

Arrow keys

When arrow keys are used for moving the insertion point in the text, they are shown as thin arrow symbols in the logfile.

Backspace

The backspace key is shown as an 'erase backward' symbol.

Mouse selection

 are | usually | _mass

Text selection with the mouse is rendered as a mouse symbol, which is followed by a box showing the text selected. If the selection is too large (more than ten characters long), only the beginning and the end of the text selected are shown, with dots in between.

There are four different symbols for different ways of selecting text:

  single click (and drag) with the mouse

  double click (and possibly drag)

  shift clicking, extending the selection

  double click with shift held down

Each of these symbols is followed by the text selected.

When the cursor is placed within the written text for insertion of new text, the logfile shows a cursor symbol with a context of 5 characters of the text on each side, preceded by a single mouse symbol:

  lm__is│_one__

Menu commands

```
Selected menu item 'Cut' using command-key
```

Menu commands are simply written out with an indication of whether the mouse or a command-key shortcut was used.

Scrolling

  scrolled 24 pixels (to 33, 271)↑

  scrolled 295 pixels (to 33, 295↓

  scrolled 33 pixels (to 33,0)→

Scrolling is shown in the logfile as a symbol showing how the scrolling was made by the user: by holding down the cursor at the arrow of the scrollbar, by clicking in the scroll area, or by dragging the box in the scroll bar. After the icon, there is an indication of the number of pixels scrolled, followed by an arrow indicating the direction of the scroll (where up means towards the beginning of the text).

If scrolling is performed automatically by the system, for example by the user's making a command which moves the cursor to a position outside of the text window, only the length of the movement in pixels and the arrow are shown.

In addition to the icon-based logfile presentation, one may also select Text-only logging. This is a more verbose representation in ASCII format which is not as legible, but can easily be interpreted by other programs.

— 10 —

FINDING SOMETHING TO WRITE ABOUT: STRATEGIC AND AUTOMATIC PROCESSES IN IDEA GENERATION

Mark Torrance, Glyn V. Thomas and Elizabeth J. Robinson
University of Birmingham

Psycholinguistic accounts of language production typically have taken as their remit the description of how people translate intention into language (Levelt, 1989). They tend to start, therefore, with the assumption that would-be language producers have something to communicate and then proceed to explain how their ideas are turned into language. Real life typically is not like that. Frequently, the need to produce language precedes having anything very specific to communicate. This is most obviously true of the contexts in which language production takes the form of writing. Professional fiction writing, undergraduate essay writing, e-mail writing to friends, and even the writing of this chapter are to a large degree motivated initially by the need to produce something in writing. What that something is not a given, provided before writing has started. Discovering what to say is part and parcel of the writing process.

Adequate theories of the writing process need, therefore, to account not only for the way ideas are translated into text, but the way the writer generates them in the first place. At least two different ways of theorizing idea generation in writing are possible. The models of text production that currently dominate writing research (or, at least, currently are most cited in writing research articles) describe writing as the conscious and analytical application of specific cognitive strategies in pursuit of rhetorical goals (Bereiter & Scardamalia, 1987; Hayes & Flower, 1980a). Idea generation is characterized as an explicit and effortful process involving deliberate and strategic search for ideas. Research on human memory, by contrast, has had considerable success in accounting for established memory retrieval phenomena in terms of automatic and implicit processes that lie outside the rememberer's immediate control (Raaijmakers & Shiffrin, 1981).

In this chapter we discuss in more detail the different roles that automatic and strategic processes might play in idea generation. We then present research which sheds some light on the relative importance of strategic and automatic processes in the ways in which a sample of student writers produced appropriate ideas for inclusion in an essay. First, however, it seems important to get a clearer idea of the nature of the problem: What exactly does "produce appropriate ideas" mean?

The idea generation problem

For most writing tasks, value is placed on breadth, appropriateness, and originality of ideas. This is particularly true in educational contexts. These criteria tend, however, to be loosely specified and subjectively evaluated. Research into writers' idea generation processes necessitates a more formal way of conceptualizing the idea generation problem. This formalism needs to offer both a means of evaluating ideas and of theorizing the processes by which they are generated.

Newell and Simon (1972) made a distinction between two different ways of talking about a problem. There is the way in which problem solvers represents that task to themselves and there is an abstract description of the problem that includes all possible solutions or partial solutions that solvers might consider. Researchers can gain some understanding of solvers' representation of the problem by observing their behavior as they try to solve it. The description of all possible paths to the solution is harder to achieve. With most problems, and particularly ill-structured problems like writing tasks, the only way to get a good approximation of possible ways of tackling the problem is to look at the way in which it is solved by a large number of people.

The problem of finding content for an essay can usefully be broken down in the same way. In the study reported in this chapter students were asked to write an essay about the pros and cons of decriminalizing drugs. Within the universal set of all possible ideas there is a subset of ideas that could be found in the solution to this task. We will call this the *solution set*. For particular writers there is also a subset of ideas that are present within their long-term memory (LTM, the writer's knowledge of the subject area). For a writer to be able, in principle, to produce a solution to the writing task, and ignoring the possibility that a writer might gain ideas from outside sources, there must be an overlap between the solution set and the writer's knowledge. Of course an overlap between the writer's knowledge and the solution set is not enough to achieve a solution. It is also necessary for writers to search LTM to identify ideas that are contained within the solution set and translate some of these into text. Using Newell and Simon's terminology, we call the set of ideas that particular writers search through in performing a particular writing task their *problem space*. A possible relation between writers' LTM, their problem space, and the solution set is illustrated in Figure 10.1. [It is perhaps worth noting that this formalism represents how writers find content for their text as entirely a matter of search and retrieval. There is no mention of creating or generating in a literal sense. We will not justify this position here except by saying that, as we discuss later, this is how idea generation was modeled by Hayes and Flower (1980b). Throughout this chapter we will use *idea generation* and *idea retrieval* interchangeably to refer to the process by which writers find content for their text.

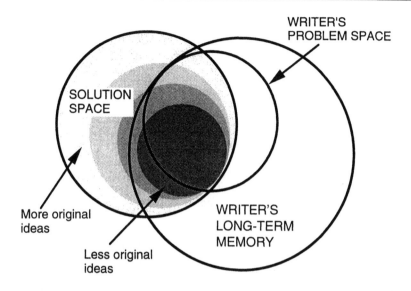

Figure 10.1. One way of conceptualizing the idea generation problem.

So much for formalizing the idea generation problem. The obvious next question is how, practically, do you go about identifying a particular writer's problem space and a particular task's solution set? Describing a writer's problem space is, in principle at least, straightforward. You just need to make a list of all the ideas that they consider while writing the essay. (Note that here and throughout this chapter we use "idea" to refer only to ideas that constitute content, or potential content for the essay. We do not consider ideas about how content might be expressed.) Obtaining a precise description of the solution set is harder. An approximation to the solution set is, however, possible by listing all the ideas contained within a large set of essays written in response to the particular writing assignment that is being considered. The larger the number of essays, the closer the approximation to the solution set. This follows Newell and Simon's (1972) strategy for defining the task environment.

This approach to defining the solution set also suggests a strategy for operationalizing idea originality. We assume that an idea is original in the context of a particular writing task if it exists within that task's solution set and is not generated by many writers when performing that task. This a somewhat rough-and-ready definition and contrasts with the more writer-centered account of creativity outlined by Sharples in chapter 7 of this volume. It does, however, appear to have some intuitive validity and, importantly for our present purposes, is easily measurable. Introducing an originality measure is important because it makes it possible to address a range of questions to do with the efficacy of different search strategies. Writers whose finished essays contain more original ideas may search through a larger set of ideas than less original writers but subsequently reject some of the more mundane ones. Alternatively, original writers' problem spaces may contain a similar number of ideas but, through more sophisticated search strategies, some of these ideas are more out of the ordinary.

Theories of idea generation

The previous section offered a formalism for describing the task that faces writers when they have to find ideas to include in a particular piece of writing. In this section we look at existing theories of how this process of generating ideas might be implemented within the writer's mind. We will start by looking at general theories of how concepts are retrieved from LTM and then summarize writing-specific accounts of idea generation.

Retrieval from long term memory

Psychologists typically think of meaning within LTM as being represented as a network of semantically related concepts (e.g., Anderson & Bower, 1972; Raaijmakers & Shiffrin, 1981; Rumelhart, Lindsay & Norman, 1972). The retrieval process starts with a memory probe being present in short-term memory. The presence of this probe automatically results in the activation of related concepts in LTM. Thus, for example, if LTM is probed with *Father Christmas*[1] concepts within LTM such as *white beard, snow, presents,* and *chimney* that are semantically related to *Father Christmas* will also become active. This activation makes it considerably more likely that these ideas will be retrieved rather than other, less related concepts. Reading off activated concepts and presenting them in either spoken or written language is likely, in adults at least, to be more or less effortless (Bock, 1982; Bourdin & Fayol, 1995; Conway & Engle, 1994; Levelt, 1989, p. 21).

Whether or not a specific idea is retrieved is dependent on the strength of the association between it and the memory probe. This means, therefore, that what is retrieved is critically dependent on the probe's make up. Raaijmakers and Shiffrin (1981) argued that this probe consists of several separate cues, the number limited by short-term memory capacity. Some of the cues within the probe remain constant. Others, however, are continuously modified during the retrieval process. This modification occurs in two situations. First, each time a new concept is retrieved it replaces one of the nonpermanent cues (chosen at random) and so itself becomes part of the probe. Second, if, after several attempts, the probe fails to retrieve anything, the nonpermanent cues are purged and replaced with the next few concepts to be retrieved.

For tasks in which people are required to retrieve as many concepts as they can on a single theme (e.g., makes of car) the model makes two predictions. First, it predicts that rate of concept retrieval will be rapid at first but will slowly tail off. Second, the model predicts that concepts will be generated in clusters. Several ideas will appear in a rush followed by a lull in production. Plotting number of concepts generated so far against time for a single writer will therefore produce a scalloped curve with steadily decreasing gradient. These patterns of retrieval for this kind of task are well established in

---

[1] Father Christmas is known in some parts of the world as Santa Claus.

the memory research literature (Bousfield & Sedgwick, 1944; Graesser & Mandler, 1978).

Two things stand out in this brief summary of existing theories about concept retrieval. First, the content of the probe is a crucial determinant of the nature of peoples' concept-generating behavior. Second, a fully automatic procedure for determining the content of the memory probe can result in the successful generation of a large number of concepts of a given theme. Is this, therefore, all there is to idea generation during the writing process? Intuitively, this would seem unlikely. When people perform real-world tasks they appear, at least in some contexts, to make use of explicit control strategies to guide knowledge retrieval (Walker & Kintsch, 1985). Is writing one of the contexts in which these control processes play an important role, and, if so, what form might they take?

Idea generation during writing

Flower and Hayes' problem-solving model and Bereiter and Scardamalia's knowledge-telling and knowledge-transforming models of writing provide similar descriptions of how ideas are generated (Bereiter & Scardamalia, 1987; Hayes & Flower, 1980b). Both of these accounts describe idea generation in terms of three stages. These are summarized in Figure 10.2. First, the writer identifies a memory probe that is used to explore long-term memory. Second, the output from the search is evaluated. Third, and optionally, if the idea passes this evaluation it is written down. Which ideas make it into the finished document, therefore, is contingent on at least three factors: the nature of the probe, whether or not relevant content in present in LTM, and the criteria by which it is evaluated.

How might the writer construct the probe? The most obvious source of concepts for the probe is the writing assignment and in some situations probes provided by the assignment may be all that are necessary to complete a writing task adequately. This is likely to be true when the task is simple, like those typically given to primary schoolchildren. The assignment may, for example, be adequate as the sole source of cues if they tap a particularly rich vein of associations within the writers' LTM. In these cases, Scardamalia and Bereiter described the writing process as knowledge telling..

However, probes derived directly and solely from the writing assignment will not always generate sufficient ideas for the writing task. As noted earlier, when retrieval is focused on a single category, retrieval rate decelerates. It may also be that in order to generate original ideas writers need to go beyond the assignment to generate their own cues. One possible source of these additional cues is an analysis of the rhetorical demands of the writing task. Scardamalia and Bereiter (1985) suggested that mature writing is often marked by the careful management of the interaction between rhetorical and content spaces, a process they called knowledge transforming. Similarly, Flower and Hayes (1980a) argued that "defining the rhetorical problem" is a central and essential process in identifying what to say.

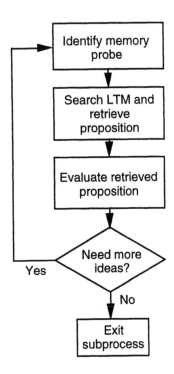

Figure 10.2. Possible model of the process by which ideas are generated during the writing process (adapted from Hayes & Flower, 1980, and Bereiter & Scardamalia, 1987, p. 8).

On the basis of existing theories of idea generation in writing, therefore, we might make two predictions. First, as already discussed, a significant feature of the memory probes used by mature writers will be cues that relate to the rhetoric of the piece they are writing. If, for example, we asked a mature writer to write "A story about Father Christmas" we might predict that LTM would be probed with not only *Father Christmas* but also *story* or some breakdown of the elements that constitute the story genre (*set scene, develop characters, happy ending,* and so forth). Second, on the basis of the model presented in Figure 10.2, we would expect to see evaluation of just-retrieved ideas as a discrete second step after each idea is retrieved. If, for example, writers retrieve *lives in Lapland* while generating ideas for their story about Father Christmas, we would then expect them to ask themselves whether or not this was an idea they wanted to include in their writing. As well as being a significant feature of the writers' think-aloud protocols, we would also expect these evaluation processes would affect the time course of writers' idea generation process.

A study of the idea generation processes of undergraduate writers producing essays

Participants, task and procedure

In the summer of 1994 we asked 10 first-year undergraduate psychology students to write an essay about the pros and cons of legalizing drugs. The full assignment was as follows:

> Britain's approach to reducing drug abuse has focused on legislation against the use of a wide range of drugs and the prosecution of drug users. An alternative approach which some people have suggested is to decriminalize all drug use and focus resources on treatment and education. Write a short essay (around 500 words) discussing the pros and cons of both approaches.

In addition to the text of the assignment, which the students had in front of them while they wrote, we also verbally instructed them to write for an intelligent adult audience and to produce the best possible essay they could manage.

Because we were interested in both what the students normally did when planning their text and what they were capable of doing, the students wrote their essays under one of two conditions. Five of the students were required to spend at least 20 minutes planning before writing out full text. The other five were permitted to plan for as long or short a time as they wanted. Before writing the essay, all of the students were given practice at thinking aloud and only went on to the main task once they were capable of producing a fluent protocol. They were then instructed to think aloud throughout their writing process. After the initial practice session, all the students thought aloud fluently. With the exception of the minimum prewriting time in the extended prewriting condition, the students were not placed under any time constraints.

In both conditions we video recorded the prewriting period before the students started to write out full text. We then transcribed their think-aloud protocols. The completed transcripts indicated what the students said and all pauses in the protocol that lasted for two or more seconds. The results we report here are based on an analysis of these transcripts and of the text of the completed essays.

Protocol coding

Each protocol was divided into chunks bounded by pauses of two or more seconds. These chunks formed the basic unit to be coded, although to make sense of the protocol, some subdivision and combining of chunks did occur during coding. For want of a better term, we call the units that we coded *protocol elements*. In coding these elements, our intention was not to provide a full description of the writers' planning activities but simply to develop an account of how they generated content. Therefore, although our coding scheme was capable of coding all protocol elements, it was designed specifically to isolate the different activities associated with idea generation.

Each element was coded on each of four dimensions. Using four relatively simple coding dimensions made it possible to define complex events such as the generation of an idea with a precision and transparency that is not available when a larger number of codes are used (cf. Bereiter, Burtis & Scardamalia, 1988). This both lays our definitions of events open to challenge and makes it possible for others to use the coding scheme without special training. Both of these criteria need to be fulfilled if research of this sort is to have serious impact on theories of the writing process.

The four coding dimensions were as follows:

CONTENT/RHETORIC. The distinction between content and rhetorical spaces (e.g., Scardamalia & Bereiter, 1985) parallels Flower and Hayes's (1980b) distinction between a plan-to-do and a plan-to-say. Elements in content space represent what writers think and elements in rhetorical space represent how they might express these ideas in their text. Thus, *decriminalizing drugs will lead to less crime* is an element in content space whereas *put "decriminalizing drugs will lead to crime" as point number two* is an element in rhetorical space.

PROPOSITIONS / NON-PROPOSITIONS / EVALUATION CRITERIA. Following usual definitions of proposition, an element was coded as a proposition if and only if it could be assigned a truth value. We used the term *nonproposition* to refer to anything that was not an evaluation criterion but that could not be assigned a truth value. Thus, the element *decriminalizing drugs will lead to less crime* is a proposition, whereas *less crime* or *decriminalizing* on their own were coded as nonpropositions. Because protocols rarely contained full, grammatical sentences, some discretion was needed in coding elements as propositions. If, as was often the case, protocols contained an element like *pros of decriminalization* followed by, for example *less crime, less overdose, cheaper drugs* we assumed that these elements were shorthand for *if drugs are decriminalized then there will be less crime*, and so forth, and coded them as propositions.

Evaluation criteria were elements that represented criteria for evaluating propositions. Thus, *ignore illegal drugs* and *we need some more humor in this* would both have been coded as evaluation criteria. Coding for evaluation criteria seemed essential in the light of existing models of idea generation in writing. They provide the production rules within the evaluation box in Figure 10.2 that permit the acceptance or rejection of just-retrieved propositions.

SOURCE. Because the writers in our study did not have access to reference materials, elements in their protocol could only come from one of two sources; the writers' own knowledge or the assignment. An element was coded as coming from the assignment if and only if it was identical or very similar to the wording of part of the assignment statement. To distinguish between elements that had just been retrieved from the writers LTM and those that had been retrieved previously and perhaps written down as part of an outline, we coded an element that was not from the assignment but that had occurred before as being from the plan. All other elements were coded as coming from the writers' knowledge base.

EVALUATIONS/METASTATEMENTS/STATEMENTS. An evaluation was any element in which a proposition that had already cropped up in the protocol was evaluated. This may have involved its acceptance or rejection as appropriate for the essay (*I don't think stuff about drugs making you happy is appropriate here*) or just the posing of a question (*er...do I need an introduction?*). Note the distinction between an evaluation and an evaluation criterion, the former being an event in which a proposition is evaluated and the latter being a the criterion by which an evaluation might be made. Metastatements were elements that referred to the process of producing the essay (in Hayes & Flower's, 1980b terminology, elements from a plan-to-compose). These included statements like *I don't know very much about this* or *I need some more ideas here*. All remaining elements were coded simply as statements.

As a check for the reliability of our coding, an independent judge coded 425 protocol elements (33% of the total). There was exact agreement on all four coding criteria between her coding and ours of 323 (76%) of these elements. The five categories of element that we discuss in our results for this study are defined in Table 10.1.

Table 10.1
Definitions of the categories of elements used in this study

	Coding Criterion			
	Content / Rhetoric	**Source**	**Proposition?**	**Statement?**
New propositions	Content	Writer's knowledge	Proposition	Statement
Content from plan	Content	Plan	Proposition or non-proposition	Statement
Rhetorical elements	Rhetoric	Writer's knowledge or plan	Proposition or non-proposition	Statement
Elements from assignment	Either	Assignment	Proposition or non-proposition	Statement
Evaluation	Not applicable	Any	*Either* proposition and evaluation *or* evaluation criterion and statement	

Coding idea units

To determine which of the ideas generated during prewriting also appeared in the final essay and to provide an approximate description of the solution set, we submitted both the wording of the elements that represented new propositions in the protocol and the texts of the finished essays to a modified version of the propositional analysis technique described by Kintsch and van Dijk (Kintsch, 1974; Kintsch & van Dijk, 1978). Propositional analysis is a means of representing the semantics of a phrase or sentence independently of the words in which it was initially expressed. In principle, the propositional representations of two different sentences that mean the same thing will be identical. In practice, this is difficult to achieve. However, there is likely to be substantially greater similarity between the propositional representations of the two different sentences than between the sentences themselves. Our first purpose in using propositional analysis, therefore, was to provide a summary of the content of proposition elements and of sentences in the finished essay that was, to some extent, independent of the language used to express them. Our second purpose was to decompose sentences that contained several propositions into their constituent parts. For example, the sentence *because drugs are bad for you they should be banned* contains three separate propositions: P1. *drugs are bad for you*, P2. *drugs should be banned* and P3. *because P1, P2*. The notation used is not important here.

Perhaps, surprisingly, of the 1123 propositions identified in the essays and protocols using this technique, as many as 703 were unique. This suggests that a proposition is too fine grained a semantic unit to permit a useful description of the solution set. To get a clearer picture of the nature of the solution set we sorted the propositions into a smaller number of larger groups. Each group heading was itself a proposition and a proposition was made a member of the group if and only if it logically entailed the group heading. For example, the group *some drugs are illegal in the UK* had as members *crack is illegal in the UK, heroin is illegal in the UK, marijuana is illegal in the UK* and so forth. A group, therefore, might usefully be thought of as representing sets of propositions that are all tokens of the same more general idea. We refer to these proposition groups as *idea units*.

This means of classification yielded a total of 63 idea units with two or more members. A trained judge independently assigned 250 of the 608 propositions from the finished essays to the proposition groups with an agreement with the initial coding of 82%.

Results

The mean prewriting time for students in the extended planning condition was 24 minutes (*s.d.* = 5) and in the normal planning condition was 9 minutes (*s.d.* = 4). There was no significant difference in essay writing time for the two groups with a mean of 33 minutes (*s.d.* = 6) for the extended planning group and of 37 minutes (*s.d.* = 6) for the normal planning group. All the completed essays were written in a single draft with little editing, although most of the students read their text through to correct errors. The pattern of idea generation behavior in these two groups was, by and large, similar. For simplicity, unless otherwise indicated, we report combined results for the two groups.

The time course of idea generation

Figure 10.3 shows the mean cumulative frequency of the occurrence of different kinds of protocol element during the students' prewriting periods.

Two things are immediately apparent. First, the predominant activity throughout prewriting was the generation of new ideas. Students spent relatively little time either considering how best to express their ideas or looking back at propositions they had already retrieved. Second, contrary to the performance of students in single-category retrieval experiments (e.g., Bousfield & Sedgwick, 1944) the mean rate of proposition retrieval did not show a steady decrease with time. Most students did show some decrease in rate of idea generation in the final 25% or 30% of their prewriting period. This, however, appeared to be because the writers' focus shifted away from idea generation and onto either reading through the plan or putting their ideas into some sort of order. This pattern is clearly seen in the data for a single student presented in Figure 10.4. This student's prewriting, in common with that of the other students, also showed an initial phase during which attention was focused on the assignment.

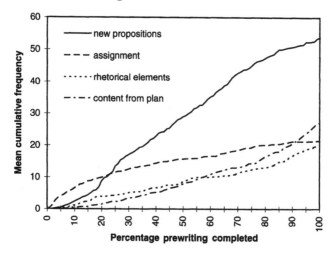

Figure 10.3. Summary of all students' prewriting activity. Mean cumulative number of protocol elements across all students against percentage of total prewriting time completed.

Consistent with previous memory retrieval research (Graesser & Mandler, 1978; Walker & Kintsch, 1985) propositions appeared in clusters giving a characteristic stepped appearance to the "new propositions" curve in the cumulative frequency graph for single subjects, of which Figure 10.4 is a typical example. All of the students showed this pattern of retrieval with a mean cluster size of just under three propositions.

In order to explore what retrieval cues the students were using and how successful these were for retrieving content, we looked at the protocol elements that immediately preceded each cluster of propositions. This analysis, shown in Table 10.2, suggested that rhetorical cues were both rarely used and, when they were used, tended to result in the retrieval of significantly less propositions than cues from either the assignment or the existing plan. (For number of clusters, $F(2,18) = 4.3$, $p = .03$. For number of new propositions in clusters, $F(2,18) = 3.5$, $p = .05$).

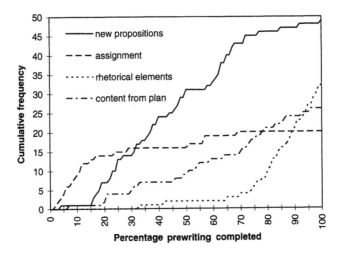

Figure 10.4. Summary of the prewriting activity of a single student. Mean cumulative number of protocol elements against percentage of total prewriting time completed.

However, the number of propositions generated through the use of a specific cues is not the only measure of its usefulness. Although rhetorical cues did not appear to be particularly successful in generating large numbers of ideas it may have been the case that those ideas that were retrieved were particularly original. Taking a single idea unit (derived from the coding strategy already described), counting the number of essays in which this idea occurred and subtracting this number from 10 (the total number of essays) gave a measure of idea originality, or at least of originality as defined earlier. Across all of the students, the mean originality rating of the ideas in clusters preceded by rhetorical elements was not significantly greater than for clusters preceded by previously retrieved content. Clusters preceded by elements derived directly from the assignment, however, contained significantly fewer original ideas than clusters preceded by other elements (mean originality ratings for clusters preceded by rhetorical elements = 7.2 [s.d. = 1.9], by previously retrieved content = 6.9 [1.44] and by assignment elements = 5.7 [.56]; $F[2,18] = 4.9$, $p = .02$). The lower originality for ideas cued by the assignment is, of course, to be expected because all the students were working from the same assignment, whereas rhetorical cues and, to a lesser extent, previously recalled content, are more likely to be unique to the individual writer.

Absent in the results reported this far is any mention of evaluation of ideas. This is because only 1.7% of the total number of protocol elements were associated with evaluating previously or just retrieved ideas or with setting evaluation criteria.

Table 10.2
Number and mean size of clusters of propositions generated during prewriting by the protocol element by which they were immediately preceded; Means for all participants, standard deviations in parentheses

	Preceding Element			
	Assignment	**Content from plan**	**Rhetoric**	**Total**
Number of clusters	6.1 (3.07)	7.9 (5.55)	3.4 (3.06)	19.9 (9.15)
Mean number of propositions in clusters	3.3 (2.0)	2.6 (1.3)	1.7 (0.96)	2.8 (1.1)

Transfer of ideas generated during prewriting to essays

Predictably, across all students there was a strong positive correlation between time spent prewriting and number of propositions generated during prewriting ($r = .78$, $p < .01$) with students in the extended planning condition producing, on average, over twice as many propositions as students in the normal planning group (70 [s.d. = 13.5] versus 29 [s.d. = 19.5]). However, the greater number of propositions generated in the extended prewriting sessions was achieved largely through students in this condition generating multiple tokens of a smaller set of ideas. Comparing the number of idea units generated rather than number propositions showed no significant difference between the extended and normal prewriting conditions.

Predictably, there was also a positive correlation between the time the students spent drafting and the number of propositions that appeared in their finished essays ($r = .64$, $p = .02$). Perhaps more surprisingly, however, there was no relationship between time spent prewriting and number of propositions in the finished essay and no significant difference in the number of propositions in essays written under the two different prewriting conditions.

The obvious next question to ask, therefore, is how many of the ideas that appeared in the finished essay were originally generated during prewriting and how many were generated during drafting. As Table 10.3 indicates, some of the ideas generated during prewriting did not appear in the final essay. However, there was also a considerable number of new ideas introduced during drafting. Interestingly, as Table 10.3 also shows, the ideas generated during prewriting and then carried over into the final essay tended to be substantially less original (according to our definition) than both those ideas that were lost between prewriting and drafting ($F[1,9] = 14.7$, $p < .005$) and those ideas that were introduced for the first time during drafting ($F[1,9] = 8.0$, $p = .02$). One possible explanation for the higher originality rating for idea units that were dropped between prewriting and drafting was that the students were simply rejecting irrelevant ideas that happened to come into their heads while they were prewriting. This did not seem to be the case, however. Although these discarded ideas tended to be of higher originality than others, their mean originality rating (6.2) suggests that, on average, they appeared in at least three of the other writers' finished essays.

There was a definite positive relation between the order in which ideas were generated during prewriting and the order in which they appeared in the finished essays (across all idea units, comparing first mention of idea unit in pre-writing with first mention in essay, $r = .49$, $p < .001$).

Table 10.3
Number and originality of ideas by when they appeared during the writing proces; Means for all participants, standard deviations in parentheses

	Mean Number	Mean Originality Rating
Ideas appearing during prewriting but not in essay	8.1 (5.1)	6.2 (0.74)
Ideas appearing during prewriting and in essay	7.2 (3.1)	4.8 (0.67)
Ideas appearing in essay but not during prewriting	16.6 (5.1)	5.8 (0.49)
All ideas appearing in essay	23.8 (4.4)	5.4 (0.27)

Discussion

In summary, therefore, most of the writers in our sample generated a number of ideas during prewriting. Search for ideas involved a cyclical process of generating cues followed by the retrieval of clusters of ideas. When drafting, the students typically incorporated a central core of the more common (or less original) of these ideas into their finished essay, but did not carry over some of the more original ones. The order with which these core ideas were represented in the finished essay closely mapped onto the order in which they were first generated. When drafting, in addition to translating the core ideas into text, the students generated some new ideas that had not been retrieved during prewriting. These new ideas were more original than the ideas carried over from prewriting.

It is possible to build two quite different accounts of the cognitive processes that lay behind this behavior. Within the tradition of seeing writing as a problem-solving activity in which the writer explicitly sets and fulfills goals, an account of the idea generation process of these students would go something like this: The students read the assignment and, using the information contained within it, combined with their own ideas about the subject, set goals for the kinds of things they were going to say. These goals made particular reference to the rhetorical demands of the writing task and fulfilled the dual function of providing cues for memory probes and criteria by which to evaluate what was retrieved. The students then probed long-term memory. As each idea was retrieved, it was evaluated and either accepted or rejected.

In deciding which propositions to keep the students tended to go for less original ideas in preference to more original alternatives. When writing their essays, however, the students evaluation criteria shifted, perhaps as a result of goal revision. Thus, when generating ideas during drafting, the students tended to select more original ideas in preference to more common place ones.

This account does not fit well with the results of this study for two reasons. First, students in the study rarely used the rhetorical demands of the writing task as a means of identifying relevant content and when rhetoric was introduced into the memory probe it was rarely effecting in retrieving a large number of ideas. Second, students rarely spent any time either setting evaluation criteria or evaluating the ideas they had retrieved. The focus of their prewriting activity appeared to be entirely on the generation of new ideas.

If the idea generation process is looked at from the perspective of current models of memory retrieval, neither of these findings is particularly surprising. Considering first the apparent inefficacy of rhetorical cues, the only situation in which a rhetorical cue will be effective in retrieving content is if the cue is already associated with a relevant idea within LTM. This will probably be the case after writers have spent some time thinking about the writing task, but is unlikely to be true when they first look at the assignment. Unless the writer has already explored his or her topic knowledge with a view to communicating it to others, there is unlikely to be any association within their LTM between this topic knowledge and rhetorical concepts.

It is also not clear what function evaluation might play during the idea generation process or how this might be achieved as a discrete process occurring after idea retrieval. Hayes and Flower (1980b) argued that writers evaluate each new idea to avoid trailing off into irrelevance. Therefore, why a writer performing the task in this study who probes LTM with *drugs* makes a note of *major urban problem* but not *rhymes with shrugs* is because if this latter idea is retrieved it is then rejected as inappropriate. Given that both have been retrieved from the same probe in order to differentiate them, the writer must introduce new information. Hayes and Flower might argue that this additional information comes in the form of a rhetorical goal to make the essay discursive and *major urban problem* is more likely to move the writer closer to this goal than *rhymes with shrugs*. But this in turn requires theorizing the process by which writers come to that conclusion. Whatever writers do to evaluate an idea is, therefore, likely to be effortful and thus show up within their think-aloud protocols. Given an appropriate memory probe, however, evaluation is unlikely to be necessary. This appeared to be the case for writers in this study. Very rarely did they explicitly evaluate ideas that they had retrieved but all managed to generate sets of ideas that were relevant to the writing task.

An alternative and more parsimonious account of the students' idea generation processes might perhaps be developed in terms of retrieval processes that occur largely automatically. The predominance of new proposition elements in the students protocols, the generation of ideas in clusters and the absence of evaluation during prewriting all point to an idea generation process that has more in common with simple models of memory retrieval than the more strategic problem-solving account developed earlier. The students' first reading of the assignment will have automatically activated relevant concepts. Search could then proceed according to the Raaijmakers and Shiffrin model with just-retrieved ideas becoming part of the memory probe. Because the students were reasonably familiar with the topic area this process is likely to have been successful in retrieving a number of relevant concepts. Stopping to explicitly evaluate these ideas as they were retrieved would have hindered rather than aided retrieval. When it came to drafting, it is possible that rather than building on the advances they had made during prewriting, the students simply repeated the same process again. Because the students still had the assignment in front of them, the same ideas were likely to be retrieved again, and because all of the students had access to the same assignment these ideas were strongly represented within the solution set. The students also generated new ideas during drafting. This may simply have occurred because of random differences in the probes used or it may have been because the students were now in a position to make use of cues associated with the rhetoric of their essays. Whatever the source of these new probes, they were less likely to be similar to those used by other writers than probes based on the assignment. Consequently, the new ideas retrieved during drafting were of greater originality.

This account suggests that prewriting did not play an important role in the students' idea generation processes and this is supported by our finding that number and originality of the ideas expressed in the finished essays ideas appeared to be independent of time spent planning prior to drafting.

Therefore, at least for the sample of writers and task used in the current study, idea generation may have been a predominantly automatic activity. This is not to say that strategic processes were entirely absent from the ways in which the students generated ideas. Students in our study generated ideas at a more or less constant rate rather than the steadily decreasing rate predicted by the Raaijmakers and Shiffrin model. A steady rate of idea generation was also found by Caccamise (1987) for idea retrieval during several different writing tasks and by Walker and Kintsch (1984) for situations in which retrieval of real-world knowledge was schema driven. This suggests that rather than automatically updating the memory probe with just-retrieved concepts the writers in this study actively sought new cues when the existing probe ceased to be effective. Hence, the students' frequently referenced back to the assignment.

The account developed here is, of course, conjectural. Much of what we observed in this study may have resulted from the choice of a writing task that drew on familiar topic and genre knowledge and of a relatively experienced sample of writers. We definitely do not want to make the strong claim that explicit analytical strategies never play an important part in writers' idea generation processes. We hope, however, that we have shown that it is at least possible to explain what superficially appears to be a complex and strategic writing subprocess in terms of relatively simple functions that are effective because of structures that already exist within the writer's long-term memory. Part of our purpose in doing this is to tentatively suggest an alternative to what we see as a predominant paradigm in theorizing the writing process. Much of the work on the psychology of writing over the years since Flower and Hayes first published their model has started from the premise that mature writing is essentially an explicit, analytic, and strategic cognitive activity. This has resulted in a profusion of increasingly complex models of writer's cognitive processes (see, for example, Hayes, chapter 1 in this volume). An alternative, and perhaps more economical strategy may be to start from the other end with the premise that writing, like speech, is largely automatic. Writing researchers would then save themselves from having to explain why many writers do not seem to set goals, define rhetorical problems, knowledge transform, and so forth, thus leaving them free to explore what needs to be added to basic, automatic processes in order to model different writers' performance.

Acknowledgments

We would like to thank Gaynor Jeffrey and Helen Jones for their help with coding and transcription. The research reported in this chapter was funded by the Leverhulme Trust.

— 11 —
THE DYNAMICS OF COMPOSING: MODELING WRITING PROCESS DATA

Huub van den Bergh
Utrecht University

Gert Rijlaarsdam
University of Amsterdam

Each process costs time. This is a main feature of processes that has received relatively little attention. To state it simply, a writing process starts and ends. In a writing process, several cognitive activities are exploited. At each moment, a writer has an opportunity to engage in a lot of different cognitive activities. The writer has to decide, be it consciously or not, which cognitive activity has to be employed to meet the ends at a specific moment. Some of these decisions are obvious (e.g., one does not generate ideas if one has not read the assignment first). Others are perhaps less obvious (in order to generate further ideas one can reread the assignment, and/or some of the text already written). And still other decisions are possible but not theorized yet. Note that in both examples a functional (means-end) relation exists between different cognitive activities.

Consider a cognitive activity such as generating ideas. It is assumed that there will be more in the beginning than in the end; one does not generate ideas if the text is already finished. The same holds for other cognitive activities; one does not revise without any written text. Hence, revising will not be encountered as frequently in the beginning as it is later in the writing process. The actual writing, formulating, has to steadily increase during the writing process. If a cognitive activity is plotted on a time axis — indicating the writing process — the frequency of occurrence is not equal at all time points. A generating curve will first increase and later decrease, a revising curve will be low at the beginning and on a certain moment there will be some increase. A writing curve will increase first and decline only at the end. Hence, cognitive activities are not distributed at random over a writing process.

It is necessary that cognitive activities during writing be organized in some way. Hence, there has to be some temporal organization. It is not until recently that attention has been drawn to this temporal organization of cognitive activities (Breetvelt, van den Bergh & Rijlaarsdam, 1994; Caccamise, 1987; Kellogg, 1987, 1988). A focus on the temporal organisation of cognitive activities elaborates the view on writing in at least two ways (see Rijlaarsdam & van den Bergh, chapter 6 in this volume).

First, a writing process can be conceptualized as a sequence of changing task situations. Because text and ideas develop during the process, the task situation changes. The developing task situation is a function of time, or to be precise, time elapsed since the start of the writing job. Therefore, the *moment* in the writing process when a cognitive activity is carried out provides relevant information. For instance, it does make a difference if a cognitive activity, like reading the assignment, is employed at the start or at the end. Obviously, "reading the assignment" can fulfill different purposes, and these purposes may well be related to differences in task situation (or the moment) in the writing process. In the beginning "reading the assignment" might be indicative of something like adapting the assignment, building a representation of task demands, whereas, in later stages "reading the assignment" might serve as a control activity to see whether one is still on the right track, or might be used as a means to generate information (cf. Breetvelt et al., 1994, in the case of writing, or Snow & Yalow, 1982, more in general). If one leaves out the time dimension — that is, the temporal organization — no indication of different purposes, or means-end relations, of a cognitive activity are available.

A second reason to incorporate the temporal organisation in theories of writing and the analysis of cognitive activities is that the temporal organisation differs between writers. Even if two writers have the same overall frequency (or proportion) of, say, generating, it is possible that they distribute this activity differently over the writing process; each writer has its own curve. The differences between these curves indicate differences in temporal organisation of both writers. This implies that the different purposes of a cognitive activity are not evenly distributed over writers.

This line of reasoning also influences our way of thinking of the relation between cognitive activities and text quality. Writers are not solely characterized by an overall frequency of a cognitive activity, but by the distribution of an activity during the writing process. Perhaps it are especially these differences between temporal organisation, which are related to differences in text quality; it is not as much a question of *if* there is a relation between a cognitive activity and the quality of writing, but *when* the relation occurs. Maybe good writers know when to engage in a certain kind of activity. And, therefore, it is more a question of when a cognitive activity is related to text quality, instead of a relation between overall frequencies of cognitive activities and text quality.

The purpose of this chapter is to provide different ways to analyze quantitatively the temporal organisation of cognitive activities. Also, the analysis of the interrelation between the temporal organization of cognitive activities and their relationship with text quality will be dealt with. We will not go into detail on theoretical aspects of the temporal organization, but focus on ways to entangle the relation between cognitive activities, temporal organisation, and text quality. We will start very simple, but gradually the models to be analyzed become more complex. Nevertheless, these complex models are clearly worthwhile, because there is much information to be gained from them. For one thing, these models allow for the testing of specific hypotheses concerning the differences between writers, tasks, the interrelations between cognitive activities and the relations with text quality — and, hence, the development of testable theories of the writing process.

A distinction is made among three questions: Does the probability of occurrence of a cognitive activity changes as a function of time? (See Rijlaarsdam & van den Bergh, chapter 6 in this volume.) Do the differences between writers change during the writing process? Does the correlation between cognitive activities and text quality change over time?

The data used in this chapter are the same as those used in chapter by Rijlaarsdam and van den Bergh (Chapter 6 in this volume) and concern structuring remarks in thinking aloud protocols[1]. *Structuring* refers to the selecting, relating and ordering or outlining of ideas. That is, we infer an act of structuring from statements like *"first ..., then ...," "... is related to ...,"* and so forth in thinking-aloud protocols. Self-evaluations appear from verbalizations like *"I better order this first,"* or, more generally, self-instructions to carry out an act of structuring. All essays were rated by four judges on five aspects of text quality. As the ratings of different aspect proved to be indistinguishable and the jury rating proved to be reliable (a = .93), all scores were summed to one indicator of global text quality.

A correlational analysis

In this section we show with a rather simple analysis of some of the changes in patterns of cognitive activities over the writing process. This type of analysis is comparable to the analysis in studies of Caccamise (1987) and Kellogg (1987, 1988). Although some of the secrets of the relation between the changing task situation and cognitive activities are revealed by this type of analysis, there are some aspects that can only be exposed by a bit more complex analysis.

Data preparation
Typically, in online writing process studies there is a different number of observations per respondent. Because of the freedom of the writer, each writer is allowed a different number of protocol segments, pauses, and the like. As there is no way to correlate variables with different numbers of observations, some data manipulations have to be performed. Usually these manipulations concern the aggregation of the observations per writer. In the majority of the studies, all observations per writer are aggregated to one frequency, or in some more recent studies a fixed number of episodes (3, 5, etc.) is distinguished (see for instance, Levy & Ransdell, chapter 8 in this volume).

---

[1] The data come from Breetvelt (1991) and concern thinking aloud protocols of 22 ninth-grade students who were writing a documented argumentative essay with documentation available. The students were trained to verbalize their thoughts while writing in a previous session. The thinking aloud protocols were analyzed by two raters, who agreed on most verbalizations (contingency coefficient = .98). Differences between both raters were resolved afterward in a discussion.

The researcher has to make a decision on the number of episodes to be distinguished for each writer. As there is no theory — although there are some pretheoretical notions — that prescribes the number of episodes in which the writing process has to be divided, this is a rather arbitrary decision; one can choose to distinguish three, four, five, or any other number of different episodes. Note, however, that the results will differ depending on the number of distinguished episodes.

There are two criteria to define episodes: First, each episode (for a given writer) contains the same number of observations (protocol fragments). Second, the writing process is divided in equal time units. From a statistical point of view the first criterion is to be preferred.[2] For the sake of simplicity, we divide the writing process into three equal parts, each consisting of one third of the total number of activities of a writer.[3] The data gathered consist (at least) of a large number of codes for different cognitive activities. If the occurrence of the target activity is coded to one and all other activity to zero, the data can be aggregated in such a way that for each episode of each writer one score remains (a count of occurrences in each episode). This results in three scores per writer, with one for each episode. The resulting data matrix is shown in Table 11.1.

For the first writer, seven out of each 100 cognitive activities in the first episode concern structuring. In the second episode six out of each hundred cognitive activities pertain to structuring. In the last episode, the first writer did not exhibit structuring activities.

Each researcher has a choice between the analysis of proportions or frequencies. In most studies frequencies have been preferred (Breetvelt et al., 1994; Caccamise, 1987). In keeping with previous research we also present the total number (i.e., the frequencies) of structuring activities per respondent per episode in Table 11.1. For the first writer, the frequency of structuring remarks are 27, 25, and 0, in the first, second, and third episode, respectively, indicating that the total number of cognitive activities per episode is somewhat over 390.

Data analysis

First, concentrate on differences in the distribution of structuring remarks over the writing process. The mean proportions as well as the mean frequencies are summarized in Table 11.1. The mean proportion of structur-

---

[2] The precision with which a writer can be characterized at a given episode depends on the number of observations in this episode. If one allows for different numbers of observations for a writer in different episodes — as is the case with the time criterion — one has to take these differences in precision into account in the statistical procedure. Unfortunately most statistical techniques do not allow for such quintessence, therefore the first criterion, in which each episode consists of (more or less) an equal number of observations (for each writer) has to be preferred.

[3] If the time per cognitive activity is available, one could use this time variable as a more adequate proxy variable for changes in task situation. Sometimes the time a writer engages in each cognitive activity is not available. Therefore, we use both the time variable and the sequence numbers as proxy-variables for changes in the task situation.

Data analysis

First, concentrate on differences in the distribution of structuring remarks over the writing process. The mean proportions as well as the mean frequencies are summarized in Table 11.1. The mean proportion of structuring activities decreases during the writing process. In the first episode the mean proportion equals .03; 3 out of each 100 cognitive activities is a structuring activity during the first third of the writing session. During the second episode 2, out of each 100 activities concerns structuring, whereas during the last episode, only 1 out of 100 activities pertain to structuring. A t test showed that there are no differences in mean proportions of structuring activities between the first and second episode ($t(21) = 1.37$; $p = .187$), but there are significant differences between both the first and third and the second and third episode ($t(21)$ is respectively 3.0 and 2.51; $p < .05$).

Table 11.1

Data example for the analysis of proportions and frequencies of structuring remarks for a correlational analysis with three episodes (Ep = Episode) and the means and standard deviations per episode

Writer	Proportions			Frequencies			Rating
	Ep 1	Ep 2	Ep 3	Ep 1	Ep 2	Ep 3	
1	.069	.058	.000	27	25	0	122
2	.024	.012	.012	4	2	1	87
3	.060	.062	.009	8	5	1	128
4	.044	.019	.005	8	4	1	94
5	.010	.022	.059	2	5	5	88
6	.035	.012	.000	11	4	0	82
7	.006	.000	.000	1	0	0	120
...							
22	.050	.000	.000	3	0	0	75
Mean	.030	.024	.011	6.59	5.91	1.64	101.44
s.d.	.025	.022	.015	7.22	7.34	1.96	15.879

For the frequencies, the same pattern emerges, although the decrease in frequencies from the second to the third episode seems more marked than the same difference in proportions. That is, the frequencies in the first two episodes do not differ significantly ($t(21) = .94$; $p = .358$), but in the last episode the frequency of structuring activities is clearly less then either the first or second episode ($t(21)$ equals respectively 3.18 and 2.87; $p < .01$).

For both the proportions as well as the frequencies, there is a clear variation between episodes. For the frequencies, however, the differences between writers fall in the third episode, whereas such a decrease is not as clear for the proportions. Hence, there is clear difference in the number or proportion of structuring remarks over the three episodes.

Figure 11.1 shows that the differences between writers are relatively large. This holds as well for the proportions as for the frequencies. As the same two writers are marked in both figures, it is obvious that the ranking of writers with regard to either proportions or frequencies differs. Take for instance the Writer A, which has a high frequency of structuring activities during the first and second episode (27 and 25, respectively). Proportionally, however, this writer does not stand out as clear. Also, for Writer B, a clear difference appears between both figures. Therefore, the analysis of proportions and frequencies are not totally comparable.

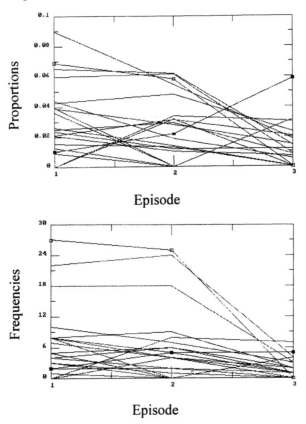

Episode

Episode

Figure 11.1 Mean proportions (top) and frequencies (bottom) of structuring per writer per episode. (Open squares = Writer A, Solid squares = Writer B).

The analysis of proportions or frequencies is likely to produce different results because two writers with the same number of structuring activities may vary with respect to the total number of verbalizations. This difference in total number of verbalizations is not taken into account in the analysis of frequencies. There are, however, two reasons why proportions are to be preferred. First, writers are more adequately characterized by proportions, as

20 structuring remarks out of a total of 200 is quite different from 20 out of 40. Second, the total number verbalizations is a function of the capacity to verbalize or fluency. This implies that the frequency that a cognitive is encountered depends on verbal fluency. Hence, high verbalizers are likely to have high frequencies in all episodes, and low verbalizers have low frequencies in all episodes. Thus, the correlation of frequencies between episodes is confounded with the total number of verbalizations. Consequently, correlations based on frequencies will be overestimated to a unknown height.

Table 11.2 shows the correlations for structuring. The difference between the analysis of proportions and frequencies clearly shows if the correlations below the diagonal (proportions) are compared with those above the diagonal (frequencies). It is shown that the correlations between episodes for proportions differ from those for frequencies; the correlations between the frequencies in each episode are clearly higher than those for proportions. Hence, it can be inferred that total number of activities artificially increases the correlations between episodes. Or, to put it differently, high verbalizers in one episode are likely to be high verbalizers in another episode.

Table 11.2

Correlations between proportions of structuring activities per episode and text quality (below diagonal), and between frequencies per episode and text quality (above diagonal)

	Episode 1	Episode 2	Episode 3	Rating
Episode 1	"	.89*	.09	.77*
Episode 2	.68*	"	.31	.72*
Episode 3	.05	.21	"	.11
Rating	.60*	.55*	-.10	"

$*$ $p < .05$.

As can be seen in Table 11.2. the correlation between the first and second episode is rather high (irrespective of whether proportions or frequencies were analyzed). Hence, high structurers in the first episode are likely to be high structurers in the second, and low structurers in the first episode are low structurers in the second episode. The amount of structuring in the third episode is unrelated to the previous episodes.

Table 11.2 also shows the correlations between text quality and structuring activities. Obviously, these correlations are higher between the first two episodes than for the last episode, irrespective of whether proportions or frequencies are analyzed (although, in general, the correlations for the frequencies are somewhat higher).

Thus, the proportion or frequency of a cognitive activity (i.e., structuring) changes over time. The difference between writers are more or less constant only during the start and middle of writing process. Furthermore, the relation between this cognitive activity and (ratings of) text quality change over time; that is, in the first and middle episode of the writing process there is a relatively strong relation between the number of structuring activities and text quality.

There are, however, four main problems with the previous analysis. The first concerns the variance within episodes. The proportion in each episode — or the mean of structuring events — is based on a number of observations for each writer, but writers do not stick to one cognitive activity in one episode. Up to this point, writers have been characterized by their proportion in each episode. But writers do not continuously carry out .069 structuring activities during Episode 1 (see Writer 1 in Table 11.1). Note that the proportion is just a mean, which implies that there is some within-episode variance too; in each episode there is some within-writer variance in the occurrence of an activity. The previous analysis did not take into account the within-writer variance, but assumed that all variance in each episode is between-writer variance. Failing to do so undoubtedly results in what is referred to as *aggregation bias* (Berstein, 1990; Cheung, 1990). Aggregation bias refers to failures that are likely to be introduced if the data are analyzed at a higher level (means per episode) instead of an analysis at the level of the observations. This aggregation bias is the result of failing to take into account the within-writer variance. This hints at the possibility that an aggregated variable (a proportion or a frequency, for that matter) is not exactly the same as the activity itself; the occurrences of an activity are not equal to the sum of occurrences or the proportion of occurrences. Proportions, for instance, consist of two parts: the number of occurrences and the total number of observations. The same proportion could be the result of different numbers of occurrences (in combination with different numbers of observations/verbalizations). Hence the same figure can mean different things. Therefore, both the within-individual variance and the between-individual variance must be modeled in each episode.

The second problem concerns the number of observations. In writing process research, the number of writers is usually quite low. If the data are aggregated to one observation per writer (per episode) the power in the statistical analysis will be quite low (i.e., the a priori chance to reject the null-hypothesis is quite low). Fortunately, there are a lot of observations per writer, as each protocol fragment is a different observation. If we make use of this information, then the power of the analysis increases substantially. In the next section we show how both these problems can be resolved.

The third problem concerns the number of episodes. No explicit theory prescribes the optimal number of episodes to distinguish; this is the researcher's decision. Unfortunately, it makes a difference whether three or five episodes are distinguished (van den Bergh, Rijlaarsdam & Breetvelt, 1993, and Breetvelt et al., 1994).[4] Ideally, however, we should not make arbitrary decisions with regard to the number of episodes. Why should one divide a continuous variable like time into episodes, if it is possible to use all information available? Therefore, we treat time as a continuous variable later (see *A growth model*).

---

[4] Consider the table shown in the footnote continuation at the bottom of the next page. The same data are used there to calculate the correlations in five episodes (below diagonal correlation for proportions, above diagonal correlations for frequencies).

A fourth problem pops up as soon as some writers took more than one writing assignment. In correlational analysis, one has to treat different assignments separately. One should not aggregate over assignments, as the consequences for the correlations will be awkward (not only is the within-episode-within-writer variance component left out, but also the within-writer-between-assignment variance). Some of the extensions of the latter multilevel can be adapted to this situation, and other extensions are also (briefly) covered later. A further advantage of these multilevel models is that not all writers have to take all assignments.

A fixed occasion model

The first problem with the correlational analysis pertains to the distinction of the within- and between-writer variance. If writing is viewed as a minilongitudinal study, the objective of the analysis pertains to "*identifying ... intraindividual change and interindividual patterns of intraindividual change in...development*" (Baltes & Nesselroade, 1979, p. 7). That is, the interest lies in intraindividual changes in a cognitive activity over the distinguished episodes, as well as in ways these patterns are ordered. So, a model has to be specified in which for each episode or occasion, the within- as well as the between-individual variance next to the means can be estimated. As the number of episodes or occasions is fixed (by the researcher), this model is called a *fixed occasion model* (Goldstein & McDonald, 1988). If only one episode or occasion would be distinguished, a one-way analysis of variance (with writers as levels) would do the job; the mean, as well as both variance components are estimated (see, for example, Bryke & Raudenbush, 1992). We have, however, chosen to distinguish three episodes. Therefore, we have to specify a multilevel model (see, for instance, Goldstein, 1987, 1995; Raudenbush & Bryke, 1992).

Multilevel modeling has become a popular technique in analyzing data that are hierarchical ordered. Note that this is the case in the analysis of writing process data; cognitive activities are nested within writers. As the writing strategy of different writers may differ, the occurrence of cognitive

	Ep1	Ep2	Ep3	Ep4	Ep5	Rat
Episode 1	'''''	.70*	.72*	.71*	.08	.47
Episode 2	.32	'''''	.65*	.70*	.21	.76*
Episode 3	.19	.14	'''''	.87*	.30	.37
Episode 4	.56*	.28	.47	'''''	.29	.42
Episode 5	-.12	.23	.06	.13	'''''	-.06
Rating	.47	.76*	.29	.41	-.10	'''''

There are considerable differences between the analyses of frequencies and proportions. Further, the differences between the analysis based on three episodes (Table 11.2) and an analysis based on a categorization in five episodes speak for themselves. The only conclusion to draw is that there are some problems related to a categorization of the writing process in episodes.

activities may differ between writers. This is merely another way of saying that all cognitive activities cannot be considered as independent observations, and we should take this dependency between observations into account in the analysis, or risk serious inferential errors (cf. Bryke & Raudenbush, 1992; Cronbach, 1986; Goldstein, 1987, 1995; Hox, 1994).

Data preparation

The data for a fixed occasion multilevel model can be represented in many ways.[5] A convenient way is expressed in Table 11.3. Each observed cognitive activity is represented in the data file by means of one record. Therefore, the number of observations varies between writers. For instance, the first writer has made 1016 verbalizations, whereas the 22nd writer has made only 362. Hence, instead of an artificial reduction of the number of observations as in the correlational analysis, we use the information of all observations.

The process variable is a binary variable, indicating only whether or not a verbalization was scored as structuring. The cognitive activities are sorted within individuals in order of occurrence in the protocol; activity number 1 precedes 2 and number 2 precedes number 3, and so on. The fourth variable indicates the episodes (1, 2, and 3). Exactly the same variable was used to aggregate the data per writer (per episode) for the correlational analysis. From this variable indicating the episodes, three dummy-variables (D1, D2, and D3) are constructed. D1 is "turned on" only if an activity is observed in the first episode, and "turned off" otherwise, D2 and D3 are "turned on" if an activity is observed in the second or third episode, respectively.

Table 11.3
Example of data for the analysis of a fixed occasion model

Writer	Process Number	Process	Episode	D1	D2	D3
1	1	0	1	1	0	0
1	2	0	1	1	0	0
...						
1	339	0	1	1	0	0
1	340	0	2	0	1	0
...						
1	676	1	2	0	1	0
1	677	0	3	0	0	1
...						
1	1016	0	3	0	0	1
2	1	0	1	1	0	0
...						
22	362	0	3	0	0	1

---

[5] Note that the data in the contribution of Janssen, van Waes & van den Bergh (chapter 12 in this volume) were analyzed also by means of a fixed occasion model. Instead of different occasions, dummies indicating the different types of pauses in either the thinking aloud or the silent condition were specified. Hence, (4 types of pauses x 2 conditions =) eight dummies are used to specify the different types of pauses. Just as with the model specified in Equation 1, the within- and between- variance components for each pause type are estimated.

Model and analysis

For each episode, a model describing the data consists of three parts: a mean, a characterization of each writer (as a deviation of the mean), and a characterization of each observation within a writer (as deviation from the mean of that writer). If Y_{ij} is the ith ($i = 1, 2, ..., N_j$) cognitive activity of writer j ($j = 1, 2, ..., J$), the model can be written as:

$$Y_{ij} = \beta_1 * D1_{ij} + \beta_2 * D2_{ij} + \beta_3 * D3_{ij}$$

$$[\; e_{1ij} * D1_{ij} + e_{2ij} * D2_{ij} + e_{3ij} * D3_{ij} + \qquad\qquad [1]$$

$$u_{10j} * D1_{ij} + u_{20j} * D2_{ij} + u_{30j} * D3_{ij} \;] \; .$$

The model in Equation 1 consists of two parts: a fixed part and a random part (between square brackets). In the fixed part for each episode, the mean number of structuring activities (or any other activity for that matter) is estimated (β_1, β_2, and β_3). These regression weights are the mean of the occurrences of the activity analyzed, or the probability of occurrence in a specific episode.

The random part of the model consist of six residual scores; three characterizing writers in the consecutive episodes (u_{10j}, u_{20j} and u_{30j}) and three characterizing each observation of writer j (e_{1ij}, e_{2ij} and e_{3ij}). As Y_{ij} is a dichotomous variable, the latter residual scores are binomially distributed (Goldstein, 1991). Therefore, they are a function of the mean estimates.[6] The random terms — u_{1j}, u_{2j} and u_{3j} — denote the deviation of Writer j from the grand mean in the respective episodes. Consequently, the mean of Writer j in, for instance, Episode 1, equals ($\beta_1 + u_{10j}$). These residuals scores between writers are assumed to be normal distributed with an expected mean of 0.0. Of course, the residual scores at Level 2 — the between-writer level — are allowed to covary; writers who were observed in the first episode are also observed in the other episodes.

The proportions for a cognitive activity usually are very small (e.g. only 7 out of each 100 cognitive activities concern structuring for Writer 1 (see Table 11.1). Hence, it is very difficult to demonstrate that the probabilities of occurrence differ from zero. Therefore, it makes sense to use a logit transformation. In that case, the end points of the scores are stretched. So, it is not the probabilities per episode that are estimated, but the logit of the probabilities.

Note that the model does not pose any arbitrary restrictions to the data with regard to the number of observations in each episode. It does not matter if for one writer there are hundreds of observations in each episode, and for other there are only tens.

---

[6] Suppose, p denotes the mean of a cognitive activity (in one episode), the (within individual) variance (in that episode) equals $p (1 - p)$. Therefore, the Level 1, or within-writer variances, are not presented in the subsequent table(s).

The data used in this example of a fixed occasion model are the same as presented earlier.[7] Table 11.4 presents the parameter estimates and their standard errors. The mean estimates (fixed parameters) as well as the between-writer variances are quantified. The mean estimates (logits) vary from -3.45 (Episode 2) to -4.32 (Episode 3). By means of a so-called expit transformation,[8] which is the reverse of a logit transformation, the results can be calculated back to proportions. These proportions are shown to vary from .031 to .013. The differences in proportions between the first and third and between the second and third episode are significant (χ^2 = 7.14; $p < .05$ and χ^2= 12.72; $p < .05$, respectively), whereas the differences in the relative number of structuring activities in the first and second episode do not differ (χ^2 = 1.33; $p > .05$).[9] The mean development of structuring can be visualized as a curve that starts .026 and is more or less stable to the middle (.031), and declines thereafter (.013).

Table 11.4
Parameter estimates for a fixed occasion model (standard errors parenthe-sized)

	Episode 1	Episode 2	Episode 3	Rating
	Mean Estimates			
Logit	-3.64 (.18)	-3.45 (.17)	-4.32 (.24)	101.7 (3.35)
Proportion	.26	.31	.13	
	Covariances between writers (correlations above diagonal)			
Episode 1	.75 (.20)	.57	.30	.65
Episode 2	.40 (.14)	.66 (.16)	.34	.75
Episode 3	.29 (.22)	.31 (.15)	1.25 (.38)	.09
Rating	8.82 (2.20)	9.59 (1.80)	1.55 (3.75)	246.09 (74.28)

Turning to the random effects, it appears that the between-writer variances are more or less equal during all three episodes (χ^2 < 1.11 in all cases; $p > .05$). That is, in each episode, the difference in structuring activities between writers is more or less equal.

From the covariances, the correlations between episodes can be calculated.[10] If a significance level of .05 is used, which is a rather severe criterion considering the small number of participants in this study, the correlations

---

[7] For the analysis several software packages are available (ML-3, MLn, HLM and VARCL). Because of the greater flexibility we prefer ML-3 or MLn over both other packages.

[8] An expit or inverse logit transformation is defined as:

$$expit \left[\ln \frac{p}{(1 - p)} \right] = \frac{e^p}{(1 + e^p)}.$$

[9] A contrast analysis can be used (see Goldstein, 1987, p. 17). If H_0 is true, then the resulting testing statistic will be distributed approximately as chi-square.

[10] The correlation between two variables, x and y, is calculated as:

$$r_{xy} = \frac{\text{covariance (x , y)}}{\sqrt{\text{variance (x) * variance (y)}}}$$

between the first and second, and the second and third episode are interesting. The covariance coefficient between the first and third episode failed to reach significance (i.e., |covariance/standard error| < 1.96). Writers who structure often during the first episode tended to do the same during the second, and those who structured often during the second tended to do the same during the third episode. However, there is no relation between the proportion of structuring activities during the first and third episode. Hence, only a relation between the proportion of structuring activities can be demonstrated in two adjacent episodes, signifying that the order of writers is not constant during the writing process.

From the residual scores for each writer in each episode (see Equation 1), curves for each writer can be approximated. These curves can be plotted in either the estimated logits or, as proportions (see Figure 11.2).

As can be seen from a comparison of the left and right parts in Figure 11.2, the logit transformation merely stretched up the bottom end (because there are no observations in the upper end, i.e., high proportions) of the scale; structuring activities are rare. It appears that there are differences between writers in the occurrence of structuring during the writing process. For instance, in the first episode, Writer A is high and Writer B a low structurer, but in the third episode Writer A is a low and Writer B a (relatively) high structurer.

Table 11.4 also shows the correlations between the residual scores per writer and text quality. These correlations can be estimated if a slight modified version of the model in Equation 1 is used. That is, in this case, we specify a multivariate response variable, consisting of scores of cognitive activities and scores indicating text quality. Hence, the response variable now is denoted as Y_{hij}, where the subscript h indicates whether a score pertains to a cognitive activity or to text quality. Next, we add a dummy-variable as explanatory variable, $QUAL_{hij}$, to estimate the mean as well as the between-writer variance in quality scores. The dummy variables for the three episodes are set to zero if a score indicates text quality. Because each writer took only one assignment, no within-writer variance for text quality can be estimated. Hence, the model can be written as:

$$Logit\ (Y_{hij}) = \beta_1 * DI_{1ij} + \beta_2 * D2_{1ij} + \beta_3 * D3_{1ij} + \beta_4 * QUAL_{2ij}$$

$$[\ u_{1j} * DI_{1ij} + u_{2j} * D2_{1ij} + u_{3j} * D3_{1ij} + u_{4j} * QUAL_{2ij}\ ]\ , \quad [2]$$

$$(\ h = 1,\ 2\ )\ ,$$

in which $QUAL_{2ij}$ is the dummy indicating the ratings of text quality.[11] The within-writers residuals score is not presented in Equation 2 because the within-writer-variance(s) is a function of estimates of the mean(s). Therefore, they are not parameters to be estimated in a true sense (see note 6). As can be seen in Table 11.4 there is a rather high correlation between structuring activities and text quality in the first two episodes, whereas in the last episode there is no relation between this cognitive activity and text quality.

Comparison

If the results of the correlational analysis and the fixed occasion model are compared, some differences are revealed. As can be seen, the estimated proportions in the fixed occasion model do slightly differ from those calculated directly (compare Table 11.1 and 11.3). Also, the correlations between episodes and between episodes and text quality show slight differences. At first glance, one could conclude that not many differences are revealed overall. However, at a second glance some dissimilarities become apparent. First, the fixed occasion model is more powerful, which appears from the correlation between the second and third episode. Second, in the multilevel analysis, the observations are considered to be nested within individuals (within episodes). Therefore, all information is used, which results in a different ranking of (some) individuals (compare for instance Figure 11.1a with 11.2b). In the majority of the activities analyzed thus far (see, for instance, Breetvelt et al. 1994; van den Bergh, Rijlaarsdam, & Breetvelt, 1992, 1993) a clear difference between the unilevel and multilevel estimates appeared. The latter are the correct population estimates (see Bryke & Raudenbush, 1992, p. 34-36). In the unilevel model the score of each writer in each episode is treated equally, irrespective whether it is based on 10 or 1,000 observations, as only one score per writer (per episode) is used. In the multilevel model, however, the differences between writers in numbers of observations are accounted for.

A growth model

The main disadvantage of the models just described concerns the classification into three episodes. Why distinguish episodes, or this number of them? If we, for instance, had distinguished five episodes in the analyses above, not only the variances between writers within episodes, but also the correlations with text quality would have changed (see note 4).

In general there are at least three reasons why an analysis based on episodes is only the last resort. First, if we distinguish some number of episodes, it is hard to infer what happens in one episode. Does the number of cognitive activities stay equal and only changes at the next episode? Probably

---

[11] This type of model can only be estimated using ML3 (Prosser, Rasbach & Goldstein, 1991) or MLn (Goldstein, 1995). Other programs, like VARCL or HLM, do not allow for variables to be random at higher levels but not at lower levels.

not. It is highly unlikely that changes in the number of cognitive activities only occur at arbitrarily-chosen points. Second, the same line of reasoning holds for the correlation between cognitive activities and text quality. Does the magnitude of the correlation only change at the arbitrary episode boundaries? Third, dividing the writing process in equal size segments does not do justice to differences in length of writing. That is, it is assumed that all writers need the same amount of time to finish the writing assignment. It seems unnecessary to dwell on the justifiability of these three assumptions. Hence, the models presented thus far are too rigid; we need a more flexible type of model.

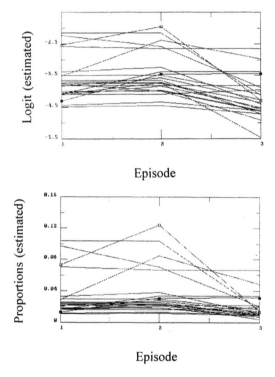

Figure 11.2. Estimated Logits (top) and proportions (bottom) in a fixed occasion model (see Equation 3; Open squares = Writer A, Solid squares = Writer B).

The main problem consists of categorizing cognitive activities into episodes. Suppose, the occurrence of a cognitive activity is a function of the time elapsed since the start of the assignment.[12] That is, probability is

---

[12] If the time elapsed since the start of writing is not available, the serial number indicating the order of the cognitive activities can be used as a proxy variable.

described as a function of time. The question is, of course, what type of function is appropriate to describe the changes in occurrence of a cognitive activity over time. Many types of function seem suitable (see for instance, Burchimal, 1989; Goldstein, 1979; Healy, 1989). We prefer polynomials (Goldstein, 1979) in which powers of time are used as explanatory variables; the probability of a cognitive activity is described in terms of $(time)^0$, $(time)^1$, $(time)^2$, $(time)^3$, and so on. Polynomials are known for their flexibility. Depending on the number of coefficients (i.e., powers of time) and their numerical values, polynomials can take almost any shape. Furthermore, the results of a polynomial analysis are relatively easy to interpret. Hence, the objective of these growth curve analyses is to estimate the occurrence of cognitive activities as a function of powers of the elapsed time. If the elapsed time is denoted with the symbol t, then the occurrence of an activity is written as a function of t^0, t^1, t^2, t^3,.... (note that $t^0 = 1$). The number of powers needed to model the occurrence of a cognitive activity is an empirical matter, so one can use as many explanatory coefficients as deemed necessary. Suppose Y_{ij} is the occurrence of a chosen activity — for instance, structuring — at moment i ($i = 1, 2, ..., N_j$) of writer j ($j = 1, 2, ..., J$). The response variable, Y_{ij}, has to be modelled as a polynomial function of t_{ij}:

$$Logit\ (Y_{ij}) = \beta_0 * t_{ij}^0 + \beta_1 * t_{ij}^1 + \beta_2 * t_{ij}^2 + ... + \beta_p * t_{ij}^p .\qquad[3]$$

The model poses no restrictions on the number of cognitive activities (N_j) per writer; the number of observations for two writers can be different or the same, this does not affect the model. In the fixed part of the model, there are p explanatory variables (i.e., powers of t_{ij}). The first regression weight (β_0) indicates the intercept; the mean occurrence of an activity at $t_{ij} = 0$. The second regression weight (β_1) symbolizes the linear change in occurrence with t_{ij}, the third regression weight (β_2) denotes the quadratic change, the fourth (β_3) the cubic change, and so on. The actual number of explanatory variables (p) is empirically determined, and need not be defined a priori.

Following these ideas, we must distinguish between the within-individual changes in occurrence, as well as the between-individual patterns in occurrence of a cognitive activity. Then we can estimate a growth curve (for an activity) for each writer and the mean growth curve for all writers. Writers might differ with respect to some or all regression weights specified in Equation 3. For instance, one writer might have a low intercept, but a high linear change, and another writer might have a medium intercept and a slow linear change. This comes down to estimating different regression weights for each writer. Or, to put it differently, to estimating a mean regression weight (the β's) and a variance between-writers around this mean weight. The differences between writers are defined in the random part of the model (between square brackets):

$$Logit\ (Y_{ij}\ ) = \beta_0 * t_{ij}^0 + \beta_1 * t_{ij}^1 + \beta_2 * t_{ij}^2 + ... + \beta_p * t_{ij}^p +$$

$$[e_{ij} + u_{0j} * t_{ij}^0 + u_{1j} * t_{ij}^1 + ... + u_q * t_{ij}^q].$$

[4]

Writers may differ with respect to the intercept (β_0), therefore the term u_{0j} characterizes Writer j's position on the intercept. Hence, the intercept of writer j equals ($\beta_0 + u_{0j}$). The same holds for the linear coefficient as well as the other random coefficients — for example, the linear change for Writer j equals ($[\beta_1 + u_{1j}] * t_{ij}^1$), the cubic coefficient ($[\beta_2 + u_{2j}] * t_{ij}^2$), and so on.

In order to highlight the possibility that the number of fixed parameters differs from the number of random coefficients, different subscripts (and superscripts) are used in both parts of the model (p in the fixed part, and q in the random part). Generally, the number of fixed parameters will be larger than the number of random parameters.[13] In effect, different growth curves are allowed for different writers. Writers may differ with respect to intercept ($\beta_0 + u_{0j}$), the linear change in an activity ($\beta_1 + u_{1j}$), the quadratic change with time ($\beta_2 + u_{2j}$), and so on. We assume these residuals characterizing the different writers are normally distributed with an expected value of zero. Because Y_{ij} is a dichotomous variable, e_{ij} is binomially distributed. Therefore, the variance of this parameter is a function of the fixed parameters (see note 6).

There are two rules of thumb to decide on the necessary number of regression weights in a given situation. Both rules are a consequence of the general axiom that the model has to be as sparse as it can be. Therefore, first, the last (fixed) regression weight (β_p) has to have a significant contribution for the description in the mean changes. And, second, a higher order term is not allowed in the model, if a lower order term (except the intercept) does not reach significance. Thus, if, for instance, the regression weight for the cubic term reaches significance, but the quadratic coefficient does not, then the cubic term is left out of the model.

As can be seen in Equation 4, the residuals are a function of time. As soon as the variances are taken, the time variable appears in a quadratic form in the variance (i.e., variance (u_{qj}) = $u_{qj}^2 [t_{ij}^q]^2$). Hence, if the random part of the model consists of only the intercept and the linear component, then the between-writer variance is a function of t_{ij}^2. If, the cubic term also appears in the random part of the model the between-writer variance is a function of t_{ij}^4. Or, more generally, differences between writers in the changes in cognitive activities are modeled in terms of variance heterogeneity.

---

[13] Our experience is that although a fourth- or even a fifth-order polynomial is sometimes necessary to describe the changes in means, three parameters (the variance of the intercept (σ_{u0}^2), the variance in the linear component (σ_{u1}^2) and the cubic component (σ_{u2}^2) suffice for the random part.

Data preparation and analysis

An example of the data to be analyzed is presented in Table 11.5. Note that the data are essentially the same as presented in Table 11.3. They are only represented in a different way.

Table 11.5 presents four variables that relate to time. The first concerns the length of each activity in seconds. This length is accumulated for each writer, which results in the writing time in seconds. In essence, this variable can be used as a time variable in the analysis.

Before starting to estimate the parameters, one has to raise the time variable. In doing so, one will get very large values if powers of writing time in seconds are used as explanatory variables (for instance, 4726^4). These high values for the explanatory variables result in extremely low values for the corresponding regression weights; one could even be confronted with serious problems due to arithmetic precision. Therefore, the time variable has to be rescaled. First, time is expressed in minutes rather than in seconds. Second, the mean time (31.324 minutes) is subtracted, and the result is divided by 10. Therefore the rescaled variable equals zero at 31.324 minutes after the start. The result is a new, rescaled variable, which can be raised to powers without getting extreme values too soon (compare, for instance, time to the fourth power in seconds 4726^4 with the rescaled value of 4.744^4).

Table 11.5
Example of data for the analysis of growth curves

| | | | | Writing time in | | |
Writer	Sequence Number	Structure	Length	Sec	Min*	Rescaled (min)*
1	1	0	63	63	1.05	-3.06
1	2	0	7	70	1.17	-3.02
1	3	0	1	71	1.18	-3.01
1	4	0	9	80	1.33	-3.00
1	5	0	14	94	1.57	-2.96
1	6	1	22	116	1.93	-2.94
1	7	1	5	121	2.02	-2.93
1	8	0	1	122	2.03	-2.93
1	9	0	18	140	2.33	-2.90
...						
1	115	0	11	4724	78.75	4.75
1	1016	0	1	4736	78.77	4.74
2	1	0	101	101	1.68	-2.96
2	2	0	196	297	4.95	-2.64
...						
22	1	0	195	195	3.25	-2.81
22	2	0	2	197	3.28	-2.80
...						
22	362	0	1	2901	48.35	1.70

*Note: In an analysis, the explanatory variables are not rounded to two decimal places.

After these data manipulations, we estimate the model parameters with either the EM-algorithm (as in HLM, Bryke & Raudenbush, 1992); Fishers scorings algorithm (as in VARCL, Longford, 1989), or with iterative generalized least squares (as in ML3 or Mln, (Goldstein, 1987, 1995). Table 11.6 displays the results of this analyis of structuring.

First we concentrate on the mean change in (logit) of the probability of structuring. To describe the mean change in (the logits of) this probability a third order polynomial is necessary because the cubic term does attribute to the description of the mean change. From these fixed estimates, the means for each point in time during the writing process can be calculated; multiplication of the regression weights and the (rescaled) value for time and addition of the results gives the mean value for (the logit of) the probability to encounter structuring activities. Afterward an expit transformation (see note 8) can be used to rescale the estimates to probabilities. For instance, at $t = -1.0$ (which equals about 21 minutes after the start) the mean probability for structuring activities equals expit (-3.240) = .038 (see also Figure 6.3 in Chapter 6).[14]

Table 11.6
Parameter estimates for growth curves for structuring (standard errors in parentheses; see also Equation 7)

Parameter	Estimates (s.e.) Fixed effects		
b_0 (*t^0_{li})	-3.653 (.162)		
$b1$ (*t^1_{li})	-.318 (.087)		
$b2$ (*t^2_{li})	-.072 (.025)		
$b3$ (*t^3_{li})	.023 (.008)		
$b4$ (*$Qual_i$)	101.700 (3.350)		
	Covariance matrix between writers (correlations above diagonal)		
	Structure T0	**Structure T1**	**Quality**
Structure T0 (s^2_{u0})	.373 (.149)	-.239	.619
Structure T1 (s^2_{u1})	-.032 (.044)	.048 (.026)	-.775
Quality (s^2_{u2})	6.049 (2.696)	-2.716 (1.171)	256.100 (74.260)

The random part consists of two parameters: the within-writer variance component and the between-writer variance component. The between-writer

---

[14] One nice thing about the polynomial growth curves is, that from the fixed parameter estimates the time points at which the decrease or increase (in structuring activities) are at a maximum or minimum can be approximated. Setting the first order derivative to zero (-.318 -2 * .072 * t + 3 * .023 * t^2 = 0; -3.13 £ t (rescaled) £ 8.87) gives -1.33 and 3.39. Hence, at 18 miutes after the start the decrease in structuring activities stopped, and increase is noted after 65 minutes.

part of the model consists of two random parameters. The variance of the intercept (σ^2_{u0}) and the variance of the linear change in structuring activities (σ^2_{u1}) proved to be necessary to describe the differences between writers. As the time variable is rescaled (see Table 11.5), the variance of the intercept denotes the variance at (±) 31 minutes after the start of writing ($t_{ij} = 0$). At this moment the variance (of the logit) equals .37. Therefore, the mean occurrence equals -3.65 with a standard deviation of (ö.372 =) .61. Hence, writers differ with respect to the value of the intercept (β_0).

a

b

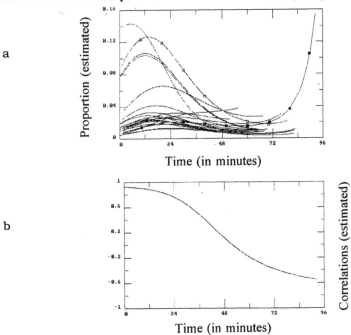

Figure 11.3a, b. Individual cures for the relation between structuring activities and time during writing (top: Open squares = Writer A, Solid squares = Writer B) and the correlation between the proportion of structuring activities and text quality (bottom).

The mean value is -.32 for the linear change in structuring activities (β_1). Therefore, there is a general decrease in the proportion of structuring. There appears to be some variances around this mean value for linear decrease (s^2_{u1} = .048). Hence, writers differ with respect to the decrease over time. Expressed in proportion, this comes down to that for one writer the decrease in proportion structuring in cognitive activities equals .36 per 10 minutes, whereas for another writer this decrease equals .49 per 10 minutes. Hence, the growth curves of different writers not only differ with respect to the intercepts, but also with respect to the slopes (see Figure 11.3a). Or, to put it differently, the temporal organization of writing process with respect to structuring activities clearly distinguishes between writers.

From both parameters, the between-writer-variance can be estimated at each given point in time. Bear in mind that both the covariance of intercept and slope ($\sigma_{u0,\,u1}$) and the variance of the slope (σ^2_{u1}) are a function of t_{ij} and t^2_{ij}, respectively. In general, the variance between writers at time T equals $\sigma^2_{u0} + 2 * T *\sigma_{u0,\,u1} + T^2 * \sigma^2_{u1}$. For instance, at real time 0, our rescaled value of t_{ij} equals -3.13 (see Table 11.5), therefore the variance between individuals is estimated as $.373 + 2 * (-3.13) * (-.032) + .048 * (-3.13)^2 = 1.04$. After 1 hour, the rescaled value of t_{ij} equals $[(60 - 31.324)/10]$. Therefore, the between-writer variance is estimated as .59. One and a half hours after that start, the between-writer variance is 1.67. Hence, the differences between writers in structuring activities first increase and then decrease.

In Figure 11.3a each line symbolizes the proportion (or probability of occurrence) of structuring activities of one writer. From these lines it is possible to "follow" the writing process with respect to structuring for each writer. First, it shows that the lines for different writers vary in length, indicating that some writers took more time to complete the assignment then others. Second, some writers organized their writing process quite differently. For instance, five writers start immediately with structuring remarks in order to decrease their structuring activities after about 20 to 25 minutes. Writer B, who starts structuring again at the end, is an exception. For the majority of writers, however, there are less marked differences over the writing process, although there is a little bulge about 20 minutes after the start.

To estimate the relation between the changes in occurrence of structuring activities and text quality, the data have to be reorganized, and two dummy variables have to be introduced. For every writer the rated text quality must be added to the response variable. The response variable consist either of ones and zeros if a cognitive activity is denoted, or as another number if it concerns text quality. Hence, we have a multivariate response variable, Y_{hij}, where the subscript h denotes whether a score concerns a cognitive activity or text quality. Two dummy variables in the explanatory part of the model define whether a parameter for a cognitive activity is estimated or a parameter for text quality. These dummies can be denoted as ACT_{hij} and $QUAL_{hij}$. The model to be estimated now reads:

$$Logit\ (Y_{hij}) = ACT_{1ij} \left[\sum_{p=0}^{p=P} \beta_{p0} * t^p_{1ij} \right] + \beta_{P+1} * QUAL_{2ij} +$$

$$[\ ACT_{1ij}\ (\sum_{q=0}^{q=Q} u_{qj} * t^q_{1ij}\ ) + u_{Q+1\,j} * QUAL_{2ij}\ ]\ , \qquad [5]$$

$$(\ h = 1,\ 2\ )\ .$$

As there is in this example only one score per respondent available for text quality, the variable text quality is not random at Level 1 (within writers). Of course, the residual scores at Level 2 (between writers) are allowed to covary; and these covariances are the parameters we are interested in. The covariance between text quality and cognitive activities and the variance between writers in activities are a function of t_{1ij}. (As $t_{1ij} * ACT_{1ij}$ equals zero if a score does not concern a cognitive activity. We have used t_{ij} in Table 11.6, to keep in line with the univariate model in Equation [4]).

The estimated covariance matrix represents the covariance matrix at the intercept (i.e., at the value where the rescaled time variable equals zero.) Hence, at this moment, the covariance between structuring and cognitive activities equals 6.05, which corresponds with a correlation of .62 (see Table 11.6). Hence, ±31 minutes after the start of the assignment, there is rather strong relation between structuring and text quality; those that engage in acts of structuring half an hour after the start have, in general, written good texts.

From the estimates, the correlation between cognitive activities and text quality can be approximated at any given point in time. To estimate the correlation, we calculate the variance between writers in activities, as shown before. For every specified point in time $t_i = T$ the variance between writers in this example can be approximated as: $\sigma^2_{u0} + 2 * T * \sigma_{u0, u1} + T^2 * \sigma^2_{u1}$. For the covariance term, only the parameter indicating the covariance with the linear change depends on time. Hence, at moment T the covariance between a cognitive activity and text quality equals $\sigma_{u0, u2} + T * \sigma_{u1, u2}$. Hence, the correlation between structuring and text quality after 10 minutes (rescaled value of σ: -2.1) equals: $[6.04 + -2.1 * (-2.71)] / [\ddot{o}.37 * 246.1] = .88$. This procedure can be repeated for every point in the measured time interval. Hence, the correlation between structuring activities is time dependent; starting highly positive, and decreasing until -.63 after about 2 hours of writing (see also Figure 11.3b). If we had not accounted for time, then the net result would only be slightly positive.

Calculation of the correlations between changes in cognitive activities and text quality is straight forward. The interpretation of these correlations, however, is sometimes cumbersome. The first aspect to take into account is the size of the standard errors. Due to the limited number of writers in this example the standard errors of both the concerning covariances (covariance [intercept, text quality] and covariance [linear component, text quality]), as well as the variance of text quality are relatively large. As the correlation is a ratio of the first two and the last term (see note 10), the standard error of the correlation has to be large too, although we cannot calculate the standard error exactly. Because we cannot suggest a very high precision for the correlation, we should interpret the correlation with some care.

The second aspect of the interpretation concerns the changes in height of the correlation coefficient with time. As shown, the correlation is rather high in the beginning but gradually drops until a value of -.60 is reached. The problems of interpretation arise from the fact that a three-dimensional figure is represented in a two-dimensional space; the differences between individuals in changes in (relative) occurrence of a cognitive activity are related to differences (between individuals) in text quality. So, every point in time shows exactly this relation. Hence, if the correlation between structuring activities and text quality equals .84 (at $t = -1.63$), it says that the writers who undertook (relative) many structuring activities after one quarter of an hour wrote a higher quality text then those who did not undertake structuring activities at this moment. However, these writers do not need to be the same writers who did undertake many structuring activities 5 minutes after the start of writing, when the correlation between structuring activities and text quality is (about) just as high. Hence, the correlation and changes in correlations should be interpreted along with the estimated polynomials (see Figures 11.3a and 11.3b). Given the changes in correlation with time, it is not very informative to generalize to the relation between cognitive activities and text quality; we cannot generalize over time during writing. It is not as much a question if there is a correlation between a cognitive activity and text quality, but a question of when there is a correlation between both variables.

A third aspect concerns the differences in time the writers used to finish the assignment. As can be seen in Figure 11.3a, some writers finished their text well before the hour, whereas others took more time to complete their texts. Therefore, the correlation coefficient is based on different numbers of respondents (after 85 minutes, for example, it is actually based on one writer). Therefore, one should be very careful in interpreting the correlation between structuring and text quality after, say 70 minutes.

A growth model: Some further possibilities

It is quite simple to generalize a growth model to the case two or more cognitive activities are to be modeled simultaneously. In that case a multivariate response variable has to be constructed. For each cognitive activity a different growth curve and different variance components, for the necessary terms, have to be estimated (Grender & Johnson, 1994). Suppose, each cognitive activity is denoted with a dummy variable, say ACT_{1ij}, for the first cognitive activity, and ACT_{2ij} denotes the second cognitive activity. The model to be estimated in this case is in essence the same as the model described in Equation 4. The only difference is that there are two polynomials, one for each cognitive activity. Consequently, there are more fixed as well as random coefficients. If there are only two cognitive activities in the analysis, the model to be analyzed can be written as:

$$Logit\ (Y_{hij})\ =\ ACT_{1ij}\ (\ \sum_{p=0}^{p=P} \beta_{1q} * t_{1ij}^{p}\ )\ +\ ACT_{2ij}\ (\ \sum_{r=0}^{r=R} \beta_{2r} * t_{2ij}^{r}\ )\ +$$

$$[Act_{1ij}\ (\ \sum_{q=0}^{q=Q} u_{1q} * t_{1ij}^{q}\ )\ +\ ACT_{2ij}\ (\ \sum_{s=0}^{s=S} u_{2s} * t_{2ij}^{s}\ )\ ]\ , \tag{6}$$

$$(\ h\ =\ 1,\ 2\ )\ .$$

The product of the dummy variables for the cognitive activities with the time variables gives an unique set of explanatory variables (powers of time) for each cognitive activity (P for the first, and R for the second cognitive activity). Or, to say it in another way, for each cognitive activity a different polynomial is estimated in the fixed part of the model. The same also holds for the random part of the model; for each cognitive activity, the necessary number of random parameters can be estimated. Note that, in accordance with Equation [4], the number of random parameters (Q for the first, and R for the second activity) differs from the number of fixed parameters (P and R, respectively). As there are no a priori restrictions posed on the covariances between the random parameters, all covariances are estimated. Again, the covariances and variances (of both activities) are a function of (squared) powers of t_{ij}. Therefore, the correlation between both activities changes over time (see Rijlaarsdam & van den Bergh, chapter 6, in this volume, for an example).

However, the model does not take into account any dependencies between cognitive activities. That is, if all distinguished cognitive activities are analyzed simultaneously, an increase in some activities implies a decrease in other activities (as the probability that cognitive activity a occurs equals one, there is always something going on). Such dependencies can be taken into account, by posing constraints on the fixed parameters ($ß_{1p}$ and $ß_{2r}$. At each time point the probabilities have to sum to unity (see Goldstein, Prosser & Rasbach, 1991, p. 77-79).

The model described in Equation 6 can easily be extended to the case that an indicator of text quality is available. The covariance coefficients between the residual scores for each cognitive activity (u_{qj} and u_{sj} respectively) and the residual scores for text quality indicate the strength of the covariance. And, again, the correlations between both cognitive activities and text quality can be approximated.

A second generalization of the multilevel models concern the case that (some of) the writers wrote more than one text. In that case, the data of the different text can be analyzed simultaneously. There are several ways to adjust the model. The simplest solution, however, is to estimate different parameters for each assignment (just as was the case for the analysis of two or more activities). According to the multilevel way of analysis, it seems more appropriate to build a model from the hierarchical structure of the data because observations are nested within assignments, and assignments are nested within individuals. Hence, a two-level model might not suffice, but a three-level model, in which the within-assignment variance, the between-assignment variance, and the between-writer variance are separated, might be preferred. The choice between both types of adjustment of the model to more writing assignments is partly dependent on the number of assignments; if only two or three assignments are taken, the first solution might be preferable, but if there are more assignments taken, the second solution might be favored. The reason behind this choice resides in the assumption of normality; if only two or three assignments are taken, it is not clear whether the assumption that the residual scores are normally distributed can be satisfied (Longford, 1989).

Conclusions

Analyses of cognitive activities as a function of time as a proxy variable for changes in the task situation might be worthwhile for development of insights in the writing process. It elaborates and refines our view on writing in many ways. It has been shown, by means of some examples, that the moment during the writing process a cognitive activity is carried out provides relevant information on the writing process itself. Moreover, the differences between individuals in the moments they engage in certain cognitive activities can be modeled by means of multilevel modeling. Simpler ways to entangle the relation between moment during the writing process and cognitive activities, however, are possible. The presented correlational analysis is one example of this type of analysis. The more complex multilevel models not only circumvent the stringent assumptions of more traditional analyses, but they are clearly in the advantage when it comes to avoid arbitrary choices, and they may provide ample opportunities for interpretation. This concerns not only the changes in occurrence of a cognitive activity during writing, but also the relation with product quality. Although the influence of "time" on changes in the probability of occurrence of a cognitive activity — as well as the changes in the relation between a cognitive activity and text quality — has been shown only by means of an example, for no major cognitive activity did the relation with text quality stay constant during the writing process (Breetvelt et al., 1994). That is, for cognitive activities like reading the assignment, generating information, revision, and so on, the differences between writers seem to change during the writing process.

Also, the relation with text quality does seem to change during writing. However, the correlation coefficients between the probability of occurrence of a cognitive activity and text quality should be interpreted in terms of a correlation and not in terms of causes and effects. Although the latter interpretation is appealing, only a coincidence between two variables has been observed. Due to the lack of manipulated variables, interpretations in terms of causes and effects are hazardous, as many rival hypotheses cannot be eliminated.

It has been shown that a complicated growth curve analysis is worthwhile, not only because of its statistical advantages, but also for the reduced number of arbitrary decisions, and therefore the possibilities for interpretation. The most important value of multilevel models is flexibility, which allows the researcher to avoid making arbitrary decisions and data reduction. The correspondence between the complex process under study, the data collection, and the statistical model is as close as can be. As a result, the estimated coefficients are more accurate, because within-writer variance is included (fixed occasion model) and time is used as a continuous variable (growth model). Arbitrary decisions as the number of episodes are avoided (growth model only), as is aggregation bias (growth and fixed occasion model). An additional advantage is the increase of statistical power, especially in writing process studies, which are generally characterized by small numbers of subjects. The most striking result is that multilevel models have the impact of individualization: Not only general trends in processes are estimated, but also the individual deviations from the general trend. Those individual variations are the key for research in the quality of processes.

— 12 —
EFFECTS OF THINKING ALOUD
ON WRITING PROCESSES

Daniël Janssen
Utrecht University

Luuk van Waes
University of Antwerp

Huub van den Bergh
Utrecht University

Concurrent thinking-aloud protocols are an important source of information about cognitive processes of writers. Our understanding of writing as a mental act has increased immensely since the introduction of thinking aloud and protocol analysis in writing research. Researchers like Hayes and Flower have demonstrated that it is actually possible to gain "direct" insight into the cognitive processes of writers at work and the problems they meet when producing text. That knowledge of writers' problems and writing strategies can be and is fruitfully used in writing instruction.

However, although this research technique has been used quite often during the last two decades (cf. Stratman & Hamp-Lyons, 1994, for a review), it has been criticized as well. Several researchers have questioned the reliability and validity of protocol analysis findings (see Smagorinsky, 1989, for an overview). One of the major objections against the method is that thinking aloud may be *reactive*. That is, the writers' cognitive processes may be disrupted by the fact that they are writing and talking out loud at the same time. If so, this would be a serious threat to the validity of thinking aloud and protocol analysis.

Although several researchers have mentioned the problem of reactivity, few studies have tried to investigate the interference of this research technique empirically. There is only one suitable way to do this: by conducting an experiment in which writing processes of subjects in a silent condition are compared to processes of writers in a concurrent protocol condition. This comparison should be based on criterion data, a measure of the underlying processes. Effects of verbalization would then appear as differences in the criterion data between the two conditions (Russo, Johnson, & Stevens 1989, p. 760).

In this chapter we propose a research method that can provide the essential, cognitively relevant criterion data for such an experiment. Furthermore, we report the outcomes of two experiments in which we have used this research method to measure the reactivity of thinking aloud in writing processes.

Before discussing these experiments, we present a classification of observation methods used in writing research. From this classification model, we derive some specific characteristics of thinking aloud as opposed to, for instance, retrospection and text analysis. The model also provides information on the nature of possible criterion data that can be used in experimental studies into reactivity. In addition, we make a plea for empirical research on reactivity and we will evaluate the research on reactivity of thinking aloud in writing so far. In the next two sections the experiments and the choice for criterion data are discussed. In the first experiment we investigated the effects of thinking aloud in a complex 1-hour assignment in which the writers had to do much knowledge transforming. The writing assignment in the second experiment was simpler and more of a knowledge-telling nature.

Classification of observation methods used in writing research

Up to the 1980s, researchers were mainly interested in the quality of written texts. Because of the shift in writing research toward more process-oriented research, new research techniques and methods were introduced. The work of Flower and Hayes (1980, 1981, 1983) influenced the way in which research was designed. In particular, research methods from social sciences and cognitive psychology were introduced in writing research. Thinking aloud and protocol analysis started to influence writing research and theory building at large.

However, still other research techniques were developed to observe and to analyse cognitive processes of writers. In the following model we classify these methods along two axes (cf. Janssen, 1991; Van der Pool, 1995). On one axis we classify the observation methods as *synchronous* or *asynchronous*. When we use synchronous observation methods, we gather information about the cognitive processes during the writing process itself. With asynchronous observation methods, cognitive data are gathered after the writing act.

On the other axis we classify the methods along a continuum between *directness* and *indirectness*. *Direct* refers to observation methods that claim to provide relatively direct[1] evidence about the cognitive processes of writing (Flower & Hayes, 1983, p. 217). *Indirect* research methods obtain cognitive information by inferring cognitive data from process or product characteristics.

Table 12.1
Classification of observation methods in cognitive writing research

	Direct observation	Indirect observation
Synchronous data collection	Concurrent protocols	Process characteristics
Asynchronous data collection	Retrospective protocols	Product characteristics

Concurrent protocols

Concurrent protocols or thinking-aloud protocols are classified as the result of direct, synchronous observations. These observation methods ask people to report about their cognitive activities continuously during the writing process. (cf. Smagorinsky, 1994, for a review of research using TA protocols)

---

[1] No method claims full directness. The step from observations to data will always require an induction. All methods are thus indirect, but some are more direct than others.

Retrospective protocols

Retrospection, on the other hand, can be classified as a direct, asynchronous method. Here, individuals reflect about their writing process and explain why they made certain choices after they have finished (parts of) their text. (cf. Greene & Higgins, 1994, for a review on the possibilities and limitations of retrospective protocols).

Process characteristics

An inventory of the methods used for indirect synchronous observation of the writing process produces the following nonlimitative list: *invisible writing* (e.g. Blau, 1983, asked people to write a text with an iron pen without ink); observers' protocols and video observation (elaborate observations made it possible for the researcher to analyse, for example, general behavior during writing sessions, the evolution of texts written on paper or on screen, eye movements, and so on.; e.g., Matsuhashi, 1981, 1982, 1987). The use of the computer for writing added more possibilities: *video conversion cards* that make it possible to continuously store the information on the computer screen to a video image on a video recorder (De Vet, 1994; Levy & Ransdell, chapter 8 in this volume). Researchers may also use *screen grab programs* that make a graphic copy of the computer screen to a data file at regular intervals (e.g., Jansen, 1994) or *keystroke recording* by which every keystroke and pause is recorded, making possible a replay of the entire writing process afterward (e.g., Börner, 1989; Severinson Eklundh & Kollberg, 1993; Flinn, 1990a, 1990b; Ransdell, 1990; van Waes, 1988).

Product characteristics

With indirect observation methods, we do not ask writers to express their cognitive activities themselves, but we try to infer them ourselves. Text analysis has been frequently used to identify patterns in written texts, especially on the basis of revisions found in the text (Faigley & Witte, 1981, 1984, on revisions; Sanders & van Wijk, chapter 13 in this volume, on text structure).

Need for empirical research on reactivity

As indicated earlier, in the last two decades concurrent protocols or thinking aloud protocols have become very popular in writing research. Most of this research was based on the general (theoretical) presupposition that under normal conditions concurrent thinking aloud protocols may slow down the performance, but do not influence either the elements of the process or the outcomes. The foundation for this claim can be found in the bible for protocol analysts: Ericsson and Simon's (1993) *Protocol Analysis*. Ericsson and Simon (pp. 79-80) distinguish three different levels at which subjects can verbalize their thought processes and thought content. At Level 1 verbalization is simply the vocalization of covert articulatory or oral encodings. There are no intermediate processes, and the subject needs expend no special effort to communicate his thoughts. At Level 2, the verbalization involves description of the thought content. Ericsson and Simon assigned to this level all verbalizations that do not bring new information into the focus of the individual's attention, but only label information that is held in a compressed internal format or in an encoding that is not isomorphic with language (e.g., information about odors). At Level 3, individuals explain their thought processes or thoughts. An explanation of thoughts, ideas or hypotheses or their motives is not simply a recoding of information already present in short-term memory, but requires linking this information to earlier thoughts and information attended to previously.

On the basis of a review of 30 empirical studies in which verbalizations are used, Ericsson and Simond conclude that the studies give no evidence that verbalizations on Levels 1 and 2 change the course or structure of thought processes. The additional verbalization only slows down the task performance moderately. On the other hand, in Level 3 studies, in cases where subjects are stimulated to verbalize thoughts that would normally receive no conscious attention, the cognitive processes may be disturbed. This might be the case when an experienced writer is asked to verbalize local grammatical or spelling decisions.

However, Russo, Johnson and Stephens (1989) challenged Ericsson and Simon's theory. Russo et al. systematically tested the reactivity of thinking aloud in a variety of dissimilar tasks: a verbal task (anagrams), a numerical task (choosing between two simple gambles), a pictorial task (Raven's progressive matrices), and the mental addition of three-digit numbers. The experimental strategy contrasted concurrent verbalization with a silent (control) condition. (Apart from these two conditions, three types of retrospective protocols were examined.) Russo et al. found a significant alteration in accuracy for two out of four tasks and a general prolongation of response time in the concurrent TA condition.

Russo et al. (1989) concluded that Ericsson and Simon's theory is not yet fully adequate to provide sufficient assurance whether or not thinking aloud will interfere with the natural task performance.[2] Ericsson and Simon (1993, p. xxviii) refered to this study as "rather puzzling" and admitted that the findings are inconsistent with their theory. Apart from some technical remarks, they especially supported the possibility that the subjects' attention may have been inappropriately divided between the task and the verbal report. This explanation, however, does not fully account for the differences in reactivity that Russo et al. found in their experiments. If there is an effect of instruction, one would expect a comparable reactivity in all the tasks, which was not the case.

On the basis of Ericsson and Simon's theory, many researchers have claimed that concurrent verbalization during writing could not influence the writing process and the cognitive processes involved. In terms of Ericsson and Simon, a writing task may be classified as an ill-defined task of both Level 1 and 2. A writing task is called ill-defined because well-defined solutions and exact scoring are possible (Dobrin, 1986). When writers are given the proper instruction, verbalizations can be of Levels 1 and 2 because in protocols writers both

---

[2] We limit the problem of reactivity of TA protocols to the discussion whether the production of TA protocols influences the "natural flow" of the writing process or not. The problems that arise in interpreting TA protocols and using them as a basis for theory are beyond the scope of this contribution (cf. Steinberg, 1986, and Dobrin, 1986).

report activities requiring little translation to an oral code (e.g., rereading), and activities requiring more recoding (e.g., explanation of chosen communicative strategy). If writing requires only Level 1 and Level 2 verbalization, no disruption of the process is to be expected.

Cooper and Holzman (1983), however, first raised some methodological questions about the use of thinking-aloud protocols in general. In particular, they questioned the methodological approach in the work of Flower and Hayes. They state (p. 290) that Flower and Hayes' claim that protocols provide direct access to writers' cognitive processes cannot be granted on theoretical and methodological grounds, and that the way in which protocols are elicited raises serious questions about their validity. In addition, Stratman and Hamp-Lyons (1994) commented that "researchers interested in composing processes have assumed that when subjects engage in a text-revision or text-analysis task, their 'reportable' short-memory contents are in an orally compatible form, fairly easy to verbalize, and therefore that reactivity effects will be slight (e.g., Flower & Hayes, 1981, 1984). This assumption, however, has never been put to test" (p. 96). In the extensive review of Ericsson and Simon (1993), no explicit reference is made to any experimental study in which writing was the main activity. Therefore, one can only speculate whether the findings of these experimental studies can be extrapolated to writing research. Ericsson and Simon did note, however, that — even with think-aloud instructions that clearly ask only for verbalization of information in short-term memory — individuals may present descriptions of complex mental operations instead, operations for which descriptive terms are not readily available. Our conclusion should be clear: The only way to obtain a clear insight in this matter is through empirical research focusing on the reactivity of thinking aloud in writing tasks.

Related experimental research on reactivity of thinking aloud in writing processes

As mentioned earlier, the first researchers to raise questions about the reactivity of thinking aloud protocols on the writing process and the written product were Cooper and Holzman (1983, 1985). They discussed the limitations of the research technique in writing as a reaction to the studies by Flower and Hayes. After this it took more than 10 years before any empirical research was reported that provided experimental data to approve or disapprove these assumptions. Stratman and Hamp-Lyons (1994) reported the results of their pilot research and Ransdell (1995) and also Levy and Ransdell (1995) reported the results of experimental studies on the impact of generating thinking-aloud protocols on the narrative writing of college students.

Stratman and Hamp-Lyons

In a pilot study, Stratman and Hamp-Lyons (1994) compared the results of 12 subjects revising a faulty text under thinking-aloud (TA) and non-thinking-aloud (non-TA) conditions in a counterbalanced design. They tried to explore possible reactivity on three output measures: error detection/removal; content changes (meaning changes at the microstructural and macrostructural level, cf. Faigley & Witte 1981, 1984); and structural changes to the organizational pattern. Stratman and Hamp-Lyons concluded that TA slightly depressed the subjects' ability to detect and remedy information organization errors (e.g., cohesion errors on sentence level); the TA condition appeared to slightly enhance the detection of faulty pronoun references; the TA condition appeared to make little difference in subjects' ability to detect phrase-level redundancies and word-level errors; TA seems to stimulate the production of new sentences, but in total fewer sentences were altered by word or phrase additions; and TA does not seem to interfere with writers' text organization processes.

These researchers very cautiously concluded that they doubt the plausibility of the theoretical statement that the TA condition merely reduces the amount of certain kinds of verbal processing, without fundamentally altering the nature of the processes themselves. Stratman and Hamp-Lyons admited that, on the basis of their pilot research, it is impossible to firmly contradict this hypothesis and say it can be seen as "suggesting, at most" (1994, p. 108).

Ransdell

Ransdell (1995) also looked for empirical evidence for protocol validity and TA reactivity. Her 38 students from an introductory psychology class wrote a letter on a computer to a close friend under three conditions: thinking-aloud condition, silent condition, and silent condition with retrospective replay[3]. All students wrote for 12 minutes in each condition (counter-balanced order). The dependent variables were words composed per minute, total number of words, mean clause length, total number of clauses, and clauses composed per minute.

As hypothesized by Ericsson and Simon, writers in Ransdell's experiment wrote significantly more slowly in the TA condition than in the no-protocol and retrospective replay conditions. Also, a slower rate of clause creation was found in the TA condition. The total number of words or clauses and the mean clause length were unaffected by condition in the experiment. She concluded that "at least from the vantage point of this preliminary study, reactivity is limited to rate, not the nature of these processes." (Ransdell, 1995, p. 97)

In her analysis Ransdell ignored all process information. However, we think that this kind of information is very useful for describing effects of thinking aloud on writing. For instance, we can conclude from her data that writers in the silent condition delete more text while writing than writers in the other conditions. Otherwise, we can hardly explain the fact (somehow overlooked by Ransdell) that the writers in the silent-condition produced more words per minute than in the other conditions, but end up with texts of equal length after 12 minutes of writing. This can only be caused by more in-process revisions (deletions) in the TA condition.

---

[3] For the replay, a special memory-resident (TSR) software program unobtrusively collected all keystrokes within a word-processed text file and then played them back in real time (Ransdell, 1990).

Levy and Ransdell

One of the researchers' goals in Levy and Ransdell (1995) was to investigate the impact of concurrent verbal protocols on the writing process, in general, and on writing profiles, in particular. They set up a 12-week writing study in which 10 undergraduates wrote several compositions in self-selected genres (40-minute composition periods). After 5 weeks, the writers were instructed in the concurrent verbal protocol technique, and from then on they had to produce TA protocols during the writing sessions. They also had to respond to beeps that were presented to them throughout the writing.

From their analyses, the researchers concluded that the effects of thinking aloud were negligible. In comparisons of TA and non-TA sessions, they found no significant differences in reaction time to the secondary task or in the number of words.

It may be clear that based on the empirical research described in this section, it is not possible to draw final conclusions on the reactivity of thinking aloud. Stratman and Hamp-Lyons do find traces of reactivity in a somewhat articificial task that cannot fully be compared with normal writing. Ransdell (1995) and Levy and Ransdell (1995), in contrast, used more common writing assignments, but they did not provide adequate criterion data to establish whether or not the cognitive processes changed as an effect of thinking aloud. To gain more insight into reactivity, we conducted two experiments. The design, choice of dependent variables (criterion data) and outcomes of these studies are discussed in the next two sections.

Experiment 1: Writing a complex text

Design

In the first experiment, 20 people wrote a business report of about two pages in two different conditions. In one condition we asked the participants to write and produce concurrent thinking aloud protocols (TA condition); in the other condition no thinking aloud instruction was given (non-TA condition or "silent" condition). In the TA condition, writers were reminded of their verbalization task when they fell silent, according to Ericsson and Simon's standards ("please keep talking"). In both conditions the subjects wrote their text on a computer word processor (WordPerfect 5.1). A Latin-square design minimized the effects of carryover (Table 12.2).

Both conditions used the software program Keytrap to register the writer's activities (van Waes & Van Herreweghe, 1995). This tool is a terminate and stay resident program. Because it is resident, it can work without disturbing the normal use of a word processor.

In the thinking-aloud condition, participants were instructed to say out loud whatever they are thinking about when writing. They had the opportunity to warm up and practice verbalizing and writing for about 5 minutes. Their verbalizations were recorded on an audio-cassette. The recorder was visible on the desk, next to the computer.

Table 12.2
Experimental design for Experiment 1

Group	Session 1		Session 2	
1	non-TA	Assignment A	TA	Assignment B
2	TA	Assignment A	non-TA	Assignment B
3	non-TA	Assignment B	TA	Assignment A
4	TA	Assignment B	non-TA	Assignment A

Note: $n = 5$ in each group.

Keytrap registers all keystrokes and all pauses between keystrokes. In our first experiment, we used a minimum pause length of 3 seconds for practical reasons: The amount of shorter pauses in a 1-hour writing session would have been too large for a detailed analysis (see van Waes, 1991a).

Because Keytrap does not interfere with the use of the word processor, the writing process cannot be disturbed by this observation technique. This makes it possible to combine in the TA condition a direct concurrent observation method (thinking aloud) with an indirect concurrent observation method (Keytrap). Thus, we are able to create two different writing conditions (TA vs. non-TA) with a comparable basis for analysis, the data output of the Keytrap-program.

Writers

Twenty students from a Business School in Zwolle (The Netherlands) participated in this experiment. All were ±21 years old, used to writing business reports, and were experienced in the use of word processors (WordPerfect). They were paid for participating in the experiment.

Writing assignment

In both conditions the subjects received written instructions describing the aim, the audience and the context of the business report. Assignment A can be summarized as follows:

> For many years your company has provided employees with scholarships to help them through college. However, many employees leave the company shortly after graduation. The personnel manager has done some research on this matter: he interviewed employees still in college and employees that had handed in their notice. He has also made some calculations from which it became obvious that giving scholarships has not been a good investment.
> It is your task to write a recommendation report in which you analyze the problem and stipulate possible solutions.

Additional information and statistical data were also provided, but this information was presented in such a way that the students could not simply copy the information from the assignment to their report. In Assignment B the students were asked to write an advisory report for a bank on the use of credit cards.

The students wrote reports of about two pages in 1 hour. There was a period of about 2 weeks between the writing sessions.

These assignments were designed to trigger a type of writing that Bereiter and Scardamalia (1987, p. 10) called knowledge transforming as opposed to knowledge telling. We knew that our students had no previous experience with these kind of reports so they could not rely on ready made plans and discourse models. They had to transform their knowledge and the information in the assignment and invent the text by means of problem analyses and goal setting. As we discussed later, in Experiment 2 we tried to evoke a different kind of writing that could be characterized as knowledge telling.

Dependent variables: Online data

We used pause data as dependent variables in these experiments.[4] In terms of the methodological classification presented earlier, our method of data registration can be characterized as indirect and synchronous. We have operationalized "effect" or "influence" in terms of changes in the real-time organization of the writing processes. An analysis of pause duration in combination with pause location (in the text and in the process) should enable us to estimate the effect of thinking aloud on cognitive processes in writing. Ideally, we need an elaborated theory to explicate the relationship between online data and "hidden" cognitive operations. Unfortunately such a theory does not yet exist (see Sanders & van Wijk, chapter 13 in this volume). Nevertheless, we believe that pause analysis can be a very useful tool in writing research; it has been used successfully in psycholinguistic research (Levelt, 1989) as well as in writing research (Matsuhashi, 1981, 1982, 1987) for many years. To substantiate this claim, so-called real-time analysis must be given further thought.

In real-time research, a writing or language production process is perceived as a process that takes place over an amount of time that can be described in terms of overt behavior (Kowall & O'Connel, 1987). In this behavior the covert cognitive operations become apparent. In other words, the cognitive operations can be induced from online behavior.

The central idea in online writing research is that in the unmarked (hypothetical) case a text is created without any interruptions. In such a case, all time is taken up by physical activities, that is,the time necessary for writing or typing things down or production. Deviations indicate writing problems. These deviations provide the researcher with information on the cognitive processes of writers when performing a writing task. For instance, in addition to producing text, writers may pause or read the text produced so far. In such cases, pausing suggests planning or problem-solving activities. Furthermore, the order in which the text segments are produced may differ from the actual order of the segments in the final text. Writers may add or delete words, sentences or paragraphs at any time during the process. These kinds of deviations form the basis for real-time analyses. It can be substantiated that behavioral observations like these are useful for cognitive research. Pauses (defined by duration and location), for

---

[4] Here we limit the analysis of this experiment to a pause analysis. However, we also carried out a revision analysis (cf. Janssen et al., 1994). This analysis shows that there was no significant difference between the number of revisions in both conditions and that there was no interaction between the level of revision and the condition.

instance, reflect different kinds of operation involved in problem solving or other kinds of planning (see Matsuhashi, 1981)

As mentioned earlier, it is possible to interpret pauses in terms of cognitive operations by examining the location of pauses in the process, the location of pauses in the text, the differences in pause duration.

If the location in the process is determined, there are two distinct possibilities:

> production ⇨ pause ⇨ production *after* the pause
> production ⇨ pause ⇨ production *before* the pause

In behavioral terms we describe a pause in the first possibility as a planning pause: after producing a segment of the text, the writer halts in order to plan the following segments and subsequently produces it. Such a sequence within sentences, we characterize as a pause used for formulating, in particular microplanning (Levelt, 1989; van Waes, 1991a, 1991b). Pauses between sentences may reflect moments of macroplanning in which propositions are retrieved from memory and linked to previously expressed propositions (Levelt, 1989). Pauses between paragraphs, on the other hand, have probably been used for planning at higher levels: for generating content, organizing, and rhetorical planning (Flower & Hayes, 1981).

Pauses that cause alterations in the text produced so far, are more likely to reflect monitoring and (the planning of) revisions. In such cases, the writer detects an error, makes a diagnosis, and repairs the error comfortably (Levelt, 1983). Finally, differences in pause duration can help us to unveil certain aspects of cognitive processes: the more and the longer the delays, the more cognitive operations are required by the output (Butterworth, 1980, pp. 155-156). A corollary of this may be that pauses within processes of text production are hierarchically structured. Within this hierarchy, longer pauses reflect planning processes of a molar nature, but shorter pauses indicate planning of an atomic nature (cf. Butterworth & Goldman-Eisler, 1979; Henderson, et al. 1966).

Hypotheses

On the basis of the literature reviewed three possible hypotheses can be brought forward:

THE WRITING PROCESS IS THE SAME IN BOTH WRITING CONDITIONS. In this hypothesis we claim that the production of TA protocols doesn't influence the way in which writers organize their writing processes. The concurrent verbalization of cognitive processes should be considered as an activity in which thoughts are expressed that are normally not verbalized aloud. From this point of view the observation method is not reactive.

THE WRITING ACTIVITIES ARE THE SAME, BUT THE PAUSES ARE LONGER IN THE TA CONDITION. Based on the Ericsson and Simon's theory, we could predict that the cognitive writing activities themselves are not influenced by the observation method, and that only the duration of the pausing time would vary between both conditions. The increased pause length in the TA condition is due to the time needed for the verbalization of the (conscious) cognitive processes.

THE WRITING PROCESS IS DISTURBED IN THE TA CONDITION. In this hypothesis the underlying assumption is that TA observation methods are reactive. The production of TA protocols does not only prolong the writing process, but also influences the organization of the process and the underlying cognitive activities. The reactivity could affect very specific levels or cognitive activities, but could also be variable and unpredictable.

Results

In our design all writers participated in both conditions. Consequently, the observations in the conditions are not independent, but nested within individuals. Therefore, effects of conditions can be concealed by the variance within individuals. And because we were only interested in the effects of conditions and not in the performance of individual writers, individual variances were isolated by multilevel analysis. With this statistical technique, it is possible to estimate the variance between individuals and within individuals separately and run tests for significance conformly (Goldstein, 1987; van den Bergh & Rijlaarsdam, chapter 11 in this volume). In the present research, we used contrast analysis to test the differences between regression weights on significance. This procedure roughly results in an asymptotical distributed chi-square.

To assess the effects of thinking aloud, we defined pauses by position in Table 12.3: Within sentences, between sentences and between paragraphs. Subsequently, we tested if the mean pause length and the estimated amounts variance (within individuals and between individuals) differ in both conditions.

Table 12.3
Pause duration per position (silent versus TA)

	Silent				Thinking Aloud			
	Mean	n	S^2_{bi}	S^2_{wi}	Mean	n	S^2_{bi}	S^2_{wi}
Within sentences (ws)	7.0	1355	1.2	46.9	8.0	1478	0.7	70.7
Between sentences (bs)	10.4	876	5.7	136.0	12.7	923	12.2	234.9
Between paragraphs (bp)	13.4	507	10.9	223.6	18.3	491	21.8	456.4

Note: S^2_{bi} = estimated variance between individuals
S^2_{wi} = estimated variance within individuals

In both conditions, pauses within sentences are shortest and the pauses between paragraphs are longest ($p < .05$). On the average, writers' pauses were shorter in the silent condition ($\chi^2_{ws} = 6.1$; $\chi^2_{bs} = 9.7$ and $\chi^2_{bp} = 11.48$, *df* = 1; $p < .05$), as expected. In both conditions the pause duration increased with the text level. This could be an indication that differences in pause duration indicate different levels of *planning*. Furthermore, writers paused longer in the TA condition, just as Ericsson and Simon predicted.

However, the differences in variance (within and between individuals) present a different picture. First, the amount of variance *within individuals* proves to be larger in the TA condition ($\chi^2 > 49$; *df* = 1; $p < .05$ on all three levels). So a single subject varies more when writing and thinking aloud at the same time. Second, thinking aloud seems to create differences between individuals. On two levels, between sentences and between paragraphs, there is a greater amount of variance between individuals (χ^2_{bs} = 6.5 and χ^2_{ta} = 10.9; df = 1; p < .05). Within sentences the variance appears to be smaller, but analysis shows that the differences on this level are nonsignificant (χ^2_{ws} = -0.47; df = 1; p > .05).

Because the means and the variances differ, we must assume that we measured on different scales in the two conditions. Although the amount of variance between individuals was relatively small, the reliability (ρ) of our measurement was very high (ρ_{taws} = .73 all others $\rho \geq$ .90).

Table 12.4 presents the correlations between the pauses on different levels of planning in both conditions. In the diagonal are the standard deviations (printed bold). As will become clear, these results provide additional information on the reactivity of thinking aloud.

Table 12.4
Correlation matrix for pause data in Experiment 1

	1	2	3	4	5	6
1. TA - within sentences	**.83**					
2. TA - between sentences	1.00	**3.49**				
3. TA - between paragraphs	.66	.81	**1.66**			
4. Silent - within sentences	.24	.42	.20	**1.08**		
5. Silent - between sentences	.63	.93	1.00	.53	**2.39**	
6. Silent - between paragraphs	-.25	.46	.56	.22	.46	**3.30**

Here we see that, in general, pauses in the TA condition correlate higher than pauses in the silent condition. For instance, the correlation between pauses within sentences and between sentences was 1.00 in the TA condition and only .53 in the silent condition, and they correlated .66 with pauses between paragraphs in the TA condition but only .22 in the silent. Between the conditions there was no meaningful relation between the pauses within sentences (ρ = .24). Some writers thus paused longer in the TA condition while others pause shorter. However, the correlation between the pauses between sentences was very high. In general, writers paused longer when planning sentences in the TA condition. The correlation on the paragraph level was rather low (ρ = .56). On the basis of observations in one condition, we can only predict pause length in the other condition adequately in 56% of the cases.

In other words, the effect of the method differed with the text level or as we would claim: the level of planning. The effect of thinking aloud was predictable between paragraphs. On the other levels, the patterns become more capricious. In conclusion, we have found an interaction between conditions, level of planning and pause length.

Experiment 2: Writing a simple text

Design

In the second experiment 28 individuals wrote a simple explanatory text (see Sanders & van Wijk, chapter 13 in this volume) of about 3/4 of an A4-page under TA and non-TA condition. The design was basically the same as in Experiment 1. In the TA condition we again asked participants to write and to verbalize everything that came into their mind. In this condition they were also stimulated to think aloud when they fell silent (*please keep talking*). In the silent condition, we gave no verbalization instruction. For this experiment, we also used the same method of process registration: Keytrap. In the thinking aloud condition, all verbalizations were visibly recorded. To minimize sequential effects, we used a Latin-square design.

In collecting the data, we were assisted by several students who participated in a course on the validity of thinking aloud and protocol analysis. One of their final assignments consisted of designing and conducting the experiments. The assistants were free to use five equivalent assignments we had made in advance (see *writing assignment*) as long as they were balanced in the design.

Writers

Twenty-eight students from the faculty of the Humanities, University of Utrecht, participated in this experiment. They were ±21 years old, advanced students who have had ample experience in writing and the use of word processor (WordPerfect). They contributed to the experiment voluntarily.

Writing assignment

The students received a written assignment in which the aim, the audience and the context of the text to be produced were described. The students were asked to describe or explain some typical Dutch (folkloristic) events or customs to a foreign visitor of our country: *Explain to someone not familiar with the topic, for instance a Japanese tourist what "Event X" is.*

The events or customs were:

Koninginnedag ("Queens day" on which the birthday of our queen is celebrated);

Elfstedentocht ("Eleven cities tour": a large skating event in the Dutch province of Friesland);

Sinterklaas (Saint-Nicolas, the Dutch equivalent of Santa Claus, who celebrates his birthday on the 6th of December by giving children presents);

Riding a bicycle;

House party (Large scale dancing event with house music).

The students were asked to write a text on this topic in about 20 minutes. There was a period of about 1 week between both writing sessions (thinking aloud and silent). This assignment was designed to trigger the kind of writing processes that Bereiter and Scardamalia (1987, p. 10) called knowledge telling. The structure of these text is highly conventional and planning the text may be considered unproblematic. Writers may follow either action or event lines or combine both (see Sanders & van Wijk, chapter 13 in this volume). Additional problem solving is not required because the writer's goals are given, and the knowledge stored in long-term memory can be used accordingly in the text.

Dependent variables

The dependent variables were much the same as in the previous experiment: we used online pause data to measure the effect of thinking aloud on the writers' cognitive processes. However, in the first experiment we distinguished pauses within sentences, between sentences and between paragraphs. In the second experiment we divided the pauses within sentences, pauses within word groups (e.g., full Nominal Phrases, Verbal Phrases, etc.) and between word groups. Because the production of word groups is considered highly automated and thus requires hardly any planning, differences in pausing behavior *within* word groups might be a strong indicator for reactivity. In order to do so, we had to reconsider our minimum pause length. In Experiment 1, 3 seconds was the minimal value. In Experiment 2, we used .5 seconds, due to the shorter assignment, neglecting most of the pauses within words which were of no interest to us, and still measure pauses within word groups.[5]

Because we had no theory that would predict different effects of TA for knowledge telling writing, our hypotheses remained unchanged from those given earlier.

Results

Because all subjects wrote a text in both conditions, as in the first experiment, we used a multilevel analysis. We estimated "text" or "assignment" effects separately and revalued "condition" effects accordingly (see Experiment 1).

To assess the effects of thinking aloud we have scored pauses by position: within word groups (*wwg*), between word groups (*bwg*), between sentences (*bs*) and between paragraphs (*bp*). After this, we have tested if the mean pause length and the estimated amounts variance (within individuals and between individuals) differs in both conditions.

Table 12.5 reveals the same pattern as Table 12.3. Again, in both conditions, the pauses within word groups were shortest and the pauses between paragraphs were longest. Pauses between word groups were shorter than pauses between sentences, but longer than pauses within word groups (all differences were significant at .05 level). We also measure a difference in pause length between sentences and between paragraphs in the silent condition, but this difference disappeared in the TA condition.

Comparing the two conditions, we found that, on the average, writers' pauses were shorter in the silent condition (χ^2_{wwg} = 3.93; χ^2_{bwg} = 4.02; χ^2_{bs} = 4.31; df = 1; p < .05). On the highest level of planning (between paragraphs) we found no differences (χ^2_{bp} = 0.63; df = 1; p > .05). These results were almost as expected. In both conditions the pause duration increased with the level of planning, as was the case in Experiment 1. Furthermore — with ex-

---

[5] Pauses within words are basically key-finding and spelling errors. We consider these as artifactual because they are inherent to the writing medium, the computer.

ception of the paragraph level — writers paused longer in the TA condition, just as Ericsson and Simon predicted.

Table 12.5
Pause duration per position (Silent versus TA)

		Silent			Thinking Aloud			
	Mn	n	S^2_{bi}	S^2_{wi}	Mn	n	S^2_{bi}	S^2_{wi}
Within word groups	1.5	854	0.04	1.5	1.9	994	0.1	1.9
Between word groups	1.9	2636	0.10	4.7	2.2	3033	0.2	4.8
Between sentences	3.0	736	0.50	8.5	3.8	770	0.6	9.5
Between paragraphs	3.8	265	0.04	10.1	3.9	237	1.0	11.7

Note: S^2_{bi} = estimated variance between individuals
S^2_{wi} = estimated variance within individuals

Again, we examined differences in variance (within and between individuals). In Experiment 1, the variance within individuals was significantly higher on all levels and the amount of variance between individuals was higher between *sentences* and *paragraphs*. In this experiment we found an overall effect on variance ($\chi^2_{overall}$ > 3.84; df 1; *p* <.05), but no effect at the separate planning levels.

Because the average number of observations between paragraphs was low and the variance within individuals is rather high, the reliability on this level is very low in both conditions: ρ_{sbp} = .40; ρ_{tabp} = .42. On all other levels the reliability of the measurement was higher (.62 < ρ < .83).

Table 12.6
Correlation matrix for pause data in Experiment 2

	1	2	3	4	5	6	7	8
1. TA within word groups	**.25**							
2. TA between word groups	.68	**.50**						
3. TA between sentences	.11	.36	**.79**					
4. TA between paragraphs	.18	.09	.50	**1.02**				
5. Silent within word groups	.57	.73	.08	.02	**.19**			
6. Silent between word groups	.64	.97	.28	-.03	.73	**.30**		
7. Silent between sentences	.09	.32	.71	.53	.23	.36	**.68**	
8. Silent between paragraphs	-.16	.15	.54	.69	.11	.18	.56	**.20**

Table 12.6 presents the correlations between the pauses on different levels of planning in both conditions. In the diagonal we report the standard deviations.

In contrast to our former experiment, pauses tend to correlate somewhat higher in the silent condition than pauses in the TA condition. But these differences are not very meaningful.

Comparing the two conditions in terms of the correlations on the separate planning or text levels, pauses were more highly correlated in this experiment. The correlation within word groups was low (. 57) but the correlation between word groups high (. 96). The correlations between sentences and between paragraphs as both fair (.73 and .69). However, we still found different correlation on different pause levels. Thus, in this experiment, thinking aloud works out differently depending on the nature of planning process observed: planning words, word groups, sentences or paragraphs. The effect of thinking aloud was most predictable between word groups, less predictable between sentences and paragraphs and unpredictable within word groups. In other words, the effect of thinking aloud on pause duration varied with the text or planning level. Once again, we found an interaction between conditions, level of planning, and pause length.

Conclusions

We started our experiments with three hypotheses: TA has no effect at all on writing behavior, TA only lengthens pause duration, and TA disturbs the writing process, that is, does more than just stretching out pause length. Both experiments point out that neither of the first two hypotheses is correct. The first hypothesis must be rejected because in the TA condition, pause time increased significantly on almost all levels in both experiments. The second hypothesis is also falsified. In the first experiment we discovered that as a result of thinking aloud, variances within and between individuals changed on all planning levels. In the second experiment, we found an overall effect on variance. Secondly, we measured interaction effect between conditions, level of planning and pause length in both experiments. In the two conditions, pause time correlates differently on the distinguished pause locations in the texts.

However, comparing the two experiments,we conclude that the effect of thinking aloud is larger in complex (knowledge transforming) writing than in simple writing processes of a more knowledge telling nature. For one thing, the effects on the variance within and between individuals established on (almost) all planning levels in the first experiment were absent in the second. We only measured an overall effect there. Moreover, the correlation pattern between the planning levels in the two conditions is similar. Nevertheless, TA proved to be reactive in both experiments.

The somewhat different effects of TA in the two experiments can be caused by writing task differences and by differences in operationalizations. To start with the latter, we measured the pauses with greater resolution. We took a great number of very short pauses into account that would have been neglected in normal thinking-aloud research and that were neglected in Experiment 1. These short pauses cannot reflect higher levels of planning that would have lead to verbalizations in thinking-aloud conditions. In Experiment 2 we thus compared thinking aloud and silent writing on a level on which they might be expected to be more alike: the lower, more automated levels of planning. This would explain the smaller differences in Experiment 2.

Nevertheless, in our opinion the assignment in Experiment 1 would be more suitable for thinking-aloud research than the one in Experiment 1. For Ericsson and Simon's theory makes clear that only heeded information can be verbalized. Only information that receives conscious attention during writing will be reflected in thinking-aloud protocols. Therefore, we assume that writing tasks that engage problem solving — as is the case in knowledge transforming — lead to more informative protocols. Simple (knowledge telling) writing, by definition, is more automated, and knowledge telling protocols are less useful for protocol analysis because a large number of the verbalizations consist of accompanying vocalizations of translating processes, revealing hardly anything of conscious planning processes. This was the case in our experiments. In Experiment 2, a large majority of the verbalizations were translations, whereas in Experiment 1, the protocols revealed more planning on a higher rhetorical level. In Experiment 1, thinking-aloud also appeared to be reactive.

Of course, there is no such thing as pure knowledge telling or pure knowledge transforming. But the assignments in the two experiments call for a different kind of writing, and certainly lead to different kind of texts. Therefore, we think it is safe to conclude that the reactivity of thinking aloud may very well vary with the writing task.

Should we now abandon the thinking aloud method? No, in general this is not a sensible thing to do. All methods have limitations, all methods have problems of validity. But we do think that writing researchers using thinking aloud and protocol analysis should build in empirical checks to make sure that reactivity is absent or, at least, not disturbingly present. We fully agree with Russo et al. (1989) who stated that

> until a theory of protocol generation can fully specify the conditions of invalidity, the only assurance of nonreactivity is empirical...In spite of the substantial reactivity we have observed and the absence of a fully adequate theory of protocol generation, we do not conclude that concurrent verbal protocols are invalid and should be avoided. All methods risk some invalidity and trade-off costs for benefits. On the basis of our own experience with verbal protocols and other process trading data...we believe that nothing can match the processing insights provided by a verbal protocol. Given their unique benefits, the challenge is to identify and reduce causes of their invalidity. (p. 767)

Russo et al. emphasize that Ericsson and Simon's theory is not fully adequate in predicting the effects of thinking aloud. Protocol validity can therefore only be based on an empirical check, not on theoretical assurances (Russo, et al., 1989, p. 759). Of course, on the basis of our experiments we can only agree. Moreover, in writing research, researchers should establish empirically whether TA forms a threat to validity. Keystroke registration and the kind of analyses we provided in this chapter can be of use there. It accommodates researchers with an unobtrusive instrument and cognitively relevant criterion data.

Acknowledgments

The data for Experiment 1 were collected by W. Wassenaar. Daniël Janssen, Joost Schilperoord and Luuk van Waes were responsible for the research project. Huub van den Bergh reanalyzed Wassenaar's statistical data. The basic module of the Keytrap program was developed by IBM Belgium for the University of Antwerp. The application programs and several updates were programmed by H. Pauwels.

— 13 —

TEXT ANALYSIS AS A RESEARCH TOOL: HOW HIERARCHICAL TEXT STRUCTURE CONTRIBUTES TO THE UNDERSTANDING OF CONCEPTUAL PROCESSES IN WRITING

Ted Sanders
Utrecht University

Carel van Wijk
Tilburg University

Since the early 1970s, composition researchers have shown a consistently growing interest in process issues. The cognitive approach received its major impetus when Hayes and Flower (1980) introduced their writing model. This line of research, however, also had its drawback: the idea took root that processes can not be inferred from products (cf. Witte & Cherry, 1986). This conviction has been challenged fiercely by Bereiter and Scardamalia (1983). They pointed to the need to know what rules less skilled writers actually use and how these rules differ from those of experts. Because the most direct way to discover these rules is by analyzing texts, they argued for research that approaches texts as complex phenomena exhibiting internal lawfulness.

To show how text analysis can be used to identify writing strategies, we will discuss in detail results from two research projects. The central textual feature in these analyses is the hierarchical structure of a text. These structures are obtained with a text-analytic method called the Procedures for Incremental Structure Analysis (PISA; Sanders & van Wijk, 1996). The chapter starts with a brief introduction of this method. After that, we discuss the application of PISA and the interpretation of PISA-structures in terms of cognitive processes, first for texts obtained with a free writing assignment, and then for texts obtained with the highly structured sentence combining task. The chapter ends with concluding remarks and some further perspectives.

Text analysis: Considerations and requirements

Text analysis can be a useful tool for gaining insights into a writer's mental representation, provided that it focuses on essential characteristics of a text and its underlying representation. Text structure and discourse coherence are such constituting principles. Without them, texts would not be but a random set of utterances (see, among many others, Van Dijk, 1977; Hobbs, 1990; Mann & Thompson, 1988; Sanders, Spooren, & Noordman, 1992). It is for this theoretical reason that our analysis focuses on text structure, rather than, for instance, stylistic or syntactic characteristics (see also van Wijk, 1992). More specifically, we focus on hierarchical structure. Hierarchical structure accounts for the intuition that the ordering of information in a text usually varies from important to unimportant — where the important information is situated highest. It also accounts for the intuition that language users know what a text is about at a certain moment. The text can handle a certain topic for some time, then digress somewhat, to return to the initial topic. These digressions from and returns to the main line can be represented graphically by means of a hierarchical structure (Polanyi, 1988; Sanders, 1992).

A more practical reason for analyzing text structure is that it enables us, in principle, to compare texts that differ in content or genre. For instance, if you want to compare an explanation of a technical apparatus with a person description of a popular rock musician or an opinion essay on nuclear energy, a content-analysis will not reveal many similarities between these texts. By contrast, hierarchical structure places texts in a format that opens many possibilities for a comparison. This is shown for explanatory texts in this chapter, and for descriptive and argumentative texts in van der Pool (1995) and van Wijk (1995) respectively.

An outline of PISA

PISA has been developed to analyze expository texts, varying from simple descriptions to technical explanations (van der Pool, 1995; Sanders & van Wijk, 1994).[1] The method is strongly influenced by earlier work in text linguistics and functional linguistics, especially the Rhetorical Structure Theory (Mann & Thompson, 1988) and the Linguistic Discourse Model (Polanyi, 1988). The basic operation performed by PISA is that it decides on the hierarchical positions of the consecutive segments in a text. This requires that the text be divided in parts before the analysis actually starts. These parts or segments correspond in most cases to a main or subordinate clause.[2] How PISA actually decides on the

---

[1] Recently the PISA-approach has also been applied to the domain of argumentative texts (Schilperoord, 1996; Van Wijk, 1995). The analysis of this genre, however, places heavy demands on world knowledge and inferencing capacity and for that reason, the analysis proceeds in a far less procedural way (i.e., more intuitively). An important reason for this difference is that expository texts are topic-centered and dominated by ideational or semantic coherence relations (e.g., cause-consequence, list; Sanders et al., 1992), whereas argumentative texts are more speech-act oriented and dominated by epistemic or pragmatic coherence relations (e.g., claim-argument, concession).

[2] Segments are identified on the basis of syntactic form. Basically we follow Mann and Thompson's (1988, p. 248) criterion: each clause is a segment, except that restrictive relative clauses, clausal subjects, and complements are considered parts of their host clause rather than separate units. To these, however, we add as segments of their own the following three types of subclausal structures:

- the second conjunct in a coordination of clauses provided only one major constituent does not reappear (see (1); contracted elements are indicated with dots).

linking of each segment, is explained briefly in the following paragraphs (for a detailed presentation, see Sanders & van Wijk, 1996).

To secure PISA's psychological plausibility, two properties of cognitive processing have been incorporated. First, people process language with some guidance: in text production they have plans (Hayes, chapter 1 in this volume). For this reason, we include two discourse schemes in PISA, which determine the global organization of the text. The *actionline* consists of a sequence of actions or events that explain how the topic is used, manufactured, operated etc. The *propertyline* consists of a list of predications that describe the topic's features, parts, properties, and so on. These discourse schemes were identified in our corpus studies, and resemble the *declarative* and *procedural strategies* proposed by Paris and McKeown (1987).

Second, people process language in an incremental way, that is, "a processing component will be triggered by any fragment of characteristic input," and "this requires that such a fragment can be processed without much lookahead — i.e., that what is done with the fragment should not depend on what will be coming in later fragments" (Levelt, 1989, p. 24). This processing regularity has been incorporated in PISA by having text segments processed in their linear surface order without a preceding global inspection of the text, that is, PISA considers the first segment, and attaches it to a discourse scheme or the topic.[3] Then it moves to the following segment, attaches it to the evolving structure, and so on for each following segment until the text ends (cf. Polanyi, 1988).

For each text segment four decisions have to be made:

1. What segment features underlie its connection to the text? These features have been grouped under three categories: sentence forms, anaphors, and lexical meanings.

2. To which other segment does the segment connect? In principle this can be any segment in the text, in reality candidates appear to be the topic, a discourse scheme or a directly preceding segment.

3. What is the hierarchical position of this connection? There are two possibilities: by coordination or by subordination.

4. What is the relational meaning of this connection? The link is interpreted in terms of a coherence relation, e.g., *sequence, cause* or *specification.*

- nonrestrictive appositions and infinitive clauses, i.e. subordinated clauses without a tensed verb (see (2)).
- major constituents that give a rephrasing or elaboration of the directly preceding one as is evidenced by a marker of the type *for instance* or *i.e.* (see (3) below).
  - (1) John likes fishing / and ... hates hunting
    John likes fishing / and Pete ... hunting
  - (2) Tom has a fine car, / a Ford Mustang
    Tom went upstairs / to finish his home work
  - (3) Pete likes to visit exotic countries / such as Brasil and India
    Pete has been almost everywhere, / e.g., Russia and China

[3] In each of our corpora subjects received an instruction which, among other things, always included the topic, for example, give an argument about *nuclear energy* or an explanation of the *telephone.*

Procedural aspects of PISA

To secure its objectivity and feasibility, PISA incorporates two other requirements. First, the analysis makes use of a well-defined knowledge base, that is, a text analyst has lost the privilege of an unbounded appeal on world knowledge. At present the knowledge available is restricted to two categories: knowledge of lexical meanings, for instance, *to belong* is a state verb and *to dial* an action verb; *poverty, hunger,* and *accident* refer to negatively evaluated situations; and knowledge of discourse regularities, for instance, a fronted adverbial clause stating a problem or goal is usually followed by one or more main clauses specifying the corresponding solution or instrument.

Second, the analysis proceeds in a procedural way, that is, the decisions an analyst has to take when analyzing a text are specified as production rules (condition-action pairs). A simplified example runs as follows: "*If* an if-clause precedes its main clause, *then* check whether its content expresses a goal, problem, or condition. *If* it expresses a goal, *then* subordinate the main clause to it with an Instrument-relation and check the if-clause for referential overlap with preceding text. *If* the current segment contains a referential expression with the antecedent in a preceding segment, *then* subordinate the current segment to the preceding segment with a Specification-relation."

Text analysis: Implementation and interpretation

As a short, and therefore somewhat impressionistic introduction to PISA, we discuss the analysis of the text presented in Table 13.1. This text is an explanation of the telephone written by a 17-year-old grammar school student.[4]

Input of PISA

The input for the analysis consists of a text split up in text segments. The text in Table 13.1 has already been segmented: Main clauses are numbered according to their order of appearance in the text, dependent clauses are marked with an *a, b,* and so forth, added to the number of their host clause (for segmentation rules, see note 2). We refer to individual segments with their code preceded by an *s* (e.g., s2, s13a and s22d).

---

[4] The text is taken from a set of over 100 explanations written by pupils of Grade 8 and Grade 12 (12 and 16-17 year-olds). Each pupil wrote an essay about either a technological topic (*the telephone*) or a cultural one (*Saint Nicholas,* the Dutch version of Santa Claus). The instruction was a situation sketch in which the pupil was asked to respond to a request for explanation (so their text can be regarded as a long conversational turn). The sketch went more or less as follows: In a foreign country you are reading a Dutch magazine. A native is looking over your shoulder and starts asking questions about an article with lots of pictures of *Topic.* He is completely ignorant about that *Topic* and you start to explain it to him: "A *Topic* is a ..."

Table 13.1

Explanation of the telephone by a 17-year-old grammar school student

Segment	Text
1	A telephone is an instrument with which you can reach someone who lives out of your neighborhood.
2	The telephone consists of a part on which you put that instrument through which you speak and listen.
3	This is called a horn.
4	The horn is connected with a wire to the instrument where you put the hook on.
5	On this part there is a dial
5a	which has little digits on it.
6a	To get in touch with someone
6	you turn those digits which correspond to a certain someone.
7	Then in that person's home rings the bell
7a	that is in the telephone
8	and then he or she knows that he/she is being called.
9	Then you can have a conversation,
9a	provided of course that you have lifted the horn,
9	about all kinds of things.
10a	When the conversation is over
10	you put the horn on the other part of the telephone.
11	The conversations pass through an exchange
11a	where all phone calls are processed.
12a	If you can't get in contact with those that you wanted to call
12	that can be defect in the exchange.
13a	If someone else is already calling the person you wanted to call
13	then you also cannot get in contact.
14	This is called "the busy signal."
15a	If you don't know someone's digits
15b	(this is called telephone number)
15	then you can look that up in a telephone book.
16	You look for the area where someone lives
17	and then look up his name.
18	Then you can find the telephone number.
19	All wires needed for the contact between people cross the whole country.
20	These are the telephone wires.
21	The telephone comes in very handy
21a	because you can pass on things very quickly
21b	especially if for instance someone dies.
22	You can also contact foreign countries with it,
22a	so that I can call you,
22b	native,
22c	if you possess a telephone
22d	and if I am back again in Holland

Operations of PISA

The analysis starts with the activation of some relevant discourse knowledge, in this case, the general topic descriptor *Telephone* and two discourse schemes, the *actionline* (a sequence of actions or events) and the *property*-line (a list of static descriptions). All three of them appear at the left hand side of Figure 13.1.[5]

The actual analysis then proceeds incrementally, that is, segments are attached to the evolving structure in their linear order without any prior inspection of text following it. Each segment is inspected for linguistic features such as connectors, pronouns, auxiliary verbs, and ellipsis, and for specific contents such as semantic type of main verb and phrases stating a goal or problem. For each segment, the features that are detected, are fed into a production system (an ordered set of *if-then* rules). This system represents a coherence expert who knows what potential role each individual feature plays in establishing coherence, how to weigh these features when they co-occur, and how to decide on the connection of a segment to the existing text structure.

Output of PISA

The PISA analysis results in a hierarchical and a relational text structure, that is to say a fully connected tree with an interpretative label attached to each connection.[6] In this chapter, we confine ourselves to the hierarchical structure (see Sanders et al., 1992, 1993, for further details on *relational structure* and the meaning of *coherence relations*). Figure 13.1 presents the hierarchical structure assigned to the telephone explanation.[7] Following this structure from left to right (i.e., in the direction the text is read) it shows us that this explanation is organized as follows.

The text starts with a description of the topic: First, properties of the telephone are specified (s1 to s5a), and then actions to operate the machine (s6a to s10). The latter part is organized as a *response* line: s6a mentions a goal and s6 to s10 state how this goal can be achieved. Because this specification is given in detail, as a sequence of actions, it is marked as an *R2* (global specifications are marked as *R1*; De Bruin, 1995). Segment 10a is a special case, a fronted *when* clause that helps sequencing the line of actions. In such a case a double

---

[5] This initialization remains the same over topics, i.e., the analysis of the Aluminum-rewrites and the Telephone-explanations start the same way. It differs, however, over genres (see Van Wijk, 1995, for the discourse schemes of a (pro-contra) argumentation).

[6] Sanders and Van Wijk (1996) report on PISA as it was first developed in Sanders (1992, chapter 5). Since then, however, the analytic system has been extended on the basis of further research on text corpora. The most important extensions concern the treatment of fronted if/when- and purpose-clauses (De Bruin, 1995) and of postposed, so-called continuative relative clauses (cf. Daalder, 1989). The analyses in this chapter are made with this augmented version.

[7] The relational structure of the first ten T-units reads as follows: s1 Specification(property); s2 List(s1); s3 Specification(s2); s4 List(s3); s5 Specification(s2); s5a Specification(s5); s6a Specification(action); s6 Instrument(s6a); s7 Sequence(s6); s7a Specification(s7); s8 Sequence(s7); s9 Sequence(s8); s9a Condition(s9); s10a Situation(s10) & Sequence(s9); s10 Sequence (s9).

attachment is made: a primary one to the main clause (the closed line with s10), a secondary one to the response line (the dotted line). From s11 to s14 we see a number of local elaborations. Both s12a and s13a are followed by an *R1*, that is, a general response to the problems (a single segment expressing, in these cases, a diagnosis and a consequence).

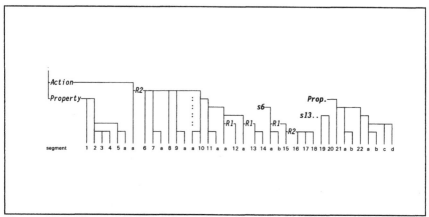

Figure 13.1. Hierarchical structure of telephone explanation.

From s15a onward the structure becomes fragmented. The cluster s15a to s18 is in itself neatly organized: s15a mentions a problem followed by both an *R1* and *R2*. This problem, however, is related to s6 (*dialing the number without knowing the number*). To connect s15a-s18 with s6 we have to cross the connection lines of s7 to s14. In other words, this attachment is discontinuous. This is also the case with s19-s20 (associated with s13) and s21-s22d (attached to *property*-line).

Results of PISA

The cognitive interpretation of this PISA-structure proceeds as follows. First, we have to notice that the text can be split in two parts. The first part runs from s1 to s9a, the second one from s10a onward.[8] These text parts can be conceived of as results of the action plans specified below. Each plan consists of an intention-strategy-procedures triplet (van der Pool & van Wijk, 1995).

1   *Basic action plan*
    Intention   I want to generate an explanation of Topic *X*
    Strategy   Make use of relevant genre cues
    Procedures   1. Describe characteristics of *X* (= fill in property line)
              2. Describe functioning of *X* (= fill in action line)

---

[8] Cf. *standard portion* and *signaled portion* in the experiment of Scardamalia, Bereiter, & Goelman (1982).

2   *Remedial action plan*
   Intention   I want to generate still more content
   Strategy   Make use of text-internal cues
   Procedures   1. Take a cue from last segment
               2. Take a cue from last paragraph
               3. Return to Topic descriptor

Plan 1 underlies the production of the first part (s1-s9a). The two *topic-lines* were generated, and after segment 9a the writer could have dropped the pen. But apparently he did not find his text adequate for reasons we can only guess at (e.g., "short texts don't look clever" or "this text is not informative enough"). The writer decided to continue content generation with Plan 2, and while carrying out this plan, he switched procedures.

At the start, text extensions (s10a-s14) were made following the first procedure "Take a cue from last segment:" s10 added a follow-up action to s9, the action closing the response line; s11 went back to *conversation* in s10a, s12 to *exchange* in s11, and s13 to *contact* in s12.

Then the writer started to follow the second procedure: a search for cues in the last paragraph (that is, the *action* line). First he went back to the initial step in using the telephone, dialing a number. In s15 to s18 he explained how to find such a number. Then he went back to the process as a whole: s19 and s20 explained how wires make telephone contact possible.

And, finally, the third procedure was tried: s21 to s22d went back to the Topic descriptor *Telephone*. And in doing so the writer also managed to return to the situation motivating his communicative intention: He directly addressed the native who had asked for this explanation.

This case study illustrates how text analysis may shed light on the plans writers use in generating content. Of course, results like these have to be evaluated in the same way as those obtained with thinking aloud: as "some reasonable guesses about what the subject was doing" (Hayes & Flower, 1980, p. 6). At present, text analysis plays a heuristic role: It contributes more to the understanding of conceptual processes in writing than to the actual testing of these ideas.

In the remainder of this chapter we discuss another aspect of the writing process: how do writers proceed in (re-)organizing content? We make use of exercises known as *sentence combining*. The topic of this writing task and the conditions under which it is performed differ sharply from the free writing task discussed so far. The choice for such different tasks and topics was also made to underscore the general usability of PISA as an analytic instrument.

Sentence combining: Origin and history

Sentence combining (SC) was introduced in a large scale developmental study by Hunt (1970). He used the so-called aluminum-passage presented in Example 3. The input lines are numbered for ease of reference, they do not occur in the actual task. We refer to them with their number preceded by an *L* (e.g., L3 and L21). Individuals were instructed to read this text closely, and then to rewrite it in a better way. Task performances follow a highly general and regular pattern: Young subjects simply copy the input text. But when subjects grow older, they gradually apply more and more elisions and embeddings, thus increasing the syntactic integration of the text.

In rewriting this passage, three qualitatively distinct performances can be distinguished: the novice, advanced, and expert performance (for a formal definition of these competence levels, see van Wijk, 1995). To illustrate these performance types, we present examples drawn from a set of over 100 SC-protocols produced by Grade 8 pupils and college freshmen. The texts in Examples 4, 5, and 6 were written by a 12-year-old student and two college freshmen.

Aluminum

Example 3

Directions: Read the passage all the way through. You will notice that the sentences are short and choppy. Study the passage, and then rewrite it in a better way. You may combine sentences, change the order of words, and omit words that are repeated too many times. But try not to leave out any of the information.
1. Aluminum is a metal. 2. It is abundant. 3. It has many uses. 4. It comes from bauxite. 5. Bauxite is an ore. 6. Bauxite looks like clay. 7. Bauxite contains aluminum. 8. It contains several other substances. 9. Workmen extract these other substances from the bauxite. 10. They grind the bauxite. 11. They put it in tanks. 12. Pressure is in the tanks. 13. The other substances form a mass. 14. They remove the mass. 15. They use filters. 16. A liquid remains. 17. They put it through several other processes. 18. It finally yields a chemical. 19. The chemical is powdery. 20. It is white. 21. The chemical is alumina. 22. It is a mixture. 23. It contains aluminum. 24. It contains oxygen. 25. Workmen separate the aluminum from the oxygen. 26. They use electricity. 27. They finally produce a metal. 28. The metal is light. 29. It has a luster. 30. The luster is bright. 31. The luster is silvery. 32. This metal comes in many forms.

Example 4 — Novice *performance*: 1. Aluminum is a metal and abundant. 2. It has many uses. 3. It comes from bauxite. 4. Bauxite is an ore 4a. and looks like clay. 5. It contains aluminum and several other substances. 6. Workmen extract these other substances from the bauxite. 7. and then they grind it. 8. They put it in tanks with pressure in them. 9. The other substances form a mass. 10. They remove the mass with filters 11. and a liquid remains. 12. Then they put it through several other processes. 12a. and yield a chemical. 12b. that is powdery and white. 13. This chemical is alumina. 14. It is a mixture. 15. And it contains aluminum and also oxygen. 16. Workmen separate the aluminum from the oxygen with electricity. 17. Then they finally produce a metal. 18. The metal is light. 18a. and has a luster as well. 19. This luster is bright and silvery. 20. This metal comes in many forms.

Example 5 — *Advanced performance*: 1. Aluminum is an abundant metal with many uses. 2. It comes from bauxite, 2a. a clay-like ore 2b. that contains besides aluminum several other substances as well. 3a. In order to extract these substances, 3. workmen first grind the bauxite 3b. and then put it in tanks 3c. where due to the pressure the other substances form a mass. 4 After that they remove this mass with filters. 5. The liquid that remains, is put through several other processes. 5a. until they yield a chemical. 6. This white powder 6a called alumina, is a compound of aluminum and oxygen. 7. The workmen separate the aluminum from the oxygen with electricity. 8. And finally a light metal is produced with a bright, silvery luster 8a. that is available in many forms.

Example 6 — *Expert performance*: 1. Aluminum is an abundant, light-weight metal with a bright, silvery luster 1a. that is extracted from bauxite, 1b. a clay-like ore. 2a. To obtain aluminum in its pure form, 2. the other substances need to be removed. 3. First, the bauxite is ground 3a. and put in tanks 3b. where pressure makes the other substances form a mass 3c. that is filtered out. 4. The remaining liquid is put through several other processes 4a. until these yield a white powder 4b. called alumina. 5a. After this compound of aluminum and oxygen is split by electrolysis, 5. pure aluminum results, 5b. a metal with many uses 5c that is made available in many forms.

The descriptive indices computed on the three rewrites show a pattern identical to that found in other studies (see Table 13.2). The more sophisticated a rewrite, the less words and T-units[9] a writer uses to present the same information. This leads to a dramatic increase in the two classic indices to determine task performance: average T-unit length and the average number of input sentences per T-unit.

The regularity of this developmental pattern, first revealed in Hunt (1970), is still an unparalleled empirical success (for a replication in Dutch, see Reesink, Holleman-van der Sleen, Stevens, & Kohnstamm, 1971). It has been the basis for a number of course books for writing training (see e.g., Strong, 1973; Daiker, Kerek, & Morenberg, 1986). The effectiveness of these courses has been well attested by highly controlled experiments (Kerek, Daiker & Morenberg, 1980). Hillocks (1986, p. 151) adhered to Cooper's (1975) conclusion, namely, that no other single teaching approach has ever consistently been shown to have such a beneficial effect on syntactic maturity and writing quality.

Table 13.2
Descriptive indices characterizing rewrite performances

	Novice	Advanced	Skilled
Number of words	135	115	98
Number of T-units	20	8	5
Average T-unit length	6.75	14.38	19.60
Average number of input lines per T-unit	1.60	4.00	6.40

This practical success, however, has been based on a collapsing theoretical basis. Hunt (1970) saw sentence combining as an application of Chomsky's Aspects Model of transformational generative grammar. The input text represented a set of kernel sentences that the writer had to integrate by applying optional transformations. Task performance depended on the number of these transformations one could apply in a single cycle. In the next 15 years, however, course books started to place less emphasis on syntax, and the transformational component of the aspects model lost its cognitive relevance. This lead to a situation that de Beaugrande (1985, p. 61) characterized as follows: "Sentence Combining has drifted steadily further away from its own theoretical

---

[9] A Minimal Terminable Unit or T-Unit is "one main clause plus any subordinate clause or non-clausal structure that is attached to or embedded in it" (Hunt, 1970, p.4).

inception and has even survived the ultimate discrediting of the original theory with little obvious damage. We thus have an application for which there is no longer a theory."

In our view, the failure to give a theoretical account of sentence combining was caused by the idea that *because* writing proficiency can be *described* in syntactic terms, it should also be *explained* in terms of sentence formulating processes. In the following section we will argue that an explanation in terms of conceptual processes appears more plausible: Rewrites differ because the underlying mental representation of the input texts differ. Such an explanation is in line with the earlier suggestion to consider the effects of sentence combining in terms of a better command of rhetorical principles and the standards of good writing (Harris & Witte, 1980).

Sentence combining and conceptual processing

Our reconstruction of the decisions underlying the rewriting of an input text proceeds in three steps. They are illustrated on the three example texts presented in Examples 4, 5, and 6.

The first step is to analyze the texts by means of PISA (see Figures 13.2a-13.4a). The texts have been segmented according to the PISA-input rules. Below each segment, the numbers are presented of the input lines integrated in it. Inputs that were reduced to subclausal structures (e.g., prenominal adjective, prepositional phrase), are placed under their host clause and marked with "<."

The PISA structures reveal striking differences between performances. The novice rewrite shows a rather flat, additive structure with a sudden jump from *property-* to *actionline*. The advanced rewrite has a structure with more hierarchical depth (less direct attachments to *property-* and *actionline*), a few double linkings (the dotted lines), and an explicit introduction of the *actionline* (a goal is mentioned). The expert rewrite displays a structure with still more depth, an elaborated start of the *actionline* (both the goal and a realization in general terms are mentioned), more double linkings, a radical move of some inputs (e.g., the lines 28 to 31 went to the very beginning of the text), a deletion of one input, and a merging in two other cases.

The second step is to recover from these PISA-structures their underlying mental representations. For texts written spontaneously, this step is a difficult one to take. Writers tend to leave out a considerable amount of information from a text, trusting that their readers will be able to add it again by activating background knowledge and making inferences (e.g., Crothers, 1978). A sentence combining task, however, controls for this behavior: All the input content is given in the task. This enables us to reconstruct underlying mental representations by simply unfolding observed PISA structures (see Figures 13.2b-13.4b).

This unfolding is done as follows: First, temporal adverbial clauses and continuative relative clauses (all clauses with a double linking) are directly at tached to the *actionline*. Then the subclausal embeddings are added as sepa-

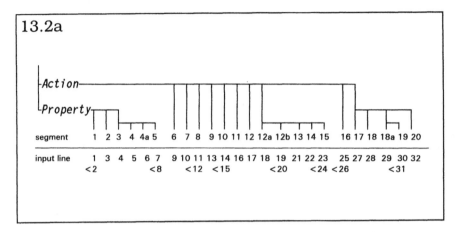

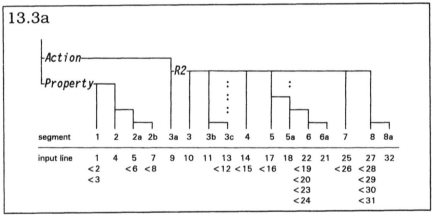

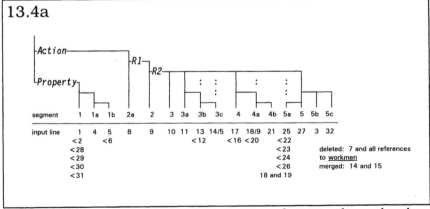

Figures 13.2a, 13.3a, and 13.4a. PISA-structure of novice, advanced and expert performance. (Topic: Aluminum)

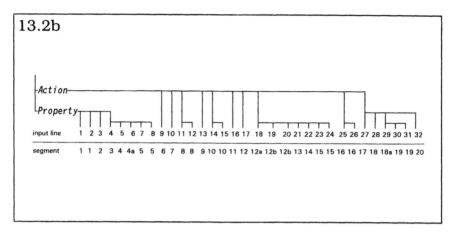

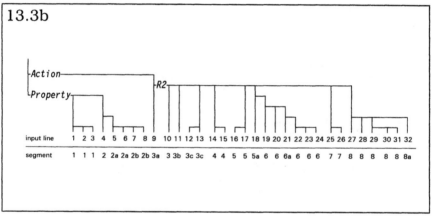

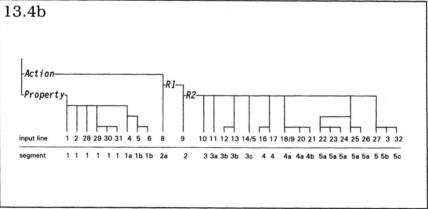

Figures 13.2b, 13.3b, 13.4b. Representation of novice, advanced and expert performance. (Topic: Aluminum)

rate structural adjuncts; the coherence relation is derived from the grammatical form of the input (e.g., a conjunct as in *bright and silvery* is an addition, a prenominal adjective as in *white powder* is a specification, a prepositional phrase as *with filters* is an instrument).

The third step is to derive from these representations for each input line a detailed inventory of all its interpretations. It appears that most lines are poly-interpretable; they can be understood in more than one way. Because subjects differ in the way they make use of these ambiguities, they process the text at different levels of understanding (Schank & Lebowitz, 1980). Table 13.3 summarizes how these differences in understanding came about in the three exemplary rewrites. For each subject it is spelled out how the inputs have to be interpreted in order to obtain the representations depicted in Figures 13.2b, 13.3b and 13.4b.

The differences between writers converge in two independent factors: First, the more skilled a writer, the better the grasp on the possibilities to realize referential continuity. This appears from the following changes: A pronoun gets assigned to another antecedent (e.g. in L2 the antecedent of *it* changes from *aluminum* to *metal*) and a full NP is replaced by another plausible candidate (e.g., in L7 *bauxite* by *ore*, in L21 *chemical* by *powder*).

Second, the more skilled a writer, the better the understanding of an input's meaning. This becomes apparent in the following changes: An input line gets connected with a more specific coherence relation (e.g., in L16 *Sequence* is replaced by *Result*, in L12 *Specification* by *Cause*), an input line is re-ordered, rephrased or recast (see Table 13.4), and an input line is moved to a new location (e.g., L3 may be placed after L27).

This inventory of input-interpretations allows for a specific description of the procedural knowledge writers have needed to produce rewrites like those in Examples 4, 5, and 6. Below, we discuss each performance in generalizing terms, as a representative of a commonly observed performance level.[10]

The novice performance

In a novice performance, writers stick very closely to the literal text. Inputs are left unchanged except for the commonly made re-ordering of constituents in L12 (see Table 13.4). Coherence is discerned on the basis of two procedures that take the form of static prescriptions: a pronoun in subject position refers to the subject of the preceding clause, and a clause with an action verb describes a consecutive event or action.

The first procedure explains why the repeatedly occurring pronoun *it* gets its antecedent is such a rigid way; the second explains why the Sequence-relation prevails. Both procedures are followed strictly with one obvious excep-

---

[10] In terms of the theory of Bereiter and Scardamalia (1987), the novice performance results from basic knowledge telling, the advanced performance from sophisticated knowledge telling, and the expert performance from knowledge transforming (for a formal definition, see van Wijk, 1995). The differences between performances can also be characterized in terms of genre; the text evolves from a description into a full-blown explanation.

Table 13.3

Interpretations of input lines underlying rewritings in novice, advanced and expert performances

#	Input line	Novice	Advanced	Expert
1	Aluminum is a metal	—	—	—
2	It is abundant	It=Aluminum	It=Metal	It=Metal
3	It has many uses	It=Aluminum	It=Metal	>L27 It=Metal
4	It comes from bauxite	It=Aluminum	It= Aluminum	It=Metal
5	Bauxite is an ore	—	—	—
6	Bauxite looks like clay	—	Bauxite<Ore	Bauxite<Ore
7	Bauxite contains aluminum	—	Bauxite<Ore	+Delete L7(=L4)
8	It contains several other substances	It=Bauxite	It=Ore	+Recast L8=Actions
9	Workmen extract these other substances from the bauxite	L9=Actions	+Rephrase L9=Actions	+Rephrase Instrument L8
10	They grind the bauxite	Sequence L9	Instrument L9	Specification L9
11	They put it in tanks	Sequence L10	Sequence L10	Sequence L10
12	Pressure is in the tanks	+Re-order	Cause L13	Cause L13
13	The other substances form a mass	Sequence L11	Result L11	Result L11
14	They remove the mass	Sequence L13	Sequence L11+Re-order	Sequence L11 +Re-order
15	They use filters	Instrument L14	Instrument L14	+Recast L14/15
16	A liquid remains	Sequence L14	Result L14	Result L14
17	They put it through several other processes	Sequence L16	Sequence L14	Sequence L14
18	It finally yields a chemical	Sequence L17 It<They	Result L17	Result L17 Chemical<powder
19	The chemical is powdery	—	+Rephrase	+Recast L18/19
20	It is white	It=Chemical	It=Powder	It=Powder
21	The chemical is alumina	—	Chemical<Powder	Chemical<Powder
22	It is a mixture	It=Chemical	It=Alumina	It=Alumina
23	It contains aluminum	It=Chemical	It=Mixture	It=Mixture
24	It contains oxygen	It=Chemical	It=Mixture	It=Mixture
25	Workmen separate the aluminum from the oxygen	Sequence L18	Sequence L17	Sequence L17
26	They use electricity	Instrument L25	Instrument L25	Instrument L25
27	They finally produce a metal	Sequence L25	Sequence L25	Sequence L25 Metal<pure Aluminum
28	The metal is light	–	–	>L2
29	It has a luster	It=Metal	It=Metal	>L2 It = Metal
30	The luster is bright	–	–	>L2
31	The luster is silvery	–	–	>L2
32	This metal comes in many forms	Sequence L27	+Rephrase	+Rephrase

Note. = means refers to, < means is replaced by, > means moved after.

Table 13.4
Reformulation types of input lines

Re-order: Only surface form is changed	
L9 Workmen extract these other substances	⇨ These other substances are extracted (by workmen)
L12 Pressure is in the tanks	⇨ In the tanks there is pressure
L14 They remove the mass	⇨ The mass is removed (by them)
Rephrase: Content is slightly adapted	
L9 Workmen extract these other substances	⇨ Workmen have to extract these other substances
L19 The chemical is powdery	⇨ The chemical is a powder
L32 This metal comes in many forms	⇨ This metal is available in many forms
Recast: Content is substantially changed	
L8 It contains several other substances	⇨ It has to be cleared from these other substances
L14 They remove the mass	⇨ They filter out the mass
L15 They use filters	
L18 It finally yields a chemical	⇨ It finally yields a powder
L19 The chemical is powdery	

Note. The recasts of L14/15 and L18/19 are referred to as *merging*.

tion: Most young writers already recognize that a clause with the verb *use* has an instrumental relation with the preceding clause (see Table 13.3, L15 and L26).

Although superficial, the novices' strategy suffices to obtain a coherent reading of the text. At only two occasions it leads them into trouble. The major problem shows up at the transition from *property* line to *action* line (from L8 to L9).[11] Many of the young writers (and even a number of the adult ones) fail to see that L9 states the goal for the actions discussed in the remainder of the text (as in Example 7a). They misinterpret L9 as the first action in a sequence. A 12-year-old wrote the juxtaposition in Example 7b; a college freshman the more eloquent, but just as erroneous subordination in Example 7c. In fact, the most interesting observations with the Aluminum passage concern the struggle with this topic line transition.

Before writers fully recognize L9 as the global organizer of the *action* line, several phases of a growing awareness can be identified. This development proceeds more or less as follows. First, writers let L9 and L10 change places (see Example 7d). Thus, they solve the problem only locally; L9 still stands in the wrong relation with the remainder of the text. Then writers escape from the problem by deleting L9. And, finally, they dissociate L9 from the *action* line, and attach it to the *property* line, either as a specification or a consequence (see

---

[11] The minor problem concerns the end of the text. Some writers treated L32 as the last member of the actionline. Apparently they did not take the adverb *finally* in L27 seriously (because it also occurred in L18?).

Examples 7e-f). In that case, they very often also add notices such as *follows* and *with a rather complex procedure.*

- *Example 7a.* In order to extract these substances, workmen first grind the bauxite and then put it in tanks etc., etc.
- *Example 7b.* Workmen extract these other substances from the bauxite and then they grind it.
- *Example 7c.* Before the workmen grind it, they extract the other substances.
- *Example 7d.* Workmen grind the bauxite and thus extract these other substances. Then they put it in tanks, etc.
- *Example 7e.* Bauxite contains aluminum and several other substances that are extracted by workmen.
- *Example 7f.* Bauxite contains aluminum but also several other substances. That's why workmen extract them from it.

The advanced performance

In an advanced performance, writers deviate more than once from the literal text; they reorder and rephrase a fair number of input clauses (for examples, see Table 13.4). They also understand that L9 states the goal of the action described in the subsequent inputs. Coherence is established along the same lines as novices do, but now procedures need to be conceived of as dynamic rules: They (a) check whether a pronoun in subject position can refer, in a plausible way, to a nonsubject of the preceding clause, and (b) inspect clause content, especially main verb, for cues for the coherence relation.

The first procedure explains why the pronoun *it* gets its antecedent in a flexible way; the second explains why the result relation occurs more often. This more active approach to pronoun resolution also underlies some input rephrasings. In a number of cases, the noun in subject position is replaced to make it equal to a nonsubject constituent of the preceding clause (e.g., *bauxite* is replaced by *ore* in L6 and L7). The greater concern for clause content seems to depend most on a better understanding of verb semantics. Apparently, it takes some time before one learns to recognize the resultative connotations of verbs like *form* (L13), *remain* (L16), and *yield* (L18).

The expert performance

In an expert performance, writers treat the input text in a very liberal way; they reorder, rephrase and even recast inputs (for examples, see Table 13.4). They also introduce the *action* line more carefully: L8 states the goal, L9 the realization in general terms.[12] Experts use the advanced writer's procedures to establish coherence, but with one important addition. Where advanced writers faithfully follow the input text when building their representation, expert writers take a more independent position: They critically review the text before

---

[12] In Figures 13.4a and 13.4b, the realization of the goal in general terms (L9) is marked with *R1*, the realization in specific terms (L10-32) with *R2*.

making their representation final. Expert writers add two procedures to the repertoire of the advanced writer: They (c) check clauses for informational relevance, and (d) check the text for thematic continuity.

Procedure (c) explains why input L7 is deleted: It states nothing but the reverse of L4. It also explains why a number of inputs undergo changes. By passivization of, among others, L11 and L14 references to *workmen* can be deleted; it is trivial that they are doing the job (see Table 13.4, the reorders). The superfluous mentioning of *chemical* in L18 and L19 is removed by merging both inputs (see Figure 13.4, the recasts).

Procedure (d) accounts for the positional shift of inputs. The sloppy presentation of properties of the metal aluminum is improved by placing those concerning the natural material at the beginning of the text (L1, L28-L31), and those concerning the commercial product at the end (L3, L32).

Conclusions

Consider an alternative explanation for the sentence combining data: Writers differ in their mental representations of the sentence combining text. As a result, they prepare different conceptual structures or preverbal messages (Levelt, 1989, p. 73) as input for their formulating system. This change in input causes that different sets of syntactic procedures become activated, and different surface forms are generated.

In other words, differences in conceptual processing appear to be essential for our understanding of sentence combining. The hierarchical and relational structure assigned to the information in the input text is the main determinant of the conceptual chunks fed into the sentence generator. Writers appear to have a strong tendency to formulate in a main clause content directly linked to the *action* or *property* line, and to formulate with each of these main clauses in one syntactic package all content subordinated to it in the mental representation.

These two formulating strategies explain for the larger number of observed rewrite operations. They are not sufficient, however, for a full understanding of sentence combining performance. Advanced and expert writers make a number of more subtle reformulations that have not yet been touched upon. Some questions remain: What arguments underlie the decision to subordinate a member of the *action* line to another member, for instance as a continuative relative clause or a temporal adverbial clause (see Examples 8a-8c)? And what arguments underlie the direction in which such a subordination is made: to the left (see Example 8b) or the right (see Example 8c)?

- *Example 8a*. They put the bauxite in tanks. *Then the other substances form a mass*. Then they remove it with filters.
- *Example 8b*. They put the bauxite in tanks *where the other substances form a mass*. Then they remove it with filters.
- *Example 8c*. They put the bauxite in tanks. *After the other substances have formed a mass*, they remove it with filters.

In this chapter we have substantiated a text analytic approach to writing research. This approach has proven to yield highly systematic descriptions of regularities in language behavior, both in structured tasks (such as sentence combining), and in free writing assignments (such as telephone explanations, person descriptions and pro-contra argumentations) (Sanders & van Wijk, 1994, 1996; van der Pool, 1995; van Wijk, 1995). These results show that text analysis deserves to be one of the basic methodologies in psycholinguistic research on text production. Text analysis yields insights into the knowledge structures that direct the composing process and the decisions underlying the selection and organization of the information in the text. Yet, it remains to be found out how, during the actual course of composing, this knowledge is used and these decisions are made. Therefore, text analysis should not be practiced in isolation of other methods (see also Bereiter & Scardamalia, 1983). To get a grip on processing aspects, our (offline) text analyses are now combined with online techniques, such as pause-measurements and key capturing programs (Janssen, van Waes, & van den Bergh, chapter 12 in this volume; Sanders, et al., 1996; Schilperoord, 1996). This puts the cognitive claims of the text analysis to the test. Initial results indicate that this combination of methods makes for a very fertile approach. Most importantly, the online manifestations seem to underpin our central claim that the structure of a text reflects conceptual decisions of the writer.

Acknowledgments

We would like to thank the editors, Dick Hayes, Hans Hoeken, Leo Noordman, and Jan Renkema for their comments on an earlier draft of this paper.

INDIVIDUAL DIFFERENCES AND APPLICATIONS

— 14 —
A Qualitative-Quantitative Study of Preschool Writing: Its Development and Contribution to School Literacy

Iris Levin
Tel Aviv University

David L. Share
Haifa University

Evelyn Shatil
Haifa University

It is well known that children construct their concepts of writing long before being exposed to formal instruction in reading or writing at school. To describe the progress of writing, written productions of young children were classified into categories, and these categories were ordered according to scales assumed to capture a developmental progression. Partly overlapping scales have resulted from writings of children exposed to different languages: Spanish (Ferreiro & Teberosky, 1979), Italian (Pontecorvo & Zucchermaglio, 1990), French (Gombert & Fayol, 1992), English (De Goes & Martlew, 1983; Scarlett, 1989) Chinese (Chan, 1992; Chi, 1988), and Hebrew (Levin, Amsterdamer, & Korat, 1966; Tolchinsky Landsmann, & Levin, 1987).

Most scales include an early form of writing, prior to letters, described as scribbles, pseudo-letters, or mock letters. Next, writing involves a string of random letters unrelated to the target utterance, primarily taken from the child's name. Finally, writing is determined by letter sound correspondences, often called *invented spelling*.

Despite the impressive similarity in the development of early writing across cultures and languages, little is known about the links between children's level of writing and other aspects of literacy. Two assumptions, frequently made in the literature, have rarely been empirically substantiated. First, preschoolers' level of writing is conceived as one of the major expressions of their emergent literacy (Clay, 1975, 1987; Garton & Pratt, 1989; Temple, Nathan, & Burris, 1982). Hence, level of writing should be correlated with performance on concurrent tasks assessing emergent literacy. Second, writing in preschool is assumed to promote competencies serving as starting points for coping with learning formally to read and write (Clay, 1975; 1987; Garton & Pratt, 1989; Temple, Nathan, & Burris, 1982). Thus, writing level should predict future progress in reading and writing in school. The aim of our chapter is examine these assumptions.

The chapter is divided into four sections. The first presents features of Hebrew orthography as a background for understanding children's writing. The second part presents a new scale of children's writing in Hebrew, based on the productions of 349 kindergarten children recruited from a wide SES range. Our scale differs from most others in its level of specification. Rather than trying to capture only the major, qualitatively different categories of writing, we added finer distinctions, some distinct qualitatively but others quantitatively, from each other. Thus, we attempted to create a more precise scale, and to increase the probability of finding statistical links with other variables. The third part presents the relations between kindergartners' level of writing, on the one hand, and between their general ability and literacy as measured by Clay's Concepts about Print, on the other. It further examines whether kindergartners' writing predicts their future progress in conventional reading and writing in first grade. The final part describes educational implications.

Unique features of Hebrew orthography

To explain the evolution of children's writing in Hebrew, the orthography must first be described succinctly. Three aspects will be dealt with: the Hebrew voweling system, the morphophonological vowel *H*, and final letters.

The Hebrew writing system (see Appendix 14.1) is considered predominantly consonantal. It represents the consonants in a relatively complete, systematic, and consistent fashion (Ravid, 1988; Shimron, 1993), and vowels are marked less efficiently. In fact, Hebrew has two voweling systems. The dominant system is inconsistent and incomplete.[1] It is composed of four letters only, AHWY, called *matres lectionis* or "mothers of reading." The letter *H* mostly marks the phonemes, /a/ and /e/, but only at end of a word. Occasionally, the letter *A* also functions as a vowel, in words with idiosyncratic spelling such as "mom," which is *ima* written AMA. The letter *Y*, which mainly marks the phoneme /i/, and the letter *W*, which mainly marks the phonemes /o/ or /u/, appear in many words, but are missing in many others that include these phonemes. This standard called "deficient" spelling was supplemented, about 40 years ago, by another standard, labeled "plene" spelling, in which *Y* and *W* appear in most words having these phonemes. Although plene standard is believed to have facilitated Hebrew reading, it has created a situation of no common standard for vowel transcription, which is indeed often inconsistent across and within texts.

The second voweling system in Hebrew is optional, and composed of diacritic marks. These marks are short lines and/or dots placed mainly underneath the letters, but also above, between, or within them. It is a complete system, with every vowel phoneme represented. Its difficulty stems though, from its redundancy. Every vowel phoneme has two to four different options

---

[1] This surface inconsistency is governed by a complex system of rules, mostly unknown to nonprofessionals.

of marking, and in order to know which option applies to which word, a complicated rule system has to be mastered, an accomplishment prevalent among professionals such as linguists or Hebrew teachers but rare among other literate adults. This system is used only where assistance in reading is required, such as in children's books, poetry, or prayer books. A fluent reader rarely writes or reads texts with diacritic marks. Preschoolers rarely use the system of diacritic marks in their writing. School-age children do so almost only when obliged in classwork. We will examine only the use of the dominant system of AHWY letters.

The poor representation of vowels by letters in Hebrew orthography is explained by the structure of the language (Yanay & Porat, 1987). Most content words in Hebrew consist of two elements: a consonantal root and an associated morphological pattern of affixes (Berman, 1978). By transforming the root, a family of words is derived carrying a common core of meaning. For example, the root k-l-t is the basis of verbs such as *kalat* (absorbed) and *hiklit* (recorded); of nouns like *miklat* (shelter), *kelet* (input), and *taklit* (record). Because words with a common root usually differ on the vowels but share the same root consonants, the consonants carry the core meaning of the word.

The vowel letter *H* differs from the rest in that its use is governed by position. As a vowel, it appears only in the final position of a word, and only in words ending with a simple CV syllable, known in Hebrew as an "open syllable," such as nemal*a* (ant), written NMLH. Note that the *H* does not mark the /a/ sound in the middle of the word, only at the end. In words ending with CVC, labeled a "closed syllable," such as name*l* (port), written NML, the *H* is not required. The other vowels, *Y*, *W*, are not limited to a position in a word, and appear both in the middle and the end.

H also functions as a morpheme in the gender-number system of nouns, verbs, and adjectives, denoting singular-feminine terms. For instance, *pila* (she-elephant) is written PYLH, in contrast to *pil* (he-elephant), written PYL, and to *pilot* (she-elephants), written PYLWT. It should be stressed that the gender-number system is pervasive throughout the language because every noun is syntactically either masculine — e.g., *sefer* (book), written SPR — or feminine — e.g., *sifra* (digit), written SPRH, and its form determines that of its accompanying verb, adjective, and so on — e.g., *sefer adom* SPR ADWM for "red book" and *sifra aduma* SPRH ADWMH for "red digit," with the feminine forms of the noun and adjective both marked with an *H*.

Five Hebrew consonants, MNCPK each have two written forms: one regular and one final. When one of these letters occurs at the final position of a word, it is written in its final form. Otherwise, it is written in its regular form. This double form has been found as early as the third century BC, in Hebrew and in related orthographies (Diringer, 1958). Final letters are believed to have assisted in reading texts without word separation.

We expected that the distinction between regular and final letters would be appreciated only by highly advanced kindergartners. We assumed that this difficulty would stem from several sources, some of which may be parallel to the difficulty of learning to leave spaces between words, and of using uppercase letters among children writing English. To comprehend the system of final letters the child has to grasp the word unit, so as to understand that final letters appear in the final position of words. In the same vein, to learn to leave spaces between words, in Hebrew or in other orthographies, requires becoming aware of the conventional segmentation of text into words. This achievement is rare among kindergartners. Learning the use of capital letters at the primary positions of sentences requires becoming aware of the sentence unit, a related, and perhaps an even more difficult task. However, the distinction between lower and upper case letters may be facilitated by the fact that each letter in the alphabet has these two forms. In contrast, the distinction between final and regular letters in Hebrew may be relatively difficult to acquire because of the scarcity of final letters, that is, there exit only five final letters in the alphabet. We expected therefore, that final letters would be replaced by many children with regular letters, or used for other functions.

Hebrew is written from right to left. Hence, the pages of Hebrew books, magazines, and the like, are sequenced in the opposite direction to English, and writing or reading of each line starts from the right margin.

The analysis of Hebrew orthography led to the following three main expectations: First, early attempts to write with letters representing the required phonemes will be limited to consonants. Vowels will be acquired later, and their mastery will often lag behind that of consonants. Second, the use of the vowel *H*, will show special features such as overgeneralizing its use to the middle position of words. Finally, the distinction between regular and final letters will be a late achievement.

The writing scale

The writing test

Each kindergartner was asked to write three pairs of words. The pairs were chosen to represent various contrasts: *pil-nemala* (elephant-ant), contrasted in size of referent, to assess children's semantic considerations in early writing, (e.g., Ferreiro & Teberosky, 1979; Levin & Tolchinsky Landsmann, 1989; Levin & Korat, 1993). The pair *lasim-simla* (to put-a dress), involved two words composed of the same syllables in different orders, to assess children's phonological considerations (e.g., Gombert & Fayol, 1992; Tolchinsky Landsmann & Levin, 1987). The pair *sefer-sipur* (book-story) involved two derivations of the same root and was designed to assess children's morphological considerations in writing (Levin & Korat, 1993; Levin, Amsterdamer, & Korat, 1996).[2] The writings produced were used to construct a scale of the development of writing in kindergarten.

---

[2] A fourth pair, which we used *aba v'ima*, "mom and dad," will be ignored to save space.

Writing levels

Children's writings were classified into six major categories: *drawings, symbolic-graphic signs, random letters, elementary-, intermediate-,* and *advanced-consonantal writing.*

With the exclusion of drawings, the five categories of writing were further divided into 13 subcategories, assumed to compose a ranked scale. This categorization was used to score the writings of each child. Scoring was carried out collaboratively by two of this chapter's authors, who were blind to the child's performance on other tasks. Scoring was based on all six writings produced by the child, because comparing different productions helped in the classification. For instance, when a child used the same letters in writing different words, it was taken to mean that the choice of letters was random, even though for a particular word a letter (or two) was used that coincided with the word's phonemes. Similarly, when children used letters for writing some words and numbers for writing other words their writing was classified as a mixed system. Finally, mastery in using vowels depended on the variety of vowels used across writings.

Interjudge reliability was tested by classification of 90 protocols, carried out by an independent judge, after instruction in using the scale. These protocols were randomly selected by taking about 25% of protocols from each category. The Pearson correlation between our classification and that of the judge was .96, ($p < .001$), indicating high reliability.

DRAWINGS: Drawings were excluded from further quantitative analyses under the assumption that a drawing does not represent a level in the evolution of writing (Gombert & Fayol, 1992; Levin, Korat, & Amsterdamer, 1995). Instead, children who draw when requested to write are assumed to have chosen to redefine the task for their own purposes. We believe that they have chosen to do so because they refuse to write nonconventionally. Refusals among advanced children, due to awareness of limitations to perform conventionally, have been reported for other literacy related tasks (Gombert & Fayol, 1992; Tolchinsky Landsmann & Levin, 1985; Sulzby, 1985; Sulzby, Barnhart, & Hieshima, 1989).

Among the 29 children who drew in response to the request to write, two provided unexpected evidence that they knew how to produce writing at some level. Ortal (Figure 14.1) introduced into her drawings of "book" and "story" linear scribbles of the kind we would have classified as symbolic-graphic signs, had they been produced alone, and not embedded within drawings. Khen (Figure 14.1) inserted scattered Hebrew letters into his drawing of "story," thereby showing he could have written in random letters, had he chosen to do so. Hadar (Figure 14.1) classified as using a mixture of symbolic-graphic systems, produced drawings four times on the request to write. Then she spontaneously switched into writing random letters, proving she could do it, but initially preferred not to. Figure 14.1 displays examples of drawings that include signs of writing.

SYMBOLIC-GRAPHIC SIGNS. This category includes two subcategories: *pseudowriting* and *mixed graphic-symbolic systems*. Examples are shown in Figure 14.2.

Figure 14.1. Examples of drawings including signs of writing.

Pseudowritings (Level 1) were composed of arbitrary signs, mostly of unidentifiable source, differing in shape across children. A few pseudowritings include a single arbitrary sign per word. Others include prolific signs that fill up the page in no particular order. Most pseudowritings, however, were governed by at least some of the graphic characteristics of conventional writing: linearity, division into units, and unidirectionality. The writing of Oshrit (Figure 14.2), is composed of very simple linear forms — a straight line, a dot, a broken line, and so on. Noam's (Figure 14.2) writing consists of closed random shapes. Karlin's (Figure 14.2) writing includes a variety of forms, from simple to very complex ones. Each of these children seems to have a unique "handwriting," which is the rule for pseudowritings. But their productions can be identified as writing, because they include arbitrary shapes, separated into units, written in a horizontal line, often from right to left (the conventional direction of Hebrew writing).

Name (age)	Oshrit (1) (6;5)	Noam (1) (6;2)	Karlin (1) (5;8)	Idan (2) (6;4)	Shay (2) (5;11)
Elephant					
Ant					
Book					
Story					
To put					
Dress					

Figure 14.2. Examples of graphic symbolic systems (1,2).

Writings labeled *mixed graphic-symbolic systems* (Level 2) were composed of units mostly of identifiable source, that is, Hebrew letters, numbers, geometrical shapes (e.g., squares), Latin letters, and the like. Some children mixed signs from different systems within the same writing, suggesting a failure to discriminate between them. Most children in this group, however, used signs from the same system in each piece of writing but varied systems across writings, as though discriminating between them but unclear as to the difference in their function. Idan (Figure 14.2) mixed Hebrew letters and numbers within several of his writings. Shay (Figure 14.2) wrote each word with signs from the same system, but used different systems for different words: simple pseudowritings, geometrical shapes, numbers, and well-shaped Hebrew letters.

RANDOM LETTERS: Writing in this category consists of a string of random Hebrew letters. This writing reflects the general characteristic of conventional writing in that the letters are arrayed horizontally, in a single direction, frequently in the conventional Hebrew direction — from right to left. Examples are displayed in Figure 14.3.

Name (age)	Uri (3) (6;1)	Re'ut (4) (5;8)	Einav (5) (6;7)
Elephant	·זז א	הותנ	ד'א̱ש̱ג
Ant	·ז·ז א	י̱צ̱פ̱ש	ל̱ב'ג
Book	א ז·ז	̱נ̱ו̱נ	א̱ב̱ג
Story	א̱זז·ז	?¡ה̱צ̱ם·	י·ת̱ב
To put	א·ז·ז̱ד	̱ז̱צ̱שם̱	א'ב̱ת̱נ
Dress	אז·ז·ז	̱ם̱ם̱ו̱ב̱ש	ת̱ב̱א̱ב

Figure 14.3. Examples of writing in random letters (3, 4, 5).

The letters used are random, in the sense that they do not represent the required sounds. However, their choice is determined by environmental exposure and graphical simplicity. Children often used letters of their own name, as well as the first letter of the alphabet (Aleph) probably because these letters are the first to be introduced to them by adults. They also used letters having predominantly simple square shapes (Reish, Waw) probably because it was easier for them to mentally construct their graphic schemes.

Random letter writings were classified into three subcategories (3, 4, and 5), which differed in the repertoire of letters used. In assessing this factor, we took into account the fact that children used different numbers of letters in writing a word. Summed over six words, the number of letters written varied in the range 12 to 39, the lowest number produced by those using two letters per word, the highest produced by those who wrote as many letters as they could get into a line, across the page. Because writing fewer letters limited the variety of letters produced, we estimated the variety of the child's repertoire by a type/token index (i.e., the proportion of different letters out of the total number of letters written). According to this index, random letter writings were divided into three groups: 3. *low* (up to 30%), 4. *medium* (31% - 40%), and 5. *high* (41% and up), percentages of different letters out of total number of letters produced. The cutoff points were statistically determined, to result in as equal subgroups as possible.

Uri's (Figure 14.3) writing illustrates low variety of letters. He wrote 25 letters in total, composed of four different letters (16%), all taken from his own name. The first word he wrote (for "elephant") was simply his name, and the subsequent words were made up of the same letters in different order. Re'ut (Figure 14.3), demonstrates medium variety. She wrote 26 letters, including 9 different letters (36%). The first word she wrote was composed of her name-letters in a mixed order. Subsequent words included some of these letters along with others. Einav's (Figure 14.3) writing, classified as high variety, wrote 25 letters, including 11 different ones (44%). Her first word includes 2 of her name-letters and 5 others. Her second and third words each included an additional name letter, along with new letters. Thus, for Uri, his name seems to have provided the entire available repertoire, for Reut the preliminary accessible repertoire, and for Einav it was probably one of various sources.

ELEMENTARY-CONSONANTAL WRITING: The progress from writing in random letters to phonetic writing is a significant step, taken gradually. Phonetic writing involves reconceptualizing the symbolic function of the written system, that is, recognizing that the written form of the word is determined by its phonological structure. The evolution of phonetic writing involves becoming able to segment words into phonemes, and this demands some level of phonological awareness. It also requires retrieval of the letters carrying the corresponding sound value. Examples of elementary-consonantal writings are displayed in Figure 14.4. The figure's title includes the conventional spelling of each word in capital letters. Each example includes a transcription of the spelling of a word written by a child, to enable comparisons between the child's writing and the conventional spelling. Note that Hebrew writing is from right to left, but the transcription is from left to right.

Elementary-consonantal writing in Hebrew includes only consonants. The reason for children's initial preference for consonants over vowels is related, we suggest, to the structure of Hebrew language and its orthography, described earlier. Level 6 was assessed in writing with elementary representation of consonants, without vowels, including the possible use of random letters too.

Random letters seem to appear intermingled with phonetic writing, for two reasons. Children who succeed in retrieving only a single sound from a word, often remain unsatisfied with writing a single letter for the whole word or utterance. Hence, they add a few letters to create a sufficiently long string. In some cases, the addition may be governed by a more rigid rule, stating that writing should include a fixed number of letters, often three.

Ferreiro and Teberosky (1979) suggested that preschoolers, from a certain phase on, construct a constraint that an utterance to be read deserves more than a single letter. They called this the "minimal quantity principle." Children were observed to obey this principle in various studies (Freeman &

Whitsell, 1985; Levin, Korat, & Amsterdamer, 1995; Pontecorvo & Zuccher-maglio, 1990; Tolchinsky Landsmann & Karmiloff-Smith, 1992; Tolchinsky Landsmann & Levin, 1985).

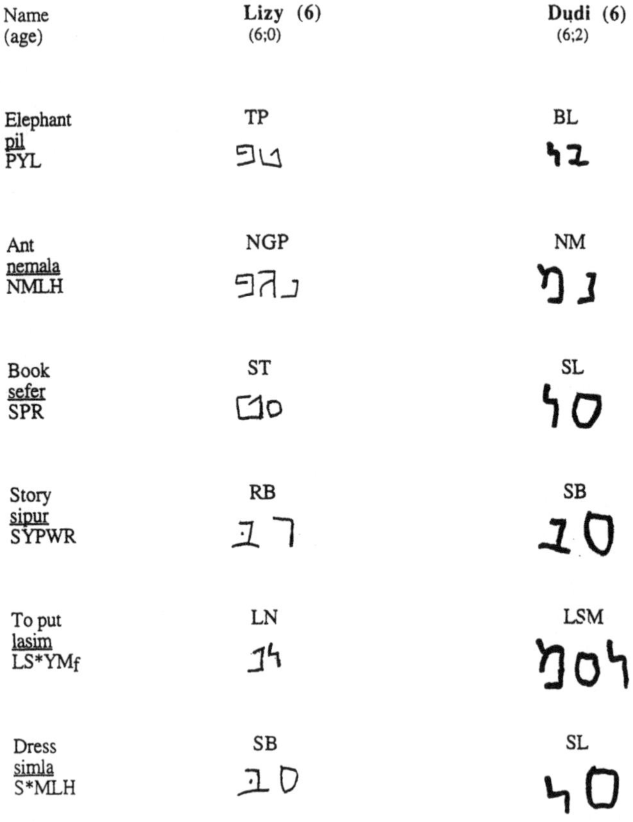

Name (age)	Lizy (6) (6;0)	Dudi (6) (6;2)
Elephant pil PYL	TP	BL
Ant nemala NMLH	NGP	NM
Book sefer SPR	ST	SL
Story sipur SYPWR	RB	SB
To put lasim LS*YMf	LN	LSM
Dress simla S*MLH	SB	SL

Figure 14.4. Examples of writing at elementary consonantal level (6).

The inclusion of random letters may appear in children who succeed in segmenting the word into its sounds, often into consonants or syllables, and who try to represent each sound with a letter. However, they may be unfamiliar with letters representing some of the required sounds, and hence they compromise on random letters. Others know the names of the letters that stand for the required sounds ("*I don't know how to write Reish*") but unable to retrieve their shape, they use other letters instead.

Lizy (Figure 14.4) in all of her writing combines a phonetic letter, representing one of the required sounds, with one or more random letters. For five words, the phonetic letter she wrote designated the initial consonant, and for one word, *sipur* (story), it was the final consonant. Perhaps she refrained from writing the initial consonant for *sipur*, as she did for the rest, because it would have meant repeating the same letter she used for the previous word (*sefer*). And because the initial letter for her carries the word's meaning, she preferred to discriminate between successive words by writing another letter. Accordingly, she may be able to segment the last consonant too, but makes do with the first one. The predominance of writing the initial letter suggests that her difficulty stems mainly from word segmentation, because the first sound is easier to segment.

In five words, Lizy seemed to be writing syllabically, that is, one letter per syllable. Thus, the number of random letters she added was not random, but rather phonologically determined. For *pil*, however, she wrote two letters despite its being monosyllabic. She did this probably because of the minimum quantity principle, described earlier: She viewed writing as requiring more than a single letter. For her, the random letter holds the place of a syllable when she is unable to represent its particular sound.

Dudi (Figure 14.4) writes phonetically without random letters (except for L instead of R). His letters represent the required, or close to the required, consonantal sounds. For instance, for *pil* (elephant), he wrote BL. Furthermore, not all required consonants are represented in his writing. Although all initial sounds were represented, the middle and final sounds were frequently missing, like when he wrote SL for *simla* (dress), and NM for *nemala* (ant).

There could be three reasons for the omission of consonants. First, children may fail to perform an accurate segmentation, omitting sounds harder to separate, like the final consonant in a CVC syllable. And indeed, writing SL for *simla* was a relatively frequent occurrence. Second, children may write syllabically, and suffice with a letter per syllable. Thus, for *sefer* (book) Dudi wrote SL and read the two letters as *se-fer*. Finally, children may feel satisfied having written a few of the required letters, and choose not to carry through the process to its end. This may explain Dudi's writing NM for *nemala* (ant).

The scale levels presented here are based on the assumption that progress in Hebrew writing is primarily determined by consonant writing. The major levels are of elementary-consonantal writing, intermediate-consonantal writing and advanced consonantal writing. Since we assumed that vowels are mastered later than an equivalent mastery of consonants, each level of consonant writing — elementary, intermediate and advanced — is divided into subcategories up to the equivalent vowel writing. Moreover, we assumed that children may progress in consonant writing while lagging behind in vowel writing so that they may use advanced consonant writing without any vowels.

The inconsistency and complexity of conventional vowel writing led us to expect a wide variety of vowel constructions, including overgeneralizing vowel writing in words where they should be missing, as well as using vowels in illegal positions (e.g., *H* in the middle of a word). Final letters were expected to be mastered late.

INTERMEDIATE CONSONANTAL WRITING: This category consisted of intermediate representation of the consonants. This level was defined as representing at least half of the consonants, but not all of them. It rarely includes a random letter, though it does include letters representing similar sounds (B for P, TS for S, etc.), or homophonic letters carrying the required sound (S instead of S*, see Appendix 14.1). This category was divided into three subcategories, according to the level of vowel representation: 7. no vowels; 8. elementary vowels; and 9. intermediate vowels. The examples are displayed in Figure 14.5.

Name (age)	Efrat (7) (5;9)	Adi (8) (5;9)	Yeela (9) (6;4)
Elephant pil PYL	PL	PYL	PYL
Ant nemala NMLH	ML	NML	NHLH
Book sefer SPR	SR	SHBR	SPHR
Story sipur SYPWR	SP	SWR	SPHR
To put lasim LS*YMf	LS	LSYM	LSM
Dress simla S*MLH	SL	SYML	SMLH

Figure 14.5. Examples of writing at intermediate consonantal level without (7), and with elementary (8), and with intermediate (9) vowels.

Efrat (Figure 14.5) represents most consonants by correct or by homophonic letters and uses no vowels (Level 7). Her performance is better than the previous example, in that she includes no consonant with inexact or incorrect sound value. Her performance was somewhat better on the first sound than on the rest. She missed the initial sound once, writing ML for *nemala* (ant). The middle and final sounds she ignored twice, as for *sipur* (story) she wrote SP, and for *simla* (dress) she wrote SL (S* represented by an homophonic letter).

Level 8 was assessed in intermediate writing of consonants along with elementary writing of vowels. The introduction of vowels signals a shift in the child's conception of written language, from consonantal to partly phonemic. Elementary vowel writing was assessed in children who used a vowel at least once, but who came up with, at most, only two types of vowel letters (e.g., *Y* and *H*). Frequently, children used the wrong vowel-letter, *H* instead of *Y* for instance, and/or placed the vowel in the wrong position, such as writing CVC as CCV.

Adi (Figure 14.5), illustrating Level 8, used the correct vowel *Y* for /i/ in two words, *pil* and *lasim*. However, she overgeneralized the usage of *Y* for /i/ by writing it in *simla*, conventionally written without that vowel, SMLH, both in "deficient" and in "plene" modes. She used the vowel *H*, but only incorrectly. She wrote *sefer* (book), with *H* after the *S*, while this vowel conventionally appears only at the final position of words. Similarly, she did not put an *H* at the end of *nemala* (ant) and *simla* (dress) where it is required to designate a feminine morpheme. With respect to consonants, she wrote only letters carrying the appropriate sounds, though not exactly obeying the conventional Hebrew orthography. For instance, in *lasim* she used a regular *M*, which should be a final *M*.

Level 9 designates an intermediate writing of both consonants and vowels. Intermediate levels are not yet entirely conventional: Most vowels are used, but some are missing or exchanged with other vowels, and at times they are incorrectly positioned. Consonants are mostly correct, but the orthographic system is not yet mastered. Final letters are replaced by regular ones, and homophonic letters are also used.

Ye'ela (Figure 14.5) erred on some consonants. In *lasim* and *simla* which are conventionally written with an S*, she used the more frequent homophonic letter -S. Finally, *lasim* that should end with a final *M*, was written with a regular *M*. Her vowel writing was again only partially correct. She appropriately used *Y* for /i/, in *pil*, but omitted it in *sipur* and *lasim*. She used *H* correctly at the end of *nemala* and *simla* but added it incorrectly in *sefer* (book) and *sipur* (story) to mark other vowel phonemes.

ADVANCED CONSONANTAL WRITING: This category composed of writings that included all consonants, either written with the required letters or with homophones. Final letters were sometimes replaced by regular letters. The category was divided into four subcategories, according to the level of vowel representation: 10. no vowels; 11. elementary vowels; 12. intermediate vowels; and 13. advanced vowels. The examples are displayed in Figure 14.6.

Noa (Figure 14.6) wrote only in consonants, all carrying the required sounds without vowels (Level 10). She exchanged the conventional S for its homophonic S* in *sefer* and *sipur*, and vice versa in *lasim* and *simla*. In addition, she ended *lasim* with a regular, rather than a final *M*.

Neta (Figure 14.6), illustrating advanced consonants and elementary vowel writing at Level 11, used several vowels, mostly in their required positions, but none of them was the required one. She systematically replaced the vowel *H* standing for /a/ by *A*. Thus, for *simla* that is written SMLH she wrote SMLA, and for *nemala* that is written NMLH she wrote NMLA. This occurred in other children's writings, and is interpreted by us as stemming from the letters' name. Note that *H* is called "Hey" and *A* is called "Aleph." Because Hebrew consonantal letters' names start regularly with the sound that they represent (Beth for /b/, Daleth for /d/, etc.) children may conclude that the sound /a/ is marked by Aleph, rather than by Hey (see, Levin, Korat, & Amsterdamer, 1995). In addition, Neta wrote *H* in *pil* instead of *Y* that stands for /i/, and she placed this *Y* where *H* is conventionally positioned, at the end of the word instead of in the middle. In contrast with her vowel difficulties, she wrote all consonants using either correct or homophonic letters.

Name (age)	Noa (10) (5;9)	Neta (11) (5;5)	Ayelet (12) (6;4)	Tom (13) (6;4)
Elephant pil PYL	PL בֿל	PLH פֿלה	PYL פֿיל	PYL פֿיל
Ant nemala NMLH	NML נמל	NMLA נמלא	NML נמל	NMLH נמלה
Book sefer SPR	S*PR שבר	SPR ספר	SPR ספֿר	SPR ספר
Story sipur SYPWR	S*PR שבר	SPAR ספאר	SYPWR סיפור	SYPWR סיפור
To put lasim LS*YMf	LSM לסב	LSM לסא	LSYMf לסים	LSYMf לסים
Dress simla S*MLH	SML סבל	SMLA סמלא	S*ML שמל	S*YMLH שמילה

Figure 14.6. Examples of writing at advanced consonantal level without (10), with elementary (11), with intermediate (12), and with advanced (13) vowels.

Ayelet (Figure 14.6), illustrating advanced consonants and intermediate vowel writing (Level 12) used two vowels, *Y* and *W*, correctly throughout her writings. Whereas many children at lower levels used *Y* for /i/, few used *W* for /u/. The later mastery of *W* may be related to the fact that *Y* stands mostly for one voweling sound /i/, whereas *W* stands for two /o/ and /u/. As for *H*, she omitted it altogether, showing her limited knowledge of the written morphological system. Ayelet also used another voweling system, that of diacritic marks, and did so partially correctly. She correctly marked the sounds /i/, /u/, and /a/, but failed on /e/. Her writing of consonants was perfect, including the correct use of regular and final letters, and the later acquired, word-specific knowledge as to which words are written with S and which with S*.

Tom (Figure 14.6) illustrates Level 13, the highest in our scale, of advanced consonant and vowel writing. Tom deviated from convention in one vowel and one consonant. He added Y to mark /i/ in simla, where it is omitted by convention, thus showing his lack of acquaintance with this particular word, and/or with the rule that Y regularly does not appear before a Shwa (a rule explicitly known mostly by experts such as language teachers). He replaced S for S* in lasim. Such a replacement is a local spelling mistake that is avoided only by having the written lexicon of that particular root.

No child in our sample of kindergartners succeeded in writing all six words correctly. Although these were mundane, simple words, well known to kindergartners, their spelling involved an advanced mastery of the complex system of AHWY vowels, the distinction between regular and final letters, and the correct choice between homophonic letters.

Two concluding remarks

I. CONSONANTS VS. VOWELS. Because in Hebrew the consonants carry the core meaning of the word, and concomitantly, because in Hebrew orthography vowels are relatively deficient, the question arises as to whether Hebrew preschoolers would represent consonants earlier than vowels. Such a trend was documented in a previous study based on a relatively limited sample of Hebrew-speaking children (Levin, Amsterdamer, & Korat, in press). A similar trend of acquiring consonants before vowels was reported by Kamii (1986), who studied English-speaking children. However, Ferreiro and Teberosky (1979) studying Spanish speakers, and Pontecorvo and Zucchermaglio (1990), examining Italian speakers, reported that some children go through a phase of syllabic writing when each syllable is marked by a vowel. Subsequently, syllabic writing grows into syllabic-alphabetic writing, representing either only the vowel or the consonant, or both. Finally, the children construct alphabetic writing, which converges with conventional writing in these languages.

Kamii attributed the difference between languages to prosodic factors, Spanish being syllable timed while English is stress-timed. Ferreiro claimed that English speakers do not write in vowels because their vowels stand for multiple pronunciations. We propose that Hebrew writers start with consonants because of the latter's morphological importance, and owing to the relative deficiency and/or obscurity of written Hebrew voweling system.

To compare vowel and consonant writing quantitatively, we used the writings of pil and nemala, conventionally written PYL and NMLH ("elephant" and "ant"). The word pil PYL is spelled with two consonants (PL) and one vowel (Y), and nemala NMLH with three consonants (NML) and one vowel (H). In these words, "plene" and "deficient" spellings converge. Note the complete representation of consonants and the deficient marking of vowels in nemala. The following analyses are based on 86 children who wrote at least some phonetic letters (Levels 6-13).

Our data clearly demonstrate that these children structured the spelling of consonants prior to that of vowels. Whereas 41 children spelled all five consonants correctly, only nine did so with the two vowels. Among the 41 who succeeded on consonants, seven also correctly spelled the vowels. In contrast, of the nine children who succeeded with vowels, only one mis-spelled a consonant. The earlier emergence of consonantal writing is apparent also in the following: Thirteen children spelled the words only with correct consonants, missing both vowels (i.e., writing PL and NML) but no child spelled the words only with correct vowels (i.e., writing Y and H).

II. AGE AND SES. The scale presented is assumed to capture a developmental process that is promoted by children's immersion in a literate culture. Hence, level of writing is expected to be related both to the children's age and to their exposure to, and experience with, books and print. We examined the effect of age on level of writing by calculating the average age of children whose writings were classified according to the major categories.

Table 14.1

Average age and SES status by level of writing

Level	Age	SES
I Symbolic graphic signs (n = 66)	5;11	-.11
II Random letters (n = 140)	6;1	-.17
III Elementary consonantal writing (n = 26)	6;0	+.11
VI Intermediate consonantal writing (n = 35)	6;0	+.45
V Advanced consonantal writing (n = 25)	6;0	+.62

Contrary to expectation, there was no relation between level of writing and age (see Table 14.1). Previous analyses based on similar scales revealed systematic increases in age with level of writing (e.g., Gombert & Fayol, 1992; Levin, Korat & Amsterdamer, 1995). The reason for this discrepant result may be twofold: In the present work the age range examined was relatively constrained, to about a year and a half, but in the former studies it was 2 to 3 years. Second, our sample included a wide range of socioeconomic strata, a factor that could have obscured the age effect.

SES was measured by averaging the Z scores for five variables: parents' education, parents' occupation, number of children in the family, number of people per room, and country of origin. The last variable was scored lower for families that immigrated to Israel from Islamic countries (Sephardic) than families coming from the West (Ashkenazi). Generally speaking, sephardic families are of a lower educational and economic levels in Israel. Consequently, country of origin is considered relevant to SES assessment. The relation we found between SES and a child's writing level is interpreted as an outcome of the relationship between home literacy and SES. In sum, writing level, assessed by our scales, is related both to age and exposure to home literacy.

The quantitative study: Early writing and its relation to emergent and to formal literacy

Two questions concerning early writing motivated our quantitative analyses: To what extent is early writing related to preschool emergent literacy, and whether it contributes to predicting acquisition of conventional reading and writing in school. Early attempts at writing may merely represent a developmental curiosity with little significance for mature literacy skills. Alternatively it may constitute an essential foundation for these skills. Emergent literacy was measured here by Clay's (1987) Concepts About Print, adapted to Hebrew by Wohl (1986). It tested print-related knowledge such as the ability to recognize in a book a word and a letter, to identify where one begins and ends reading a line, a page, or a book. This factor has already been found to be related to the child's home literacy on the one hand (Box & Aldridge, 1993), and to later reading acquisition, on the other (Day & Day, 1984; Lomax & McGee, 1987).

Writers

The study was carried out in two waves, the first at the end of the kindergarten school year (May-June 1991), and the second at the end of first grade (May-June 1992). A total of 349 children, 173 boys and 176 girls, were recruited from 20 kindergartens in the Haifa urban area, selected to represent a wide range of socioeconomic levels. Their mean age was 6.0, with a range of 5.5-7.2, in years and months. A year later, 313 of these children were re-examined, 154 boys and 159 girls, studying in 14 classes in five schools. The rest were excluded because they either left the area or were retained in kindergarten.

Tests

WAVE 1: KINDERGARTEN TESTS. In the first wave,[3] four tests were administered individually to each child: The Writing Test described earlier; Concepts About Print were assessed by a Hebrew adaptation (Wohl, 1986) of Clay's (1987) test. In this test the possible range of scores was 0-16. The mean score gained was M = 10.66, s.d. = 3.69, and the range 1-16. Vocabulary was assessed with the Peabody Picture Vocabulary Test (Hebrew version, Solberg & Nevo, 1979). The test contained 110 items of increasing difficulty, scored according to the author's manual. The mean score was M = 50.10, s.d. = 6.98, and the range 19-66. Intellectual ability was measured by Raven's Colored Progressive Matrices (Raven, 1986, Sets A and B). The mean score gained was M = 9.77; s.d. = 3.76; and the range 1-23.

WAVE 2: 1ST GRADE TESTS. Nine tests were developed for the second wave[4]: four tests of spelling, two of oral word reading, and three of reading compre-

---

[3] Many tests were administered, but only four mentioned here will be examined in this chapter.

[4] As above, more tests were administered.

hension. Spelling and reading comprehension tests were administered collectively to entire classes. Word reading tests were administered individually. The spelling tests included a dictation test composed of 20 common words; a homophone dictation test that included 20 words (each having a homophonic-heterographic counterpart, like the word *kar*, that may mean "cold" or "pillow," spelled QR or KR, respectively). Each homophone was embedded in a sentence read to the children; an orthographic choice test (Olson, Kligl, Davidson, & Foltz, 1985) for visual word recognition was produced by us in Hebrew. Children were presented with a list of 20 words, each spelled in two ways, and were asked to select the correct spelling; a Homophone Choice test was composed of 16 sentences, each including two homophonic words spelled differently, such as the word *kol*, written either KL or QWL, meaning "all" and "voice," respectively. Children were asked to choose the item that matched the sentence in which these two words were embedded. A spelling score was computed by averaging the Z-scores computed for each of the four tests.

The Oral Word-Reading measures included one untimed, the other timed, Oral Word Reading. The untimed test, measuring reading accuracy, was composed of a list of 114 written words, including diacritic marks. The words varied in length and syllabic complexity, with the shorter, simpler words appearing at the beginning of the list. The timed test, measuring reading speed and accuracy was composed of a list of 56 written words. The children were asked to read aloud the words as quickly as possible and were stopped after one minute. A word reading score was computed by averaging the Z-scores computed for each of the two tests.

The tests of Reading Comprehension included a Sentence Comprehension test composed of 21 sentences, varying in length, followed by a comprehension question in multiple-choice format; an Expository Paragraph Comprehension test, and a Narrative Comprehension test, each composed of three to four passages. Each passage was followed by 5-7 questions to be answered by selecting a true or false response. The total number of questions was 36. A reading comprehension score was computed by adding the raw scores across the three tests.

Intercorrelations within and between grades

Table 14.2 presents intercorrelations between children's scores obtained in kindergarten and in first grade. The intercorrelations support three general conclusions: First, early writing was significantly related to general early literacy, measured by Concepts about Print ($r = .45$, $p < .001$), to vocabulary measured by Peabody ($r = .23$, $p < .001$), and to general IQ measured by Raven ($r = .33$, $p < .001$). These results are in line with conceiving early writing as promoted by children's exposure to, and early experience with books and print; with viewing writing as a linguistic competency, and with the assumption that early writing, just like later, is a problem-solving process.

Second, children's achievements in reading and writing in first grade were significantly intercorrelated, a finding already well established in the literature (e.g., Shanahan, 1984; Zutell, 1992). Here, this finding primarily serves to support the validity of our Hebrew measures for Grade 1 spelling, word reading, and reading comprehension. As expected, spelling was significantly correlated with oral word reading ($r = .58$, $p < .001$) and with reading comprehension ($r = .54$, $p < .001$). Word reading, in turn, was significantly correlated with reading comprehension ($r = .47$, $p < .001$).

Table 14.2

Intercorrelations between measures of Writing Level, Concepts About Print, Literacy and IQ (n = 259)

	2	3	4	5	6	7
1. Writing (K)	.45**	.33**	.23**	.40**	.28**	.42**
2. Print C (K)		.31**	.35**	.33**	.21**	.59**
3. Raven (K)			.20**	.18*	.12	.31**
4. Peabody (K)				.22**	.07	.37**
5. Spelling (1)					.58**	.54**
6. Word Re (1)						.47**
7. Read Com (1)						–

**$p < .001$, *$p < .01$

Note.   Writing=Level of writing in Writing Test;
Print C = Concepts About Print (Clay, 1985) adapted;
Raven = IQ by Colored Progressive Matrices (Raven, 1986);
Peabody = Peabody Picture Vocabulary Test (Solberg & Nevo, 1979) adapted;
Spelling = Score combined across 4 tests: Regular dictation, Homophone dictation, Orthographic choice, and Homophone choice.
Word Re = Score combined across 2 tests: Untimed and Timed oral word reading.
Reading Com = Score combined across 3 tests: Sentence comprehension, Paragraph comprehension: Expository, and Paragraph comprehension: Narrative.
(K) = Administered in Kindergarten; (1)=Administered in Grade 1.

Finally, early writing and concepts about print, both assessed in kindergarten, were significantly correlated with reading-writing achievements in first grade. They were correlated with spelling ($r = .40$, $p < .001$, $r = .33$, $p < .001$), with word reading ($r = .28$, $p < .001$, $r = .21$, $p < .001$), and with reading comprehension ($r = .42$, $p < .001$, $r = .59$, $p < .001$), respectively. In contrast, Vocabulary and IQ measured in kindergarten, were significantly correlated with reading comprehension ($r = .37$, $p < .001$, $r = .31$, $p < .001$), and with spelling ($r = .22$, $p < .001$, $r = .18$, $p < .01$), but not with word reading ($r = .12$, ns, $r = .07$, ns). It can be seen that both early writing and print concepts consistently outperformed general vocabulary and IQ in the prediction of Grade 1 reading and spelling.

Predicting reading-writing acquisition from early writing

Having suggested that early writing reflects, in part, linguistic competency and general problem-solving ability, as well as general orientation to books and print assessed by Concepts About Print, the question arises as to whether early writing makes a unique contribution to Grade 1 reading and spelling, or is merely a proxy for these more general factors.

We expected to discover such a unique contribution, particularly to spelling, less so to word reading, and least to reading comprehension. Reading comprehension, being a complex competency (Stanovich, 1993) was expected to be explained more than spelling and word reading by Vocabulary, IQ, and Concepts About Print. Table 14.3 presents hierarchical regressions predicting each of these Grade 1 achievement measures. After removing the variance explained by Vocabulary, IQ and Concepts About Print, level of word writing in kindergarten still accounted for significant variance, in spelling (7%), word reading (4%) and reading comprehension (2%) in first grade.

Table 14.3
Hierarchical regressions predicting first-grade spelling, word reading, and reading comprehension

	Statistic	
Step and variable assessed in kindergarten	**R^2 changes**	**F to enter**
	First grade Spelling	
1. Peabody Vocabulary	.075	10.54***
Raven IQ		
2. Concepts About Print	.059	17.85***
3. Early Writing	.066	21.49***
	First grade Oral Word Reading	
1. Peabody Vocabulary	.014	1.89
Raven IQ		
2. Concepts About Print	.033	9.15**
3. Early Writing	.044	12.64***
	First grade Reading Comprehension	
1. Peabody Vocabulary	.190	31.17***
Raven IQ		
2. Concepts About Print	.197	84.93***
3. Early Writing	.018	8.13**

***$p < .001$, **$p < .005$
Note. Regressions are based on $n = 256$.

These data indicate that preschoolers' early attempts at writing are far from mere developmental curiosity. In fact, our interest in the issue of predictive validity was prompted by colleagues' skepticism regarding the relevance of preschooler's playful attempts at writing to conventional in-school literacy skills. Not only were we reassured to find consistently significant correlations but found ourselves pleasantly surprised at the strength of the relationship. Indeed, the finding that early writing outperformed general verbal and non-verbal ability attests to the importance of domain-specific knowledge in early literacy and reaffirms the modular nature of expertise in early reading and writing. The finding that early writing was not simply a stand-in for general concepts about print points to the importance of both productive and receptive aspects of written language understanding.

Early writing, not unsurprisingly, made the strongest unique contribution to in-school spelling. The contribution to word decoding no doubt also reflects a child's understanding of the alphabetic principle. The more modest relationship between our preschool writing scale and reading comprehension emphasizes the greater role of general problem solving skills and linguistic competence in the latter. Collectively, these relationships confirm the fact that literacy begins well before formal schooling.

Educational implications

It should be made clear in advance that educational implications are not directly derived from experimental findings. Such implications are based on an apriori theoretical prism, through which the findings are viewed. The interpreted findings are then taken as supportive of educational implications that are consistent with the theory. This circular state of affairs means that the very same data would lead to different implications by researchers differing in their theoretical outlook. Our framework is an integration of the developmental model of Piaget, and the socio-historical model of Vygotsky. We view our data as supportive of the claim that children construct their knowledge of the written system in their attempts to make sense of that cultural object. This in no way denies the critical mediating role of informal and semi-formal input of parents and peers concerning the written code.

The predictive contribution of the level of preschoolers' writing to their progress in reading and writing in first grade, could be taken to mean that children with a low writing level at preschool, are at risk of failing in reading and writing in school. It should be stressed that reading and writing, are the major goals of schooling in first grade, and difficulties in acquiring these skills can have long lasting negative effects for children's schooling careers. Consequently, it could have been implied that educators should diagnose early preschoolers' writing level and institute well structured, formal, intervention to promote the writing of the weaker students, so as to improve their readiness for school, hoping to immunize them against future failing. This is not the educational implication we endorse.

We believe that formal assessment of children's level of writing or reading should be postponed to school. It should be done late enough to allow children first to try cope with this endeavor in their own way and pace. It should be early enough so that the gap between students does not become too vast to overcome. Formal teaching should also not take place in preschool. It should be postponed to a time when the majority of students can gain from it. Does this mean that our data does not have any educational-pedagogical-practical implications? This is not our view.

We believe that preschool teachers should develop their understanding of children's process of gaining insight of the written system. Then they will respect the cognitive work that children put into this endeavor. Knowledgeable teachers will tend to encourage children to explore writing (or reading, for that matter) without too hasty attempts to impose on them the mastery of conventional writing. What is viewed as ignorant errors by the less insightful teacher (e.g., the mixture of drawing and letter writing; the deletion of all vowels by a child with advanced consonantal writing) can be interpreted by the educated teacher as serious and creative attempts on the part of the child to make sense of the cultural representational system of writing.

The more knowledgeable the kindergarten teacher, the better she or he may be able to provide the appropriate scaffolding for the child. Children who write in pseudo-letters and children who struggle with phoneme-grapheme correspondences, will find different experiences as relevant, challenging and fruitful. The observant kindergarten teacher will be able to offer differential activities that will suit their different needs.

School teachers, who formally introduce children to reading and writing can also gain from insightful understanding of children's early attempts to write. Rather then viewing the newcomers to school as *tabula rasa* or as all having the same knowledge base, and expect them to progress neck to neck, these teachers will respect the concepts that children have constructed, via transaction with parents and teachers in preschool, and be aware of individual differences.

While we do not recommend formal instruction in writing or reading in preschool, we whole-heartedly encourage the promotion of literacy of preschoolers. Writing, as a communicative-representational competence, can be smoothly integrated into children's play. Children can write signs, recipes, notes, cards, or even texts as part of their sociodramatic games. After all, they frequently play adult roles, and the adults they know frequently use writing and reading in functional ways. To encourage children to play with and communicate via graphical notations, to the extent that it suits their needs, would lead them to explore the conventional writing system, as well as invent and try out nonconventional notations. The more curious they will become with respect to writing, the more they will discover the functionality of writing, and the more they will gain feelings of self efficacy in this area, the more literate they will grow.

The facilitation of early literacy in preschool is particularly important among underprivileged communities. The correlation we found between SES and level of writing, suggests that children growing up in less literate or less enriching homes are delayed in school-related competencies even prior to formal schooling. To close the emerging gap we must facilitate the development of literacy in preschool, particularly among children of lower SES.

Finally, we would like to stress that promotion of literacy should be a dominant but not an exclusive goal of preschool. Preschool should foster other cognitive competencies (e.g., mathematics), social reasoning, artistic sensitivity, and motor skills, to mention but a few important goals. This is particularly important for children who develop slow in literacy. A pluralistic approach helps to provide each child with experiences of efficacy, which would promote the child's motivation to explore, experience and learn.

Appendix 14.1

Hebrew letters as presented by Latin letters in describing written forms:

א	= alef	ב	= beth	ג	= gimmel	ד	= daleth	ה	= heh
ו	= waw	ז	= zayin	ח	= het	ט	= tech	י	= yod
כ	= kaf	ל	= lamed	מ	= mem	נ	= nun	ס	= samekh
ע	= a'yin	פ	= peh	צ	= zadik	ק	= kuf	ר	= reish
ש	=Sh or S=shin			ת	= taf				

Note. 1. Teth and taf which have the same sound /t/ are noted by the same letter (T).

2. Shin is noted by Sh when pronounced /sh/, and by S* when pronounced /s/.

3. M, N, C, P, K have two written forms: Regular and final. When a final letter is used it is maked by f (e.g., M$_f$ for final M).

— 15 —
THE PARADOX OF WRITING APPREHENSION

Robert Madigan, Patricia Linton, and Susan Johnson
University of Alaska Anchorage

Many adults feel anxious when confronted with writing tasks, experiencing self-deprecating thoughts and concerns about how their written work will be received. For these individuals, writing is an unpleasant, unrewarding activity that they actively avoid. Daly and Miller (1975a) proposed the term *writing apprehension* to describe these reactions and developed a self-report inventory to assess it.

Writing apprehension has been the subject of considerable research since that time, much of it reviewed by Daly (1985). In general, two dramatic and consistent effects of writing apprehension have been documented: distress associated with writing and a profound distaste for the process. Both lead to marked avoidance behaviors. For apprehensive writers, avoiding potential writing demands can be an objective in selecting a college class (Daly & Miller, 1975b), choosing a college major (Daly & Shamo, 1978), or making a career decision (Daly & Shamo, 1976). These avoidance behaviors, and the pain accompanying writing, persist despite the fact that the actual skill of apprehensive writers may differ little from that of their peers in the types of writing typically required in college and on the job. Faigley, Daly, and Witte (1981) found no differences in the quality of argumentative essays written by apprehensive and nonapprehensive writers, although the two groups did differ on more personal, narrative essays.

It should be stressed that the literature on writing apprehension is complex, and many variables appear to determine whether or not a difference is found between the writing of apprehensive and non apprehensive writers. Writing apprehension is most likely to affect writing quality when time constraints are in place (Kean, Gylnn, & Britton, 1987), or when the topic requires a narration of personal experiences (Faigley et al., 1981). But the fact that performance differences disappear in other situations, such as argumentative essay writing, suggests to us that afflicted writers may not have fundamental writing skill deficiencies. This poses an interesting paradox about writing apprehension: On the one hand, apprehensive writers report distress over their writing abilities and, on the other, objective ratings of their writing fail to find serious, consistent shortcomings.

This chapter reports several new findings that clarify the nature of writing apprehension and address this apparent paradox. In the first study, a resolution to the paradox was sought through a new, fine-grained analysis of the writing behavior of apprehensive and nonapprehensive students. By analyzing the fluency of text production and writers' syntactic sophistication, we looked for evidence that would support the apprehensive writers' belief that writing is somehow harder for them or that they are less skilled at it. The data from this study suggested a new model of writing apprehension, which was tested in two additional experiments.

Experiment 1

This experiment examined the writing of apprehensive and nonapprehensive writers to determine whether there were differences in fluency, syntactic complexity, or holistic quality of the work when writers were given unlimited time to produce simple expository essays. The fluency and syntactic complexity analyses reported here represent new approaches to searching for subtle deficits in the writing skills of apprehensive writers that might justify their negative convictions.

Fluency
Fluency, the speed with which words are produced, has not previously been examined in connection with writing apprehension. It is a potentially important dimension of the writing experience for apprehensive writers. If writing is truly harder for apprehensive writers, then words may come more slowly to them. Apprehensive writers may produce texts equal in quality to those of nonapprehensive writers, but do so with greater effort, making writing more painful. In Experiment 1, a word processing program logged the length of time writers paused before producing each word during the composing process to allow the relation between fluency and writing apprehension to be examined.

Syntactic complexity
In addition, the essays produced by the participants were subjected to holistic quality and syntactic feature analyses. Because the essays did not involve personal narration, we did not expect to find holistic quality differences associated with writing apprehension. Syntactic complexity was another matter. Syntactic complexity refers to the structural characteristics of individual sentences in written works. It may be that the distress felt by apprehensive writers results in simpler prose, and therefore measures of syntactic complexity might reveal evidence of actual writing deficits in apprehensive writers. Such measures offer the best chance of detecting any fine-grained differences in the texts produced by apprehensive and nonapprehensive writers.

In fact, some syntactic differences have been reported. Daly (1977) found that apprehensive writers produce fewer words in their essays, use relatively fewer commas, and relatively fewer adverbs. Burgoon and Hale (1983) found that apprehensive writers use shorter words. However, Faigley et al. (1981) found such syntactic differences associated with writing apprehension only when the assigned essay topics required narration of personal experiences and not when topics were more impersonal, as in argumentative essays. In this study we brought new measures of syntactic complexity to bear on the works of apprehensive and nonapprehensive writers to determine whether sentence-level structural differences might be detected when expository essays were written on impersonal topics.

The selection of a measure of syntactic complexity was based on Cheung and Kemper's (1992) review of 11 different approaches. One promising technique examined the proportion of *left-branching constructions*. A left-branching subordinate construction is a clause or verbal phrase that occurs before the main verb, as in the sentence "The person *who owns the car* is here." It can be contrasted with a *right-branching subordinate construction*: "Fettuccine is the dish *that I usually order*." Kemper (1988) found that sophisticated writers make more extensive use of left-branching syntactic constructions. A left-branching construction requires more planning on the writer's part because the point of the sentence must be delayed while the left-branching elaboration is developed (Kemper, Kynette, Rash, Sprott, & O'Brien, 1989). We calculated the proportion of left-branching constructions in the writing of apprehensive and nonapprehensive participants as a further comparison of the syntactic complexity of the two groups.

Method

PARTICIPANTS. A total of 75 students from psychology classes at the University of Alaska, Anchorage, received extra credit for participating in the experiment. Fifty-eight participants, whose writing apprehension scores on the Daly and Miller (1975a) measure were in the upper and lower thirds of the sample formed the apprehensive and nonapprehensive groups compared in this study. The 30 low-apprehension writers had a median age of 24; there were 20 men and 10 women. The high-apprehension group contained 28 writers, 9 men and 19 women, with a median age of 21. Both groups contained students from freshmen to seniors.

PROCEDURE. Students wrote essays in response to two assigned topics: "What governmental agency do you have the strongest feelings about — either positive or negative? Analyze the source of those feelings," and "Analyze the most important skills for a new college instructor."

One essay was written in a quiet room; only the data from that condition are reported here. The second essay was written in a "distraction" condition in which the writers heard irrelevant speech played through earphones at a moderate level as they wrote. The speech was part of a symposium on cognitive psychology recorded at a conference — students typically reported that it was dry and uninteresting. Writers were instructed to ignore the tape and write an essay that addressed the assigned topic. The data from the distraction condition is analyzed later in this chapter. The essay topics were counterbalanced across the two writing conditions.

Participants were given unlimited time to write their essays, although most took less than 30 minutes for each. Immediately after finishing an essay, students completed a thought-listing questionnaire used to assess the self-talk they recalled engaging in during the writing process. The measure was patterned after one developed for use with test anxiety by Sarason, Sarason, Keefe, B. Hayes, and Shearin (1986). Further details and findings about the self-talk measure are presented later in the paper.

The essays were typed at a computer terminal using a word processing program that stored two time measures associated with the production of each word: a pause time, measured from the end of the last word to the first letter in the current word; and a typing time, measured from the first letter in the current word to the word delimiter at its end (e.g., a space, comma, or period). The program allowed writers to perform simple editing operations, such as inserting and deleting text. The pause times were used in the fluency analyses.

Results

The results reported here are from writing samples collected in the condition where students wrote in a quiet room. The first set of analyses examined the pause time between words in writers' essays. Pause times were examined for two different syntactic structures, noun phrases and right-branching subordinate clauses.

NOUN PHRASE FLUENCY OF APPREHENSIVE WRITERS. Noun phrases were selected because they typically represent a single, specific concept ("the big, red barn"). The average pause time per word within a noun clause is a measure of the lexical access time required to assemble that particular idea in the text.

Only simple noun phrases found after the main verb and consisting of at most an article, adjectives, and a noun were examined in this analysis. Several types of more complex constructions were excluded: phrases beginning with a preposition, phrases with participles or gerunds, and phrases in which editing operations took place before the phrase was completed. In cases where the noun phrase was substantially repeated within the essay, only the first occurrence was analyzed.

The pause time for each phrase was calculated as the total of the pause times for each word in the phrase divided by the number of words. The distribution of these times is highly skewed, with most times under a second but some much longer. Because of this, we used the median of a sample of seven noun phrases as the typical pause time for each writer. If fewer than seven noun phrases were available, all were used in the calculation of the median.

The results showed that nonapprehensive writers produced noun phrases slightly faster than apprehensives, .86 versus 1.07 seconds per word, *s.d.* = .37 and .34, respectively. However, this difference was not statistically significant ($p > .08$). There was no convincing evidence of superior lexical access by nonapprehensive writers.

RIGHT-BRANCHING CLAUSE FLUENCY OF APPREHENSIVE WRITERS. The second fluency analysis examined right-branching subordinate clauses. Because the right-branching constructions occur after the main verb, they may reflect less preplanning than earlier clauses and therefore are more likely to indicate the time required to spontaneously generate a new proposition in the text.

Pause times for right-branching subordinate clauses were determined for the first four words of each eligible clause. Word 1 was always a transition word beginning the clause such as a subordinating conjunction (that, when, if, etc.) or a relative pronoun (who, which, etc.), and the next sequential words in the clause were identified as Words 2, 3, and 4. If a transition word was omitted ("Here is the car [that] I want"), the first word of the clause ("I") was called Word 2 and Word 1 was considered to be missing for that observation. Clauses that contained editing operations initiated before the clause was completed were excluded from this analysis. The writer's typical pause time was taken to be the median of the pause times observed for the first five eligible right-branching clauses in their essay. If there were fewer than five clauses, then all available clauses were used.

In Figure 15.1, the pause times observed for the first four words of right-branching clauses are presented. Like the noun phrase data, there are no significant group differences, $F(1,37) < 1$. Taken together, the two fluency analyses revealed no basis for apprehensive students' belief that writing is somehow harder for them than for other students.

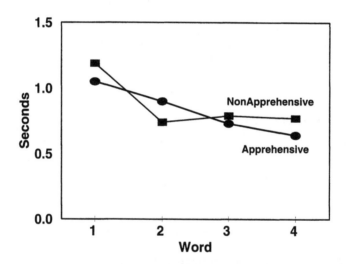

Figure 15.1. Mean pause times for the first four words of right-branching clauses in the essays of apprehensive and nonapprehensive writers. Pause times are measured from the last character of one word to the first character of the next and exclude typing times. Word 1 was always a transition word such as "where" or "that."

HOLISTIC QUALITY RATINGS. The writing samples analyzed above were given holistic writing quality ratings by two independent raters following the procedure described by Johnson, Linton, and Madigan (1994). Writing quality was defined as "a subjective term, referring to the writer's ability to express thoughts in a clear, organized and interesting manner." This holistic approach to writing quality differs from the analytical approach of Ransdell and Levy (chapter 5 in this volume) in which raters are asked to make 13 separate judgments of textual features that are then summed together to arrive at a final writing score. In the holistic approach, judges sort the essays into six groups based on their overall impression of the quality of expression. Holistic judgments have generally proven to be reliable and useful measures of writing quality (White, 1985) and have previously been used to assess the work of writing apprehensive people (Faigley et al., 1981).

There were no significant quality differences between the two groups. On a 6-point quality scale, apprehensive participants wrote essays with a mean rating of 3.31 (s.d. = 1.96); nonapprehensives had a mean of 3.90 (s.d. = 2.58). Although the mean quality ratings of essays written by apprehensive writers were somewhat lower, there was not a significant difference ($p > .09$) in the holistic quality of essays from the two groups.

SYNTACTIC COMPLEXITY. The last analysis compared the sentence-level syntactic structure of the essays written by the two groups. Each sentence in the texts was parsed to identify syntactic structures containing verb or verb-like constructions. These included main and subordinate clauses, as well as phrases constructed with gerunds, participles, and infinitives. The proportion of left-branching constructions was calculated and found to be .15 (s.d. = .09) for apprehensive writers and .14 (s.d. = .08) for nonapprehensives. The difference is not significant.

Discussion

In Experiment 1, participants were given unlimited time to write an expository essay. Despite the application of new methods of textual analysis, no support was found for a writing deficiency view of writing apprehension. On every measure, apprehensive writers performed slightly, but not significantly, lower than nonapprehensives. There was simply no evidence that the writing of apprehensive students is deficient in any way when compared to the writing of their nonapprehensive peers. The overall finding of Experiment 1 is that the essays of apprehensive and nonapprehensive writers are indistinguishable. The data serve only to underline the paradoxical discrepancy between the subjective beliefs of apprehensive writers and objective analyses of their writing skill.

One final point about Experiment 1 deserves comment. The final sample of apprehensive and nonapprehensive participants contained a sex imbalance with a preponderance of females in the apprehensive group and males in the nonapprehensive group. This appears to be a characteristic of this particular sample and not a general finding. Daly (1985) reviewed previous studies on gender differences in writing apprehension and found them to be inconsistent. Other work by us, such as the data set reported in Experiment 2, has not shown a gender effect.

Experiment 2

In Experiment 2, the search for a resolution to the paradox of writing apprehension is extended to factors outside the writing process. In planning this experiment, we turned to research on test anxiety to identify possible variables that might give rise to writing apprehension. In particular, we examined the role of ongoing, negative thoughts during the writing process as a possible mediator of apprehension. Wine (1980) developed a model of test anxiety that proposes such a mediating process. In her "direction of attention" hypothesis, she suggested that people who experience test anxiety turn cognitive processes inward and become preoccupied with negative thoughts about their situation. The experience of test anxiety is then directly mediated by these unpleasant distracting thoughts. Several studies present data consistent with Wine's hypothesis (Galassi, Frierson, & Sharer, 1981; Sarason, 1984). If writing apprehension involves a similar mediating mechanism, then the apprehensive person would be one who engages in self-deprecating, negative thoughts during the writing process; the net effect is to produce writing apprehension. Experiment 2 examines the possible role of negative self-talk as a mediator of writing apprehension.

Structural equation modeling (Hayduk, 1987) was used to examine several models of possible relations. This technique can be a powerful way to explore complex relations among a number of variables. For this study, causal modeling was applied to writing apprehension, holistic writing quality, and two additional clusters of variables representing self-talk and writing aptitude.

Self-talk variables

Following Wine's (1980) lead, we selected two measures related to self-talk during the writing process. When participants finished writing, they were asked to recall self-talk that may have occurred by completing a questionnaire. Trait anxiety was also measured as a potential mediator of self-talk patterns. Watson and Clark (1984) reviewed evidence showing that trait anxiety affects the way people react to stress by increasing distracting cognitions. Thus it is possible that trait anxiety may contribute directly to writing apprehension by increasing negative self talk.

Writing aptitude variables

Two measures of writing aptitude were included in the modeling analysis to examine their relationship to writing apprehension. A measure of working memory capacity was selected because of evidence linking it to writing skill (Kellogg, chapter 3 in this volume; Madigan, Johnson, & Linton, 1994; Ransdell & Levy, chapter 5 in this volume). The language usage subtest of the AS-SET test (American College Testing Program, 1983) was included as a second indicator of writing skill. This test measures knowledge useful for effective writing, such as word usage conventions, punctuation, and grammatical rules. In the structural equations, language usage and working memory measures were combined into a writing aptitude measure and related to writing apprehension.

Figure 15.2 shows the conceptual framework for the experiment. Broken lines in the figure indicate the specific paths to be examined in the study. The design allows both writing-related and self-talk variables to be simultaneously evaluated for their contributions to writing apprehension.

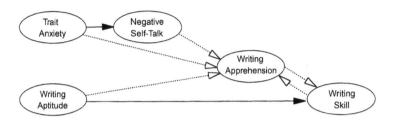

Figure 15.2. Structural models examined in Experiment 2. Broken lines indicate paths to be tested in the analysis. Solid lines represent paths present in all models.

Method

WRITERS. First-semester English composition students (49) and freshmen general psychology students (52) participated in the study. English composition students were part of a larger study and were paid $25 for their participation; psychology students received optional course credit. The sample of 101 students included 38 men and 67 women. Ages ranged from 18 to 58, with a mean age of 22.8.

MEASURES AND PROCEDURE. A writing sample was collected from each of the students in response to the following prompt: "What government agency or program do you have the strongest feelings about — whether positive or negative? Analyze the source of those feelings." The samples were given independent holistic quality ratings by two experienced English composition instructors following the procedure described by Johnson et al. (1994).

The thought-listing measure described in Experiment 1 was used to assess student self-talk during the composing process. The questionnaire contained 8 negative and 10 positive statements. Students were asked to check any statement that was "an idea, thought, or feeling that you had while you were working on your writing assignment." Examples of a positive and a negative statement were "I am doing a good job," and "I'd rather that other people didn't read this." The number of negative thoughts was used in the structural equations.

The Daly and Miller (1975a) measure of writing apprehension was administered. Eysenck's Neuroticism Scale (Eysenck & Eysenck, 1968) was used as an index of trait anxiety. The working memory measure was modified from one developed by Daneman and Carpenter (1980), which required participants to read a series of sentences out loud, remembering the last word of each sentence. This approach has been widely used in the studies of the relation between working memory and reading comprehension (Daneman &

Carpenter, 1983; Dixon, LeFevre, & Twilley, 1988; King & Just, 1991; Mac-Donald, Just, & Carpenter, 1992). It differs somewhat from the measure used by Ransdell and Levy in chapter 5 of this volume, which uses a language production task to measure working memory.

Writers in this experiment saw sentences that varied from 9 to 15 words in length presented on a computer screen. After finishing a group of sentences, writers were prompted to recall the last words of each in any order except that the last word of the last sentence could not be given first. Three practice sets were provided, with two sentences in each set. Writers were subsequently given additional sets: first one with three sentences, then four sentences, and finally five sentences. Three replications of each set size were presented. Writers' scores were the total number of last words correctly recalled. All measures used in the study were individually administered in a testing session lasting about 3 hours.

Results and discussion

The correlation matrix for the six variables is presented in Table 15.1. Five structural models were constructed to test the paths identified in Figure 15.2; the details of the models and their fit to the data are given in Table 15.2. A complete presentation of Model 1, the most parsimonious explanation of the data, is shown in Figure 15.3. All paths shown have coefficients that are significant ($p < .05$); other possible paths identified in Figure 15.3 were not significant.

Table 15.1
Correlations among the variables of Experiment 2

	Variable				
	2	**3**	**4**	**5**	**6**
1. Eysenck N Scale	.05	.09	.34*	.21*	.02
2. Working Memory Span		.41*	-.03	-.04	.31*
3. Language Usage Test			.05	-.11	.38*
4. Negative Self-Talk				.48*	-.10
5. Writing Apprehension					-.19
6. Writing Sample Rating					

* $p < .05$.

The model of Figure 15.3 depicts writing apprehension as an experience heavily influenced by negative self-talk, a finding compatible with Wine's (1980) proposal for test anxiety. The path between trait anxiety and negative self-talk supports the conclusion of Watson and Clark (1984) that trait anxiety predisposes people to react to stress with negative, distracting cognitions. Actual writing skill in this sample is best predicted by working memory capacity and language usage skill, not writing apprehension. The fact that there was no significant path between apprehension and writing skill confirms the findings of Experiment 1 and other previous work.

Experiment 2 suggests a resolution to the paradox of writing apprehension. It appears that writing apprehension may be a self-inflicted wound that is not systematically related to objective writing skill. Apprehensive writers experience genuine distress in writing situations, but the distress arises not because their writing skills are dramatically worse than those of their peers but rather because of critical, self-deprecating thoughts that occur during the writing process. We now turn to a third experiment that provides additional elaboration and clarification of this view.

Table 15.2
Alternative models for writing apprehension

Path From	To	Model 1	2	3	4	5
Trait Anxiety	⇨Self-Talk	.41*	.41*	.42*	.41*	.42*
Aptitude	⇨Writing Skill	.61*	.59*	.61*	.61*	.62*
Self-Talk	⇨Apprehension	.56*	.57*	.55*	.55*	.56*
Apprehension	⇨Writing Skill	–	-.20	–	–	–
Writing Skill	⇨Apprehension	–	–	-.19	–	–
Trait Anxiety	⇨Apprehension	–	–	–	-.03	–
Aptitude	⇨Apprehension	–	–	–	–	-.19
Coefficient of Determination		.48	.48	.48	.48	.51
Chi Square		7.13	4.07	3.92	7.07	4.50
df		11	10	10	10	10
Adjusted Goodness of Fit		.96	.97	.97	.95	.97

*$p < .05$.

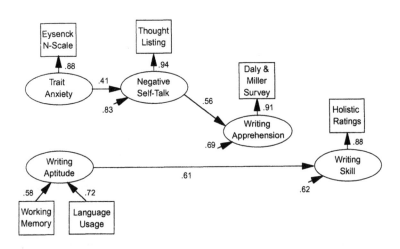

Figure 15.3. The structural model best describing the covariance matrix of Experiment 2. Test reliabilities were used to establish paths between latent variables and observed measures except in the case of working memory and language usage. All paths shown have coefficients significant at $p < .05$.

Experiment 3

We next compared reports by apprehensive and nonapprehensive writers of self-talk patterns during writing assignments that placed different demands on the writer. Students wrote two essays, one in a quiet room and the other while listening to a lecture presented over a headset. Pilot testing had indicated that writing in this distraction condition was difficult and demanding.

We suspected that the distraction condition might differentially affect the self-talk patterns of apprehensive and nonapprehensive writers. This prediction was derived from the significant path shown in Figure 15.3 between trait anxiety and negative self-statements. To the extent that negative self-statements during writing are stable characteristics of apprehensive writers, those afflicted may not be sensitive to the objective difficulty of the writing task and instead may show similar negative self-talk patterns regardless of the assignment. Nonapprehensive writers, on the other hand, might worry more about their performance when the task is more challenging. In Experiment 3, we expected that only nonapprehensive writers would report more negative self-statements under the high demand of the distraction condition.

Results and discussion

Experiment 3 was carried out at the same time the data for Experiment 1 were collected. The relevant methodological details were described earlier. Immediately after writing essays in a quiet condition or a distraction condition, students completed a thought-listing questionnaire to report any thoughts or ideas they experienced during the writing process. These data are presented in Figure 15.4.

Apprehensive writers appear to change their self-talk patterns little between the quiet and the distraction conditions. Separate t tests for reported positive and negative thoughts failed to show significant changes ($p > .10$). However, nonapprehensive writers significantly increased reported negative self-talk ($p < .01$) and decreased positive self-talk ($p < .05$) in the distraction condition.

It should be pointed out that the apprehensive writers do appear to change self-talk patterns in the same direction as nonapprehensive writers, but do so much less dramatically and to a degree that does not reach statistical significance. The data thus provide additional support for the self-inflicted wound account of writing apprehension. Apprehensive writers appear to be little more distressed by a truly hard writing assignment than one not so hard. This finding also provides further insight into the paradox of writing apprehension. If the self-talk patterns of apprehensive writers are relatively insensitive to the actual difficulty of writing assignments, then distressing writing experiences occur on almost every writing occasion, further reinforcing their distaste for the writing process and their erroneous beliefs about writing skill deficits.

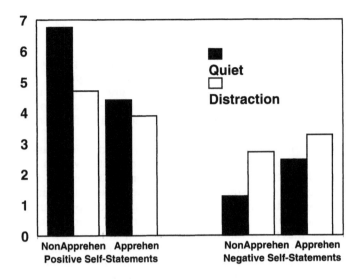

Figure 15.4. Self-talk pattern of apprehensive and nonapprehensive writers in Experiment 3.

Conclusions

The data presented here suggest a resolution to the paradox of writing apprehension. We found writing apprehension to be a psychological phenomenon that has little to do with the demand of the writing task or the quality of the texts produced. Although persons who are writing apprehensive believe that they are poor writers, we find their actual work indistinguishable from work written by nonapprehensive writers. The one difference between apprehensive and nonapprehensive writers we identify is that the experience of writing is more painful for apprehensives; they suffer before, during, and after the writing task because they worry more than nonapprehensives about how their work will be received. It is pain without gain.

This conclusion does not mean that all writing apprehensive writers are good writers; it means only that the distribution of writing skill in apprehensive writers is no different from the distribution of writing skill in their unafflicted peers. What distinguishes the two groups appears to be their patterns of self-talk. Writing apprehension is a manifestation of evaluation anxiety and appears to have much in common with test anxiety. Like test anxiety, it is mediated by negative self-talk. Writing apprehensives judge themselves and their own text harshly; they fail to perceive that their text and the facility with which they produce it are much the same as those of nonapprehensives writing under the same conditions.

Our finding that self-talk is a crucial variable is consistent with data on the treatment of writing apprehension. Boice (1985) increased the amount of writing produced by apprehensive college faculty members with a program that reduced negative self-talk and increased cognitions related to coping with writing tasks. Salovey and Haar (1990) examined treatments for writing apprehension by directly comparing the efficacy of instruction in the writing process with a combination treatment that added cognitive therapy to the writing process instruction. The cognitive component focused on the elimination of negative self-talk and the substitution of positive coping thoughts. Only the combination group showed improvements in actual writing performance, supporting the contribution of self-statements to writing skill.

Our conclusions apply to expository writing with no time constraints. We selected this setting because previous work suggested it might be one where the paradox of writing apprehension would be particularly glaring. Other types of writing, such as personal narrative or writing under time pressures, have been found to be associated with poorer performance by apprehensives when compared with nonapprehensives (Faigley et al., 1981; Kean et al., 1987). Characteristics of the writing situation may interact with writing apprehension in these settings to produce the observed performance decrements. For example, when time pressures are applied, the time lost through negative self-talk may be costly for the final product. When students are required to write personal narratives, the focus on the writer as subject may add to the evaluation anxiety and increase negative self-talk to the point where it interferes with the composing process. These interpretations are testable and would shed additional light on the mechanisms of writing apprehension.

These findings have important implications for pedagogy. Writing apprehension in students is frequently a concern for instructors. Not only do apprehensives themselves believe they are handicapped by their affliction, so too do some of those who assign or evaluate writing. Writing instructors may design course requirements to minimize apprehension among students by changing writing assignments; some writing textbooks place emphasis on devices to make students more comfortable. Experiment 3 suggests that different types of writing assignments are not likely to reduce writing apprehension among susceptible students. Successful treatment appears to require that patterns of negative self-talk be changed.

Acknowledgments

Portions of the data in this chapter have been presented at the 4th annual meeting of the American Psychological Society (APS) in San Diego, June, 1992, and the 7th annual meeting of APS in Los Angeles, June, 1995. The authors express their thanks to Tricia Wilson, John Holt, Tom Peterson, Jennifer Blackwell, Chris Kleinke, Donna Kleppin, Genie Babb, Anne Lazenby, Joseph Kane, Jodi Kindred, Lisa Lund, Anne Pfauth, Todd Ostendorf, Viorica Marian, and Sarah Bumpus for their help with the experiments.

— 16 —

STUDYING "REAL-LIFE" WRITING PROCESSES: A PROPOSAL AND AN EXAMPLE

Thea van der Geest
University of Twente

In the debate about approaches in writing research, the demand is often heard for one that allows writing to be seen and described as a social and collaborative process, rather than solely as an individual cognitive process (e.g., Barabas, 1990, Odell, 1985; see also Witte & Cherry, 1994). The dominant frame of analysis in the 1980s, represented by the problem-solving approach to study cognitive processes of individuals (Flower & Hayes, 1980, 1981; Hayes & Flower, 1980) considered the "world outside" the writer mainly from the point of view of the internal representations of this world the writer has built up and is building up while writing. Although this is valid from a cognitive-psychological point of view, it is not enough when one wants to describe what people actually are doing when they write in a non-instructional context (e.g., when they produce technical reports as part of their engineering work, or design an application form for student loans as part of their administrator's job, or write a marketing brochure for a bank that brings new trust funds into the market). To discriminate between the two visions of writing without falling in the trap of drawing an artificial line between the social and the cognitive aspects of writing, I will reserve the term *writing process* for the actual text production of an individual writer, including of course the planning, idea generation, reviewing one's own text and revising that is part of text production. I will use the term *document production process* when the focus is on writing in an organization, in interaction with other actors involved, rather than as an individual, cognitive process.

In chapter 2 of this volume, Hayes and Nash characterize the framework for studying writing processes as a building that is partly under construction, at the same time that other parts are still waiting to be designed. My interest in document production processes can be situated in the latter part of the building. The description of a document production process in this chapter has a dual goal: First, the chapter contains an attempt to identify features that should get a place in the design of a descriptive framework for document production processes. Second, the value of these features is demonstrated in a case of a writing process studied as a process of purposeful actions of interacting actors in an organizational context. In terms of Hayes' building metaphor: I propose how this new part of the building should be constructed, and I show a more detailed drawing for some spots in the building.

There is no agreement yet about how document production processes should be studied, and which features need to be included in our studies. Various researchers seem to study different aspects and stages of the document production process. Spilka (1990) studied document production processes in order to describe the *interaction* accompanying the writing of reports in an electrical plant. Kleimann (1993) explored the relation between *workplace culture* and the organization of the document production process in a government agency. Ede and Lunsford (1990) were particularly interested in *collaboration*. Medway (1996) analyzed the use of the *various semiotic systems* (speaking, drawing, writing) in an architects' office. Broadhead and Freed (1986) compared drafts in order to discover what for the writers in a management firm were the *reasons to change* their texts. The diversity of these and other studies in the field of professional communication makes it hard to see what we know about our research subject at the time, and where we are heading for in future research efforts.

The lack of agreement on subject and method is not really surprising, because studying real-life writing processes poses serious methodological challenges to the researcher. Due to the particulars of the processes studied, such as the "situatedness" of the process and the lengthy period of time it often expands over, researchers have to depend on methods such as case studies and ethnographic accounts. These methods do not allow generalization of findings in ways we know from experimental research, where sampling or systematic variation under controlled conditions are means to strengthen claims that go beyond the particular process or subject studied. Yin (1994) contrasted the "statistical generalization" that is feasible in experimental research with "analytical generalization" in case studies. He stated that case studies should be considered from a replication logic, rather than from a sampling logic. The cases studied are not to be seen as samples from a larger group, but as replications, from which an analytical theory is emerging than can be corroborated in a series of successive case studies. However, the minimum requirement to consider cases as replications is that they are described along the same lines, and this certainly is not the case in the studies that have been done so far. In this chapter I propose a descriptive framework for case studies of document production processes that could enable us to learn more from each others' research into professional writing.

A descriptive framework for case studies of writing at work

What characteristics of document production processes would one want to include in a framework to study and describe those processes?

Writers at work rarely work alone (Debs, 1989; Ede & Lunsford, 1990; van der Geest, 1996). They have to deal with many actors in the writing process. For example,

- The client commissioning the assignment.
- The manager who is responsible for the writing project or the umbrella project it is fitting in.
- Co-authors and other co-producers of elements of the document.
- Reviewers/content experts that will check document versions (e.g., for its technical or legal accuracy).
- Reviewers/editors that will check document versions (e.g., for its stylistic qualities).
- Support staff (e.g., librarians, information processing departments, graphic designers, printers).

We need a framework of description or analysis that takes into account the activities of all actors involved in the document production.

Because almost always more than one actor is involved, the interaction between the actors is characteristic for document production processes. The framework must allow for the description and analysis of the interaction between the actors, be it written or oral interaction (Plowman, in press; Spilka, 1990, 1993).

The actual document production is mostly embedded in a larger umbrella project, which often defines goals, plans, content and constraints for the document to be produced to a large extent (van der Geest, 1996). These process and product characteristics should be taken into account inasmuch as the ones that are dictated by the document itself.

Document production processes often expand over a long period of time (e.g., Cross, 1993). The framework should allow for studying complete processes rather than occasional writing sessions.

Real-life writing seldom starts from scratch; often writers at work draw from previous documents, from genre models, or from external sources to plan or compose their product (van der Geest, 1996; Pemberton et al., 1996). These source documents should be taken into account, together with the actual document to be produced.

When one wants to include characteristics like these in a process description and analysis, the data collection should at least cover the following issues:

1. The actors involved in the document production process.
2. The activities the actors undertake that are related to the document production process.
3. The (oral and written) communication between actors related to the document production.
4. All versions of the documents produced, including side documents such as proposal and comment sheets.
5. The information sources the actors consult.
6. The chronological order of activities, interactions and documents.

The issues proposed here are discussed later. A data set as described offers opportunities for a very wide range of explorations of the social, cultural, and organizational practices of writing at work, and at the same time allows testing of (mostly qualitative) analytical generalizations about document production processes over a number of studies, conducted in various situations.

Background of the study

The study reported here[1] is part of our research on reviewing as a recurrent, iterative activity within professional writing processes. We assume that by describing and analyzing review practices, in the end we will be able to create a knowledge basis for improvement: process-related improvements (e.g., make the review more efficient and rewarding) as well as product improvements (e.g., make documents technically more accurate). Three studies preceded the one reported here: Van der Geest (1996) interviewed professional writers and writing professionals about their activities in a document production process; Van Gemert and Woudstra (1996, in press) conducted a survey study among quality managers who participated in the production process of work instructions and quality handbooks in companies. The last two studies demonstrated that review was intricately related to planning: Problems with assignment and planning often emerged only when either the process or the product was evaluated. It became clear that in order to analyze review practices, data collection should start right at the beginning of the document production process. Also, it appeared that focusing only on the written discourse in review practices, such as commented versions, made us myopic: Most of the communication within the review was oral and took place in face-to-face meetings or over the telephone. Thus, we had to include oral communication as well as written communication.

We conducted a pilot study within an engineering firm, using various research instruments known from the professional writing process literature. We focused on the writers, their activities, and the successive versions of the document produced, hoping this would give a complete view of the production process. We used methods such as writers' logs, retrospective interviews, and comparison of drafts followed by stimulated recall about revisions. We informally evaluated the reliability, validity, and data yield in relation with the time invested by researchers and writers studied. With that experience, we started the study that is reported next.

The sector document on external safety: An exemplary case study

The small engineering firm in which we conducted our pilot study, specializes in risk analysis studies. The main clients of the engineers are government agencies and local administrations. The engineers realized that the

---

[1] The study was conducted in cooperation with Lisette van Gemert. It is part of the research program on Text in Use and Text Design of the section of Applied Linguistics, Department of Philosophy and Social Sciences, University of Twente.

technical reports were their core product, although they considered them-selves technicians, and certainly not writers. They hoped that these studies could help them in monitoring and improving the quality of their document production process and the reports produced.

During our pilot study, the engineering firm was approached for a new commission. We decided to track the complete document production process of this new report, from the very first beginning through the approval of the final version. Our research goal was to observe, throughout the process, the formulation, deliberation, and negotiation of plans, and the development and monitoring of the planned process and product features by review activities. We treated the formation of plans, their realization and the control over the realization as one ongoing process, taking together planning at one hand and review at the other hand.

The engineering firm was approached by one of the Dutch provinces, which was in the process of updating its 5-year environmental policy plan. A section within that policy plan concerned external safety (i.e., the risks caused by industries, road transport, static installations containing toxic or explosive materials like gas stations, and so on). The province asked the firm to update a section of the policy plan, that is: to produce a technical report that would describe the current provincial policy and regulations for external safety, and make an inventory of the accumulated risks within the province's territory, in the form of a "risk map." Two engineers were involved in produc-ing the report. The province was represented by a project group, consisting of five officials, most of them with a technical background. The project group was backed by a soundboard group that commented on the project approach and versions of the report. The project group manager was responsible for communicating the soundboard group's comments to the engineers.

Design of the study

Our plan was to describe the production process of a technical report, in particular the role of planning and reviewing activities by all actors involved. For this, we collected data using the following methods:

- We interviewed actors in an early stage and asked them about their goals and plans for the project and the report.
- We recorded all meetings and most of the phone calls concerning the project and had disposal of all side documents, source texts, and versions the writers saw.
- We compared successive versions of documents to track revisions at the paragraph or higher text level.
- Each time the writers offered a version for review, we interviewed the reviewers within the firm about their comments, and about what they expected the writers to do with it. We heard what external re-viewers meant with their comments when they explained them to the authors in meetings and phone calls.
- Each time the writers received comments from internal or external reviewers, we interviewed them about their interpretation of the com-ments, and about their goals and plans for revised versions.

Our data set provides data from various sources for most of the activities, so findings can be corroborated by triangulation, an important way of reducing problems with construct validity and reliability that often plague case studies. Also, the data give room to the different views the actors can have with regard to a particular activity. In practice, data collection meant that we compared document versions and talked with writers and reviewers about once every two months; these interviews each took 1 to 2 hours. The questions for writers or reviewers were semi-structured; for each interview they were slightly adapted to the current state of the documents. Tapes of interviews, meetings, and telephone conversations were transcribed.

Data collection in qualitative studies often results in large sets of data, and this is certainly the case with document production processes with several actors and a long duration. Yin (1994) and Miles and Huberman (1994) gave a number of methods for analyzing qualitative data. For our study of planning and review practice, in order to reduce the data analysis task, we decided to track six issues (four of which were content issues) that were discussed over and over throughout the document production process:

- Rhetorical: purpose and target audience for the report.
- Content 1: A list of definitions of technical terms.
- Content 2: A case description of a risk decision for city officials.
- Content 3: A map of risk sites.
- Content 4: A flow chart for deciding how to handle risk procedures.
- Process: Review procedures and communication about review procedures.

We chose these issues because they were discussed extensively, and hence we could expect the actors to remember facts and opinions, which we could relate to what was said in meetings, to document features and content. Every time one of the actors paid explicit attention to one of these topics, we saw this as a new episode for analysis.

I will use findings of the study[2] to demonstrate that a data set like ours allows a researcher to give a full descriptive account of the process (see *Process description*, next). Later, findings from other studies serve as a claim (what Yin, 1994, calls an analytical generalization) that is corroborated by the results of our case study. The case study is also used in what is commonly assumed to be the goal of case studies: An exploration is made into the of function external representations, a concept derived from cognitive psychology.

Process description

THE ACTORS. Some rhetoricians defend that writing by its nature is collaborative, even when the writer does not communicate with others while producing the text. The document at hand is always influenced by all kinds of preceding communications; writers resonate the voice of others to shape their own text. From a philosophical point of view this might be true, but it does not help much when one wants to describe a document production

---

[2] Because data analysis is still in progress, I do not deal here with the detailed results of this analysis.

process. In our case studies, we define actors from the point of view of the writers: Actors are all those the writers had direct communication with about the report to be produced. In the initial interview, we asked all actors to indicate the persons involved, their organizational background and their role in the project. Not all the participants had the same perception of who was involved; for example, the internal reviewer within the engineering firm did not know about some of the actors within the province.

These were the actors in the document production process:

Client: the province

- PG1: The project group chair was responsible for the management of the project. She also was the contact person with the engineers and the soundboard group.
- PG2: Project group Member 2 was an engineer working for the province.
- PG3: Project group Member 3 also worked for the province. These three members all worked for the Water and Environment Bureau of the province.
- PG4: Member 4 was an engineer who worked for the provincial region where most of the risk sites are located.
- PG5: Member 5 also is an engineer working for the region with most industrial risk sites.

All members of the project group gave comments on plans and drafts, sometimes in extensive, written form. Several wrote text proposals or draft versions for the final report. The comments and texts were communicated to the writers by PG1.

The project group offered versions of the report for review to a soundboard group. Because the engineers never communicated directly with the soundboard group, but only heard about their comments via the project group, we do not consider the soundboard group actors in this document production process. Their comments are represented by the project group.

Contractor: the engineering firm

- WR1: Writer 1 conferred with the client in the initial stage about the project, and wrote the first draft of three chapters. Then he fell ill, and did not return before the end of the project.
- WR2: Writer 2 was due to participate in the project on a limited scale, but replaced Writer 1 when he fell ill. He reviewed an early version of the first three chapters, and then became responsible for writing and rewriting the complete final report.
- WR3: To compensate for the absence of Writer 1, a temporary help was hired to produce part of the appendices of the report.
- IR: One of the colleagues within the firm was present at the initial meeting about the project, and was appointed as internal reviewer within the firm. His task was to review versions before they went out to the client; this, however, only happened once, for an early version of three chapters.

Subcontractor: graphical and text editing

- Editor: After an initial meeting with WR1 and WR2, the editor made a formal proposal for editing and testing the final document. She was contracted to edit the final report and pretest it with three persons from the target audience.
- Graphic designer: Forming a small company with the editor, he was informally consulted for graphic design decisions during the initial meeting.

After an initial contact about the project and the commissioning of the subcontract, the writers did not carry the subcontract into effect.

A CHRONOLOGICAL ACCOUNT OF ACTIVITIES. A writing project with a run time of over a year, with so many actors, consists of many different activities. An *activity* means an action (or set of actions) of an actor that is deliberately aimed at enhancing the production of the final document. It should be realized that an activity can serve several purposes at a time: For example, a particular meeting can serve both to limit the extent of the assignment (a planning activity) and to communicate comments on a chapter (a reviewing activity). The activity is not only defined by its aim, but also by its actor(s) and by the time it is occurring. This definition excludes all accidental events that might influence the document production process. And, according to the definition, a planned lunch meeting between the actors is an activity in the document production process, whereas an incidental meeting in a cafe where a writer comes to talk about the project with the person who happens to sit next to him at the bar is not an activity in the same process, even though this meeting might in the end be more influential than the lunch meeting. This distinction is based on practical grounds: It is virtually impossible to collect data about all the accidental events that could influence the document production process.

Table 16.1 presents a section from the chronological overview of the activities in the project, as a sample of the complete overview. Data sources for the activities mentioned are given.

The actors involved and the activities undertaken in the project in their chronological order and related with the documents produced give a fairly accurate view of what happened in the document production process. The data set is fit for descriptive research aims, ranging from a global description as presented previously to a very detailed description with citations from the various data sources.

ORAL AND WRITTEN COMMUNICATION ABOUT THE PROJECT. This section and the next are meant to demonstrate how case studies can be used in research with other than descriptive aims. This section focuses on testing a hypothesis derived from other studies, wherease in the next section, the aim of the study is explorative.

Several authors have stressed that the study of document production processes should not be limited to the analysis of written discourse (e.g., Medway, 1996; Plowman, in press; Spilka, 1993). Spilka (1993) cited studies that suggest "that, in nonacademic settings, both oral discourse...and written discourse...can be highly influential in fulfilling important rhetorical goals" (p. 71). Plowman (in press) stated that talking and writing are interfunctional. I use her assumption of interfunctionality as an analytical generalization from other studies, which serves as a hypothesis that should be tested in this case study.

Table 16.1
Sample of activities, actors, and data sources between September 13-30, 1994

Date	Activity and actors	Data sources
September 13	WR1 and internal reviewer (IR) decide on review procedure	* Audiotape of meeting * Internal note by WR1 on review procedures
September 13	IR gives comments on version	* Version with comments * Interview IR about comments (29-9)
September ?	WR2 gives comments on version	*missing version with comments*
September 21	WR2 attempts to clarify purpose of document	* Internal memo * Initial interview WR2 (22-9)
September 22	WR1 sends list of questions to PG	* Letter + internal memo
September 22	WR1 sends mainly unrevised version to client	* Version sent * Interview WR1 about review procedure, comments, and revision plans (29-9)
September 30	PG2 calls WR1 to discuss and answer questions	*missing: audiotape phone call* * Notes by WR1

The exemplary section from the previous chronological overview shows how oral and written communication in this project are interwoven; this case study corroborates the findings of the others mentioned. Writer 1 (WR1) states a view of the reviewer's task in an internal memo (WRITTEN). On the basis of this text, WR1 and the internal reviewer discuss the internal reviewer's role and the review procedure in a face-to-face meeting (ORAL). Subsequently, the reviewer works according to the procedure discussed and critiques a draft by making written notes on it (WRITTEN). The comments give the writers reasons to formulate a set of questions for the client (WRITTEN), which were discussed and answered in a telephone conversation (ORAL) with the client. Although separate activities can be discerned, it would be hard to discern separate functions for talk and text in this example. Both talk and text production. such as writing a memo or a draft, help writers and other actors to find out what they want the document to become. Studying the document production processes without paying attention to the oral interaction in the process would mean that an essential and influential part of the process would remain unobserved.

Talk in document production processes does not necessarily imply face-to-face contact. From studies of collaborative writing processes in the context of computer-supported collaborative work (see the summary in Plowman 1992; in press), it appears that writers seem to consider face-to-face meetings as the best medium for idea generation, knowledge retrieval, and global planning, because it leaves room for the uncertainties and complexities that often characterize the initial stages of text production. Spilka (1993) stressed that the moving between oral and written discourse serves to facilitate progress in the composing process and to establish agreement in an ongoing argument or discussion. The actors in her study moved more frequently between oral and written discourse during invention and planning than during writing and revision, but Spilka did not discriminate between oral discourse in face-to-face situations on the one hand and telecommunicated discourse on the other hand. Face-to-face meetings seem to be less necessary in the stage that existing texts are refined.

In the project, we saw the same preference observed for face-to-face meeting in the initial stage of the project as was noted by Plowman. Until this chapter was written, two face-to-face meetings took place. One meeting at a very early stage (April) was meant to discuss the project, for the client as a preparation for defining the project plan, for the engineering firm to help them develop their proposal. The second face-to-face meeting (July) was referred to as the "start meeting"; it served to plan the global content of the document to be produced as well as to make appointments on the project planning and management. After this start meeting, the writers did not meet face-to-face with their client for over a year. All communication in that period was by means of written text (sent by mail, e-mail or fax) or by telephone conversations. Writer 2, who became the main person responsible for writing the report when Writer 1 fell ill, never actually met the chairperson of the project group, with whom he conferred regularly by phone.

For a well-grounded study of the factors determining the document production process, data collection should expand to the oral interaction that is not face to face, such as telephone calls between actors. Because these events are often not planned long in advance or placed on the agenda, the initiative and responsibility for data collection has to be put in the hand of the actors. This in itself is already a remarkable shift from more traditional research methods.

A focus on the *written* text in the document production process obscures the vision on how actors, particularly writers and client, work toward agreement on the goals, content, and style of the document. The drafts show the results of the deliberations. Minutes of meetings might show a bit of the argumentation that underlaid the choice for the results. But only the full account of the oral and written interaction can show how the actors talked and negotiated with each other. Given the power relation between client and contractor, one can expect clients to have a dramatic impact on the document

---

3 We had obtained permission to tape face-to-face meetings between client and contractor, when it became apparent that much of the oral interaction was taking place over the telephone. New deliberations with the actors in the document production process resulted in a "phone tap." An audiocassette recorder was connected to a telephone contact within the engineering firm, and was activated by a writer anytime he had telephone contact with his client. Because it took some time to obtain permission from the actors to tape the telephone calls and to install the recording equipment properly, data from initial phone calls were missing.

production process and the resulting text, but so far, little empirical foundation has been created that could show how clients pursue, create, and execute that influence in their interaction with the writers, and to what effect in the document produced. As far as power relations and their influence on creating agreement and mutual understanding about the text between writer and reviewer have been studied, this was mainly in the context of producing scientific articles to be approved by journal reviewers (e.g., Myers, 1985), or young employees who were introduced to the organization's culture for report writing by their managers (e.g., Paradis, Dobrin, & Miller, 1985; Winsor, 1989; an exception appears in Couture & Rymer, 1991). If researchers would collect the data set as proposed earlier, they would create a basis for generalizing about this social issue toward document production processes in various organizational settings, and for different forms of collaboration between clients and contractors. Methods from the field of discourse analysis could help us to assess in detail how actors such as the client's representatives establish and maintain their personal and organizational role in the document production process.

In this section two main arguments have been presented in favor of collecting data on the talk as well as the text that is produced in the course of document production. First, talk and text are interwoven, and often serve the same function in the document production, even if they take place in separate activities. Second, a large part of the social processes, such as the negotiation between those who write the document and those who have commissioned it, remains invisible when we only collect the products of written discourse as data.

The section also demonstrates how an analytical theory from other studies, in this case a claim (hypothesis) about the interfunctionality of talk and text, can be supported by data from new case studies. In this case, functions of communication were achieved both by written and by oral discourse. We slightly refined Plowman's claim about interfunctionality, adding that oral discourse could be both face to face and distant.

MAIN DOCUMENT AND SIDE DOCUMENTS. Yin (1994) noted that a common misconception about case study research is that the strategy is only appropriate for the exploratory phase of an investigation, whereas other strategies like surveys or experimentation are better fit for describing or testing propositions. After having focused on the case study for describing the document production process and for supporting a claim about the interfunctionality of talk and text, this section focuses on the use of case study data to explore the issue of external representations.

In writing process research, little attention has been paid to texts other than drafts of the final documents. Often the writing process was considered to be staged according to the drafts produced, and changes in plans or goals were detected by comparing successive versions of the document (see e.g., Broadhead & Freed, 1986). However, studies on computer-supported collaborative writing (e.g., Neuwirth & Kaufer, 1989; Sharples & Pemberton, 1988) have revealed the relevance of "external representations" when two or more people are working together rather than separately, which is the case in most professional document production processes.

From the cognitive perspective, external representations are fascinating as a strategy writers use to alleviate the cognitive load that writing causes. They are the means writers use to visualize or verbalize "cognitive units" such as concepts or ideas, or the relation between them. They enable the writer to manipulate with elements (that can stand for ideas, but also for complete paragraphs or chapters) without or before committing them to text (Sharples & Pemberton, 1988; Wood, 1992a,b). External representations can take virtually any form: sketches, notes, jotted-down lists, outlines, diagrams, maps, a draft text, but also all kinds of idiosyncratic messages of writers to themselves.

But in document production processes, external representations play a role beyond the cognitive: They are both the stimulus and the result of interaction between the actors involved. When several actors are involved in the process, and when the production expands over a longer period of time, external representations seem to be an indispensable record of the process and a starter for further action. This exploration of the function of external representations in document production processes might be illustrated by findings from this case study.

The representatives responsible for updating the province's environmental policy plan knew the term of operation of the 1989 environmental policy plan ended in 1994, and hence they initiated talks with agencies that could contribute to sections of the new plan. The small engineering firm was one of those agencies. Before and during the first exploratory meeting, no paperwork (external representation) was available for the engineers. Members of what later became the project group just explained their ideas orally and discussed them with Writer 1 and another engineer from the firm. The meeting resulted in the agreement that the engineering firm would write a draft proposal for the project, whereas the province's representatives would write a draft project plan that would meet the requirements for projects like this one. Both the proposal of the engineering firm and the project plan of the province were an external representation of what the parties understood to be the issues agreed on in the meeting. Their understanding did not completely coincide, as could be expected. But this could only become apparent *because* an external representation was made. It helped the parties to identify issues that had remained unclear in the meeting, issues for which further discussion was needed. The drafts were the starting point for a second round of oral discussion, by telephone, after which the two plans were attuned to each other. The new versions were new external representations of ideas about the project and the document to be produced. They literally served as a contract between the actors specifying the document and the procedure to get the work done.

The observations in the case, exploring the role of main document versions and side documents, help to identify a topic that needs further research. A provisional proposition about external representations in group work could be that external representations are meant to consolidate issues that have been agreed on in oral discourse or that need agreement for further planning. It seems to depend on the stage of the project what forms of written discourse are acceptable: lists, outlines, sketches, proposals in early stages, drafts and comments in later stages. Purely idiosyncratic external representations seem only to be acceptable when they serve as a starter for oral discourse, in which the producer can explain the meaning of the representations.

Medway (1995) described how architects talked about the "virtual building" they drew in their sketches as if it already really existed. Likewise, the actors in this case discussed the external representations (in this example an early outline) as if it already *was* the document. With only the outline produced, they said things like: "Well, then you have the inventory of risk analysis studies, of what the risk picture is [in this province]. That should certainly remain in [the document]." and "Are we complete when we mention the field of environmental planning, calamity contingency plans, and registration of toxic materials?" The way actors talk about side documents seems to show that, for them, these products are as real as the draft versions of the document. They act on the side documents as well as on the successive stages of the actual document. Both types of documents serve as external representations of ideas about what the final product should be, and as a basis for further interaction and negotiation in order to reach shared meanings and consensus. A more detailed analysis of the side documents and the ways they are used and referred to in oral discourse could help to explain the role of external representations in document production processes. One thing may be clear: There is no sound reason to exclude side documents from an analysis of successive drafts of a document, when the aim is to describe a production process.

Studying writers at work

Most research on writing processes have been conducted in conditions that cannot be considered "real-life." The writing studied was either executed by students, working individually for an imaginary audience and medium as part of their course, or was prompted in a laboratory research setting. Often, the practitioners were put in situations where much of what formed their craftmanship as writers was not elicited. Important characteristics of document production processes, such as how writers and their clients define their target audience and goals, how writers interact and negotiate with each other and with those who commissioned the writing, and how the quality of drafts is assessed in review cycles, these process characteristics remain invisible when we keep studying the writing of nonacademics within the limits of academic institutions. This chapter contains a proposal for a different approach.

If the focus remains on questions such as how and why professionals act like they do in document production process (a situation over which there is little control), the strategy of case study research is appropriate. This chapter stresses the importance of regarding the selected cases as replications; in order to increase the number of analytical generalizations that can be made from separate studies, start with collecting identical data sets. These data sets should cover issues that traditionally have remained out of scope in writing process research: the oral discourse between actors, the side documents, and the sources of information and text (including models, style sheets, and previous editions of the same document) used by the writers. The additional data allow a study of writing as more than just a cognitive process: They are an empirical foundation for propositions about the social dimensions of writing.

Studying real-life writing processes is not easy; conducting case studies and working with qualitative data, in general, is laborious. Having executed several studies of real-life writing, one can imagine why many scholars prefer research in controlled conditions, where they can exclude a large part of the multitude of factors that can affect their research object, and where they can single out small issues for study. Yet, one main reason to conduct real-life writing studies has remained unmentioned in this chapter. That is, it is extremely rewarding to conduct writing research in all kinds of profit and nonprofit organizations. It shows how writing is in the center of important issues in the society, such as in this case the safety of citizens and the legitimacy of government decisions. The writers studied do not need to be convinced of the need to communicate, which often seems a problem with students. They have vigorous debates among each other and with reviewers about issues at all levels of text production, from purpose and audience to spelling and graphics, and all actors know their decisions really matter. One can see them apply sophisticated strategies to perform the task assigned, negotiating with other actors both about the writing project and about the text to be written. Researchers should be grateful to the professionals that give them the opportunity to deepen research insights about writing processes and to improve their instruction to the next generation of practitioners now populating the classrooms.

— 17 —

REWRITING: THE ARTS AND SCIENCES OF IMPROVING EXPOSITORY INSTRUCTIONAL TEXT

Bruce K. Britton
University of Georgia

Good writing is largely a matter of rewriting. This chapter describes three methods of rewriting expository instructional text to improve its learnability. Two of the methods have been applied by us to rewriting expository instructional text that was originally written by others. We have tested the rewritten instructional texts against the original texts for instructional effectiveness. The results showed a large and consistent advantage in favor of rewritten texts, on tests of learning designed to be fair to both the original and rewritten texts (Britton, 1995a; Britton & Gulgoz, 1991; Britton & Tidwell, 1991, 1993; Tidwell, 1992). These two methods are scientific in the sense that they are based on the observation of phenomena of naturally occurring expository instructional texts (Britton, 1992; Britton, van Dusen, Glynn, & Hemphill, 1990), supplemented by experimental investigation of them, leading to their theoretical explanation, and resulting in a systematic procedure that can accomplish the complex task of rewriting expository instructional text to increase its learnability. Our third method is more like an art, and has not yet been tested empirically.

Briefly, the three methods are:

1. *The Coherence Revision Method*, in which the coherence relations among parts of a text, which tend to be disorderly in naturally occurring expository instructional texts, are made orderly to afford comprehension (this method is derived from the Kintsch & van Dijk, 1978, model, as explained in Britton & Gulgoz, 1991; Gulgoz, 1989).

2. The *Diagnosis-Treatment Revision Method*, in which the reader's misconceptions are diagnosed by a special test of cognitive structures, and these misconceptions are then used to guide repairs of the text that obviate the misconceptions of those who read the repaired text (Britton & Tidwell, 1991, 1993; Tidwell 1992);

3. The *Method of Good Examples*, in which original and rewritten versions of the same texts are identified for which the rewritten version has been found by empirical test to be markedly superior to the original. Such originals and their rewritten counterparts are then presented side-by-side to the writer, to provide guidance in the rewriting process (based on Britton, Van Dusen, Gulgoz, & Glynn, 1988; Gulgoz 1989; Tidwell, 1989).

Coherence Revision Method

Three levels of revision

A coherent text is marked by an orderly relation of its parts that affords comprehension. Important relations are found at several levels of expository text. At the concept/word level, coherence requires that when a concept that is referred to in one part of a text is used again in another part of the text, it should be recognized for what it is — namely, another instance of the same concept — and not mistaken for a different concept. This orderly relation among the concepts of a text can often be achieved by using the same word or phrase for the concept on its later occurrences as on its first.

But naturally occurring texts frequently use different words for the same concepts. For example, Tables 17.1 and 17.2 show some of the concepts for which a variety of different terms were used within two 1,000 to 2,000 word Air Force texts used in our studies. We have found this phenomenon to be quite general among naturally occurring expository instructional texts (Britton, 1992; Britton et al., 1990).

The effect of this practice on the comprehension of readers is likely to be dire, unless the readers are able correctly to infer, on each occasion, the identity of the concept the author intends for them to think of. For example, consider a text such as the following (from the beginning of the text referred to in Table 17.2, which is summarized in the Appendix, and was one of the texts on which we tested the coherence revision method):

> Title: Air War in the North, 1965
>
> By the Fall of 1964, Americans in both Saigon and Washington had begun to focus on Hanoi as the source of the continuing problem in the South. As frustrations mounted over the inability of the ARVN to defeat the enemy in the field, pressure to strike directly at North Vietnam began to build.

Table 17.1
Different terms used for important concepts in the Nuclear Strategy Text

Nuclear Forces	Nuclear forces, nuclear weapons, weapon systems, the force, capabilities, nuclear power, warheads
Nuclear war	Nuclear war, nuclear exchange, nuclear hostilities, nuclear attack
The to-be-attacked nation	potential adversaries, another nation, inferior state, side, party, attacked systems, an opponent
Employment strategy	Employment strategy, usage plans, firing strategy
The attacking nation	A nation, one's state, attacking systems, the possessor, the holder, side, the powerful state
Nuclear strategy	Nuclear strategy, strategy, strategic choices, strategic options

Table 17.2
Different terms used for important concepts in the Air Force Rolling Thunder passage

North Vietnam	North, Hanoi, enemy, communist, its, enemy, leadership, North Vietnam Leadership, they, them, Democratic Republic of Vietnam, DRV, North Vietnamese
American officials	Americans, members of the Johnson administration, U.S., civilian advocates, those, Joint Chiefs, JCS, they, military leaders, government, Washington, civilians, other senior officials, American policymakers, some officials
Bombing attacks	strike directly, aerial extension, bombing attacks, they, campaign, attacks, bombing, power, operations, bombing operations, Rolling Thunder, air raids, retaliatory strikes, air power, sorties, bombing campaign, strikes, air war

If the reader assumes that "the North" refers to one thing, "Hanoi" another, and "the enemy" a third, or that "Saigon" refers to one thing, and "the South" another, then comprehension will suffer. Orderly relations among these parts of the text can be restored by using the same terms (or appropriately prepared-for contractions of the terms) as follows:

Title: Air War in North Vietnam, 1965

By the Fall of 1964, Americans in both South Vietnam and Washington had begun to focus on North Vietnam as the source of the continuing war in South Vietnam. As frustrations mounted over the inability of the South Vietnamese army to defeat North Vietnam in the field, pressure to strike directly at the North began to build.

Another disorderly relation often found in naturally occurring expository instructional texts occurs when an essential concept is left implicit, as is the "Americans" among whom "frustrations are mounting" and "pressure is building." Readers who are unable to infer the correct concept will be at sea.

The Given-New contract is another orderly relation that affords comprehension. According to the Given-New contract, the canonical order of mention of the ideas in a sentence is to present first the Given (sometimes called Old) idea(s), and then the New idea(s). When the order Given-New is followed, the readers can begin by using the Given idea to move their mental pointer to the location of that idea, and then when the New idea arrives, attach it to that location. To prepare for an example, begin by dividing the second surface sentence of the original Vietnam text into three natural parts:

1. As
2. frustrations mounted over the inability of the ARVN to defeat the enemy in the field
3. pressure to strike directly at North Vietnam began to build.

Parts 2 and 3 are actually independent sentences and they are related by Part 1's preposed conjunction "as."

To illustrate the Given-New contract, consider Part 2. Which part of it is Given and which is New? Is it all New? Is the first part Given, and the second part New? If the reader cannot correctly infer the relation of the sentence to the rest of the text, then comprehension will not be afforded.

After some analysis, we concluded that the Given part is "the inability of the ARVN to defeat the enemy in the field" because it refers back the idea that ended the previous sentence, "the continuing problem in the South." That is, "the inability of the ARVN to defeat the enemy in the field" is "the continuing problem in the South." "If the ARVN had been able to defeat the enemy in the field, then there would not have been a problem in the South (or at least not the problem being considered here). The Given appears in the second part of the sentence.

The new part is that "frustrations mounted." It appears at the beginning of the sentence. Because in English the canonical order is Given followed by New, the reader expects the Given to appear first. If the Given part is moved to the first position, the readers' likely expectations will be met, and comprehension will more likely be afforded; hence, the Coherence Revision Method proposes:

> 2.' The inability of the ARVN to defeat the enemy in the field
>   caused frustrations to mount.

[This sentence is still subject to several disorders in its relations to the rest of the text, some stemming from the use of different phrases or words for the same concepts in the previous sentence ("the inability of the ARVN to defeat the enemy in the field" for "the continuing problem in the South," as well as "ARVN" and "enemy"), and some from the missing intended concept "Americans." Therefore, it was subject to further revisions.]

Sources of disorderly coherence relations

Why does naturally occurring expository text have such coherence problems? There are several reasons (Britton, Gulgoz, & Glynn, 1993). One reason is a consequence of the fact that naturally occurring expository text is often written by experts in the subject matter of the text. Experts in any domain have very large, well developed, and highly interconnected knowledge structures in their domain, and they have developed and used these knowledge structures extensively over many years. Because of the experts' extensive practice, these knowledge structures are often highly automatized, and the expert normally moves about in them with great facility. Often, the expert will jump from one idea to the next without having to move laboriously through the intermediate ideas that a novice would need to know in order to understand the connections that the author uses automatically. When the experts come to write expository instructional texts, they will tend to write as they think, and the consequence will be texts with coherence problems for the novice. But the experts do this because these coherence problems do not arise when experts read their own text. For example, experts know perfectly well that "the North" is the same as "Hanoi," "the enemy," and "North Vietnam," that "the continuing problem in the South" is "the inability of the

ARVN to defeat the enemy in the field," and that it is among the Americans that frustrations were mounting and pressure was building. Because experts cannot see that there is any comprehension problem, they are likely to allow these potential coherence problems to remain in the text, leading to the need for the Coherence Revision Method.

A second reason for the coherence problems of naturally occurring expository instructional text arises from the normal revision process for such texts. If an expository text is about an important field, the field will normally be making progress over time, and this leads to the need either for new editions of the same text, or for completely new texts on the topic. New editions are usually cheaper to produce when much of the old text can be saved. So often the new edition is prepared by modifying some parts of the old edition, removing other parts, and inserting new material. And often the new edition is prepared by new subject matter experts. These are ideal conditions for the creation of coherence problems. This is because the sections that are removed may contain coherence links needed for comprehension of succeeding sections that were not removed, and the new inserted sections may refer to the same concepts in different ways than the old sections. This is exacerbated when the new edition is prepared by a different subject matter expert than the old edition. Also, books assembled by committees virtually guarantee these same sort of coherence problems. Because the new editions must often be produced to a strict deadline, there may be no time allocated for anyone to ever read over the entire text looking for coherence problems, so that the full brunt of them is only encountered by the ultimate consumers, namely the students who must try to learn from them.

A third reason for the ubiquity of coherence problems is that writers seem to have a strong tendency to change the way they refer to concepts. This tendency is called *elegant variation*, and Fowler (1965) had this to say about it:

> It is the...writers...intent rather on expressing themselves prettily than on conveying their meaning clearly, and still more those whose notions of style are based on a few misleading rules of thumb, that are chiefly open to the allurements of elegant variation...the...victims [are] first terrorized by a misunderstood taboo, next fascinated by a newly discovered ingenuity, and finally addicted to an incurable vice...there are few literary faults so widely prevalent. (p. 148).

Yet these strictures seem to have had little effect on writers and editors. For example, the well established Italian journalist who edited John Paul II's (1994) text said that

> A dutiful respect for a text in which every word counts obviously guided me in the editing work I was requested to do. I limited myself...to the suggestion of a synonym where a word was repeated in the same paragraph... (Messori, 1994, p. vii).

My hypothesis for the source of elegant variation is that when children are taught to write text in school, they are typically assigned a length criterion, that is, to write so many lines or paragraphs or pages. But because they may have great difficulty in coming up with enough ideas to meet the length criterion, some develop the trick of presenting the same ideas over again in different words, thereby recycling a set of ideas to meet the length criterion. Those who do so most successfully are likely to get good grades on the assignment because they meet the length criterion, and this encourages them to continue the practice.

Evidence for success of the Coherence Revision method

The Coherence Revision Method has been tested on the text used here as an example, which was a 1,000-word Air Force text on the history of the Rolling Thunder Operation during the Vietnam war (Britton & Gulgoz, 1991), and also on a 2,000-word Air Force text on the Nuclear Strategy concepts underlying the doctrine of Mutual Assured Destruction (Britton, 1995a, 1995b). In both cases, we gave the original and the revised versions of the text to separate groups of about 40 Air Force recruits, and then we measured how closely the recruits' knowledge matched the knowledge that the original authors of the text thought the readers should have.

The tests we gave to the recruits were made up from only the original texts, and those tests had been taken by the authors of the texts (an Air Force Major for the Rolling Thunder text, and an Air Force Colonel and college professor for the Nuclear Strategy text). In the case of the Nuclear Strategy text, the co-authors themselves actually made up the test. Also, our revision was not influenced by the test they made up, because we had completed our revision before we asked them to construct the test from their original text. We also did the three parts of the Coherence Revision Method separately on the Nuclear Strategy text, and tested them separately to find out which ones were effective. In both cases, the full Coherence Revision Method was very successful. Table 17.3 shows the results.

Table 17.3
Two tests of the Coherence Revision method: Correlations of separate groups of Air Force recruits (n = 40) with the authors' original structure

	Rolling Thunder Text (Britton & Gulgoz, 1991)	**Nuclear Strategy Text** (Britton, 1995a)
Original text	.08	.29
Repeated-Concepts Revision	–	.41
Given New Revision	–	.43
Full Coherence Revision Method	.52*	.48*

For tests of the Coherence Revision method using correlational techniques, see Britton et al. (1990); Britton, van Dusen, and Gulgoz (1991); and Kintsch, Britton, Fletcher, Kintsch Mannes, and Nathan (1993). For tests of an individual differences model of the process by which good and poor readers succeed or fail in reading expository instructional texts, see Britton (1993) and Britton, Kyllonen, Eisenhart, Stennett, and Gulgoz (1995). For proposed extenstions of the method, see Britton (1994).

But can writers apply the method? The answer is that some can do it, as shown by Gulgoz (1993). The participants were four pre-Masters graduate students from the Department of Psychology at Auburn University at Montgomery. In the Training Phase, the subjects were told about Kintsch's model, and the techniques derived from it which I described earlier; tried the techniques on the first section of the Air Force Rolling Thunder Passage, as homework; came to a session to show their work, discuss it, and get feedback; did the same with the second section, the third section, and a textbook excerpt about Australian sheep.

Then they tried out the method on two other textbook excerpts, with the success shown in Table 17.4.

Table 17.4
Results of the test phase on textbook excerpts

		Correct Changes	Extra Changes Congruent with Processes	Other Changes Irrelevant and Wrong
Theory of Contentinal Drift	Mean (Range)	57% (43-71%)	2.25 (1-3)	1.75 (2-3)
Pollution of Chesapeake Bay	Mean (Range)	79% (67-100%)	2.75 (2-4)	.5 (0-1)

Diagnosis-Treatment Revision method

The goal of this section is to describe an effective and easy-to-use method for diagnosing the knowledge structures that learners have after reading a text, and then treating the text by repairing it, so that the readers of the repaired version will learn from it more of what the author intended them to learn. The section is based on Britton and Tidwell (1995). The method, called the *Cognitive Structure Testing System* (CS), identifies misconceptions, missing conceptions, and inconsistencies in learners' knowledge after reading a text. In this section, we describe its use to diagnose the state of novices' knowledge after reading a to-be-revised text, so researchers can intervene adaptively to repair the text to move new novices' knowledge toward the knowledge the author intended them to have.

The basic diagnostic procedure of the CS method is straightforward. After the students read the to-be-revised-text, we give them a CS test, which provides a picture of their current knowledge structure in the area of the text. The same test has previously been given to the author of the text, or to experts who have read the text. The author's or experts' responses supply the intended knowledge structure for the text. Then we compare each student to the experts. Discrepancies between the experts and the students can be read off directly by superimposing the graphical representation of the student's knowledge on the expert's graphical representation (the CS program provides the graphical representations online). Such discrepancies signal misconceptions.

The CS test data that provide the pictures of the student's and expert's knowledge are collected by selecting the most important elements (e.g., terms or propositions) in the text, constructing all possible pairs of them, and presenting each pair for a rating of relatedness on a 6- or 7-point scale. These relatedness ratings tell which elements are related to each other, and the strength and direction of those relations. Because the test began by choosing the most important terms in the text, the relations between those terms are likely to be the most important relations in that text. (With our CS computer program, such tests can be constructed online by simply selecting the elements; the rest of the test construction process is done automatically, and the test can then be administered immediately.)

How do we use these data to get the pictures of the most important parts of the knowledge structures of students and experts? We use the assumption that a knowledge structure, like any structure, comprises a set of elements connected by relations. The whole of any structure comprises the sum of its parts (at least), and an exhaustive inventory of those parts is given by listing all possible pairs of the elements and their relations to each other. Because the CS program collects data on each of those parts, we can build up the whole structure from it. The ratings of relatedness that the CS test provides are interpreted as distances, links, weights, and in other ways, and analyzed and presented graphically and numerically in several different forms to help with diagnosis and repairs of students' misconceptions. (In the CS computer system, we can now provide online graphics and some numerical analyses of the ratings, including multidimensional scaling solutions, network diagrams, and measures of harmony, and it would be inexpensive to add online analyses of tree structures, correlations, distances, factor analysis and clustering.)

Repairs of the text to shift the novices toward the experts' structure are immediately suggested by these analyses. Text repairs implemented by Britton and Tidwell (1991, 1993) and Tidwell (1992) included adding explicit links between elements of the text information, disambiguating the text, and adding information. These repairs were markedly successful in substantially reducing misconceptions of new groups of novices.

Graphical diagnosis

For an example of a CS analysis, consider the pattern of responses of Subject 14 (an Air Force recruit in the 11th day of basic training) for the relatedness of the term *Graduated Response Strategy* to 11 other terms (after reading the text on Operation Rolling Thunder summarized in the Appendix) shown in the top panel of Figure 17.1. The plotted points are the scale values that this learner chose for the degree of relatedness of each pair of the terms listed on the ordinate to Graduated Response Strategy. (The CS computer system provides such plots immediately after the test is completed.) This subject responded that the Graduated Response Strategy was very closely related to Members of the Johnson Administration, President Johnson, Civilian Advisers, Psychological, Rolling Thunder, and Failure; more distantly related to Maxwell Taylor and Robert McNamara; and very distantly related to Military Advisers, Success, and Military Strategy.

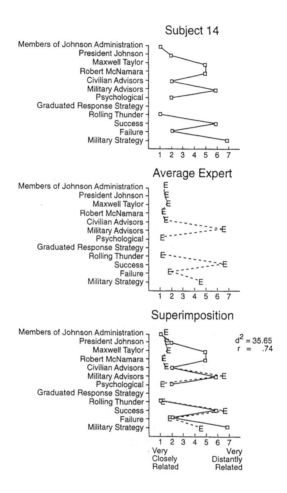

Figure 17.1. Subject 14 compared to the average expert for the term "Graduated Response Strategy."

To diagnose the student's misconceptions about the Graduated Response Strategy, the first step is to compare the student's conceptions to the correct conceptions. The correct conceptions are provided by the responses of the average expert, plotted in the second panel of Figure 17.1. (These were the average of the responses of seven subject matter experts, including a former

U.S. ambassador, three military historians, and three high-level military personnel; their responses were correlated about .8, so they were combined; see Britton & Gulgoz, 1991, Experiment 2.) Graphical comparison of this student's mental structure to that of the experts can easily be accomplished by superimposing the two profiles, as shown in the bottom panel of Figure 17.1. Obviously, this student deviates from the experts on the terms *Maxwell Taylor* and *Robert McNamara*, indicating misconceptions in those areas. To repair those misconceptions, the instructor should intervene with some supplementary information on how Taylor and McNamara relate to the Graduated Response Strategy.

Figure 17.1 shows only one twelfth of the results of this CS test: the rest is given by the plots for the other 11 terms. We have used the complete set of plots to plan reparative interventions; then we have tested the effects of those interventions on the novices' knowledge structures. Based on these and other graphics, interventions have reduced the novice's misconceptions: Nearly all misconceptions found in 83 Air Force recruits were eliminated by adding a few sentences to the 1,000 word Air Force text summarized in the Appendix (Britton & Tidwell, 1991, 1993; Tidwell, 1992).

Other graphics provided by the CS program depict the knowledge structures that underlie the ratings. For example, the network analysis of the average CS data of the seven subject matter experts (for the same terms) is shown in Figure 17.2, using the Pathfinder program of Schvaneveldt (1990). (The CS computer system provides this graphic online for each individual.) We interpret this picture to mean that the Graduated Response Strategy was the central concept for the experts, surrounded by the various characters favoring its adoption — Civilian Advisers, President Johnson, Robert McNamara, Maxwell Taylor, Members of the Johnson administration — by its major characteristic of being psychological, and by its implementation, the Rolling Thunder operation, which was a failure. At the periphery of the representation are the Military Strategy proposed by the Military Advisers, with the notion of Success most distant from everything. In contrast, the Pathfinder analysis of a group of novices who read the same text is shown in Figure 17.3. The CS program also provides online a graphic of a multidimensional scaling analysis (Shepard, 1962) for each individual learner. Tree analyses (Sattath & Tversky, 1977) could also be provided.

With practice these graphical displays have been used to diagnose novice's misconceptions, missing conceptions, and inconsistencies in their mental structures, and to devise effective interventions that repair the problems. Writers and instructors can be taught to do the same, and therefore these techniques hold great promise for improving the effectiveness and efficiency of rewriting.

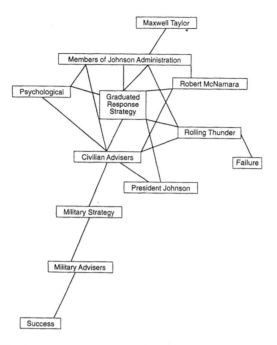

Figure 17.2. Average expert's Pathfinder Network after reading the text summarized in the appendix.

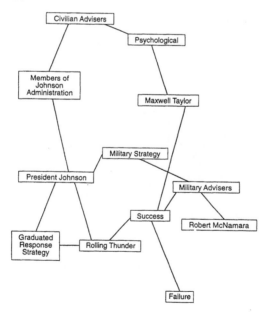

Figure 17.3. Average novice's Pathfinder Network after reading the text summarized in the appendix.

Numerical diagnosis

An even more automated system for diagnosis and repair is feasible and needs to be tested. To be automatic, it must be based on computable measures of discrepancies from expert structures. Of numerical measures of the discrepancy between the experts and the novice, the most obvious is the distance between the novice's profile and the experts. We have also found that the correlation between the novice's profile and the expert's is a useful measure. Both measures are shown in the bottom panels of Figures 17.1 and 17.4. For example, the .74 correlation in Figure 17.1 is consistent with the graphical impression of relatively high correspondence. To illustrate the usefulness of these measures, consider Participant 38's profile for the Graduated Response Strategy, shown in the top panel of Figure 17.4.

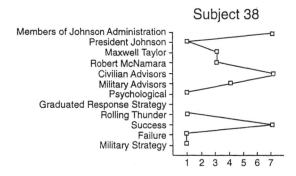

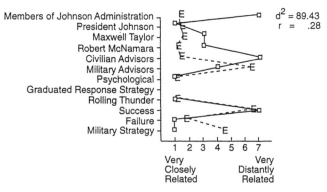

Figure 17.4. Participant 38 compared to the average expert for the term "Graduated Response Strategy."

It is evident graphically from the bottom panel that this subject's misconceptions are much more widespread than Participant 14's. This is also evident from comparing the distances and correlations shown in the bottom panels of Figures 17.1 and 17.4. In this case, the distances and correlations provide essentially the same information. This is partly because the correlation — the "pattern" of responses — is one of three components of the distance; the other two components are the "level" (i.e., the mean) and the "scatter" (Cronbach, 1991; Cronbach & Gleser, 1953). In some cases, each of these three components have provided different information that is useful.

Harmony diagnosis

We have also developed a completely new type of analysis, that diagnoses whether there are internal inconsistencies in each participant's knowledge structure, and specifies their locations (Britton & Eisenhart, 1993). These analyses may allow us to maximize the impact of reparative interventions by targeting them at the weak points of the novices' mental structures. We call these internal inconsistencies *disharmonies*, which mean locations of low or negative harmony, where the degree of "harmony" (McClelland & Rumelhart, 1988; Smolensky, 1986) refers to the balance (Heider, 1958), consonance (Festinger & Carlsmith, 1959), or internal consistency of the relations among the elements of the mental structure. For example, according to Heider's balance theory, if ideas about the relations among three persons are such that A likes B, A likes C, and B likes C, that is a balanced structure; its harmony is 1.0. (Harmony values range from a maximum of +1 to a minimum of -1.) On the other hand, if A likes B, and A likes C, but B dislikes C, that is an unbalanced structure. The harmony of this situation is .333, indicating substantial disharmony. Because people seek harmony in their knowledge structures, such an imbalance may lead individuals to think that B and C may become more positive to each other, or A become more negative to B or C; each of these would increase the harmony of this mental structure.

Similarly, cognitive dissonance arises when two or more cognitions are inconsistent with each other, as in the classic experiment in which a subject who has just done a very boring task is induced to lie to someone about the interestingness of the task for a paltry $1 (Festinger & Carlsmith, 1959). The results indicate that the subject feels very dissonant (i.e., disharmonious) about lying in this situation, because the idea that one does not lie without adequate compensation is belied by his act. Because people seek harmony, and the subjects in this condition have already lied and taken the dollar, they tend to increase their positive evaluation of the interestingness of the task, thereby increasing their harmony. The dissonant feeling is less likely to occur in subjects who accept a payment of $20 for lying. According to harmony calculations, situations where cognitive dissonance arises have low or negative harmony (i.e., high disharmony) compared to situations where the cognitions are consonant (see also Read & Miller, 1993).

Our program adds to this line of research the idea that knowledge structures in memory can also be characterized by their harmony. That is, a person's knowledge structure for a subject matter area can be balanced, consonant, and internally consistent, in which case it fits together well and makes sense as a whole: This situation would correspond to a high value of harmony. Alternatively, a memory structure can be unbalanced, dissonant, or inconsistent, in which case it does not fit together well, and does not make sense: This corresponds to a low harmony value.

For an example of a knowledge structure in memory that is internally inconsistent, consider a learner who believes that two things that are opposed to each other are both positively related to something else. In terms of the passage summarized in the Appendix, an example would be the belief that the Graduated Response Strategy was a rousing success, that President Johnson favored the Graduated Response Strategy, and that President Johnson was not at all a Success. Such a memory structure is internally inconsistent in the same way as Heider's unbalanced structure described previously, in which A is positive toward B and C but B is negative toward C (if A corresponds to the Graduated Response Strategy, B to Success, and C to President Johnson). An easy way to see this inconsistency in verbal terms is to compare a verbal statement of the unbalanced structure to its balanced alternative. In this case, the unbalanced structure can be stated as:

1. The graduated response strategy was a success.
2. President Johnson favored the Graduated Response Strategy.
3. President Johnson was not a success.

A balanced alternative is:

1. The Graduated Response Strategy was not a success.
2. President Johnson favored the Graduated Response Strategy.
3. President Johnson was not a success.

Formally, these balanced and unbalanced structures can be represented as in the top panel of Figure 17.5. The links labeled with +1 are excitatory ones, corresponding to a rating on the CS test of "very positively related," and those labeled -1 are inhibitory ones, corresponding to "very negatively related."

The calculation of harmony scores begins by simulating the process of thinking about the ideas with regard to each other. The thinking process implemented here is spreading activation. This simulated thinking is intended to be of the same kind that goes on when the verbal statements of the set of ideas are thought about. For example, in thinking about the verbal statements of the unbalanced structure, once all three terms are in mind, the statements tell us to link Graduated Response Strategy excitatorially to the idea of Success, and also excitatorially to the idea of President Johnson, and to inhibitorially link Success to President Johnson. Then think about each pair of ideas with regard to the others, by spreading activation appropriately (i.e., as specified by the links). All is well until the third statement, which asks about President Johnson as opposed to Success. When negative activation is spread toward Success, it conflicts with the positive activation previously established by Success's excitatory link to the Graduated Response Strategy. This conflict causes a reexamination of the first statement, which causes a reexamination of the second statement, and so on. At the end of the process, reconciliation of these ideas is not feasible.

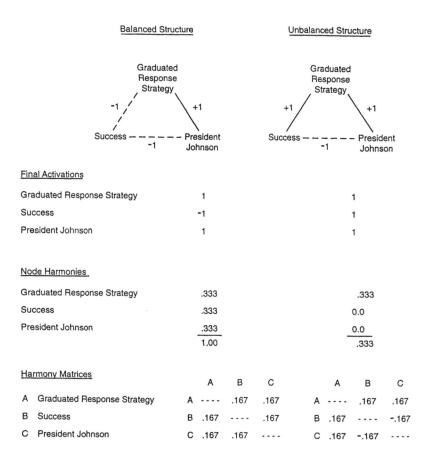

Figure 17.5. Balanced and unbalanced structures, final activations, and harmony for nodes and links.

Similarly, the operation of the harmony calculating program begins by getting all three ideas in mind (by setting the activations of the terms to small random values), and then during the simulated thinking process, each idea tries to satisfy the constraints it has with other ideas. The process can be followed by spreading activation along the links in the top right panel of Figure 17.5. For example, if an individual starts out thinking about the Graduated Response Strategy, it tries to excite Success and President Johnson because it is positively related to them. But then Success and President Johnson try to make each other have opposite values, because they are inhibitorially related to each other. But of course, to the extent that Success and President Johnson satisfy their constraint by having opposite values, the Graduated Response Strategy cannot successfully make both of them have the same value. Similarly, to the extent that the Graduated Response Strategy is able to constrain Success and President Johnson to have the same value as it, they cannot also have different values from each other. So no perfect solution is possible: Because the constraints cannot all be satisfied, harmony is necessarily less than one.

In contrast, consider the ability of the balanced structure to satisfy its constraints. In processing the verbal statements for it, individuals begin with all the ideas in mind, and then the statements tell them to link the Graduated Response Strategy inhibitorially to the idea of Success but excitatorially to the idea of the President Johnson, and also to inhibitorially link Success to President Johnson. Similarly, the operation of the harmony calculating program begins by setting the activations of all the ideas to small random values, and then Graduated Response Strategy tries to make President Johnson have the same value as it. It also tries to make Success have an opposite value from it. Success cooperates by also trying to make Graduated Response Strategy have an opposite value from it. Similarly, President Johnson is cooperating by trying to make Graduated Response Strategy have the same value as it, and trying to make Success have an opposite value from it. All the ideas are cooperating with each other because their constraints are internally consistent. So a perfect solution is possible: Graduated Response Strategy and President Johnson are both activated maximally (+1), and Success is -1. All the constraints can be satisfied simultaneously: Harmony is +1.

The main evidence for our harmony hypothesis comes from a series of five experiments, three of which were reported in Britton and Eisenhart (1993). The results show that inharmonious structures are found significantly more often among the less capable learners, and among those who read less clear texts. But experts have highly harmonious structures for consistent texts in their subject matter area. In unpublished research, we have shown that individual's harmony values correlate positively with their judgments of ease of understanding texts, and that people seek more harmonious memory structures. Further research is underway.

In the harmony calculations, each rating of relatedness on the CS test is interpreted as the degree of association (excitatory or inhibitory) between the two terms of the pair. So the complete set of ratings for a subject provides the subject's associative knowledge about the terms or propositions, with the knowledge expressed as an associative matrix whose entries are the relatedness ratings between each term and each other term. Such a matrix can also be pictured following the conventions of Figure 17.5. Figure 17.6 shows such a drawing. It shows the CS ratings of the author of the text that is summarized in Appendix 17.1, by Major R. C. Earhart, then a history professor at the Air Force Academy. The convention is that solid lines indicate positive links, and dashed lines negative links, as in Figure 17.5. For example, Figure 17.6 shows that the link between Graduated Response Strategy and President Johnson is positive, but there are negative links between Success and both Graduated Response Strategy and President Johnson. (This subset of relations is consistent with the balanced structure in Figure 17.5.)

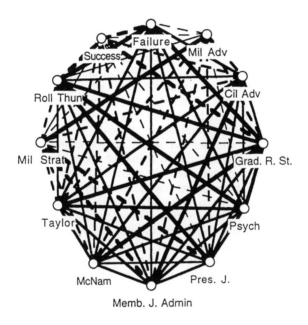

Figure 17.6. Major Earhart's associative structure for the Air Force Rolling Thunder text.

We then simulate the individual's thinking about this entire matrix. This corresponds to the process of thinking that often takes place after individuals have learned some body of knowledge about a subject matter area. For example, after any chapter has been read, the reader will have a knowledge structure that is composed of the ideas in that chapter in relation to each of the other ideas in that chapter. If thinking about that knowledge structure ensues, the reader may come to a conclusion about how well the set of ideas in the chapter "makes sense" or "fits together." Our algorithm for calculating harmony guarantees that if the relations in a knowledge structure form a consistent, consonant and balanced structure, they will have a high overall harmony score, but if they are inconsistent, dissonant or unbalanced, they will have a low overall harmony score. The overall harmony score is interpreted as the subject's feeling of comfort, confidence, consistency and certainty about his knowledge of the subject matter as a whole. The overall harmony of Figure 17.6 is .96. The overall harmonies of the structures in Figure 17.5 are the sums of either the bottom or the next-to-bottom panels.

Up to this point we have discussed only the overall harmony of memory structures considered as a whole. But for cognitively diagnostic assessment and rewriting the text, it is even more useful to know the specific locations of disharmonies in the student's knowledge structure because interventions can then be targeted at inconsistencies. The disharmonious locations represent the ideas and relations about which the student is most uncertain. These are the things that learners ought to ask questions about, but normally they can only do so if they are metacognitively skilled enough to be able to identify the loci of their uncertainty. However, with our system, even if learners lack those metacognitive skills, researchers can help by pointing out to the rewriter those areas where our calculations indicate they have inconsistent structures. These are areas where they ought to feel uncertain, because calculations indicate inconsistencies in their knowledge structures.

This system is the first to provide this information on the specific locations of disharmonies. For example, in the case of the structures in the top panel of Figure 17.5, the second panel shows example activations of the nodes after the system has finished thinking about the structure. The third panel shows the resulting harmony associated with each node; notice that for the unbalanced structure some nodes have zero harmony. (The harmony values are scaled to be from -1 to +1.) The bottom panel shows the entire matrix of harmonies output by the system, with the negative entries representing disharmony. This shows the harmonies associated with specific links in the knowledge structure: the link between B and C is the most problematic one in the unbalanced knowledge structure. Low harmony nodes (B and C) and links (between B and C) are the topics that learners should feel moved to ask questions about.

This corresponds to the common experience in which when individuals feel uncomfortable about some knowledge structure — say, one that they have built from a chapter, article, or talk — they can specify which are the ideas that are disharmonious, so they can say that "this idea doesn't make sense" or "this idea doesn't fit with the other ideas," and so on. A common response to this feeling of disharmony is to seek further information (e.g., by asking a question). But less competent learners may be unable to specify the locations of their uncertainty accurately enough to be able to ask questions directed at their areas of uncertainty. Because the system can identify those locations, our rewriting can take them into account. (In the CS program, the CS test results are used to calculate harmony scores for each subject.[1] The harmony scores are provided online.)

---

[1] The CS program calculates harmony as in McClelland and Rumelhart (1988; pp. 50-52) and Smolensky (1986). The individual's ratings of relatedness are interpreted as weights on the links between all the terms in a connectionist network. The initial activations of the terms are set at small random values, and then activation is spread until the network settles to stable final activation values. (The average of several runs can

Challenges for the Diagnosis-Treatment Revision Method

We have confirmed that the CS system can effectively diagnose and re-pair cognitive structures in Britton and Tidwell (1991, 1993) and Tidwell (1992); repairs substantially reduced the discrepancies that had diagnosed between experts and novices, as shown in Table 17.5.

Table 17.5

Shifts of novices' structures toward experts' knowledge structures[a]

	Original Version	**Revised Version**
Text 1	.22[b]	.86[*]
Text 2	62	.86[*]

[*]$p < .05$ different from original version
[a]From Britton & Tidwell (1991)
[b]Numbers are correlations of novices' relatedness ratings with experts' relatedness ratings.

An important challenge is to improve the relation between the diagnoses and the repairs. Britton and Tidwell (1991) and Tidwell (1992) depended on their knowledge of the subject matter area to devise effective and efficient repairs. These repairs were very easy to do: Once we saw what the novices did not understand, we simply put it into the text. Whether this will be a generally useful procedure is a matter for further research. As the automatic diagnosis program improves, the cognitive load of the diagnosis phase on the rewriter will be reduced, freeing capacity for devising effective repairs. Automatic repair procedures should also be investigated intensively because of their efficiency advantages

---

be used.) The harmony calculation is based on the goodness-of-fit between the product of the final activation values and the weights. To calculate goodness-of-fit, the product of each pair of final activation values is multiplied by the weight between them. This provides the harmony associated with the link between that pair.

For example, if two terms were rated as being very closely related, the weight on their link is +1, and if their final activations are the same as each other (i.e., either both +1 or both -1) then the product of the final activations and the weight is either +1 x +1 x +1 = +1 or -1 x -1 x +1 = +1, which both give a maximum harmony of +1. Similarly, if the two terms were rated as being very distantly related, the weight on their link is -1, and if their final activation values are different (i.e., one is +1 and the other is -1) then their harmony is +1 x -1 x -1 = +1, which is also maximum harmony. But if the weight is, e.g., -1 and the final activations are the same, e.g., +1 and +1, then the harmony is -1 x +1 x +1 = -1, which is minimum harmony. Or if the weight is +1 and the final activations are +1 and -1, then the harmony is -1. Intermediate values of weights and activations produce intermediate harmonies.

These harmonies are then displayed for each link, aggregated across individual nodes to provide a harmony value for each node, and aggregated across the set of nodes to provide an overall harmony value.

A second challenge is to improve experts' or rewriter's ability to select terms that will be maximally diagnostic for novice's structures. Schvaneveldt (1992) suggested that the selection of maximally diagnostic terms is a "black art." To deal with this problem we designed our computer program to make it easy for experts to quickly try out sets of terms on themselves as well as on novices. In addition, we developed some useful term-selection guidelines for experts to use to select terms. Further research is needed to test these techniques.

A third challenge is to develop automatic methods for integrating the harmony analyses with the information about discrepancies from the experts' structure, and linking the results to optimal repair strategies. It appears likely that novices may be most susceptible to intervention in areas of their knowledge structure about which they feel most uncertain. Therefore, it may be possible to exploit areas of correspondence between the misconceptions and the disharmonies to use relatively small text interventions to induce large changes in knowledge structures.

In conclusion, the Cognitive Structure Testing system has been shown to be an effective method for rewriting text to shift novice's knowledge structures toward experts' in one subject matter area (Britton & Tidwell, 1991; 1993; Tidwell, 1992). We believe that this can be generalized to other subject matter areas. From the beginning, our goal has been to develop educational systems for real-world application. The CS computer program described here is available for general use, and the generality of its effectiveness must be tested.

Method of Good Examples

The third method for improving military textbooks has not yet been tested. But it can be used even more easily than any of the other methods. I call it the *Method of Good Examples*. It is based on a series of studies on 88 pairs of texts (Britton, 1986; Britton et al., 1989; Gulgoz, 1986; Tidwell, 1989; Van Dusen, 1988). All these texts had been revised by others (Graves & Hodge, 1971; Graves & Slater, 1988; Hirsch, 1970; Kern, Sticht, Welty, & Hauke, 1976). In each pair, one was an original text, and the other was the revised version of that text.

We tested how much was learned from each of these 88 texts on separate groups of students. The results for one set of texts are shown in Table 17.6. The main things to notice here are, first, that the average text was improved, as shown by the mean difference at the bottom of the table. Second, notice that some of the texts were much more improved than others. The ones that were much improved are called the Good Examples. Tables 17.7 and 17.8 show others of the data sets, and they have Good Examples too.

In order to show writers how to improve instructional text, all of the Good Examples — and only the good examples — should be given to writers with the following instructions: "Here, do it like these people did." I bet this would work, but it has not yet been tried.

Table 17.6
Improvement of Kern et al. (1976) revisions (Data from Britton et al., 1989)

Text Topic	Original Version Retention	Revised Version Retention	Retention Difference
Nuclear weapons	33	55	+22
Tank crew duties	43	63	+20
Firing at a sniper	57	77	+20
Controlling shock	60	77	+17
Foot patrols by MPs	49	64	+15
Blasting caps	29	41	+12
Placing radio antennas	61	73	+12
Duties of rifle squad leaders	32	35	+3
Using radar to check vehicle speeds	43	44	+1
Care of the feet	61	61	0
Mean	47	59	+12

Table 17.7
Improvement of Robert Graves (1971) revisions (data from Britton et al. (1989)

Text Topic	Original Version	Revised Version Retention	Retention Differences
History of a century	27	45	+18
Medieval view of science	17	34	+17
Liberty	13	29	+16
Arms control	32	43	+11
Future of humankind	9	17	+8
Weights of stars	31	37	+6
Running down of the universe	24	29	+5
Struggles for existence	41	40	-1
Archeological report of Wooley	34	33	-1
Effects of steam power	39	36	-3
Whitehead's view of physical nature and living nature	23	19	-4
Scientific analysis	38	27	-11
Mean	27	32	+5

Table 17.8
Improvement of E.D. Hirsch (1970) revisions (Data from Tidwell, 1989).

Passage	Original Version Retention	Revised Version Retention	Retention Difference
Art forms	37	48	+11
Friendship	50	58	+8
T.V. violence	49	55	+6
Weather	35	40	+5
Isolation	44	49	+5
Laetrile	54	58	+4
E.R.A.	52	56	+4
Time vs. Newsweek	49	52	+3
Caesarean sections	61	64	+3
Witchcraft	57	58	+1
Genetic research	44	45	+1
Moral decay	54	54	0
Live drama vs. T.V. drama	60	60	0
Family size	58	58	0
Adoption policies	60	59	-1
Student revolution	42	41	-1
Human rights violations	52	48	-4
Admission quotas	47	41	-6
Mean			+2

Acknowledgments

This research was supported by ONR Grant 442-8041–01, AFOSR grant 89-0515, and OERI Grant 117A 2007. The intellectual assistance and encouragement of Susan Chipman, Jamie Eisenhart, Patrick Kyllonen and Abraham Tesser was indispensible throughout, as was the programming assistance of Cathy Brooks, Andrew Lech, and Rohit Wangeo. Anne Reynolds helped by independently selecting the CS terms for the Air Force Vietnam text. Ray Christal, Gail McKoon, William Montague, Roger Ratcliff, Wallace Sinaiko, and George Sperling provided valuable comments on earlier versions of these ideas.

Appendix 17.1

This Appendix provides a brief description of how the CS test was constructed for the text that is briefly summarized below. (The entire Original text (Earhart, 1978; U.S. Reserve Officer's Training Corps., 1985) is available on request from the first author.)

The text began by describing some *members of the Johnson Administration*, including *President Johnson*, who had *civilian advisers*, including *Robert McNamara* and *Maxwell Taylor*, as well as *military advisers*. The military advisers proposed the *military strategy*, which was (roughly) to bomb North Vietnam very heavily. The civilian advisers proposed instead the *graduated response strategy*, which was to bomb North Vietnam a little and then pause to see if that had "broken their will;" if it hadn't, the bombing would be escalated gradually. Since the focus was on breaking the North Vietnamese will, this was described in the passage as a *psychological* strategy. Johnson chose the graduated response strategy, and the resulting operation was codenamed *Rolling Thunder*. *Success* and *failure* could be attributed to various persons, policies, actions, and consequences in the passage.

The CS Test

The 12 italicized terms in this summary were selected by Bruce Britton in conjunction with Anne Reynolds to represent important topics of the text. All possible pairs of these terms were presented to subjects in random order, each with a 7-point scale ranging from *very closely related (1) to very distantly related (7)*.

— 18 —

SELF-REGULATION AND STRATEGY INSTRUCTION FOR STUDENTS WHO FIND WRITING AND LEARNING CHALLENGING

Steve Graham & Karen R. Harris
University of Maryland

In a study examining students' knowledge of the writing process (Graham, Schwartz, & MacArthur, 1993), a fifth-grader provided us with a very cogent description of what good writers do when they write:

> They brainstorm ideas...then think about it and then write about it ...look it over to see how to make it all fit in right...then they do a final copy and go over that; and then if it is still not right, they do it again.

This exposition was a reminder of more sophisticated descriptions of the writing process furnished by some of the novelists, playwrights, and other professional writers interviewed for the literary magazine, the *Paris Review*. When planning *The Naked and the Dead*, for example, Norman Mailer indicated that he developed extensive notes, including a long dossier on each character and charts outlining the action and the interaction of the characters (Plimpton, 1967). In describing his writing habits, Truman Capote reported that he repeatedly reworked what he wrote, writing the first draft in longhand, revising in longhand, revising again at the typewriter, and revising yet again after letting the manuscript set for a week or more (Cowley, 1958).

Planning and revising text involves the use of a variety of self-regulation procedures such as goal setting, seeking information, reviewing notes, and previous drafts of text, evaluation, organizing and transforming ideas, and checking and monitoring (Graham & Harris, 1994a). Skilled writers also use these and other self-regulation strategies to help them manage the writing task, their behavior, and their working environment. Many professional writers, for instance, indicate that they use strategies such as goal setting, self-monitoring, and environmental structuring to help them regulate their output and bolster motivation. Erica Jong, the author of the *Fear of Flying*, noted that she sets a goal to write 10 pages a day in longhand (Safire & Safire, 1992). Other writers get started writing each day by working in a specific place or following a well defined routine. For example, Toni Morrison, author of *Beloved* and *Tar Baby*, indicated that she gets up at 5:00, makes coffee, goes to a hotel room she keeps for the purpose of writing, watches the sun come up, and then begins to write (Burnham, 1994).

Children who find learning challenging

In contrast to skilled writers, children who experience difficulty learning in school employ a different, less sophisticated approach to writing — one that minimizes the role of planning, revising, and other self-regulation strategies (Englert, Raphael, Anderson, Anthony, Stevens, & Fear, 1991; Graham, 1990; McCutchen, 1988). They typically convert writing tasks into tasks of telling what one knows, doing little planning or reflection in advance or during the act of writing. Any information that is somewhat topic appropriate is retrieved from memory and written down, with each preceding phrase or sentence stimulating the generation of the next idea. Little attention is directed at rhetorical goals, the organization of the text, the needs of the audience, or the constraints imposed by the topic. This retrieve-and-write process typically functions like an automated and encapsulated program, operating largely without metacognitive control.

An important goal in writing instruction for students who find learning challenging, therefore, is to help them incorporate additional self-regulatory procedures into their writing, so that they become more resourceful, reflective, and goal oriented. An obvious means for accomplishing this objective is to confront this automated retrieve-and-write strategy head on by explicitly teaching these students to upgrade or even replace their existing writing strategies with more sophisticated procedures, those requiring the use of the same types of self-regulatory procedures used by skilled writers.

In this chapter we describe a program of research designed to investigate the effectiveness of this approach with students with learning disabilities. The children participating in these studies were primarily in the upper elementary grades, received special education services, scored within the normal range on measures of intelligence, and experienced difficulty learning to write and, in most cases, learning to read. We first examine several studies focusing on a specific self-regulatory process, either self-monitoring or goal setting. This is followed by the analysis of a broader-based approach, where specific planning and revising strategies were taught in conjunction with other self-regulation procedures such as goal setting and self-monitoring. Specific procedures for helping writers become more strategic are also presented by Sharples (chapter 7 in this volume) and Reece and Cumming (chapter 19 in this volume) as well as by Flower (1981), Kellogg (1987), and Bereiter and Scardamalia (1982).

Self-monitoring and goal setting

Monitoring output

One of the most striking characteristics of the writing of students with learning disabilities is that they produce very little of it. Their papers are inordinately short, containing little detail, description, or elaboration (Graham, Harris, MacArthur, & Schwartz, 1991). Although it is possible that their relatively short compositions are due to a lack of knowledge or interest in the types of topics they are asked to write about, it also appears that they terminate the composing process too soon — before accessing what they do know. In a study by Graham (1990), fourth- and sixth-grade students with learning disabilities spent only 6 to 7 minutes when writing an opinion essay, generating only 26 and 41 words, respectively. When prompted to write more, however, the students' text became two to four times longer, with approximately one half of the prompted material being new and useful information.

One way that some professional writers regulate their writing output is by monitoring their productivity. For example, Irving Wallace, a contemporary novelist, indicated that he often kept a chart of how many pages he wrote each day. According to Wallace, the practice of monitoring his literary output helped him establish discipline over his writing, "its figures scolding me or encouraging me" (Wallace, 1971, p. 65). We examined if a similar method would have a positive effect on the writing output of students with learning disabilities (Harris, Graham, Reid, McElroy, & Hamby, 1994).

Fifth- and sixth-grade students with learning disabilities who had difficulty attending to task and completing classroom writing assignments were taught two different self-monitoring strategies. One mimicked the strategy used by Irving Wallace — students counted and graphed the number of words included in each story completed. The other involved recording and graphing on-task behavior during the writing period. Students asked themselves if they were on task whenever they heard a signal delivered approximately every 45 seconds via headphones.

Both of the self-monitoring procedures had a positive and similar effect on students' behavior and writing performance. When using either one of the procedures, students were more actively involved during the writing period (on task behavior improved from 50% to 80%), generated longer stories (papers doubled in length), and wrote stories that were more engaging (the quality of students' papers evidenced a 2-point improvement on an 8-point quality scale). Although students' opinions on which method worked best were mixed, some of the participating students complained that having to wear the headphones was embarrassing and the teacher indicated that simply counting the number of words written was easier to implement as it required no special preparation.

This study illustrated that self-monitoring can have a positive effect on the writing output and working behaviors of students with learning disabilities. Whereas the study focused on the product of writing, students can also be asked to monitor how they write. They can complete a writing process checklist, for instance, noting the specific actions undertaken when writing. This might include actions aimed at arranging a time and place to write, understanding the task; planning, seeking, and organizing information; revising; obtaining necessary assistance; and self-consequating (see Harris & Graham, 1992a, for an example). In addition to serving as a reminder to engage in these processes, such a checklist provides students with important tips on how to write as well as feedback on their approach to writing.

Setting goals

When writing *Origin of the Species*, Charles Darwin became concerned because he was not able to stabilize the amount of work he completed each day. At his wife's suggestion, he began each working session by deciding how many points he would prove, representing each with a pebble in a pile on the sandwalk outside his study. Each time a point was proved and buttressed with a footnote, he knocked a pebble away from the pile (Stone, 1978).

In a study by Voth and Graham (1995), a similar strategy was used to help seventh- and eighth-grade students with learning disabilities improve their essay writing. During individual conferences with their teacher, students set goals designed to increase the number of proofs and/or refutations typically included in their papers. Proofs were the number of reasons that supported the author's premise, and refutations were the number of reasons supporting the counterposition that were discredited.

Half of the students who set goals were further taught a strategy designed to help them achieve their objectives. The success of goal setting is dependent on one's ability to put together an effective series of activities for achieving the intended outcome (Locke, Shaw, Saari, & Latham, 1981). Because students with learning disabilities often have difficulty with the self-regulation of organized strategic behavior (Harris, 1982), we anticipated that they would benefit from this additional support.

Setting goals had a positive impact on students' writing. Students who set goals wrote papers that were longer and were judged to be more persuasive than papers written by students in a control group. Teaching students to use a strategy to help them accomplish their goals, however, only augmented students' goal setting performance when they set a goal to refute reasons that ran counter to their premise. Why was the strategy unnecessary when setting a goal to include more supporting proofs? It was probably because this goal was fairly easy for the participating students to achieve, making the use of the strategy superfluous. Although the participating students rarely addressed the counterposition in an essay written before the introduction of goal setting, they almost always included at least one or two reasons to support their premise.

As with self-monitoring, goal setting can also be applied to the processes involved in writing. Robert Heinlein, author of *Stranger in a Strange Land*, for instance, noted that an important objective in his writing was to "cut away the fat" (Safire & Safire, 1992). Whereas a revising goal to shorten the papers of students with learning disabilities is probably not the best place to start (remember their compositions are typically short on ideas and details), Graham, MacArthur, and Schwartz (1995) examined if setting a goal to add information during revising was worthwhile. Similar to other children, the revising behavior of students with learning disabilities can best be described as house cleaning. Most of their revisions are aimed at trying to tidy-up mechanical errors and cleaning up speech (MacArthur & Graham, 1987; MacArthur, Graham, & Schwartz, 1991). One possible means for changing these students' preoccupation with surface-level features when revising is to assign them a revising goal that directs their attention to more substantive concerns.

To test this hypothesis, fourth- through sixth-grade students with learning disabilities were randomly assigned to one of the following three conditions. A control group was given a general revising goal to make their paper better. The two experimental groups were given a specific revising goal to "add" three things to make their paper better. As in the Voth and Graham (1995) study, half of the students in the experimental group were further taught a strategy designed to help them achieve their objective.

Students assigned the general goal to make their paper better exhibited the typical pattern of revising — they made their paper look neater and corrected errors of mechanics and usage as best they could. In contrast, students assigned a goal to add information took a more balanced approach to revising. Whereas they continued to make a comparable number of house-cleaning changes when compared to students in the control group, they made three times as many meaning-changing revisions, primarily involving additions. These changes were strong enough to have a small, but positive effect on the quality of students' writing. Neither revising behavior nor the quality of text, however, were appreciably enhanced as a result of teaching students to use a strategy designed to help them achieve their objective.

The goals used in both of the studies presented previously supplied a specific and clear standard of performance. These properties facilitate goal attainment, as they provide a clear indication of what is required, making it easier to plan how to obtain the goal as well as assess progress in achieving it (Locke et al., 1981). Many of the goals that writers set, however, are not this specific. For example, Robert Heinlein's goal to "cut away the fat" specifies the process to be used, but does not provide an objective means for determining when this is accomplished. In helping poor writers establish goal setting as an integral part of the writing process, both general writing goals (e.g., writing a funny paper) and specific product goals should be emphasized. This provides a much more comprehensive net for casting one's writing plan (Harris & Graham, 1992a).

Self-regulated strategy development

A recent emphasis in writing instruction is the explicit, context-based teaching of strategies for planning and revising (cf. Englert et al., 1991; Kellogg, 1987). Since the early 1980s, we have been involved in evaluating a theoretically and empirically based instructional model for developing writing and self-regulation strategies among students, especially children who find learning and writing challenging (cf. Harris & Graham, 1992a, 1992b). We refer to this approach as self-regulated strategy development (SRSD). With SRSD, students are explicitly taught strategies for planning and revising in combination with procedures for regulating the use of these strategies, the writing process, and undesirable behaviors (such as impulsivity or negative self-talk) that may impede performance.

The goals of SRSD

The major goals of SRSD include helping students master the higher-level cognitive processes involved in composing; develop autonomous, reflective, self-regulated use of effective writing strategies; increase knowledge about the characteristics of good writing; and form positive attitudes about writing and themselves as writers. Various forms of support for achieving these goals are contained within the model.

One form of support is inherent in the planning and revising strategies students are taught. A strategy such as outlining or semantic webbing, for instance, helps students regulate the writing process by providing structure that organizes and sequences behavior. A second form of support involves helping students acquire self-regulation skills needed to use the target strategies successfully and manage the writing process. This includes teaching students to monitor changes in their writing performance or behavior (including strategy use), set goals for improving their performance through using the target strategies, and develop an internal dialogue for directing strategy use as well as the writing process.

In developing an internal dialogue, students create personalized self-statements designed to help them manage one or more of the following processes: defining the problem (*What do I have to do?*), planning (*How should I change the strategy for this assignment?*), evaluating (*Did I do this right?*), reinforcing (*I did a great job.*), and so forth. When necessary, students may also be encouraged to develop self-statements for promoting desirable behaviors (*I can do this by working hard.*) or controlling maladaptive behaviors such as impulsivity (*Take my time.*).

Support is further provided through the methods used to teach the target writing and self-regulation strategies. As students initially learn to use these processes, the teacher supplies considerable assistance by modeling, explaining, reexplaining, and assisting whenever necessary. This scaffolding is gradually withdrawn as students become increasingly adept at using the strategies independently.

Additional support involves the use of instructional procedures to increase students' knowledge about themselves, writing, and the writing process. Model compositions are typically used to illustrate the characteristics of good writing, whereas self-monitoring, goal setting, and teacher feedback help students acquire knowledge of their writing capabilities and how to regulate the composing process.

Stages and characteristics of instruction

Six instructional stages provide the structural framework for SRSD (Harris & Graham, 1992a, 1992b). The following stages represent a "metascript," providing a general guideline that can be reordered, combined, or modified to meet student and teacher needs.

1. The teacher helps students develop the preskills, including knowledge of the criteria for good writing, important to understanding, acquiring, or executing the target strategy (*Develop Background Knowledge*).

2. Teacher and students examine and discuss current writing performance and the strategies used to accomplish specific assignments (*Initial*

Conference: Strategy Goals and Significance). The strategy, its purpose and benefits, and how and when to use it are then examined, and students are asked to make a commitment to learn the strategy and act as a collaborative partner in this endeavor. Negative or ineffective self-statements or beliefs students currently use may also be addressed at this time.

3. The teacher models how to use the strategy, employing appropriate self-instructions (*Modeling of the Strategy).* The self-instructions include a combination of problem definition, planning, strategy use, self-evaluation, coping and error correction, and self-reinforcement statements. After analyzing the model's performance, teacher and students may collaborate on how to change the strategy to make it more effective or efficient. Each student then develops and records personal self-statements they plan to use during writing.

4. The steps of the strategy and any accompanying mnemonic for remembering them as well as the personalized self-statements are memorized; paraphrasing is allowed as long as the original meaning is maintained (*Memorization of the Strategy).* This stage is included for students who have severe learning and memory problems and is not be needed by all students.

5. Students and teachers use the strategy and self-instructions collaboratively (*Collaborative Practice)* to complete specific writing assignments. Self-regulation procedures, including self-assessment or goal setting may be introduced at this point.

6. Students use the strategy independently (*Independent Performance).* If goal-setting and self-assessment procedures are in use, students and the instructor may decide to start fading them out; students are also encouraged to say their self-statements covertly in "their head."

Procedures for promoting maintenance and generalization are integrated throughout the SRSD model. These include discussing opportunities to use, and results of using, the strategy and self-regulation procedures with other tasks and in other settings; asking parents and other teachers to comment on the student's success in using the strategy; and working with other teachers to prompt the use of the strategy in their classrooms.

In addition to these components, there are several characteristics critical to the effective implementation of the model. First, interactive learning between teachers and students, consistent with the dialectical constructivist viewpoint is emphasized (Pressley, Harris, & Marks, 1992). Students are viewed as active collaborators who work with each other and their teacher to determine the goals of instruction; complete the task; and implement, evaluate, and modify the strategy and strategy-acquisition procedures. Second, instruction is individualized so that the strategies and skills targeted for instruction are designed to "upgrade" each child's current approach to writing. Teachers also provide individually tailored feedback and support and may modify the basic steps of the model (adding, deleting, or rearranging), depending on students' individual needs and capabilities. Finally, instruction is criterion rather than time based. Thus, students move through the instructional process at their own pace and do not proceed to later stages of instruction until they have met the criteria for doing so. Instruction is not terminated until students have mastered the strategy, using it efficiently and effectively. Finally, SRSD is an ongoing process in which new strategies are introduced and previously taught strategies are upgraded. For example, in teaching students how to use a peer-revising strategy, a child may initially use only two criteria to evaluate his partner's writing, identifying places in text that are unclear and places where more detail is needed (see MacArthur, Schwartz, & Graham, 1991). Later, the strategy may be upgraded to include feedback on text structure and order (see Stoddard & MacArthur, 1993).

Findings

The SRSD model has been used to teach a variety of planning and revising strategies to students with learning disabilities, including brainstorming (Harris & Graham, 1985), reading for information and semantic webbing (MacArthur, Schwartz, Graham, Molloy, & Harris, 1995), generating and organizing writing content using text structure (Danoff, Harris, & Graham, 1993; De La Paz & Graham, 1995; Graham & Harris, 1989a, 1989b; Sawyer, Graham, & Harris, 1992; Sexton, Harris, & Graham, 1995), goal setting (Graham, MacArthur, Schwartz, & Voth, 1992) revising using peer feedback (MacArthur, Schwartz, & Graham, 1991; Stoddard & MacArthur, 1993), and revising for both mechanics and substance (Graham & MacArthur, 1988).

In all of the studies conducted to date, SRSD has provided an effective means for teaching writing and self-regulation strategies. In each investigation, the quality and usually the length and structure of students' compositions improved after teaching them either a planning or revising strategy and accompanying self-regulation procedures via SRSD.[1] Effect sizes typically exceeded 1.0 (Graham & Harris, 1993). Although students usually maintained these gains on follow-up probes administered 1 to 2 months later, their success in adapting particular strategies to different writing genres (from expository to narrative writing for example) has been more variable (Graham et al., 1991). As a result, we recommend that direct and assisted practice in applying strategies across different genres be included as a routine part of instruction.

Improvements in what students write were accompanied by changes in their approach to writing. After learning a prewriting strategy using SRSD, for example, students who initially did no planning in advance consistently developed plans and ideas prior to writing (cf. Graham & Harris, 1989b). Concurrent changes have also occurred in students' knowledge of writing and their confidence in their writing capabilities, or self-efficacy. For instance, when students were taught a strategy for setting writing goals, per-

---

[1] Writing quality was measured using traditional holistic ratings. Compositions were typed and all identifying information was removed prior to scoring. Each composition was scored by two raters who were unfamiliar with the design and purpose of the study. Reliability coefficients between the two raters typically ranged between .80 – .90 .

ceptions of writing competence became more accurate and understanding of what good writers do shifted from a focus on mechanical factors to an emphasis on substance (Graham et al., 1992). Finally, students' and teachers' evaluations of SRSD have been uniformly positive. As one teacher noted, she could see "the light bulbs going on" as students learned the strategy (Danoff et al., 1993).

An example

Ray Bradbury, author of the *Martian Chronicles* and other works of science fiction, indicated that his formula for writing stories involved creating a character who wants something and then setting him or her off to find it (Bradbury, 1990). Isaac Asimov, another science fiction writer and author of the *Foundation* trilogy, used a slightly different strategy — before writing, he first decided how the story would end and the problem it centered around (Asimov, 1994). Prior to actually writing, both authors made crucial decisions about the structure of their story.

In a series of studies with fourth- through sixth-grade students, we examined if a similar strategy would help students who find learning and writing challenging create better stories (Danoff et al., 1993; Graham & Harris, 1989a, MacArthur, Graham, & Schwartz, in press; Sawyer et al., 1992). Before writing, students were encouraged to ask themselves a series of questions about the structure of their story, including questions about the story's setting, characters, and their goals; actions for achieving these goals; and the story's ending. To further help them regulate the writing process and use of the story writing strategy, they set goals for using the strategy and writing complete stories, monitored their writing output and strategy use, and managed specific aspects of their writing behavior through the use of personalized self-statements (e.g., one student used the statement, "take my time," to counter his impulsivity). The SRSD procedures for learning the strategy are described in Appendix 18.1.

Learning the "story writing" strategy and accompanying self-regulation procedures via SRSD resulted in improvements in the schematic structure and overall quality of students' writing. The following two stories (corrected for mechanical, but not grammatical errors), written by a fifth grade student with learning disabilities, illustrate the types of changes that occurred.

> BEFORE INSTRUCTION: *One day I was running in the field. It was very hot and leaves was falling. There are lots of hills and nice green grass. There are huge trees thats full of leaves. There were lots of flowers in the garden. It was a lot of shade. Lots of bushes that has leaves on it. And the summer was nice.*

> AFTER INSTRUCTION: *Once upon a time, an Indian named Rob wanted to ride a horse again. The reason why Rob wanted to ride again is because two years ago, he had an accident on the horse. Rob had got hurt bad. He had to get his legs cut off. So one day Rob went outside in his wheelchair and he seen a horse. It was all white and then Rob wheeled his chair over to*

the horse. And Rob grabbed the horse and pulled his self up.
Rob was on the horse. Then the horse took off. And the horse
was kicking and then he jumped up and Rob the brave Indian
fell off and died. He was brave so that is the end of him.

In addition to improving what students' wrote, instruction changed how they wrote. After learning the story writing strategy, most of the participating students continued to use it to develop an initial writing plan, which they modified as they wrote. Prior to instruction, students rarely did any planning in advance of writing. Learning the strategy and accompanying self-regulation procedures also had a salutatory effect on students' efficacy for writing. For example, one student noted, "Now this story writing makes sense."

Process writing and strategy instruction working in tandem

In the popular process approach to writing instruction (cf. Atwell, 1987), the cognitive processes and strategies considered central to effective writing are emphasized by encouraging students to plan and revise, providing assistance in carrying out writing processes during individual or group conferences, creating social situations where students assist each other in planning and revising their texts, and delivering process-oriented instruction through occasional mini-lessons. It is important to note, however, that cognitive processes and strategies may not receive enough attention in process writing classes, as they are often considered secondary to the development of content and communication (cf. Fitzgerald & Stamm, 1990). Moreover, explicit instruction in using specific writing strategies is uncommon in many of these classrooms (cf. Anthony & Anderson, 1987). Instead, teachers focus on facilitating children's "natural" development over long periods of time through questions and "gentle" responses during conferences, sharing, and so forth.

Students who find learning and writing challenging may require more extensive, structured, and explicit instruction (than is typically provided in process writing classes) to master the skills and processes critical to effective writing (Graham & Harris, 1994b; Harris & Graham, 1994). A considerable amount of evidence, for example, demonstrates that students who find learning challenging do not acquire a variety of cognitive and metacognitive skills unless detailed and explicit instruction is provided (cf. Brown, Campione, & Day, 1981). We have conducted several studies examining the impact of integrating strategy instruction into process writing classrooms (Danoff et al., 1993; Graham & Harris, in press; Harris & Graham, 1993; MacArthur et al., in press; MacArthur, Schwartz, & Graham, 1991). Two of these studies are considered here: One focuses on the process of revising and the other explores planning.

In the study involving revising (MacArthur, Schwartz, & Graham, 1991), 12 students with learning disabilities in fourth- through sixth-grade were taught a reciprocal peer-editing strategy to use during Writers' Workshop (Atwell, 1987), a conventional process approach to writing. The strategy prepared students to work in pairs to help each other revise their papers. Following SRSD instruction, students taught the strategy made more revisions and produced papers of higher quality when revising with peer support than students in a Writer's Workshop control group. When revising without peer support, students in the strategy group continued to make more revisions than students in the control group.

Similar results were obtained when the story writing strategy described in the previous section was integrated into fourth- and fifth-grade classes using Writers' Workshop (Danoff et al., 1993). The strategy and accompanying self-regulation procedures were taught during daily minilessons. Each of the participating classes contained one student with learning disabilities who was being mainstreamed for the entire school day. The writing performance of each of these students and one average writer from each class was monitored before, during, and after instruction using a multiple baseline design.

Following SRSD instruction, the schematic structure of stories written by both the average writers and the students with learning disabilities improved. These improvements were maintained over time. Even more importantly, the quality of students' stories improved as well. The only exception involved the fourth-grade students, who wrote qualitatively better stories immediately following instruction but did not maintain these gains over time.

The findings from these two studies demonstrate that the integration of more extensive and explicit strategy instruction into a process approach to writing can have a positive effect on both average writers and students with learning disabilities. Including strategy instruction as part of Writers' Workshop may have been beneficial in these and other studies (Graham & Harris, in press; Harris & Graham, 1993; MacArthur et al., in press), because it made important cognitive processes more visible and concrete to students.

Nourishing the development of self-regulation

In this chapter, we examined how the automated retrieve-and-write strategy used by many students who find learning and writing challenging can be addressed head-on by explicitly teaching them more sophisticated strategies — those involving the use of the same types of self-regulatory procedures used by more skilled writers. Although this is a crucial ingredient in an effective writing program (for students with and without writing problems), such instruction needs to occur in an environment in which students skills in self-regulation can prosper and grow (such as a process writing classroom). In closing, we offer several observations important to creating such a writing environment.

In a recent "Peanuts" cartoon, Charlie Brown's sister, Sally, shared her very short report on Lincoln with her class by telling them, "If I had a dime for every one of these stupid reports I have written, I would be a rich person." When students do not value writing or what they write, they are less likely to engage in the types of mental activities that epitomize skilled writing. For example, they may fail to utilize the resources at their disposal, including the specific strategy and self-regulation procedures taught in the classroom. This was aptly illustrated in another cartoon, where Calvin tells his imaginary tiger friend, Hobbes, the necessary steps for doing his homework assignment, but then promptly decides not to do it because he does not care about the assignment (Wigfield, 1994). Teachers can counter such apathy, however, by encouraging students to choose their own writing topics; assigning topics that are designed to serve a real purpose; encouraging students to share their work with others; and creating a classroom environment that is supportive, pleasant, and nonthreatening (Graham & Harris, 1994a).

An important principle in self-regulated learning is that people learn by doing (Zimmerman, 1989). Students need to have plenty of opportunities to apply the planning, revising, and other self-regulation skills learned in class (as well as those they develop on their own). What can teachers do to encourage the use of these processes? First, they can establish predictable classroom routines for writing where the use of these strategies is expected and reinforced. In the process approach to writing (Atwell, 1987), for example, students are encouraged to spend time planning, drafting, revising, and editing their papers. In addition, they can directly remind students to use specific strategies or provide them with procedural assistance in carrying them out. Three, they can assign writing tasks that lead students to use specific self-regulation processes. Not all writing tasks engender the same levels or even types of self-regulation. Durst (1989), for instance, found that analytic and summary writing resulted in the use of different self-monitoring behaviors.

Finally, the development of self-regulation in writing may be inhibited if students are provided few opportunities for managing their own behavior (Zimmerman, 1989). In classrooms with a highly structured curriculum or a restrictive code of conduct, for example, students may not have the freedom or the opportunity to take the risks necessary to develop new writing strategies or refine and extend those taught in the classroom. If we expect students to become planful, reflective, and resourceful writers, they need to exert strategic control over personal, behavioral, and environmental influences (Graham & Harris, 1994a). This includes allowing them to work on writing projects of their own choosing, develop unique interpretations or personal opinions about teacher assigned topics, construct a personal plan for accomplishing the writing task, work at their own pace, and arrange a suitable writing environment.

Appendix 18.1
Teaching a story writing strategy using SRSD

After reviewing students' writing portfolios, a fifth-grade teacher decided to teach a strategy that would help her pupils use knowledge of story parts to generate, structure, and flesh out their ideas for their papers. The majority of her students were writing stories that were missing one or more elements critical to developing and resolving the plot, and virtually all of their stories could be improved by including greater detail and elaboration, as well as more goals and actions. The teacher was also interested in helping several of her students who were particularly anxious about writing establish a stronger sense of motivation, enhanced self-efficacy, and more internal attributions (what she termed an overall, "*I can do this if I try*" attitude).

The teacher began instruction with a conference with the class (*Initial Conference: Strategy Goals and Significance*).[2] They discussed the common parts of a story, the goal for learning the "story writing" strategy (to write better stories: ones that are more fun to write and more fun to read), and how including and expanding story parts can improve a story. The teacher also described the procedures for learning the strategy, stressing the students' roles as collaborators and the importance of effort in strategy mastery.

The class then completed a more detailed analysis of the parts commonly included in a story (*Develop Background Knowledge*), focusing on the setting (characters, place, and time) and story episodes (precipitating event, characters' goals, action to achieve goals, resolution, and characters' reactions). They identified examples of these elements in the literature they were currently reading, highlighting different ways authors develop story parts. They further generated ideas for story parts using different story lines. Finally, each student examined two or three of their previous stories and determined which story elements were present in each story. At this point, the teacher showed the students how to graph the number of story parts they included in their stories, while at the same time explaining the purpose of graphing (to monitor the completeness of their stories and the effects of learning the "story writing" strategy). For students who already used all or nearly all of the story parts, the teacher discussed with them how they could improve their parts with more detail, elaboration, and action.

Next, the teacher provided a more detailed description of the "story writing" strategy. Each student had a small chart listing the strategy steps: (1) Think of a story you would like to share with others; (2) Let your mind be free as you think of ideas and work on your story; (3) Write down the story part reminder (W-W-W-; What = 2; How = 2); (4) Make notes of your ideas for each part; and (5) Write your story — use good parts; add, elaborate, or revise as you go; make sense. The story part reminder prompted students to ask themselves the following questions: (1) Who is the main character? Who else is in the story? (2) *When* does the story take place? (3) *Where* does the story

---

[2] The teacher decided to do the *Initial Conference* before *Develop Background Knowledge*.

take place? (4) *What* does the main character do or want to do? What do other characters do? What happens when the main character does or tries to do it? (6) What happens with other characters? (7) *How* does the story end? (8) *How* does the main character feel? How do other characters feel?

The teacher then asked the students what they thought the reason for each step might be. They further discussed how and when to use the strategy, making linkages to reading and writing book reports and other compositions. The teacher also emphasized the importance of student effort in mastering the strategy, and illustrated the types of things she typically says to herself to free up her mind and think of good ideas and parts when writing. After discussing how such self-statements can be helpful, students generated their own preferred self-statements, recording them on paper.

In the ensuing lesson, the teacher shared a story idea with the class that she had been thinking about, and modeled (while "thinking out loud") how to use the strategy to further develop the idea (*Modeling of the Strategy*). The students helped her plan, write, and revise her story. While composing, the teacher modeled five types of self-instructions: problem definition, planning, self-evaluation, self-reinforcement, and coping. Once the story was finished, the class again discussed the importance of what we say to ourselves and identified the functions and types of self-statements used by the teacher. Students then generated and recorded their own self-statements to use while writing. The focus was on developing self-statements that promote an "I can do" attitude. Finally, the teacher asked for recommendations on how the strategy steps and mnemonic might be made more effective. The class decided to make no changes at this point.

The teacher next asked her students to memorize (either alone or with a partner) the five-step strategy, the mnemonic, and the self-statements they planned to use while writing (*Memorization of the Strategy*). Most of the students memorized these easily, while others needed more extended practice.

Students now began to use the " story writing" strategy to write their own stories, receiving assistance from the teacher as needed (*Collaborative Practice*). During individual conferences, the teacher encouraged students to set goals to include all of the basic parts in their stories and to monitor and graph their success in meeting this objective. As students became more adept at using the strategy and self-regulation procedures, reliance on the teacher and instructional materials (charts and self-statement lists) was faded, and students were encouraged to use their self-statements covertly. Most of the students were ready for the final stage of instruction, *Independent Performance*, after only two or three collaborative experiences.

Finally, the entire class held a meeting to discuss and plan for strategy maintenance and generalization. The students discussed opportunities they might have for using the strategy in the near future, and agreed to participate in a review session at least once a month to help promote *maintenance and generalization*.

— 19 —

Evaluating Speech-Based Composition Methods: Planning, Dictation, and The Listening Word Processor

John E. Reece
*Royal Melbourne Institute
of Technology*

Geoff Cumming
La Trobe University

Writing is often difficult because it is a complex task. Writers must attend to low level demands — such as spelling, punctuation, simple syntax, and the mechanical demands of handwriting — as well as attend to higher-level aspects — such as global plans and goals. We report experiments investigating three ways that the demands of writing might be eased:

- Making a written outline plan before composing, which allows the writer to attend first to overall structure with minimal distraction from lower level processes. Then, the written plan itself serves as a reference during composition.
- Dictation, which as a composition method bypasses some of the lower level demands, and may allow faster composing, although it does not give the writer (dictator) a visible record for reference during the composition process.
- The Listening Word Processor (LWP), which is a simulated computerized speech recognition system. Writers dictate and watch their composition, which is actually keyed by a hidden typist, emerge on a computer screen almost at once. The LWP gives the advantages of dictation plus an inspectable representation of the composition so far.

We first consider the theoretical view of writing that underlies the experiments described here.

Theoretical foundations: Multiple processes, multiple levels

Early models of the composing process recognized that writing is made up of subprocesses, especially planning, generation, and revising. Planning referred to a range of activities involved with generation and organization, and was viewed as the most important process. Improving planning skills, or simply increasing the amount of time spent on planning, was held to lead to an improvement in text quality. Where early models were mistaken was in the assumption that the processes of planning, generation, and revising occurred in a fixed, linear order.

Bereiter and Scardamalia (1987) considered planning within a theoretical position that viewed written composition as an ability with both natural and problematic features. With minimum instruction, a child can learn the basic skills; this is writing as a natural skill. However, to become a skilled writer requires considerable effort: This is the problematic side of writing. Writing as a natural process is represented in Bereiter and Scardamalia's model as *knowledge telling*, whereas the problematic approach to writing is embodied as *knowledge transformation*. For our purposes, the important feature of the distinction is the posited relation with planning: Bereiter and Scardamalia presented the knowledge transforming approach as an educational imperative because it encourages more sophisticated text planning.

Bereiter and Scardamalia's distinction illuminates the somewhat paradoxical phenomenon of novice writers being able to produce large amounts of topically relevant (although not high quality) text in response to a writing task — merely by using knowledge telling — compared with expert professional writers agonizing over word choice and structure, as they use the more demanding process of knowledge transformation.

Hayes and Flower (Flower & Hayes, 1980; Hayes & Flower, 1980, 1986) developed a seminal model of composition that retained the notion of three basic subprocesses, but recognized the iterative and recursive nature of the relation between them. Writers revise not only after a first draft has been completed, but at a number of points throughout a composition session. Similarly, planning does not occur only at the beginning of a composition session; writers plan constantly throughout text production. Further, Hayes and Flower saw planning as the central process, and they, along with other composition researchers, encouraged teachers of writing to focus on the improvement of the planning skills of their students.

In addition to the view of composition as comprising a number of subprocesses, writers are also required to allocate attention to a number of levels. This theoretical notion has been explored by de Beaugrande (1984) and Bereiter and Scardamalia (1987). As well as low level demands (including spelling, punctuation, simple syntax, and the physical process of handwriting), there are also higher level demands (including global plans and goals).

Finally, the subprocesses relate to the multiple levels. Planning and revision can take place at any level of composition; a writer can plan the next word, the next paragraph, or the whole tenor of a piece of writing. Similarly, revision can take place at a number of levels; a writer might simply alter a word, or may change the overall plan.

We conclude that two central issues have been identified: planning as a key process, and composition as an activity that is cognitively demanding.

The importance of planning

Hayes and Flower (1983) emphasized that planning is a broad activity including deciding on meaning, selecting what to present to the audience, and choosing rhetorical strategies. A plan may be written or held in memory in some form, perhaps as a visual image. Planning includes prewriting and also activities during composing. Prewriting includes research, simply thinking about a topic before writing, and outlining, which involves the construction of a written or sketched outline before producing text.

A number of studies have shown that expert writers devote more time to planning than novices do. Much of this research uses the assumption that long pauses during composition are planning episodes (Matsuhashi, 1982). In an early study, Emig (1971) reported that few professional writers used outlines, but all of her participants claimed to engage in some form of planning activity before writing. Using structured interviews, Rose (1980) and Sommers (1980) concluded that good writers plan more and are more willing to make sweeping changes to their plan during composition. Stallard (1974) and Pianko (1979), studying high school and college students, found that good writers thought more about their topics before drafting, but they found little evidence of outlining by any of their writers.

Composition and information-processing load

Viewing written composition as a multiprocess, multilevel activity leads to the conclusion that composition is cognitively demanding, with a number of processes competing for limited attentional resources. Successful composing requires sophisticated switching of attention between processes and levels, running processes in parallel, or automatic processing of some demands.

Most adult writers have, to some degree, automated the low level demands of writing in that they do not need to pay much attention to spelling, punctuation, and the mechanical demands of handwriting or keyboarding. As a result, they can allocate more attention to the higher level planning demands. Children, on the other hand, appear to be particularly hampered by the low level demands of writing (Bereiter & Scardamalia, 1987), with the result that less attention can be paid to the important planning processes.

For his research on the role of planning, Kellogg (1988) adopted this view of writing as a cognitively demanding task. He reasoned that requiring preparation of an outline would lead to considerable planning taking place before text generation, and therefore to increased attentional resources being available during composition itself. Working with adult writers he found that compositions were indeed of higher quality following production of an outline, and his interpretation was confirmed by the results of an experiment using a secondary task reaction time paradigm. Interestingly, he found also that a mental outline was as effective as a written outline, indicating that it was the cognitive planning activities, rather than the physical presence of the outline that were important.

Of particular interest is the question of how planning can be supported in young writers. Requiring preparation of an outline can lessen the risk of cognitive overload during text generation. More generally, requiring explicit attention to any form of prewriting may encourage young writers to engage in more mature composition strategies, including goal setting, extensive idea generation, and consideration of overall structure.

Why speech-based composition?

Many skilled, professional writers have sung the praises of dictation. Gardner (1980), well-known for his theory of multiple intelligence, was fulsome in his praise of dictation, claiming it permits his composition rate to match his thinking rate. Many prolific authors compose solely by dictation. The blind poet, John Milton, dictated his masterpiece *Paradise Lost*. Before the advent of laptop computers and modems, journalists were regularly required to dictate stories over the telephone.

Most arguments for speech-based composition — predominantly dictation — cite its ability to bypass many low level demands during the composing process. The dictator need pay no attention to spelling, punctuation, or pen manipulation: These are confronted only later, during transcription. Additional cognitive resources are therefore available during dictation for planning, and for text generation itself. In normal written composition, by contrast, the low level demands can limit planning and hamper composition performance, as De La Paz and Graham (1994) argued.

In skilled writers, low level demands are presumably largely automated, so dictation may not substantially increase resources available for text generation. It is for young writers and writers with a learning disability that dictation should confer particular benefits.

In addition to considerations of cognitive load, dictation may offer a speed advantage. In written composition, the limited speed of handwriting may cause ideas in working memory to be lost; the hand cannot keep pace with the mind. When dictating, however, material can be composed at the normal speech rate (Gould, 1980).

A number of problems must be set against the strong arguments in favor of dictation. First, dictation is an unfamiliar composition method for most writers, and nearly all children. Speaking usually produces conversational language, yet the aim of dictation is to produce language that is appropriate in print (Haggblade, 1990). Second, dictation must be followed by transcription, which may be an awkward and unfamiliar task. Third and most substantially, there is no ongoing external representation of the composed text. For dictators to monitor text composed so far, they must either maintain and refer to a representation in memory, or relisten to a tape, both of which impose an extra cognitive load.

How important is the presence of a physical representation of the text? It may depend on the writer's strategy. Faigley, Cherry, Jolliffe, and Skinner (1985) established that writers reread their texts quite often, despite claiming to engage in little revision. Rereading can, however, also be used to assist planning. Britton, Burgess, Martin, McLeod, and Rosen (1975) found that writers could complete simple composition tasks without seeing what they produced, but that performance on more complex tasks was hampered. On the other hand, Gould (1980) showed that some writers could produce good quality text even when unable to see what they have produced, although some reported feeling uncomfortable.

There is evidence that better writers reread their texts more than remedial or immature writers do (Mischel, 1974; Stallard, 1974), and for different reasons. Paradoxically, however, there is also evidence that basic writers are more adversely affected by lack of a visual record than are more skilled writers (Faigley et al., 1985). Overall, the evidence suggests that rereading text is useful for planning. Lack of a physical record may restrict higher level planning and induce the writer to adopt a more knowledge telling composing style. A skilled writer may, however, be able to adopt compensatory strategies.

In addition to the general question of the value of dictation, this discussion raises two specific questions:

1. Does dictation particularly benefit young writers and writers with a learning or intellectual disability?

2. Would there be benefits of a text production system combining the advantages of dictation with a physical representation allowing the writer to monitor text already produced?

The next section reviews some of the literature and addresses the first question; the second question is taken up by the experiments reported later.

Research on dictation

Gould (1980) examined the use of dictation as a composition method. He described studies that involved business people and university students dictating, for the most part, simple business letters. Comparing dictation with conventional written composition, he concluded that text production method was not an important variable in defining text quality, but that dictation gave more rapid composing and longer texts. He also commented on the speed with which writers could learn to use dictation.

In an ingenious investigation, Bereiter and Scardamalia (1987) used a text production condition called *slow dictation*, which required Grade 4 and Grade 6 students to dictate at their normal handwriting speed. They argued that, by comparing normal with slow dictation, the effect of speed of production could be isolated from any effect of bypassing lower level demands. Also, the effect of these demands could be investigated by comparing slow dictation with conventional handwriting. They found that text production method had little effect on text quality, although regular dictation produced longer texts. Hidi and Hildyard (1983) and McCutchen (1987) found similar results with children from Grade 3 to Grade 8.

One interesting finding of the McCutchen (1987) study was an interaction between composition method and type of task. Expository essays produced using dictation were less coherent than narrative essays produced using either method, supporting the notion that dictation may encourage a simple sequential style of composition — Bereiter and Scardamalia's (1987) knowledge telling. This may be suitable for narratives, but less appropriate for expository, argumentative essays in which a more complex structure is often required.

No research mentioned so far found any overall improvement in text quality with dictation. Research with learning disabled students has, however, found a difference. MacArthur and Graham (1987) assessed the story production of learning disabled (LD) students using dictation, handwriting, and word processing. They found that, compared with stories produced by handwriting or word processor, dictated stories were longer, generated more quickly, and of higher quality. They concluded that the mechanical demands of writing may be particularly disruptive for learning disabled students' composing, thus giving an affirmative answer to our first question.

Graham (1990), again with LD students, used written composition and normal and slow dictation. He found that text quality did not differ between the two dictation conditions, but that both were superior to writing. He concluded that LD students' writing problems can, at least in part, be attributed to difficulties with the mechanical aspects of writing.

Rentel and King (1983) compared the dictated and handwritten stories from very young (Grade 1 and Grade 2) writers and found some superior features in the dictated stories. Similar results were found by Pontecorvo and Zucchermaglio (1989). These findings again give an affirmative answer to our first question, in this case for beginning writers.

Why, however, do most studies using adult writers show no advantage for dictation? Any benefits obtained from the easing of mechanical demands may be counterbalanced by the lack of an external representation of already-composed text. Evidence has already been presented that writers reread their text as they compose. Rereading, which may be deliberate or just a quick scan, can serve a number of functions. It allows the writer to monitor progress, perhaps in relation to a plan, to evaluate what has already been composed, and to reinforce any mental text representations. Loss of the possibility for rereading may outweigh the bypassing of low level demands given by dictation, especially for adults for whom these demands are largely automated. By contrast, for very young or learning disabled writers the easing of mechanical demands seems to predominate.

Beyond dictation: Planned dictation and computerized speech recognition

The LWP allows writers to dictate their compositions and see the text emerge on a computer screen almost simultaneously. The intention was to provide the advantages of oral composition (speed of production and bypassing of low level demands) and of a visible record. Our primary research aim was to assess how working with the LWP might alter writers' processes and products.

Gould (1980) and others discussed the idea of using a speech recognition system. Gould, Conti, and Hovanyecz (1983) evaluated "the listening typewriter": The text of dictated letters appeared in typewritten form almost at once. The aim was to evaluate a potentially technically viable system, so vocabulary was limited and editing required writers to use special formatting commands. In other words, the device was not based on a natural language interface. Results showed that writers were able to adapt quickly to using the system but there was little beneficial effect on text quality.

In two papers on computer speech recognition (Newell, Arnott, Carter, & Cruickshank 1990; Newell, Arnott, Dye, & Cairns, 1991), the aim was to assess the technique for office use, rather than to evaluate its effect on composition. In fact, there do not appear to have been any published studies investigating the use of computer speech recognition as a composition tool. This is despite the fact that fluent, accurate computer speech recognition at normal speaking rate is recognized as an important technological goal (Meisel, 1993), and computer speech recognition systems that perform impressively in restricted situations (such as emergency rooms) are beginning to become available. There can be little doubt that such systems will lead to a dramatic change in composition strategies; our research is an attempt to anticipate these developments.

A further aim was to investigate a simple and ecologically valid method of composition that both relieved low level demands and provided planning support. The method, called *planned dictation*, required writers to engage in a preproduction planning session, incorporating brainstorming and outlining, and then to refer to their written plan while dictating the composition. Our rationale was based on a view of planning as a way to foster mature composition strategies.

We started by training writers in effective planning, including idea generation, problem solving, organization of material, and outlining. We encouraged them to view planning as an important part of writing and hoped that this would, in general, promote the use of higher level planning processes and, more specifically, lead to a written plan. This could serve as a cognitive scaffold during subsequent dictation, thus at least partly substituting for rereading of text, which is not possible during dictation.

It is interesting to note the suggestions of Sharples and O'Malley (1988):

> Two other effective strategies [for managing composition's multiple constraints] are to operate an external memory, such as a written plan, and to pass responsibility for some of the constraint management (particularly that concerned with the simple rule-governed aspects of writing, such as spelling and layout) over to an automated system. (p. 282)

These comments were made with reference to a computer-based planning and writing system, but they could easily be related to planned dictation.

Planned dictation required writers to engage in preproduction planning and to produce an outline on paper that could be referred to during dictation. The LWP, on the other hand, provided a record of text as it was produced. By comparing texts produced using the LWP with texts produced using planned dictation, we hoped to separate the effects of preproduction planning from those of having available a form of textual representation during composition by dictation.

Five studies on planned dictation and the Listening Word Processor

For each of these studies, a number of measures of writing processes and products were collected. First, each text was rated holistically. Raters were provided with a marking guide that provided a detailed list of the criteria to be used when assessing a text. The markers were experienced primary and secondary school teachers, and the cross-marker reliability of the ratings was checked regularly and averaged $r = .85$.

In addition, each text was assessed using a method known as *feature analysis*. Feature analysis has been described in detail by Sharples (1985) and can be thought of as an objective method of evaluating text by decomposing a text into its constituent rhetorical and grammatical features and scoring the maturity of these features. Feature analysis is very time consuming, but a great deal of information is gained. Each text must be separated into its main clauses, and the connections between the clauses must be represented as a form of flow chart. Once this is done, the number of mature and immature text features are identified, and these form the final score for the text. Sharples (1985) argued that feature analysis provides more detailed information about composition development in young writers than other objective methods of text analysis. The use of feature analysis was based on the premise that appropriate objective measures of text content can be used to make interpretations regarding the underlying cognitive processes responsible for a composition. In our experiments, the feature analyses were reduced to two figures: the ratio of mature and immature text features per 100 words of text. Other researchers have analyzed individual features in more detail (Sharples, 1985).

Finally, a number of process measures were taken, such as text length, time spent composing, time spent in preproduction planning, number of long pauses, and so on. Text length was assessed simply by counting the number of words in the completed texts. For the first experiment, writers were videotaped as they worked, and these tapes were used to record time spent composing, time spent in preproduction planning, and pause patterns (consistent with Matsuhashi, 1982, long pauses were defined as pauses over 2 seconds long). For the remaining studies, the temporal patterns in composing were analyzed either from audio tape recordings (in the case of dictated texts and texts produced using the LWP) or via handheld stopwatch recording.

With the exception of the first study to be described, all of our research used Grade 5 and Grade 6 students as participants. This population was selected for a number of reasons. First, several authors have commented that this age is a crucial time in the development of mature composition strategies (Bereiter & Scardamalia, 1987). Second, students of this age are about to commence secondary school, which will expose them to a new set of writing demands. Third, preliminary investigations revealed that students of this age were amenable to new composition methods. Students of a younger age could be taught the principles of dictation and use of the LWP, but it required a level of training that was not feasible in the circumstances. The first study, which was more exploratory, examined the composition performance of university undergraduates. The data from all of the studies were analyzed using within-subjects analyses of variance. For brevity, only significance levels are reported.

Study 1: Planned dictation with mature writers

This first study examined the value of planning in combination with two production methods — writing and dictation — in an adult population. We wanted to test the hypothesis that a speech-based composition method — dictation — that automated several low level composition demands could be used in combination with a preproduction planning session to produce high quality compositions. In line with other researchers (Kellogg, 1988), we predicted that precomposition planning would lead to an improvement in handwritten texts, but the effect of precomposition planning on dictation was somewhat of a mystery. Our theoretical argument was that the written plan would provide a form of "cognitive scaffold," which would counteract some of the extra cognitive load imposed by dictation. We hoped that the combination of dictating with reference to a written plan would bring the best out of a composition method that had previously been considered, at best, equivalent to other methods in terms of resulting text quality. In cognitive terms, we predicted that the written plan would provide the writer's working memory with easy access to a model of the high level plans of the text, while the speech-based composition fostered translation of that plan without the burdens of low level text demands.

Sixteen university psychology undergraduates were given brief instructions on dictation and planning. For dictation, students were given a briefing sheet explaining the basic principles of dictation, and were then shown a videotape of a person dictating a composition. Planning was carried out with pencil and paper and consisted of brainstorming and creating a heading-style outline of the composition. Students again read a briefing sheet that explained brainstorming and outlining and were shown examples of both. Students were not placed under any time limit for their planning session. Each student produced four compositions on different topics, one each for unplanned dictation and writing, and planned dictation and writing. The topics were chosen to represent a range of writing genres, from argumentative to personal expository. The combination of production method and topic was counterbalanced across the 16 students. For the two planning conditions the planning session took place before production of the draft. In the planned dictation and writing conditions, students were encouraged to refer to their plan while they were dictating, although they were given the option of varying from their plan if they wished. Students were videotaped while they wrote, so that long pauses (i.e., pauses greater than 2 seconds) could be analyzed. For the dictation conditions, pauses were noted from the audiotaped dictations.

Table 19.1 summarizes the results for this study. For holistic scores, planning led to a significant improvement in the quality of both written, p = .006, and dictated texts, $p < .0001$. There was no significant difference between unplanned written and unplanned dictated texts. Of greater interest was the significant interaction between presence of planning and production method, $p = .048$. The improvement in text quality attributable to planning was greater for dictated texts than written texts. With planning, dictated texts were superior to texts produced by planned writing, $p = .046$. The results for feature analysis showed a similar main effect for the presence of planning, $p < .0001$; that is, both dictation and writing were improved by a preproduction planning session. However, the interactive effect was not evident. Feature analysis involved calculating a ratio of the number of mature text features per 100 words of text. Immature text features were not analyzed statistically because of their infrequent occurrence.

Table 19.1
Means ands standard deviations for Study 1

| | Text production condition | | | |
| | Unplanned | | Planned | |
Dependent measure	**Writing**	**Dictation**	**Writing**	**Dictation**
Holistic score[a]				
Mean	6.23	5.98	7.16	7.78
(s.d.)	*(1.58)*	*(1.46)*	*(1.43)*	*(1.11)*
Mature text features [b]				
Mean	.75	7.56	12.19	11.44
(s.d.)	*(2.35)*	*(1.71)*	*(2.07)*	*(2.03)*
Immature text [b] features				
Mean	.75	1.31	0.63	0.56
(s.d.)	*(.32)*	*(1.00)*	*(0.30)*	*(0.24)*
Text length[c]				
Mean	420.4	590.4	406.8	470.2
(s.d.)	*(93.7)*	*(116.6)*	*(75.5)*	*(66.1)*
W.P.M[d]				
Mean	10.3	21.9	8.0	13.4
(s.d.)	*(2.4)*	*(5.8)*	*(2.6)*	*(3.7)*

Note. n = 16 for all conditions.
[a]Score range = 0 - 10.
[b]Mature and immature features per 100 words of composed text.
[c]In words.
[d]Words composed per minute of nonplanning composition time.

Table 19.1 also shows results for text length. Two points here are worthy of note. First, dictated texts were longer than written texts in both the planned and unplanned conditions. Second, planning resulted in a substantial drop in the length of dictated texts, $p = .002$, but not written texts, $p = .68$. Results for pause time and time spent composing are shown in Figure

19.1. The amount of time spent on long pauses dropped substantially for both writing and dictation after a preproduction planning session, although the difference was statistically significant only for writing, p = .001. It seems that the preproduction planning session subsumed some of the planning that would be expected to take place during production.

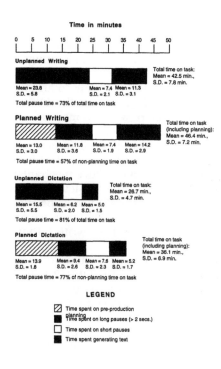

Figure 19.1 Mean pause time and time spent composing.

In summary, the most important result here was the relation between planning and text production method. In the unplanned condition, there was little difference in the quality measures of composition samples produced by either dictation or conventional handwriting. However, introducing a session of precomposition planning led to a more substantial improvement in performance for students using dictation compared with those using writing. This interactive relation between planning and text production method was also evident in some other process measures, such as text length. Also notable were the indications of a change in composing process brought about by the planning session, as evidenced by the profile of production measures. Preproduction planning seemed to foster a more "writing-like" process in those students using dictation.

As far as can be established, these results provide the first demonstration of dictation as a composition method that can result in texts of superior quality to those produced using conventional handwriting with mature writers, but Levy, Rozen, Marek, & Lea (1995) reported a similar facilitation comparing LWP-created text to text created on a conventional word processor.

Studies 2 and 3: Young writers using the LWP

In Study 2, 30 young writers (ages 10 to 12) were introduced to two new composition methods: dictation and the LWP. We predicted that the LWP would provide young writers with a text production method that embodied the best features of both dictation and handwriting: automation of low-level demands and the presence of a real-time visual record of composed text. We expected that these benefits would translate to an improvement in text quality for those compositions produced using the LWP. In cognitive terms, we expected the LWP to permit more working memory resources to be available for important high level plans, and not be taken up by low-level demands (in the case of handwriting) or the need to constantly monitor the progress of a composition (in the case of dictation). In accord with our theoretical view that poor writers have poorly developed cognitive mechanisms for monitoring their compositions and for dealing with the low-level demands of writing, we predicted that any benefits from the LWP would be more pronounced in poor writers. Finally, in line with previous findings, we expected any benefit for dictation would be present more in poor writers than in normally achieving young writers.

Students received approximately 1 hour of training (three 20-minute sessions) with each of dictation and the LWP (2 hours training in total). This training was carried out by the author on a one-to-one basis with each student. All training and testing took place in a small, private room at the student's school.

The training regimes for dictation and LWP followed similar prearranged scripts. Students were first familiarized with the composition devices. The experimenter then discussed the concept of different ways of producing text. Several themes were emphasized:

1. That compositions are not always written down.
2. That if you have the ability to tell someone a story, you have the ability to use dictation (or LWP). This was reinforced by having the student tell the experimenter a story while the experimenter tape-recorded the story. When the recording was played back, the experimenter told the student how that story could be transcribed.
3. That many people use oral composition facilities.
4. That dictation is not telling a story, it is composing a text; and that what the student said was going to be written down at a later time.

The second phase of training involved a demonstration of the new composition methods. For demonstrating dictation, the experimenter pretended to be a writer who had just received a composition task. While thinking aloud, the experimenter went through the process of considering the task and using the tape recorder to record the dictated text. It was emphasized that once the tape recorder was turned on, it should not be touched. When using the LWP, a typist sat behind a large cardboard screen so that the children could not speak directly to him. The children looked at a simple monochrome computer monitor and dictated their texts into a microphone. The typist transcribed the dictated material as it was spoken. It is important to note that the typist interpreted all punctuation, spelling, and basic formatting (as he did when transcribing the dictated texts), and instructions to reread material were given by the students to the typist in plain language (e.g., *Move down a bit please. More. That's good.*). Each student produced three compositions, one using each of dictation, handwriting, and the LWP. Three composition assignments were used, and these were counterbalanced with production method.

Study 3 was essentially a replication of Study 2, using 15 Grade 5 and Grade 6 students with poor writing skills. These students were identified by their teachers and by a writing test conducted just prior to the commencement of the study. Apart from requiring extra training (approximately 30 extra minutes for each student), the experiment with the poor writers was the same as that with the normally achieving students.

Table 19.2 shows the results for the text quality measures for both experiments. For the holistic scores of the normally achieving students, the most important result was that texts produced using the LWP received the highest mean rating and were found to be significantly better than texts produced using the other two methods, $p = .051$ (planned comparison involving LWP versus the combination of handwriting and dictation). The difference between dictated texts and texts produced using the LWP, $p = .033$, was more pronounced than the difference between written and dictated texts, $p = .38$. A different pattern of results emerged with the poor writers, however. With this group, written texts were inferior to those produced using either of the speech-based methods, but the differences were not statistically significant. Texts produced using the LWP received the highest ratings and were significantly better than written texts, $p = .019$. Similar results were found for mature and immature text features, with texts produced using the LWP demonstrating the highest number of mature text features and the lowest number of immature text features of any of the methods investigated. Despite these trends, the only notable significant result was that texts produced using the LWP showed significantly more mature text features than handwritten texts, $p = .028$.

Another set of notable results concerns production measures for both groups of writers (Table 19.3). In both cases, the profile of production measures for texts produced using the LWP was more similar to written texts than to texts produced using dictation. This disparity was greater with the poor writers. (It should be noted that long pauses were measured from audiotapes of the dictated and LWP-produced texts, but were measured using hand-timing for the handwritten texts.) For text length, time spent composing, and the proportion of composition time spent on long pauses, the figures for LWP-produced texts more closely resembled the figures for written texts than those of the other speech-based method.

Table 19.2
Text quality means and standard deviations for Study 2 and Study 3

Dependent measure	Text production condition		
	Writing	Dictation	LWP
	Normally achieving writers (Study (2)		
Holistic score[a]			
Mean *(s.d.)*	6.37 *(1.96)*	6.18 *(1.55)*	7.14 *(1.44)*
Mature text features[b]			
Mean *(s.d.)*	7.77 *(2.53)*	6.33 *(2.19)*	8.23 *(2.39)*
Immature text features[c]			
Mean *(s.d.)*	6.07 *(2.66)*	8.47 *(2.21)*	5.87 *(2.05)*
	Poor writers (Study 3)		
Holistic score			
Mean *(s.d.)*	4.32 *(1.37)*	5.57 *(2.34)*	6.07 *(1.70)*
Mature text features			
Mean *(s.d.)*	3.14 *(1.19)*	4.07 *(1.58)*	4.27 *(1.83)*
Immature text features			
Mean (s.d.)	8.27 *(2.05)*	8.73 *(2.15)*	7.60 *(3.02)*

Note. n = 30, each condition in Study 2; *n* = 10, each condition in Study 3.
[a]Score range 0 - 10.
[b]Mature and immature features per 100 words of composed text.
[c]In words.

Table 19.3
Production measure means and standard deviations for Study 2 and Study 3

Dependent measure	Text production condition		
	Writing	Dictation	LWP
	Normally achieving writers (Study (2)		
Text length[a]			
Mean *(s.d.)*	121.9 *(47.4)*	223.5 *(85.4)*	166.2 *(55.2)*
Time composing[b]			
Mean *(s.d.)*	19.83 *(4.97)*	15.93 *(5.91)*	20.95 *(5.45)*
Percentage of time spent on long pauses[c]			
Mean *(s.d.)*	72.16 *(7.45)*	43.82 *(10.91)*	65.11 *(9.93)*
	Poor writers (Study 3)		
Text length			
Mean *(s.d.)*	56.7 *(22.9)*	135.7 *(42.7)*	69.7 *(25.1)*
Time composing			
Mean *(s.d.)*	12.69 *(3.95)*	9.26 *(2.68)*	11.63 *(2.15)*
Percentage of time spent on long pauses			
Mean (s.d.)	57.66 *(10.53)*	45.59 *(8.41)*	54.81 *(9.97)*

Note. n = 30, each condition in Study 2; *n* = 10, each condition in Study 3.
[a]In words.
[b]In minutes.
[c]Long pauses were pauses longer than 2 seconds.

In summary, the results of this study were very promising for the LWP. This speech-based composition method, which provided a point-of-production external representation of composed text, resulted in compositions that were generally superior to those produced by the other two methods. Also, the LWP appeared to confer special benefits on poor writers. In line with previous research, dictated texts were found to be slightly superior in quality to written texts for poor writers, but no different from written texts for normally achieving writers.

Also important were the indications that the LWP fostered a different composing process in both normally achieving and poor writers to that seen with dictation. If long pauses are assumed to represent planning episodes, then there were indications that the LWP encouraged planning in a fashion not seen with dictation. We interpret this as follows: Because the LWP provides the writer with a visual record of their text, the writer has no need to allocate a substantial portion of working memory to maintaining some form of ongoing representation of the composition. Instead, writers can turn their attention to a consideration of higher level aspects of the composition task.

Study 4: Planned dictation with young writers

In many ways, Study 4 was a replication of Study 1, using younger writers. However, using this population raised some problems because the skills being examined, such as the ability to use planning techniques, are less developed in children than in adults. More training was required for the use of both planning and dictation. Twenty Grade 5 and Grade 6 students underwent training over a period of weeks on the use of planning and dictation. The dictation training was identical to that used in Study 2. The planning training was based around showing students videotapes of an adult engaging in the planning activities, showing students' plans and the resulting texts, and several one-to-one practice sessions (for a full description of the training regime, see Reece, 1992). In addition to brainstorming and outlining, students in this study were also encouraged to refer regularly to sheets that prompted their use of reflective planning (Bereiter & Scardamalia, 1987). Unlike Study 1, the 20 students in this experiment were matched into pairs on the basis of age, sex, teacher assessment of writing ability, and the results of a short writing and dictation pre-test conducted 1 week before the study commenced. One student in each pair received training in planning. All students received training in the use of dictation. Each student, therefore, produced two texts for the final testing session, one using each of dictation and writing, with 10 students engaging in preproduction planning.

The results are summarized in Table 19.4. Despite an analysis of holistic scores revealing only one significant main effect — planned texts were found to be significantly better than unplanned texts, $p = .007$ — the trends in the data were similar to those found in Study 1. There was little difference in the overall quality of written and dictated texts, but there was a trend for dictated texts to show a greater improvement with planning than written texts. The results for feature analysis were more complex. For both mature and immature text features there was a highly significant interaction between presence of planning and text production method, $p = .0002$ (mature), $p =$

.004 (immature). Planning led to an increase in the number of mature text features in written compositions, but the increase with dictated compositions was significantly greater. Similar results were found for the decrease in immature text features after planning. Results for various text production measures showed a similar pattern of results to that seen with adult writers in Study 1. Planning led to reduction in both the length of texts and the percentage of time spent on long pauses for both text production methods.

There was one particularly interesting comparison between the results of this experiment and the results of Study 1. In Study 1, strong and significant results were more likely to be found for the holistic score results rather than the feature analysis results. In Study 4, the reverse was true. There are several explanations for this difference. First, feature analysis was designed originally to assess the developing skills of young writers; therefore, it may have been more sensitive to differences in the quality of immature texts. Conversely, it may have been that the holistic rating system made it easier to discriminate between good, average, and poor adult texts.

Table 19.4
Means and standard deviations for Study 4

| Dependent measure | Text production condition | | | |
| | Unplanned | | Planned | |
	Writing	**Dictation**	**Writing**	**Dictation**
Holistic score[a]	6.50	5.90	7.48	7.28
Mean (s.d.)	(1.64)	(2.5)	(1.18)	(2.27)
Mature text features[b]	7.40	6.00	9.40	12.00
Mean (s.d.)	(2.35)	(1.71)	(2.07)	(2.03)
Immature text features[b]	6.00	8.00	5.10	5.30 (1.24)
Mean (s.d.)	(2.60)	(2.11)	(1.53)	
Text length[c]	136.8	219.2	140.5	165.4
Mean (s.d.)	(55.7)	(34.5)	(29.4)	(43.1)
Time spent composing[d]				
Mean (s.d.)	17.4 (5.8)	12.2 (2.9)	17.5 (3.9)	15.7 (4.4)
Percentage of time spent on long pauses[e]	70.2 (7.2)	42.2 (7.5)	64.9 (5.5)	58.5 (5.8)
Mean (s.d.)				

Note. n = 10 for all conditions.
[a]Score range = 0 - 10.
[b]Mature and immature features per 100 words of composed text.
[c]In words.
[d] In minuutes of non-planning composition time.
[e]Pauses longer than 2 sec during non-planning composition time.

In sum, the results of Study 4 demonstrated that children could be trained to plan their compositions; they could be trained to dictate efficiently; and, most importantly, they could produce high quality compositions using a combination of precomposition planning followed by dictation. Theoretically, the results supported the notions presented in Study 1 and extended these to a sample of young writers.

Study 5: Preproduction planning and the LWP

Given the advantages seen with planned dictation and the LWP, Study 5 assessed whether preproduction planning followed by production using the LWP would be particularly advantageous for young writers. This study was an attempt to combine the best features of the production methods studied so far: speech-based production, a preproduction planning session, and a continuously updated external record of composed text. Put simply, this study pitted our two best composition methods — planned dictation and the LWP — against each other, with the addition of yet another combination, planned LWP.

This study used the same 10 pairs of students used in Study 4. Students received two short remedial training sessions in the use of dictation and planning (for those students in the planning condition), followed by more extensive training in the use of the LWP, as described in Studies 2 and 3. Again, each student produced three texts, one using each of dictation, handwriting, and the LWP.

Quality and process measures are shown in Table 19.5. As was found in earlier studies, texts produced using the LWP were superior in holistic quality to those produced using the other methods. There were significant main effects for both planning, $p = .002$, and production method, $p = .011$, and a significant interaction between the two, $p = .0036$, which can best be accounted for by the lack of improvement in LWP-produced texts after planning. Consistent with the results from our other studies, planning led to a more substantial improvement in dictated texts than handwritten texts. Results for immature and mature text features for dictation and writing were similar to those from Study 4; however, planning made little difference to the number of immature and mature text features of LWP-produced texts. Statistically, the most important result was the significant interaction between text production method and planning for mature text features, $p = .0039$. Analysis of various production measures, although essentially replicating the results from previous studies with regard to LWP without planning, dictation, and writing, reinforced the notion that a preproduction planning session had little effect on composition processes when the production method was the LWP.

The two major findings from the final study were the replication of the results for planning and dictation, and the finding that training in planning had little effect on students' use of the simulated voice recognition system. When using the LWP, students produced text samples of as good quality as samples produced by planned writing or planned dictation. Put simply, planning provided no added benefit for LWP users. How can these results be interpreted theoretically? The simplest explanation is to refer to a ceiling effect: the LWP by itself is as good a method as there is; the preproduction planning session simply does not confer any extra benefits to the writer's cognitive system. This is, however, an unsatisfactory explanation.

Table 19.5
Means and standard deviations for Study 5

Dependent Measure	Unplanned			Planned		
	Writing	Dictation	LWP	Writing	Dictation	LWP
Holistic score[a]						
Mean	6.30	5.73	7.60	7.35	7.05	7.33
(s.d.)	(1.25)	(1.87)	(1.44)	(0.89)	(0.99)	(1.39)
Mature text feature[b]						
Mean	7.20	6.40	8.60	9.20	10.90	8.80
(s.d.)	(1.87)	(1.71)	(2.72)	(2.49)	(2.00)	(2.25)
Immature text featuresb						
Mean	5.60	7.50	5.30	5.20	6.50	5.90
(s.d.)	(2.41)	(2.37)	(2.63)	(1.55)	(1.96)	(1.37)
Text length[c]						
Mean	111.8	175.5	132.0	98.4	146.9	138.0
(s.d.)	(24.9)	(52.1)	(41.4)	(22.9)	(26.5)	(41.6)
Time spent[d] composing						
Mean	18.58	11.47	17.49	17.60	15.23	16.94
(s.d.)	(5.93)	(3.35)	(4.49)	(5.48)	(4.32)	(3.92)
Percentage of time spent on long pauses[e]						
Mean	67.72	45.66	64.89	63.15	59.57	62.55
(s.d.)	(5.22)	(6.01)	(8.50)	(5.70)	(6.14)	(9.38)

Note. n = 10 for all conditions.
[a]Score range = 0 - 10.
[b]Mature and immature features per 100 words of composed text.
[c]In words.
[d] In minuutes of nonplanning composition time.
[e]Pauses longer than 2 seconds during nonplanning composition time.

It was clear from observation that students in the planned LWP condition treated the plan in a similar way to those in the planned writing condition. When composing, students in the planned writing and planned LWP conditions rarely referred to their plans, whereas those in the planned dictation condition referred to their plans regularly. It seemed that students in the planned writing and LWP conditions considered the plan useful only as a way of generating and organizing material before composing. Once composing commenced, the plan was not seen as essential. Students who dictated after planning may have used the plan as a form of substitute text, and part of the improvement seen in planned dictated texts may have been due to the constant reinforcement of the plan while composing.

Despite the similarity in the strategies adopted by students in the planned writing and planned LWP conditions, it was still the case that the written text quality improved with planning, whereas planning had little effect on the quality of LWP-produced texts. It was also the case that the text length decreased with written texts after planning, whereas planned LWP texts were slightly longer than unplanned LWP texts.

One possible explanation for these results is that the benefits of precomposition planning may be dependent on the level of cognitive load in working memory during postplanning composition. If the lack of an external textual representation leads to particular difficulties for young writers, then the precomposition plan may be particularly beneficial. When an external textual representation is present, but writers are required to attend to low level details, the benefits of a preproduction plan are still present, but not as strong. If both sources of cognitive load are alleviated, as with the LWP, the benefits of a preproduction plan may be confounded by the benefits provided by the text production method per se. For example, perhaps writers found it distracting to move their attention back and forth between the written plan and the on-screen text.

A related possibility is that the planning encouraged by the LWP while composing had a more powerful influence on the quality of the final text than preproduction planning. Once composing with the LWP commenced, the strategy encouraged by the LWP might have essentially "taken over" from any effect of the preproduction planning. This implies that encouraging planning during composing might be more beneficial than a preproduction planning session, but only if a substantial proportion of the cognitive load associated with conventional composition is alleviated.

Conclusions

Previous research on speech-based composition has generally resulted in a less-than-enthusiastic endorsement for such methods, despite valid theoretical arguments for anticipating improved composition performance. For adults and normally achieving children, texts produced using dictation have rarely been shown to be superior to those produced using conventional handwriting. However, research on the use of dictation with very young children and children with an intellectual or learning disability has provided some encouraging results.

We have argued that evaluating dictation by itself — that is, with no extra support for planning — does not provide the best possible test for a speech-based composition method because of problems associated with conventional dictation, such as the lack of an external representation of text as it is being produced. Our response was to investigate two alternative speech-based composition options: planned dictation and the LWP. With planned dictation, writers engaged in preproduction planning exercises, such as brainstorming and outlining, and then dictated their texts from their plans. This was one attempt to tap into the benefits of dictation — speed of production and the automation of low level mechanical demands — while providing some form of external representation to act as a form of cognitive scaffold. The second option was a simulated computerized speech recognition system:

the LWP. Here, writers dictated and observed the text emerging on screen at point of production. Again, this method combined the benefits of dictation with the advantage of an ongoing record of the composition.

Two important results emerged from these studies. First, texts produced using these two methods were generally superior in quality to those produced using more conventional methods. Second, there was strong evidence from the analysis of pause times, text length, and other production measures, that the two experimental speech-based methods fostered a cognitive composing process different to that seen with traditional dictation.

Speech-based composition has undergone dramatic changes since Gould's seminal research on dictation. Importantly, Gould's (1980) main conclusion — that the quality of dictated texts was generally no different to that of handwritten texts — has been shown not to be generalizable to all forms of speech-based composition. With significant advances constantly being made in the area of computerized speech recognition, the future of speech-based composition seems very healthy. An LWP that does not require a typist sitting behind a cardboard screen may not be too far away.

REFERENCES

American College Testing Program (1983). *ASSET*. Iowa City: American College Testing Program.

Anderson, J. R., & Bower, G. H. (1972). Configurational properties in sentence memory. *Journal of Verbal Learning and Verbal Behavior, 10*, 29-34.

Anthony, H., & Anderson, L. (1987, April). *The nature of writing instruction in regular and special education classrooms*. Paper presented at the Annual Meeting of the American Educational Research Association, Chicago, IL.

Antos, G. (1982). *Grundlagen einer Theorie des Formulierens: Textherstellung in geschriebener und gesprochener Sprache*. [Foundations of a formulation theory: Generation of text in written and oral language.] Tuebingen: Niemeyer.

Asimov, I. (1994). *Assimov: A memoir*. New York: Bantam.

Atwell, N. (1987). *In the middle: Reading, writing, and learning from adolescents*. Portsmouth, NH: Heinmann.

Baddeley, A. D. (1986). *Working memory*. Oxford: Oxford University Press.

Baddeley, A. D. (1992). Is working memory working? The 15th Bartlett Lecture. *Quarterly Journal of Experimental Psychology, 44A*, 1-31.

Baddeley, A. D., & Hitch, G. (1974). Working memory. In G. H. Bower (Ed.), *The psychology of learning and motivation*, (Vol. 8), New York: Academic Press.

Baddeley, A. D., & Lewis, V. J. (1981). Inner active processing in reading: The inner voice, the inner ear and the inner eye. In A. M. Lesgold & C. A. Perfetti (Eds.), *Interactive processes in reading* (pp. 107-129). Hillsdale, NJ: Lawrence Erlbaum Associates.

Baddeley, A. D., Logie, R., Nimmo-Smith, I., & Brereton, N. (1985). Components of fluent reading. *Journal of Memory and Language, 24*, 119-131.

Baddeley, A. D., & Wilson, B. (1985). Phonological coding and short-term memory in patients without speech. *Journal of Memory and Language, 24*, 490-502.

Badecker, W., Hillis, A., & Caramazza, A. (1990). Lexical morphology and its role in the writing process: Evidence from a case of acquired dysgraphia. *Cognition, 35*, 205-243.

Ballay, J. M., Graham, K., Hayes, J. R., & Fallside, D. (1984). CMU/IBM usability study: Final report. [CDC Tech. Rep. No. 11]. Communication Design Center, Pittsburgh, PA: Carnegie Mellon University.

Baltes, P. B., & Nesselroade, J. R. (1979). History and rationale of longitudinal research. In J. R. Nesselroade & P. B. Baltes (Eds.), *Longitudinal research in the study of behavior and development*. New York: Academic Press.

Barabas, C. (1990). *Technical writing in a corporate culture*. Norwood, NJ: Ablex.

Bazerman, C. (1988). *Shaping written knowledge: The genre and activity of the experimental article in science.* Madison: University of Wisconsin Press.

Beal, C. R. (1990). The development of text evaluation and revision skills. *Child Development, 61,* 247-258.

Bekerian, D. A., & Dennett, J. L. (1990). Spoken and written recall of visual narratives. *Applied Cognitive Psychology, 4,* 175-187.

Benton, S. L., Kraft, R. G., Glover, J. A., & Plake, B. S. (1984). Cognitive capacity differences among writers. *Journal of Educational Psychology, 76,* 820-834.

Bereiter, C., & Scardamalia, M. (1982). From conversation to composition: The role of instruction in a developmental process. In R. Glaser (Ed.), *Advances in instructional psychology* (Vol. 2, pp. 1-64). Hillsdale, NJ: Lawrence Erlbaum Associates.

Bereiter, C., & Scardamalia, M. (1983). Levels of inquiry in writing research. In P. Mosenthal, L. Tamor, & S. Walmsley (Eds). *Research on writing; Principles and methods* (pp. 3-25). New York: Longman (a shortened version is included in their 1987 compilation).

Bereiter, C., & Scardamalia, M. (1987). *The psychology of written composition.* Hillsdale, NJ: Lawrence Erlbaum Associates.

Bereiter, C., Burtis, P. J., & Scardamalia, M. (1988). Cognitive operations in constructing main points in written composition. *Journal of Memory and Language, 27,* 261-278.

Bergh, H. van den (1988). *Examens geëxamineerd.* [Examinations examined]. Unpublished doctoral dissertation, University of Amsterdam. Den Haag: SVO. Selecta-reeks.

Bergh, H. van den (1988). Schrijven en schrijven is twee: een onderzoek naar de samenhang op verschillende schrijftaken [Writing and writing is two: A study to the covariance between different writing assignments]. *Tijdschrift voor onderwijsreseacrh, 13,* 311-324.

Bergh, H. van den, Rijlaarsdam, G., & Breetvelt, I. (1992a). Doelen stellen en tekstkwaliteit: een empirisch onderzoek naar de relatie tussen schrijfprocessen en tekstkwaliteit [Goal setting and text quality: An empirical study on the relationship between writing processes and text quality]. *Tijdschrift voor Taalbeheersing, 14,* 221-233.

Bergh, H. van den, Rijlaarsdam, G., & Breetvelt, I. (1992b). Het stellen van doelen; relaties met produktkwaliteit. *Tijdschrift voor Taalbeheersing, 14,* 221-233.

Bergh, H. van den, Rijlaarsdam, G., & Breetvelt, I. (1993). Revision processes and text quality: An empirical study. In G. Eigler & Th. Jechle (Eds.), *Writing: Current trends in European research.* Freiburg: Hochschul Verlag. p. 133-147.

Bergh, H. van den, Rijlaarsdam, G., & Breetvelt, I. (1994). Revision process and text quality: An empirical study. In G. Eigler & Th. Jechle (Eds.), *Writing: Current trends in European research* (pp. 133-148). Freiburg: Hochschul Verlag.

Berman, R. A. (1978). *Modern Hebrew structure.* Tel-Aviv: University Publishing Projects.

Berstein, L. (1990, April). *Developing an adequately specified model of state level student achievement with multilevel data.* Paper presented at the meeting of the American Educational Association, Boston.

Besner, D., & Humphreys, G. (Eds.) (1990). *Basic processes in reading: Visual word recognition.* Hillsdale, NJ: Lawrence Erlbaum Associates.

Blakeslee, A. M. (1992). Investing scientific discourse: Dimensions of rhetorical knowledge in physics. Unpublished doctoral dissertation, Carnegie Mellon University.

Blau, S. (1983). Invisible writing: Investigating cognitive processes in writing. *College Composition and Communication, 34,* 297-312.

Bock, J. K. (1982). Toward a cognitive psychology of syntax: Information processing contributions to sentence formulation. *Psychological Review, 89,* 1-47.

Boden, M. A. (1990). *The creative mind.* London: Weidenfeld & Nicolson.

Boden, M. A. (Ed.) (1994a). *Dimensions of creativity.* Cambridge, MA: Bradford Books.

Boden, M. A. (1994b). What is creativity? In M. A. Boden (Ed.), *Dimensions of creativity* (pp. 75 – 117). Cambridge, MA: Bradford/The MIT Press.

Boice, R. (1985). Psychotherapies for writing blocks. In M. Rose (Ed.), *When a writer can't write* (pp. 182-218). New York: Guilford.

Bond, S., & Hayes, J. R. (1984). Cues people use to paragraph text. *Research in the Teaching of English, 18,* 147-167.

Börner, W. (1989). Planen und Problemlösen im fremdsprachlichen Schreibprozeb: Einige empirische Befunde. In U. Klenk, K.H. Körner, & W. Thümmel (Hrsg.), *Variatio Linguarum. Beiträge zu Sprachvergleich und Sprachentwicklung. Festschrift zum 60. Geburtstag von Gustav Ineichen.* Wiesbaden: Steiner, 43-62.

Bourdin, B., & Fayol, M. (1994). Is written language production more difficult than oral language production. A working memory approach. *International Journal of Psychology, 29,* 591-620.

Bourdin, B., & Fayol, M. (1995). Working memory and writing. In C. Aarnouste, F. de Jong, H. Lodewijks, J. Simons, & D. van der Aalsvoort (Eds.), *Abstracts of the 6th European conference for research on learning and instruction.* Nijmegen, NL: Mesoconsult.

Bousfield, W. A., & Sedgwick, C. H. (1944). An analysis of sequences of restricted associative responses. *Journal of General Psychology, 30,* 149-165.

Bower, G. H. (1972). Mental imagery and associative learning. In L. Gregg (Ed.), *Cognition in Learning and Memory.* New York: Wiley.

Box, J. A., & Aldridge, J. (1993). Shared reading experience and Head Start children's concepts about print and story structure, *77,* 923-930.

Bradbury, R. (199). *Zen and the art of writing.* New York: Bantam.

Braddock, R. (1992). The frequency and placement of topic sentences in expository prose. *Research in the Teaching of English, 8,* 287-302.

Brand, A. G. (1989). *The psychology of writing: The affective experience.* New York: Greenwood Press.

Breetvelt, I. (1991). *Schrijfproces and tekstkwaliteit: een onderzoek naar het verband tussen schrijfprocessen en tekstkwalitiet bij leerlingen in het voortgezet onderwijs* [Writing process and text quality: A study into the relationship between writing processes and text quality at students in secondary education]. SCO-rapport 225. Amsterdam: SCO.

Breetvelt, I. (1991). *Schrijfproces en tekstkwaliteit (Writing process and text quality)*. Amsterdam: SCO.

Breetvelt, I., Bergh, H. van den, & Rijlaarsdam, G. (1994). Relations of writing processes and text quality: When and how. *Cognition and Instruction, 12*, 103-123.

Breetvelt, I., van den Bergh, H., & Rijlaarsdam, G. (1996). Reading the assignment and generating processes: An empirical study on the relationship between cognitive activities and text quality. In G. Rijlaarsdam, H. van den Bergh, & M. Couzijn (Eds.), *Writing research: Theories, models and methodology*. Amsterdam: Amsterdam University Press.

Bridwell, L. S. (1980). Revising strategies in twelfth grade students' transactional writing. *Research in the teaching of English, 14*, 197-222.

Bridwell-Bowles, L. S., Johnson, P., & Brehe, S. (1987). Composing and computers: Case studies of experienced writers. In A. Matsuhashi (Ed.), *Writing in Real Time* (pp. 81-107). New York: Ablex.

Britton, B. K. (1986). Capturing art to improve text quality. *Educational Psychologist, 21*, 333-356.

Britton, B. K. (1992). *Effects on learning of individual differences in inference making ability* [AFOSR Final Technical Report].

Britton, B. K. (1993). *A LISREL individual differences model of learning from instruction*. Invited address at Armstrong Labs, Brooks Air Force Base, San Antonio, TX.

Britton, B. K. (1994). Understanding expository text: Building mental structures to induce insights. In M. Gernsbacher, (Ed.), *Handbook of Psycholinguistics* (pp. 641-674). New York: Academic Press.

Britton, B. K. (1995a). *Improving instructional texts: Tests of components of principled revisions*. Paper presented at the 1995 Annual Meeting of the American Educational Research Association, San Francisco, CA.

Britton, B. K. (1995b). Improving military textbooks: A research program, computer programs, and an SBIR. Invited address presented to the Special Interest Group on Military Education and Training, 1995 Annual Meeting of the American Educational Research Association, San Francisco, CA.

Britton, J., Burgess, T., Martin, N., McLeod, A., & Rosen, H. (1975). *The development of writing abilities*. London: Macmillan.

Britton, B. K., & Eisenhart, F. J. (1993). Expertise, text coherence, and constraint satisfaction: Effects on harmony and settling rate. *Proceedings of the Cognitive Science Society, 15*, 266-271.

Britton, B. K., & Gulgoz, S. (1991). Using Kintsch's computational model to improve instructional text: Effects of repairing inference calls on recall and cognitive structures. *Journal of Educational Psychology, 83*, 329-345.

Britton, B. K., Gulgoz, S., & Glynn, S. M. (1993). Impact of good and poor writing on learners. In B. K. Britton, A. Woodward, & M. Binkley (Eds.), *Learning from textbooks*. Hillsdale, NJ: Lawrence Erlbaum Associates.

Britton, B. K., Kyllonen, P., J. F., Stennett, B., & Gulgoz, S. (1995). Learning from instructional text: Test of an individual differences model Unpublished manuscript.

Britton, B. K., & Tidwell, P. (1991). Shifting novices' mental representation toward experts': Diagnosis and repair of mis- and missing conceptions. In *Proceedings of the Thirteenth Annual Conference of the Cognitive Science Society*. Hillsdale, NJ: Lawrence Erlbaum Associates.

Britton, B. K., & Tidwell, P. (1993). Shifting novices' mental representations toward experts': Diagnosis and repairs of misconceptions. Unpublished manuscript.

Britton, B. K., & Tidwell, P. (1995). Cognitive structure testing methods: A computer system for diagnosis of expert/novice differences. In S. Chipman (Ed.) *Cognitively diagnostic assessment* (pp. 251-279). Hillsdale, NJ: Lawrence Erlbaum Associates.

Britton, B. K., Van Dusen, L. M., & Gulgoz, S. (1991). Reply to "A response to 'Instructional texts rewritten by five expert teams.'" *Journal of Educational Psychology, 83*, 149-152.

Britton, B. K., Van Dusen, L. M., Glynn, S. M., & Hemphill, D. (1990). The impact of inferences on instructional text. In A. C. Graesser & G. H. Bower (Eds.), *The psychology of learning and motivation* (Vol. 25, pp. 63-70). New York: Academic Press.

Britton, B. K., Van Dusen, L., Gulgoz, S., & Glynn, S. M. (1989). Instructional texts rewritten by five expert teams: Revisions and retention improvements. *Journal of Educational Psychology, 81*, 226-239.

Broadhead, G. J., & Freed, R. C. (1986). *The variables of composition: Process, product in a business setting*. Carbondale: Southern Illinois University Press.

Brown, A., Campione, J., & Day, J. (1981). Learning to learn: On training students to learn from texts. *Educational Researcher, 10*, 14-21.

Brown, J. S., McDonald, J. L., Brown, T. L., & Carr, T. H. (1988). Adapting to processing demands in discourse production: The case of handwriting. *Journal of Experimental Psychology: Human Perception and Performance, 14*, 45-59.

Bruin, G. de (1995). *De discourse-organiserende funktie van de vooropgeplaatste adverbiale bijzin* [The discourse-organizing function of the fronted adverbial clause]. Unpublished master's thesis, Tilburg University.

Bryke, A. S., & Raudenbush, S. W. (1992). *Hierarchical linear models: applications and data analysis methods*. Newbury Park, CA: Sage Publications.

Burgoon, J., & Hale, J. L. (1983). Dimensions of communications reticence and impact on verbal encoding. *Communication Quarterly, 31*, 302-311.

Burnham, S. (1994). *For writers only*. New York: Ballantine Books.

Burtis, P. J., Bereiter, C., Scardamalia, M., & Tetroe, J. (1983).The development of planning in writing. In B. M. Kroll & G. Wells (Eds.), *Explorations in the development of writing* (pp. 153-174). New York: Wiley.

Butterworth, B. (1975). Hesitation and semantic planning in speech. *Journal of Psycholinguïstic Research, 4*, 75-87.

Butterworth, B. (1980). Evidence from pauses in speech. In B. Butterworth (Ed.), *Language production: Vol. 1. Speech and talk.* New York: Academic Press.

Butterworth, B. (1982). Speech errors: Old data in search of new theories. In A. Cutler (Ed.), Slips of the tongue and language production. Berlin.

Buzan, T. (1989). *Use your head* (Revised Edition). London: BBC Books.

Caccamise, D.J. (1987). Idea generation in writing. In A. Matshusahi (Ed.), *Writing in real time: Modeling in production processes* (pp. 224-253). Norwood, NJ: Ablex.

Card, S., Robert, J., & Keenan, L. (1984). Online composition of text. *Proceedings of Intact '84* (pp. 51-56). Amsterdam: North-Holland.

Carey, L. J., & Flower, L. (1989). *Foundations for creativity in the writing process: Rhetorical representations of ill-defined problems.* (Tech. Rep. No. 32). Berkeley, CA: Center for the Study of Writing.

Carey, L. J., Flower, L., Hayes, J. R., Schriver, K. A., & Haas, C. (1989). *Differences in writers' initial task representations.* (Tech. Rep. No. 35). Carnegie Mellon University.

Carr, T. H., & Levy, B. A. (Eds.) (1990). *Reading and its development: Component skills approaches* (pp. 1-55). San Diego, CA: Academic Press.

Carroll, J. M. (1985). *What's in a name?* New York: Freeman.

Chan. L. (1992). *Preschool children's understanding of Chinese writing.* Paper presented at the 9th Annual Conference of the Hong Kong Educational Research Association.

Chandler, D. (1991). Writing media. *Unpublished paper,* University College of Wales, Aberystwyth.

Chandler, D. (1995). *The act of writing: A media theory approach.* Aberystwyth: University of Wales.

Chase, W., & Simon, H. A. (1973). Perception in chess. *Cognitive Psychology, 4,* 55-81.

Chenoweth, A. (1995, March). *Recognizing the role of reading in writing.* Paper presented at College Composition Communication Conference, Washington, DC.

Cheung, H., & Kemper, S. (1992). Competing complexity metrics and adults' production of complex sentences. *Applied Psycholinguistics, 13,* 53-76.

Cheung, K. L. (1990). The analysis of multilevel data in educational research: Studies of problems and their solutions. *International Journal of Educational Research* [special issue], *14,* 215-319.

Chi, M. M. (1988). Invented spelling/writing in Chinese-speaking children: The developmental pattern. In J. E. Readance & R. S. Baldwin (Eds.), *Dialogues in literacy research, 37th yearbook of the National Reading Conference.* Chicago, IL: National Reading Conference.

Clark, A. (1989). *Microcognition: Philosophy, cognitive science, and parallel distributed processing.* Cambridge, MA: MIT Press.

Clay, M. M. (1975). *What did I write?* Auckland, NZ: Heinemann.

Clay, M. M. (1987). *Writing begins at home.* Auckland, NZ: Heinemann.

Coffman, W. E. (1966). On the validity of essay tests of achievement. *Journal of Educational Measurement, 22,* 41-45.

Conway, R. A., & Engle, R. W. (1994). Working memory and retrieval: A resource-dependent inhibition model. *Journal of Experimental Psychology: General, 123(4)*, 354-373.

Cooper, M., & Holzman, M. (1983). Talking about protocols. *College Composition and Communication, 34*, 284-293.

Cooper, M., & Holzman, M. (1985). Reply by Marilyn Cooper and Michael Holzman. *College Composition and Communication, 36*, 97-100.

Coulmas, F. (1985). Reden ist Silber, Schreiben ist Gold [Speech is silver but silence is golden]. *Zeitschrift fuer Literaturwissenschaft und Linguistik, 59*, 94-112.

Couture, B., & Rymer, J. (1991). Discourse interaction between writer and supervisor: A Primary collaboration in workplace writing. In M. M. Lay & W.M. Karis (Eds.), *Collaborative Writing in industry: Investigations in theory and practice* (pp. 87-108). Amityville, New York: Baywood.

Couzijn, M., & Rijlaarsdam, G, (1996). Observational learning: Learning and transfer effects on argumentative writing. In G. Rijlaarsdam, H. van den Bergh & M. Couzijn (Eds.), *Effective teaching and learning of writing. Current trends in empirical research*. Amsterdam: Amsterdam University Press.

Cowley, M. (Ed.) (1958). *Writers at work: The Paris Review Interviews*. New York: Viking Press.

Cowan, N. (1995). *Attention and memory: An integrated framework*. New York: Oxford University Press.

Cox, B. E. (1990). The effects of structural factors of expository texts on teacher's judgments of writing quality. In *Literacy theory and research: Analyses from multiple paradigms* (pp. 137-143). Chicago, IL: National Reading Conference.

Cronbach, L. J. (1986). Research in classrooms and schools: Formulations of questions, designs, and analysis. Occasional paper, Stanford Evaluation Consortium.

Cronbach, L. J. (1991). Methodological studies: A personal retrospective. In R. E. Snow & D. Wiley (Eds.), *Improving inquiry in social science: A volume in honor of Lee J. Cronbach*. Hillsdale, NJ: Lawrence Erlbaum Associates.

Cronbach, L. J., & Gleser, G. C. (1953). Assessing similarity between profiles. *Psychological Bulletin, 50*, 456-473.

Cross, G.A. (1993). The interrelation of genre, context, and process in the collaborative writing of two corporate documents. In R. Spilka (Ed.), *Writing in the workplace. New research perspectives* (pp. 141-157). Carbondale: Southern Illinois University Press.

Crothers, E. (1978). Inference and coherence. *Discourse Processes, 1*, 51-71.

Cumming, A. (1989). Writing expertise and second language profiency. *Language Learning*. (March) 81-141.

Daalder, S. (1989). Continuative relative clauses. In N. Reiter (Ed.), *Sprechen und Hören; Akten des 23. Linguistischen Kolloquiums, Berlin 1988* (pp. 195-207). Tübingen: Niemeyer.

Daiker, D., Kerek, A., & Morenberg, M. (1986). *The writer's options; Combining to composing*. New York: Harper & Row.

Daly, J. A. (1977). The effects of writing apprehension on message encoding. *Journal Quarterly, 54,* 566-572.

Daly, J. A. (1978). Writing apprehension and writing competency. *Journal of Educational Research, 72,* 10-14.

Daly, J. A. (1985). Writing apprehension. In M. Rose (Ed.), *When a writer can't write* (pp. 42-82). New York: Guilford Press.

Daly, J. A., & Miller, M. D. (1975a). The empirical development of an instrument of writing apprehension. *Research in the Teaching of English, 9,* 242-249.

Daly, J. A., & Miller, M. D. (1975b). Further studies in writing apprehension: SAT scores, success, expectations, willingness to take advanced courses, and sex differences. *Research in the Teaching of English, 9,* 249-253.

Daly, J. A., & Shamo, W. (1976). Writing apprehension and occupational choice. *Journal of Occupational Psychology, 49,* 55-56.

Daly, J. A., & Shamo, W. (1978). Academic decisions as a function of writing apprehension. *Research in the Teaching of English, 12,* 119-126.

Daneman, M., & Carpenter, P. A. (1980). Individual differences in working memory and reading. *Journal of Verbal Learning and Verbal Behavior, 19,* 450-466.

Daneman, M., & Carpenter, P. A. (1983). Individual differences in integrating information between and within sentences. *Journal of Experimental Psychology: Learning, Memory, and Cognition, 9,* 561-583.

Daneman, M., & Greene, I. (1986). Individual differences in comprehending and producing words in context. *Journal of Memory and Language, 25,* 1-18.

Daneman, M., & Stainton, M. (1993). The generation effect in reading and proofreading. *Reading and Writing: An Interdisciplinary Journal, 5,* 297-313.

Daneman, M., & Tardif, T. (1987). Working memory and reading skill reexamined. In M. Coltheart (Ed.), *Attention and performance XII.* Hillsdale, NJ: Lawrence Erlbaum Associates.

Danoff, B., Harris, K. R., & Graham, S. (1993). Incorporating strategy instruction within the writing process in the regular classroom. *Journal of Reading Behavior, 25,* 295-322.

Darke, J. (1978). The primary generator and the design process. In W. E. Rogers & W. H. Ittelson (Eds.), *New directions in environmental design research: Proceedings of EDRA 9* (pp. 325–337). Washington: EDRA.

Day, K. C., & Day, H. D. (1984). Kindergarten knowledge of print conventions and later school achievement: A five year follow up. *Psychology in the Schools, 21,* 393-396.

de Beaugrande, R. (1984). *Text production: Toward a science of composition.* Norwood, NJ: Ablex.

de Beaugrande, R. (1985). Sentence combining and discourse processing: In search of a general theory. In D. Daiker, A. Kerek, & M. Morenberg (Eds.), *Sentence combining; A rhetorical perspective* (pp. 61-75). Carbondale IL: Southern Illinois University Press.

De Goes, C., & Martlew, M. (1983). Young children's approach to literacy. In M. Martlew (Ed.), *The psychology of written language* (pp. 217-235). New York: Wiley.

De La Paz, S., & Graham, S. (1994). Dictation: Applications to writing with students with learning disabilities. In T. Scruggs & M. Mastropieri (Eds.), *Advances in learning and behavioral disabilities*. Greenwich, CT: JAI Press.

De La Paz, S., & Graham, S. (1995). *Strategy instruction in planning: Effects on the writing performance and behavior of students with learning difficulties*. Manuscript submitted for publication.

De Vet, D. (1994). Cats: A real help for writers. In L. van Waes, E. Woudstra & P. van den Hoven (Eds.), *Functional communication quality* (pp. 183-194). Amsterdam: Rodopi.

Debs, M .B. (1989). Collaborative writing in industry. In B. E. Fearing & W. K. Sparrow (Eds.), *Technical writing: Theory and practice* (pp. 33-42). New York: MLA.

Dijk, T. van (1977). *Text and context: Explorations in the semantics and pragmatics of discourse*. New York: Longman.

Dimter, M. (1981). *Textklassenkonzepte heutiger Alltagssprache*. [Concepts of text categories in today's everyday language]. Tuebingen: Niemeyer.

DiPardo, A. (1994). Stimulated recall in research on writing: An antidote to "I don't know, it was fine." In P. Smagorinsky (Ed.), *Speaking about writing: Reflections on research methodology* (pp. 163-181). Thousand Oaks, CA: Sage Publications.

Diringer, D. (1958). *The story of the Aleph Beth*. London: Lincoln Prager.

Dixon, P., LeFevre, J. A., & Twilley, L. C. (1988). Word knowledge and working memory as predictors of reading skill. *Journal of Educational Psychology, 80*, 465-472.

Dobrin, D. N. (1986). Protocols once more. *College English, 48*, 713-725.

Durst, R. (1989). Monitoring processes in analytic and summary writing. *Written Communication, 6*, 340-363.

Durst, R. (1990). The mongoose and the rat in composition research: Insights from the RTE Annotated Bibliography. *College Composition and Communication, 41(4)*, 393-408.

Dweck, C. (1986). Motivational processes affecting learning. *American Psychologist, 41*, 1040-1048. .

Earhart, R. C. (1978). *History 202: Modern warfare and society*. United States Air Force Academy.

Eastman, C. M. (1970). On the analysis of intuitive design processes. In G. T. Moore (Ed.), *Emerging methods in environmental design and planning*. Cambridge, MA.: M.I.T. Press.

Eco, U. (1982). The narrative structure in Fleming. In B. Waites, T. Bennett, & G. Martin (Eds.), *Popular culture: Past and present* (pp. 245–262). London: Croom Helm.

Ede, L., & Lunsford, A. A. (1990). *Singular texts/plural authors: Perspectives on collaborative writing*. Carbondale: Southern Illinois University Press.

Eklundh, K. S. (1992). Problems in achieving a global perspective of the text in computer-based writing. In M. Sharples (Ed.), *Computers and writing: Issues and implementations* (pp. 73–84). Dordrecht: Kluwer.

Elbow, P. (1973). *Writing without teachers*. London: Oxford University Press.

Elbow, P. (1981). *Writing with power*. New York: Oxford University Press.

Elshout, J. (1982). Experimenteel onderzoek van intellectuele vaardigheden. *Nederlands Tijdschrift voor de Psychologie, 37*, 195-205.

Elshout, J. (1984). Expert en beginners. [Experts and novices]. In G. A. M. Kempen & Ch. Sprengers (Eds.), *Kennis, mensen en computers* (pp. 25-30). Lisse: Swets en Zeitlinger.

Emig, J. (1971). *The composing processes of twelfth graders*. Urbana, IL: National Council of Teachers of English.

Engle, R. W., Cantor, J., & Carullo, J. J. (1992). Individual differences in working memory and comprehension: Test of four hypotheses. *Journal of Experimental Psychology: Learning, Memory, & Cognition, 18*, 972-992.

Englert, C., Raphael, T., Anderson, L., Anthony, H., Stevens, D., & Fear, K. (1991). Making writing strategies and self-talk visible: Cognitive strategy instruction in writing in regular and special education classrooms. *American Educational Research Journal, 28*, 337-373.

Ericsson, K. A., & Simon, H. A. (1993). *Protocol analysis: Verbal reports as data — Revised edition*. Cambridge, MA: MIT Press.

Eysenck, H. J., & Eysenck, S. B. G. (1968). *Manual: Eysenck personality inventory*. San Diego: Educational and Industrial Testing Service.

Faigley, L., Cherry, R. D., Jolliffe, D. A., & Skinner, A. M. (1985). *Assessing writers' knowledge and processes of composing*. Norwood, NJ: Ablex.

Faigley, L., Daly, J. A., & Witte, S. (1981). The role of writing apprehension in writing performance and writing competence. *Journal of Educational Research, 75*, 16-21.

Faigley, L., & Witte, S. (1981). Analyzing revision. *College Composition and Communication, 32*, 400-414.

Faigley, L., & Witte, S. (1984). Measuring the effect of revision on text structure. In R. Beach & L. Bridwell (Eds.), *New directions in composition research* (pp. 95-108). New York: Guilford Press.

Ferreiro, E., & Teberosky, A. (1979). *Literacy before schooling*. Exeter, NH: Heineman Educational.

Festinger, L., & Carlsmith, J. M. (1959). Cognitive consequences of forced compliance. *Journal of Abnormal and Social Psychology, 58*, 203-210.

Finn, J. D., & Cox, D. (1992). Participation and withdrawal among fourth-grade pupils. *American Educational Research Journal. 29 (1)*, 141-162.

Fitzgerald, J., & Stamm, C. (1990). Effects of group conferences on first graders' revision in writing. *Written Communication, 7*, 96-135.

Flinn, J. Z. (1987a). Case studies of revision aided by keystroke recording and replaying software. *Computers and Composition, 5*, 31-43.

Flinn, J.Z. (1987b). Programming software to trace the composing process. *Computers and Composition, 5*, 45-49.

Flower, L. S. (1981). *Problem-solving strategies for writing*. New York: Harcourt Brace.

Flower, L. S., & Hayes, J. R. (1980a). The cognition of discovery: Defining a rhetorical problem. *College Composition and Communication, 31*, 21-32.

Flower, L. S., & Hayes, J. R. (1980b). The dynamics of composing: Making plans and juggling constraints. In L. W. Gregg & E. R. Steinberg (Eds.), *Cognitive processes in writing* (pp. 31-50). Hillsdale, NJ: Lawrence Erlbaum Asscoiates.

Flower, L. S., & Hayes, J. R. (1981). A cognitive process theory of writing. *College Composition and Communication, 32*, 365-387.

Flower, L. S., & Hayes, J. R. (1984). Images, plans, and prose: The representation of meaning in writing. *Written Communication, 1*, 120-160.

Flower, L. S., & Hayes, J. R. (1985). Response to Marylin Cooper and Michael Holzman, "Talking about protocols." *College Composition and Communication, 36*, 94-97.

Flower, L. S., Hayes, J. R., Carey, L., Schriver, K., & Stratman, J. (1986). Detection, diagnosis, and the strategies of revision. *College Composition and Communication, 37(1)*, 16-55.

Fodor, J. A. (1983). *The modularity of mind*. Cambridge, MA: MIT Press.

Fowler, H. W. (1965). *A dictionary of modern English usage* [Second Ed.]. Oxford: Oxford University Press.

Freedman, S. W. (1987). *Peer response groups in two ninth-grade classrooms* (Tech. Rep. No. 12). Center for the Study of Writing, Berkeley, CA: University of California.

Freeman, Y. S., & Whitsell, L. R. (1985). What preschoolers know already about print. *Educational Horizons, 64*, 22-24.

Freud, S. (1976). Creative writers and day-dreaming. In A. Rothenberg & C. R. Hausman (Eds.), *The creativity question* (pp. 48–54). Durham, NC: Duke University Press. (Original work published 1908)

Friedlander, A. (1987). The writer stumbles: Constraints on composing in English as a second language. Unpublished doctoral dissertation. Carnegie Mellon University.

Galassi, J. P., Frierson, J. T., Jr., & Sharer, R. (1981). Behavior of high, moderate, and low test anxious students during an actual test situation. *Journal of Consulting and Clinical Psychology, 49*, 51-62.

Gardner, H. (1980). On becoming a dictator. *Psychology Today, 14*, 14-19.

Garrett, M. F. (1976). Syntactic processes in sentence production. In R. J. Wales & E. Walker (Eds.), *New approaches to language mechanisms* (pp. 231-255). Amsterdam: North Holland.

Garrett, M. F. (1980). Levels of processing in sentence production. In B. Butterworth (Ed.), *Language production, Vol. 2, Speech and talk*. New York: Academic Press.

Garston, D. G. (1985). *A program evaluation and review technique machine-readable data file*. Raleigh, NC: National Collegiate Software Clearinghouse.

Garton, A., & Pratt, C. (1989). *Learning to be literate: The development of spoken and written language*. Oxford: Blackwell.

Gathercole, S. E., & Baddeley, A. (1993). *Working memory and language*. Hillsdale, NJ: Lawrence Erlbaum Associates.

Geest, Th. van der. (1996). Professional writing studied: Authors' accounts of planning in document production processes. In M. Sharples & Th. van der Geest (Eds.), *The new writing environment; Writers at work in a world of technology*. London: Springer Verlag.

Gelb, I. J. (1963). *A study of writing*. Chicago, IL: University of Chicago Press.

Gelernter, D. (1994). *The muse in the machine: Computers and creative thought*. London: Fourth Estate.

Gemert, L. van, & Woudstra, E. (1996). Writing ISO procedures: activities of writers to acquire knowledge. In *Proceedings of the 1995 International Conference of the Academy of Business Administration*. London.

Gentner, D. R. (1983). Keystroke timing in transcription typing. In W. E. Cooper (Ed.) *Cognitive aspects skilled typewriting* (pp. 95-120). New York: Springer-Verlag.

Gernsbacher, M. A. (1990). Language comprehension as structure building. Hillsdale, NJ: Lawrence Erlbaum Associates.

Gernsbacher, M. A., & Faust, M. E. (1991). The mechanism of suppression: A component of general comprehension skill. *Journal of Experimental Psychology: Learning, Memory and Cognition, 17*, 245-262.

Ghiselin, B. (1954). *The creative process*. University of California Press.

Glynn, S. M., Britton, B. K., Muth, D., & Dogan, N. (1982). Writing and revising persuasive documents: Cognitive demands. *Journal of Educational Psychology, 74*, 557-567.

Godschalk, F. I., Swineford, F., & Coffman, W. E. (1966). *The measurement of writing ability*. New York: College Entrance Examination Board.

Goldman-Eisler, F. (1968). *Psycholinguistics: Experiments in spontaneous speech*. London: Academic Press.

Goldstein, H. (1979). *The design and analysis of longitudinal studies: Their roles in the measurement of change*. London: Griffin.

Goldstein, H. (1987). *Multilevel models in educational and social research: Their role in the measurement of change*. London: Griffin.

Goldstein, H. (1991). Nonlinear multilevel models, with an application to discrete response data. *Biometrika, 78*, 45-51.

Goldstein, H., & McDonald, R. P. (1988). A general model for the analysis of multilevel data. *Psychometrika, 53*, 455-467.

Gombert, J. E., & Fayol, M. (1992). Writing in preliterate children. *Learning and Instruction, 2*, 23-41.

Gould, J. D. (1978). How experts dictate. *Journal of Experimental Psychology: Human Perception and Performance, 4*, 648-661.

Gould, J. D. (1980).Experiments on composing letters: Some facts, some myths, and some observations. In L. Gregg & E. Steinberg (Eds.), *Cognitive processes in writing* (pp 97-128). Hillsdale, NJ: Lawrence Erlbaum Associates.

Gould, J. D., Conti, J., & Hovanyecz, T. (1983). Composing letters with a simulated listening typewriter. *Communications of the ACM, 26*, 295-308.

Gould, J. D., & Grischkowsky, N. (1984). Doing the same work hard copy and with CRT terminals. *Human Factors, 26*, 323-337.

Grabowski, J., & Miller, G. A. (1996, in press). Factors affecting the use of spatial prepositions in German and American English: Object orientation, social context, and prepositional inventory. *Journal of Psycholinguistic Research.*

Grabowski, J., Hauschildt, A., & Rummer, R. (1992). Reden ueber Ereignisse: Kognitive Aufbereitungen im Sprachproduktionsprozess. [Speaking about events: Cognitive editing in the language production process.] In L. Montada (Ed.), *Bericht ueber den 38. Kongress der Deutschen Gesellschaft fuer Psychologie in Trier 1992* (pp. 168-169). Goettingen: Hogrefe.

Grabowski, J., Vorwerg, C., & Rummer, R. (1994). Writing as a tool for control of episodic representation. In G. Eigler & Th. Jechle (Eds.), *Text production: Current trends in European research* (pp. 55-68). Freiburg: Hochschulverlag.

Grabowski-Gellert, J. (1989). Facilitating experiments with verbal data? On equivalence between oral and written text production and its extension to specific situations. In P. Boscolo (Ed.), *Writing: Trends in European research* (pp. 260-271). Padua: UPSEL.

Graesser, A. C., & Mandler, G. (1978). Limited processing capacity constrains the storage of unrelated sets of words and retrieval from natural categories. *Journal of Experimental Psychology: Human Learning and Memory, 4,* 86-100.

Graham, S. (1990). The role of production factors in learning disabled students' compositions. *Journal of Educational Psychology, 82,* 781-791.

Graham, S., & Harris K. R. (1989a). A components analysis of cognitive strategy instruction: Effects on learning disabled students' compositions and self-efficacy. *Journal of Educational Psychology, 81,* 353-361.

Graham, S., & Harris K. R. (1989b). Improving learning disabled students' skills at composing essays: Self-instructional strategy training. *Exceptional Children, 56,* 201-214.

Graham, S., & Harris, K. R. (1993). Self-regulated strategy development: Helping students with learning problems develop as writers. *Elementary School Journal, 94,* 169-181.

Graham, S., & Harris, K. R. (1994a). The role and development of self-regulation in the writing process. In D. Schunk & B. Zimmerman (Eds.), *Self-regulation of learning and performance: Issues and educational applications* (pp. 203-228). Hillsdale, NJ: Lawrence Erlbaum Associates.

Graham, S., & Harris, K. R. (1994b). The implications of constructivism for teaching writing to students with special needs. *Journal of Special Education, 28,* 275-289.

Graham, S., & Harris, K. R. (1996, in press). Teaching writing strategies within the context of a whole language class. In E. McIntyre & M. Pressley (Eds.), *Skills in whole language.* New York: Christopher-Gordon.

Graham, S., Harris, K. R., MacArthur, C., & Schwartz, S. (1991). Writing and writing instruction with students with learning disabilities: A review of a program of research. *Learning Disability Quarterly, 14,* 89-114.

Graham, S., & MacArthur, C. (1988). Improving learning disabled students' skills at revising essays produced on a word processor: Self-instructional strategy training. *Journal of Special Education, 22,* 133-152.

Graham, S., MacArthur, C., & Schwartz, S. (1995). The effects of goal setting and procedural facilitation on the revising behavior and writing performance of students with writing and learning problems. *Journal of Educational Psychology*, *87*, 230-240.

Graham, S., MacArthur, C., Schwartz, S., & Voth, T. (1992). Improving the compositions of students with learning disabilities using a strategy involving product and process goal setting. *Exceptional Children*, *58*, 322-335.

Graham, S., Schwartz, S., & MacArthur, C. (1993). Learning disabled and normally achieving students' knowledge of the writing and the composing process, attitude toward writing, and self-efficacy. *Journal of Learning Disabilities*, *26*, 237-249.

Graves, M. F., Prenn, M., Earle, J., Thompson, M., & Johnson, V. (1991). A response to "Models for the design of instructional text." *Reading Research Quarterly*, *26*, 110-122.

Graves, M. F., & Slater, W. H. (1986). Could textbooks and would textbooks. *American Educator*, *10*, 36-42.

Graves, M. F., Slater, W. H., Roen, D., Redd-Boyd, T., Duin, A. H., Furniss, D. W., & Hazeltine, P. (1988). Some characteristics of memorable expository writing: Effects of revisions by writers with different backgrounds. *Research in the Teaching of English*, *22*, 242-265.

Graves, R., & Hodge, A. (1971). *The reader over your shoulder*. New York: MacMillan. (Original work published 1943).

Greenberg, M. A., & Stone, A. A. (1992).Writing about disclosed versus undisclosed traumas: Immediate and long-term effects on mood and health. *Journal of Personality and Social Psychology*. *63*, 75-84.

Greene, S. (1991). *Writing from sources: Authority in text and task*. (Tech. Rep. No. 55). Center for the Study of Writing, University of California, Berkeley, CA.

Greene, S., & Higgins, L. (1994). "Once upon a time": The use of retrospective accounts in building theory in composition. In P. Smagorinsky (Ed.), *Speaking about writing: Reflections on research methodology* (pp. 115-140). Thousand Oaks, CA: Sage Publications.

Grender, J. M., & Johnson, W. D. (1994). Fitting multivariate polynomial growth curves in two-period cross-over designs. *Statistics in Medicine*, *13*, 931-943.

Guelich, E., & Raible, W. (Eds.) (1975). *Textsorten. Differenzierungskriterien aus linguistischer Sicht* [Text classes. Differential criteria from a linguistic perspective]. Wiesbaden: Athenaion.

Guenther, H. (1988). *Schriftliche Sprache* [Written language]. Tuebingen: Niemeyer.

Guenther, K. B., & Guenther, H. (Eds.) (1983). *Schrift, Schreiben, Schriftlichkeit* [Script, writing, written language]. Tuebingen: Niemeyer.

Guenther, U. (1993). *Texte planen — Texte produzieren. Kognitive Prozesse der schriftlichen Textproduktion* [Planning of texts — production of texts. Cognitive processes in written text production]. Opladen: Westdeutscher Verlag.

Gulgoz, S. (1986). Retention differences between original and revised versions of texts. Unpublished masters thesis, University of Georgia.

Gulgoz, S. (1989). Revising text to improve learning: Methods based on text processing models, expertise, and readability formulas. Unpublished doctoral dissertation, University of Georgia.

Haas, C. (1987). How the writing medium shapes the writing process: Studies of writers composing with pen and paper and with word processing. Unpublished doctoral dissertation. Carnegie Mellon University.

Haas, C. (1989). Does the medium make a difference? A study of composing with pen and paper and with a computer. *Human-Computer Interaction, 4*, 149-169.

Haas, C., & Hayes, J. R. (1986). What did I just say? Reading problems in writing with the machine. *Research in the Teaching of English, 20*. 22-35.

Haggblade, B. (1990). Voice recognition systems: Will they encourage executives to dictate? *Business Education Forum, 44*, 18-20.

Harris, K. R. (1982). Cognitive-behavior modification: Application with exceptional students. *Focus on Exceptional Children, 15*, 1-16.

Harris, K. R., & Graham, S. (1985). Improving learning disabled students' composition skills: Self-control strategy training. *Learning Disability Quarterly, 8*, 27-36.

Harris. K. R., & Graham, S. (1992a). *Helping young writers master the craft: Strategy instruction and self-regulation in the writing process.* Cambridge, MA: Brookline.

Harris, K. R., & Graham, S. (1992b). Self-regulated strategy development: A part of the writing process. In M. Pressley. K. Harris, & J. Guthrie (Eds.), *Promoting academic competence and literacy in school.* San Diego. CA: Academic Press.

Harris. K. R., & Graham, S. (1993). Cognitive strategy instruction and whole language: A case study. *Remedial and Special Education, 14*, 30-34.

Harris, K. R., & Graham, S. (1994). Constructivism: Principles, paradigms, and integration. *Journal of Special Education, 28*, 275-289.

Harris, K. R., Graham, S., Reid, R., McElroy, K., & Hamby, R. (1994). Self-monitoring of attention versus self-monitoring of performance: Replication and cross-task comparison studies. *Learning Disability Quarterly, 17*, 121-139.

Harris, S., & Witte, S. (1980). Sentence combining in a rhetorical framework: Directions for further research. In A. Freedman & I. Pringle (Eds.), *Reinventing the rhetorical tradition* (pp. 89-98). Conway. AR: L & S Books.

Hatch. J.. Hill. C.. & Hayes, J. R. (1993). When the messenger is the message: Readers' impressions of writers. *Written Communication, 10(4)*, 569-598.

Hayduk, L. A. (1987). *Structural equation modeling with LISREL.* Baltimore: Johns Hopkins University Press.

Hayes, C. (1987). Planning in the machining domain: Using goal interactions to guide search. Unpublished masters thesis. Carnegie Mellon University.

Hayes, J. R. (1985). Three problems in teaching general skills. In S. Chipman, J. Segal, & R. Glaser (Eds.) *Thinking and learning skills.* Hillsdale, NJ: Lawrence Erlbaum Associates.

Hayes, J. R. (1989). *The complete problem solver* (2nd ed.). Hillsdale, NJ: Lawrence Erlbaum Associates.

Hayes, J. R., & Flower, L. S. (1980). Identifying the organization of writing processes. In L. Gregg & E. R. Steinberg (Eds.), *Cognitive processes in writing* (pp.3-30). Hillsdale, NJ: Lawrence Erlbaum Associates.

Hayes, J. R., & Flower, L. S. (1983). Uncovering cognitive processes in writing: An introduction to protocol analysis. In P. Mosenthal, L. Tamor, & S. A. Walmsley (Eds.). *Research on writing: Principles and methods*. New York: Longman.

Hayes, J. R., & Flower, L. S. (1986). Writing research and the writer. *American Psychologist, 41*, 1106-1113.

Hayes, J. R., Flower, L. S., Schriver, K. S., Stratman, J., & Carey, L. (1987). Cognitive processes in revision. In S. Rosenberg (Ed.), *Advances in applied psycholinguistics: Vol. 2. Reading, writing, and language processing* (pp. 176-240). New York: Cambridge University Press.

Hayes, J. R., Schriver, K. A., Hill, C., & Hatch, J. (1990). *Seeing problems with text: How students' engagement makes a difference*. Final report of Project 3, Study 17. Carnegie Mellon University, Center for the Study of Writing.

Hayes, J. R., Schriver, K. A., Spilka, R., & Blaustein, A. (1986). If it's clear to me, it must be clear to them. Paper presented at the Conference on *College Composition and Communication*, New Orleans, LA.

Hayes, J. R., & Simon, H. A. (1974). Understanding written problem instructions. In L.W. Gregg (Ed.), *Knowledge and cognition*. Hillsdale, NJ: Lawrence Erlbaum Associates.

Hayes, J. R., Waterman, D., & Robinson, S. (1977). Identifying the relevant aspects of a problem text. *Cognitive Science, 1*, 297-313.

Hayes-Roth, B., & Hayes-Roth, F. (1979). A cognitive model of planning. *Cognitive Science, 3*, 275-310.

Healy, M. J. R. (1989). Growth curves and growth standards — The state of the art. In J. Tanner (Ed.), *Auxiology '88: Perspectives in the science of growth and development*. London: Smith-Gordon.

Heath, S. B. (1983). *Ways with words: Language, life, and work in communities and classrooms*. New York: Cambridge University Press.

Heider, F. (1958). *The psychology of interpersonal relations*. New York: Wiley.

Henderson, A., Goldman-Eisler, F., & Skarbek, A. (1966). Sequential temporal patterns in spontaneous speech. *Language and Speech, 9*, 207-216.

Henderson, R. W. (1989). *EventLog*. Iowa City, IO: CONDUIT.

Henning, J., & Huth, L. (1975). *Kommunikationals Problem der Linguistik* [Com-munication as a linguistic problem]. Goettingen: Vandenhoeck & Ruprecht.

Herrmann, Th. (1983). *Speech and situation*. New York: Springer.

Herrmann, Th., & Grabowski, J. (1992). *Muendlichkeit, Schriftlichkeit und die nicht-terminalen Prozessstufen der Sprachproduktion* [Orality, written language, and the pre-terminal stages of language production]. [Reports from the Special Research Group on language and situation, SFB 245, Heidelberg/Mannheim, No. 38]. Mannheim: University, Chair for Psychology III.

Herrmann, Th., & Grabowski, J. (1993). *Das Merkmalsproblem und das Identitaetsproblem in der Theorie dualer, multimodaler und flexibler Repraesentationen von Konzepten und Woertern (DMF-Theorie)* [The feature problem and the identity problem, treated in the theory of the dual, multi-modal, and flexible representation of concepts and words]. [Reports from the Special Research Group on language and situation, SFB 245, Heidelberg/Mannheim, No. 61]. Mannheim: University, Chair for Psychology III.

Herrmann, Th., & Grabowski, J. (1994). *Sprechen — Psychologie der Sprachproduktion* [Speaking — the psychology of language production.] Heidelberg: Spektrum Akademischer Verlag.

Herrmann, Th., & Grabowski, J. (1995). Pre-terminal levels of process in oral and written language production. In U. Quasthoff (Ed.), *Aspects of oral communication* (pp. 67-87). Berlin: deGruyter.

Herrmann, Th., Grabowski, J., Graf, R. & Schweizer, K. (1996). Konzepte, Woerter und Figuren: Zur Aktivationstheorie multimodaler Repraesentate. Teil I: Repraesentationstypen [Concepts, words, and gestalts: Towards an activation theory of multi-modal representation. Part I: Types of representation]. In J. Grabowski, G. Harras & Th. Herrmann (Eds.), *Bedeutung — Konzepte — Bedeutungskonzepte* [Meaning — concepts — concepts of meaning]. Opladen: Westdeutscher Verlag.

Hidi, S. E., & Hildyard, A. (1983). The comparison of oral and written productions in two discourse types. *Discourse Processes, 6,* 91-105.

Hidi, S., & Hildyard, A. (1983). The comparison of oral and written productions of two discourse types. *Discourse Processes, 6,* 91-105.

Hilgard, E. R. (1987). *Psychology in America: A historical survey.* New York: Harcourt Brace Jovanovich.

Hill, C. (1992). Thinking through controversy: The effect of writing on the argument evaluation processes of first-year college students. Unpublished doctoral dissertation, Carnegie Mellon University.

Hillocks, G., Jr. (1986). *Research on written composition: New directions for teaching.* Urbana, IL: ERIC Clearinghouse on Reading and Communication Skills.

Hirsch, E. D. *The philosophy of composition.* (1970). Chicago, IL: University of Chicago Press.

Hjelmquist, E. (1984). Memory for conversations. *Discourse Processes, 7,* 321-335.

Hobbs, J. (1990). *Literature and cognition.* Menlo Park, CA: Center for the Study of Language and Information, Stanford University.

Horowitz, M., & Newman, J. (1964). Spoken and written expression: An experimental analysis. *Journal of Abnormal and Social Psycholoy, 68,* 640.

Hox, J. J. (1994). *Applied multivariate analysis.* Amsterdam: TT-publikaties.

Hull, C. L. (1943). *Principles of behavior.* New York: Appleton Century Crofts.

Hull, G. (1993). Hearing other voices: A critical assessment of popular views on literacy and work. *Harvard Educational Review, 63(1),* 20-49.

Hull, G. A., & Smith, W. L. (1983). Interrupting visual feedback in writing. *Perceptual and Motor Skills, 57,* 963-978.

Hunt, K. (1970). Syntactic maturity in school children and adults. *Monographs of the Society for Research in Child Development, 35*, 1-67.

Hutchins, E. (1995). *Cognition in the wild*. Cambridge, MA: MIT Press.

Ihde, D. (1979). *Technics and praxis*. Dordrecht: Reidel.

Jakobs, E. (1995). Text und Quelle. Wisenschaftliche Textproduktion unter Nutzung externer Wissensspeicher [Text and reference. Scientific text production and the use of external stores of knowledge]. In E. M. Jakobs, D. Knorr & S. Molitor-Luebbert (Eds.), *Wissenschaftliche Textproduktion. Mit und ohne Computer* (pp. 91-112). Frankfurt/M.: Lang.

Jansen, C. (1994). Computerized writing aids: Do they really help? In M. Steehouder, et al. (Eds.), *Quality of technical documentation*. Amsterdam: Rodopi.

Janssen, D. (1991). *Schrijven aan beleidsnota's. Schrijfprocessen van beleidsambtenaren empirisch-kwalitatief onderzocht* [Writing Policy Issue Papers]. An empirical-qualitative study into writing processes of governmental policy designers]. Groningen: Wolters-Noordhoff.

Janssen, D., Schilperoord, J., Waes, L. van, & Wassenaar, W. (1994). Effecten van hardop denken op het schrijfproces [The influence of thinking aloud on the writing process]. In A. Maes, P. Van Hauwermeiren, & L. van Waes (Eds.), *Perspectieven in Taalbeheersingsonderzoek*. Dordrecht: ICG Publications.

Jeffery, G. C., & Underwood, G. (1995). Working memory and semantic processing in sentence production: A comparison of spoken and written sentences. Unpublished manuscript.

Johnson, E., & Mazzeo, J. (1995). *Generalizability of tasks in NAEP*. Paper presented at the 1995 Anual Meeting of AERA in San Francisco.

Johnson, S. E., Linton, P. W., & Madigan, R. J. (1994). The role of internal standards in assessment of written discourse. *Discourse Processes, 18*, 231-245.

Just, M. A., & Carpenter, P. A. (1980). A theory of reading : From eye fixations to comprehension. *Psychological Review, 87*, 329-354.

Just, M. A., & Carpenter, P. A. (1992). A capacity theory of comprehension: Individual differences in working memory. *Psychological Review, 99*, 122-149.

Kahn, D. (1980). *Syllable-based generalizations in English phonology*. New York: Garland.

Kamii, C. (1986). *Spelling in kindergarten: A constructivist analysis comparing Spanish and English speaking children*. Unpublished manuscript.

Karmiloff-Smith, A. (1990). Constraints on representational change: Evidence from children's drawing. *Cognition, 34*, 57–83.

Kaufer, D. S., Hayes, J. R., & Flower, L. S. (1986). Composing written sentences. *Research in the Teaching of English, 20*, 121-140.

Kean, D., Gylnn, S., & Britton, B. (1987). Writing persuasive documents: The role of students' verbal aptitude and evaluation anxiety. *Journal of Experimental Education, 55*, 95-102.

Kellogg, R. T. (1987). Writing performance: Effects of cognitive strategies. *Written Communication, 4*, 269-298.

Kellogg, R. T. (1988). Attentional overload and writing performance: Effects of rough draft and outline strategies. *Journal of Experimental Psychology: Learning, Memory, and Cognition, 14*, 355-365.

Kellogg, R. T. (1989). Writing performance: Effects of cognitive strategies. *Written Communication, 4*, 269-298.

Kellogg, R. T. (1990).Effectiveness of prewriting strategies as a function of task demand. *American Journal of Psychology, 103*, 327-342.

Kellogg, R. T. (1994). *The psychology of writing*. New York: Oxford University Press.

Kellogg, R. T., & Mueller, S. (1993). Performance amplification and process restructuring in computer-based writing. *Journal of Man-Machine Studies, 39*, 33-49.

Kemper, S. (1988). Geriatric psycholinguistics: Syntactic limitations of oral and written language. In L. Light & D. Burke (Eds.), *Language and memory in old age* (pp. 58-76). Cambridge: Cambridge University Press.

Kemper, S., Kynette, D., Sprott, R., & O'Brien, K. (1989). Life-span changes to adults' language: Effects of memory and genre. *Applied Psycholinguistics, 10*, 49-66.

Kennedy, M. L. (1985). The composing process of college students writing from sources. *Written Communication, 2*, 434-456.

Kerek, A., Daiker, D., & Morenberg, M. (1980). Sentence combining and college composition. *Perceptual and Motor Skills, 51*, 1059-1157.

Kern, R. P., Sticht, T. G., Welty, D., & Hauke, R. N. (1976). *Guidebook for the development of Army training literature*. Alexandria, VA: Human Resources Resources Organization.

King, J., & Just, M. A. (1991). Individual differences in syntactic processing: The role of working memory. *Journal of Memory and Language, 30*, 580-602.

Kintsch, W. (1974). *The representation of meaning in memory*. Hillsdale, NJ: Lawrence Erlbaum Associates.

Kintsch, W., Britton, B. K., Fletcher, C. R., Kintsch, E., Mannes, S. M., & Nathan, M. J. (1993). A comprehension-based approach to learning and instruction. In D. L. Medin (Ed). *Psychology of learning and instruction* (Vol. 30, pp. 165-214). New York: Academic Press.

Kintsch, W., & van Dijk, T. A. (1978). Toward a model of text comprehension and production. *Psychological Review, 85*, 363-394.

Kleimann, S. (1993). The reciprocal relationship of workplace culture and review. In R. Spilka (Ed.), *Writing in the workplace. New Research Perspectives* (pp. 56-70). Carbondale: Southern Illinois University Press.

Klein, W. (1985). Gesprochene Sprache — geschriebene Sprache [Spoken language — written language]. *Zeitschrift fuer Literaturwissenschaft und Linguistik, 59*, 9-35.

Koch, P., & Oesterreicher, W. (1988). Sprache der Naehe — Sprache der Distanz [Language of proximity — language of distance]. *Romanistisches Jahrbuch, 39*, 15-43.

Kohler, W. (1940). *Dynamics in psychology*. London: Liveright.

Kollberg, P. (1995). *Rules for the S-notation* [IPLab Working Paper No. 36]. Department of Numerical Analysis and Computing Science, Royal Institute of Technology, Stockholm.

Kowall, S., & O'Connel, D. C. (1987). Writing as language behavior: Myths, models, methods. In A. Matsuhashi (Ed.), *Writing in real time*. Norwood, NJ: Ablex.

Kozma, R. B. (1991). The impact of computer-based tools and embedded prompts on writing processes and products of novice and advanced college writers. *Cognition and Instruction, 8*, 1-27.

Kuutti, K. (1991). The concept of activity as a basic unit of analysis for CSCW research. In L. Bannon, M. Robinson, & K. Schmidt (Eds.), *Second conference on computer supported cooperative work* (pp. 249–264). Amsterdam: Kluwer Academic Publishers.

Lansman, M., Smith, J. B., & Weber, J. (1990). Using computer generated protocols to study writers' planning strategies. Unpublished manuscript.

Larkin, J. E., & Simon, H. A. (1987). Why a diagram is (sometimes) worth ten thousand words. *Cognitive Science, 11*, 65-99.

Lawson, B. (1990). *How designers think: The design process demysified* (2nd ed.). Oxford: Butterworth-Heinemann.

Levelt, W. J. M. (1983). Monitoring and self-repair in speech. *Cognition, 14*, 41-104.

Levelt, W. J. M. (1989). *Speaking: From intention to articulation*. Cambridge, MA: MIT Press.

Levin, I., Amsterdamer, P., & Korat, O. (1996). Emergent writing in preschool: Developmental perspectives and language effects. In J. Shimron (Ed.), *Psycholinguistic studies in Israel: Language acquisition, reading and writing*. [in Hebrew].

Levin, I., & Korat, O. (1993). Sensitivity to phonological, morphological and semantic cues in early reading and writing in Hebrew. *Merrill-Palmer Quarterly, 39*, 213-232.

Levin, I., Korat, O., & Amsterdamer, P. (1995). Emergent writing among Israeli kindergartners: Cross-linguistic commonalities and Hebrew-specific issues. In G. Rijlaarsdam, H. van den Bergh, & M. Couzijn (Eds.), *Current trends in writing research: Theories, models and methodology*. Amsterdam: Amsterdam University Press.

Levin, I., & Tolchinsky Landsmann, L. (1989). Becoming literate: Referential and phonetic strategies in early reading and writing. *International Journal of Behavioural Development, 12*, 369-384.

Levy, C. M., & Ransdell, S. E. (1994). Computer-aided protocols of writing processes. *Behavior Research Methods, Instruments and Computers, 26*, 219-223.

Levy, C. M., & Ransdell, S. E. (1995). Is writing as difficult as it seems? *Memory and Cognition, 23*, 767-779.

Levy, C. M., Rozen, L., Marek, J. P., & Lea, J. (1995). *How will the word processors of 2005 affect writing?* Paper presented at the International Conference of Writing and Computers, October. London.

Lindblom, B. (1982). The interdisciplinary challenge of speech motor control. In S. Grillner, B. Lindblom, J. Lubker & A. Persson (Eds.), *Speech motor control. Proceedings of an international symposium on the functional basis of oculomotor disorders* (pp. 3-18). Oxford: Pergamon Press.

Locke, E., Shaw, K., Saari, L., & Latham, G. (1981). Goal setting and task performance: 1969-1980. *Psychological Bulletin, 90,* 125-152.

Lomax, R. G., & McGee, L. M. (1987). Young children's concepts about print and reading: Toward a model of word reading acquisition. *Reading Research Quarterly, 22,* 237-256.

Longford, N. T. (1989). *Multivariate variance component analysis: An application in test development* [Tech. Rep. No. 89-91]. Princeton, N.J.: Educational Testing Service.

Ludwig, O. (1980). Geschriebene Sprache [Written language]. In H. P. Althaus, H. Henne & H. E. Wiegand (Eds.), *Lexikon der Germanistischen Linguistik* (pp. 323-328). Tuebingen: Niemeyer.

Lutz, J. A. (1987). A study of professional and experienced writers revising and editing at the computer and with pen and paper. *Research in the Teaching of English, 21(4),* 398-421.

MacArthur, C., & Graham, S. (1987). Learning disabled students' composing with three methods: Handwriting, dictation, and word processing. *Journal of Special Education, 21,* 22-42.

MacArthur, C., Graham, S., & Schwartz, S. (1991). Knowledge of revision and revising behavior among learning disabled students. *Learning Disability Quarterly, 14,* 61-73.

MacArthur, C., Graham, S., Schwartz, S., & Shafer, W. (1996, in press). Evaluation of a writing instruction model that integrated a process approach, strategy instruction, and word processing. *Learning Disabilities Quarterly.*

MacArthur, C., Schwartz, S., & Graham, S. (1991). Effects of a reciprocal peer revision strategy in special education classrooms. *Learning Disabilities Research and Practice, 6,* 201-210.

MacArthur, C., Schwartz, S., Graham, S., Molloy, D., & Harris, K. (1995). [Case studies of classroom instruction in a semantic webbing strategy]. Unpublished raw data.

MacDonald, M. C., Just, M. A., & Carpenter, P. A. (1992). Working memory constraints on the processing of syntactic ambiguity. *Cognitive Psychology, 24,* 56-98.

MacKay, D. G., Wulf, G., Yin, C., & Abrams, L. (1993). Relations between word perception and production: New theory and data on the verbal transformation effect. *Journal of Memory and Language, 32,* 624-646.

Madigan, R. J., Holt, J., & Blackwell, J. (1993, November). The role of working memory in writing fluently. Paper presented at the annual meeting of the Psychonomics Society, Washington, DC.

Madigan, R. J., Johnson, S. E., & Linton, P. W. (1994, June). Working memory capacity and the writing process. Paper presented at the American Psychological Society, Washington, DC.

Mandel, B. J. (1978). Losing one's mind: Learning to write and edit. In *College Composition and Communcation* (pp. 362–368).

Mann, W., & Thompson, S. (1988). Rhetorical structure theory: Toward a functional theory of text organization. *Text, 8,* 243-281.

Masson, M. E., & Miller, J. A. (1983). Working memory and individual differences comprehension and memory of text. *Journal of Educational Psychology, 75(2)*, 314-318.

Matsuhashi, A. (1981). Pausing and planning: The tempo of written discourse production. *Research in the Teaching of English, 15*, 113-134.

Matsuhashi, A. (1982). Explorations in the real-time production of written discourse. In M. Nystrand (Ed.), *What writers know: The language, process, and structure of written discourse*. New York: Academic Press.

Matsuhashi, A. (1987). Revising the plan and altering the text. In A. Matsuhashi (Ed.), *Writing in real time: Modelling production processes* (pp. 197-223). New York: Ablex.

Matsuhashi, A. (1981). Pausing and planning: The tempo of written discourse production. *Research in the Teaching of English, 15*, 113-134.

McClelland, J. L., & Rumelhart, D. E. (1988). *Explorations in parallel distributed processing: A handbook of models, programs, and exercises*. Cambridge, MA: MIT Press.

McCutchen, D. (1987). Children's discourse skill: Form and modality requirements of schooled writing. *Discourse Processes, 10*, 267-286.

McCutchen, D. (1988). "Functional automaticity" in children's writing: A problem of metacognitive control. *Written Communication, 5*, 306-324.

McCutchen, D., Covil, A., Hoyne, S. H., & Mildes, K. (1994). Individual differences in writing: Implications of translating fluency. *Journal of Educational Psychology, 86*, 256-266.

Medway, P. (1995, April). *Virtual and material buildings: Language in architectural construction*. Paper presented at the 1995 Annual Convention of the American Educational Research Association, San Francisco.

Medway, P. (1996). Writing, speaking, drawing: the distribution of meaning in architects' communication. In M. Sharples & Th van der Geest (Eds.), *The new writing environment: Writers at work in a world of technology* London: Springer-Verlag.

Meisel, W. S. (1993). Talk to your computer: Voice technology lets you verbally command your computer to convert speech to text. *Byte, 18*, 113-120.

Messori, V. (1994). *Introduction to crossing the threshold of hope*. New York: Knopf.

Miles, M. B., & Huberman, A. M. (1994). *Qualitative data analysis. An expanded sourcebook* (2nd ed.). Thousand Oaks, CA: Sage.

Miller, G. A. (1956). The magical number seven plus or minus two: Some limits on our capacity for processing information. *Psychological Review, 63*, 81-97.

Miller, G. A. (1991). *The science of words*. New York: Freeman.

Miller, G. A., Galanter, E., & Pribram, K. H. (1960). *Plans and the structure of behavior*. New York: Holt, Rinehart, & Winston.

Mischel, T. (1974). A case study of a twelfth-grade writer. *Research in the Teaching of English, 8*, 303-314.

Miyake, A., Just, M. A., & Carpenter, P. A. (1994). Working memory constraints on the resolution of lexical ambiguity: Maintaining multiple interpretations in neutral contexts. *Journal of Memory and Language, 33,* 175-202.

Molitor, S. (1987). *Weiterentwicklung eines Textproduktionsmodells durch Fallstudien* [Development of a text production model by case studies] [Rep. No. 45]. Tuebingen: University, German Institute for Distance Education (DIFF).

Monahan, B. D. (1984). Revision strategies of basic and competent writers as they write for different audiences. *Research in the Teaching of English, 18(3),* 289-304.

Moravcsik, J. E., & Kintsch, W. (1993). Writing quality, reading skills, and domain knowledge as factors in text comprehension. *Canadian Journal of Experimental Psychology, 47,* 360-374.

Morris, R. G. M. (1989). *Parallel distributed processing: Implications for psychology and neurobiology.* New York: Oxford University Press.

Myers, G. (1985a). The social construction of two biologists' proposals. *Written Communication, 2,* 219-245.

Myers, G. (1985b). Text as knowledge claims: The social construction of two biologists' proposals. *Written Communication, 2,* 219-245.

Nelson, J. (1988). Examining the practices that shape student writing: Two studies of college freshmen writing across disciplines. Unpublished doctoral dissertation, Carnegie Mellon University.

Nelson, M. S., & Denny, E. D. (1993). *The Nelson-Denny Reading Test.* Boston: Houghton-Miffin.

Neuwirth, C. M., & Kaufer, D. S. (1989). The role of external representations in the writing process: Implications for the design of hypertext-based writing tools. In *Hypertext'89 Proceedings* (pp. 319-342). Baltimore, MD: Association for Computing Machinery.

Newell, A. (1990). *United theories of cognition.* Cambridge, MA: Harvard University Press.

Newell, A., & Simon, H. A. (1972). *Human problem solving.* Englewood Cliffs, NJ: Prentice Hall.

Newell, A. F., Arnott, J. L., Carter, K., & Cruickshank, G. (1990). Listening typewriter simulation studies. *International Journal of Man-Machine Studies, 33,* 1-19.

Newell, A. F., Arnott, J. L., Dye, R., & Cairns, A. Y. (1991). A full-speed listening typewriter simulation. *International Journal of Man-Machine Studies, 35,* 119-131.

Newman, W. M., & Lamming, M. G. (1995). *Interactive system design.* Wokingham: Addison-Wesley.

Nilsson, M. (1993). *Trace-it 2.0 user's manual.* IPLab, Department of Numerical Analysis and Computing Science, KTH.

Norman, D. A. (1986). Cognitive engineering. In D. A. Norman & S. W. Draper (Eds.), *User centered system design,* Hillsdale, NJ: Lawrence Erlbaum Associates.

Norman, D. A., & Rumelhart, D. E. (1983). Studies of typing from LNR research group. In W. E. Cooper (Ed.), *Cognitive aspects skilled typewriting* (pp. 45-65). New York: Springer-Verlag.

Norman, D. A., & Shallice, T. (1986). Attention to action: Willed and automatic control of behavior. In R. J. Davidson, G. E. Schwarts & D. Shapiro (Eds.), *Consciousness and self-regulation. Advances in research and theory.* (Vol. 4, pp. 1-18). New York: Plenum Press.

Nystrand, M. (1989). A social interactive model of writing. *Written Communication, 6*, 66-85.

O'Malley, C. (1988). Writers' protocols and task analysis. *Writer's Assistant working paper 3*, University of Sussex.

O'Donnell, A. M., Dansereau, D. F., Rocklin, T., Lambiote, J. G., Hythecker, V. I, & Larson, C. O. (1985). Cooperative writing: Direct effects and transfer. *Written Communication, 2(3)*, 307-315.

O'Hara, K. (1966, in press). Cost of operations affects planfulness of problem-solving.

Odell, L. (1985). Beyond the text: Relations between writing and social context. In L. Odell & D. Goswami (Eds.), *Writing in nonacademic settings* (pp. 249-280). New York: Guilford Press.

Olson, D. R. (1977). From utterance to text: The bias of language in speech and writing. *Harvard Educational Review, 47*, 257-281.

Olson, R. K., Kligl, R., Davidson, B. J., & Foltz, C. (1985). Individual and developmental differences in reading disability. In C. E. MacKinnon & T. C. Waller (Eds.), *Reading research: Advances in theory and practice. (Vol 4).* New York: Academic Press.

Oostdam, R., & Rijlaarsdam, G. (1995). *Towards strategic language learning.* Amsterdam: Amsterdam University Press.

Owen, W., & Smyser, J. (1974). *The prose works of William Wordsworth.* Oxford: Clarendon Press.

Paivio, A. (1971). *Imagery and verbal processes.* New York: Holt, Rinehart, and Winston.

Paivio, A. (1986). *Mental representations: A dual coding approach.* New York: Oxford University Press.

Palmer, J., MacLeod, C. M., Hunt, E., & Davidson, J. E. (1985). Information processing correlates of reading. *Journal of Memory and Language, 24*, 59-88.

Palmquist, M., & Young, R. (1992). The notion of giftedness and student expectations about writing. *Written Communication, 9(1)*, 137-168.

Paradis, J., Dobrin, D. & Miller, R. (1985). Writing at Exxon ITD: Notes on the writing environment of an R&D organization. In L. Odell, & D. Goswami (Eds.), *Writing in nonacademic settings* (pp. 281- 308). New York, London: Guilford Press.

Paris, C., & McKeown, K. (1987). Discourse strategies for describing complex physical objects. In G. Kempen (Ed.), *Natural language generation; New results in artificial intelligence, psychology and linguistics.* (pp. 97-115). Dordrecht: Nijhoff.

Pemberton, L., Gorman, L., Hartley, A., & Power, R. (1996). Computer support for producing software documentation; Some possible futures. In M. Sharples & Th. van der Geest (Eds.), *The new writing environment: Writers at work in a world of technology.* London: Springer Verlag.

Pennebaker, J. W., Kiecolt-Glaser, J. & Glaser, R. (1988). Disclosure of traumas and immune function: Health implications for psychotherapy. *Journal of Consulting and Clinical Psychology. 56*, 239-245.

Perkins, D. N., & Salomon, G. (1989). Are cognitive skills context-bound? *Educational Researcher*, (January – February, 1989), 16-25.

Pianko, S. (1979). A description of the composing processes of college freshman writers. *Research in the Teaching of English, 13*, 5-22.

Plimpton, G. (1958). *Writers at work: The Paris Review interviews. First series.* London: Secker & Warburg.

Plimpton, G. (Ed.) (1967). *Writers at work: The Paris Review Interviews* (Third Series). New York: Viking Press.

Plowman, L. (1992). *Talking and writing in a group writing task: A sociocognitive perspective.* Cognitive Science Research Reports. Brighton: University of Sussex.

Plowman, L. (1996, in press), The interfunctionality of talk and text. *Journal of Computer-Supported Cooperative Work.*

Polanyi, L. (1988). A formal model of the structure of discourse. *Journal of Pragmatics, 12*, 601-638.

Pontecorvo, C., & Zucchermaglio, C. (1989). From oral to written language: Preschool children dictating stories. *Journal of Reading Behavior, 21*, 109-126.

Pontecorvo, C., & Zucchermaglio, C. (1990). A passage to literacy: Learning in a social context. In Y. M. Goodman (Ed.), *How children construct literacy* (pp. 59-98). Newark, DE: International Reading Association.

Pool, E. van der (1995). *Writing as a conceptual process; A text-analytical study of developmental aspects.* Unpublished doctoral dissertation, Tilburg University.

Pool, E. van der, & Wijk, C. van (1995). Proces en strategie in een psycholinguïstisch model van schrijven en lezen [Process and strategy in a psycholinguistic model of writing and reading]. *Tijdschrift voor Onderwijsresearch, 20*, 200-214.

Pope John Paul II (1994). *Crossing the threshold of hope.* New York: Knopf.

Portnoy, S. (1973). A comparison of oral and verbal written behavior. In K. Salzinger & R. Feldmann (Eds.), *Studies in verbal behavior* (pp. 99-151). New York: Pergamon Press.

Power, M. J. (1985). Sentence production and working memory. *The Quarterly Journal of Experimental Psychology, 37*, 367-385.

Pressley, M., Harris, K. R., & Marks, M. (1992). But good strategy instructors are constructivists! *Educational Psychology Review, 4*, 3-31.

Prosser, R., Rasbach, J., & Goldstein, H. (1991). *ML3: Software for three-level analysis. Users' guide for V.2.* London: Institute of Education, University of London.

Quellmalz, E. S., Cappel, F. J., & Chou, C. P. (1982). Effects of discourse and response mode on the measurement of writing competence. *Journal of Educational measurement, 19*, 241-258.

Raaijamkers, R. G. W., & Shiffrin, R. M. (1981). Search for associative memory. *Psychological Review, 88*, 93-134.

Ramers, K. H. (1992). Ambisilbische Konsonanten im Deutschen [Ambisyllabic consonants in German]. In P. Eisenberg, K. H. Ramers & H. Vater (Eds.), *Silbenphonologie des Deutschen* (pp. 246-283). Tuebingen: Narr.

Ransdell, S. E. (1994). Generating thinking-aloud protocols: Impact on the narrative writing of college students. *American Journal of Psychology, 108,* 89-98.

Ransdell, S. E. (1990). Using a real-time replay of students' word processing to understand and promote better writing. *Behavior Research Methods, Instruments, and Computers, 22,* 142-144.

Ransdell, S. E. (1995). Generating thinking-aloud protocols: Impact on the narrative writing of college students. *American Journal of Psychology, 108,* 89-98.

Ransdell, S. E., & Levy, C. M. (1994). Writing as process and product: The impact of tool, genre, audience knowledge and writer expertise. *Computers in Human Behavior, 10,* 1-17.

Ransdell, S. E., & Levy, C. M. (1995a, March). *Individual differences in working memory, reading comprehension, and writing performance.* Paper presented at the 9th annual Florida Conference on Cognition, Perception, and Language.

Ransdell, S. E., & Levy, C. M. (1995b). Writing as process and product: The impact of tool, genre, audience knowledge and writer expertise. *Computers in Human Behavior, 10,* 1-17.

Ravid, D. (1988). *Transient and fossilized in inflectional morphology: Varieties of spoken Hebrew.* Unpublished doctoral dissertation, Tel Aviv University.

Read, S. J., & Miller, L. C. (1993). Dissonance and balance in belief systems: The promise of parallel constraint satisfaction processes and connectionist modeling approaches. In R. C. Schank & E. Langer (Eds.), *Beliefs, reasoning and decision making: Psycho-logic in honor of Bob Abelson.* Hillsdale, NJ: Lawrence Erlbaum Associates.

Redish, J. (1993). Understanding readers. In C. M. Barnum & S. Carliner (Eds.), *Techniques for technical communicators* (pp. 14-41). New York: Macmillan.

Reece, J. E. (1992). Cognitive processes in the development of written composition skills: The role of planning, dictation, and computer tools. Unpublished doctoral thesis, La Trobe University.

Reesink, G., Holleman-van der Sleen, S., Stevens, S., & Kohnstamm, G. (1971). Syntaktische ontwikkeling bij schoolkinderen en volwassenen: een replicatie-onderzoek [Syntactic development in schoolchildren and adults: A replication]. *Nederlands Tijdschrift voor de Psychologie, 26,* 335-364.

Reitman, W. R. (1964). Heuristic decision procedures, open constraints, and the structure of ill-defined problems. In M. W. Shelley & G. L. Bryan (Eds.) *Human judgment and optimality.* New York: Wiley.

Reitman, W. R. (1965). *Cognition and thought.* New York: Wiley.

Rentel, V., & King, M. (1983). Present at the beginning. In P. Mosenthal, L. Tamor, & S. S. Walmsley (Eds.), *Research on writing: Principles and methods.* New York: Longman.

Rijlaarsdam, G. (1986). *Effecten van leerlingenrespons op aspecten van stelvaardigheid* (Effects of peer response on aspects of writing proficiency, writing processes and psychological variables), Unpublished doctoral dissertation, Center of Educational Research, Amsterdam: .

Rijlaarsdam. G. (1993a, March). *Learning, whose learning? Autonomous learning in mother tongue education.* 5th International Convention on Language and Education. School of Education. University of East Anglia. Norwich, UK.

Rijlaarsdam, G. (1993b). Research in L1-Education. A review and preview of applied linguistics research for the benefit of mother tongue education. *Toegepaste taalkunde in artikelen*, 46/47 (1993: 2/3), 238 -254.

Rijlaarsdam, G., van den Bergh, H., & Breetvelt, I.. (1993, August-September). *Metacognitive activities related to text quality in written composition processes.* Paper presented to the Fifth European conference for Research on Learning and Instruction. Aix en Provence, France.

Rose, M. (1980). Rigid rules, inflexible plans, and the stifling of language: A cognitivist analysis of writer's block. *College Composition and Communication, 31*, 389-401.

Rothenberg, A. (1976). The process of Janusian thinking in creativity. In A. Rothenberg & C. R. Hausman (Eds.), *The creativity question* (pp. 311–327). Durham, NC: Duke University Press.

Rothkopf, E. Z. (1971). Incidental memory for location of information in text. *Journal of Verbal Learning and Verbal Behavior, 10*, 608-613.

Rumelhart, D. E., Lindsay, P. H., & Norman, D. A. (1972). A process model of long-term memory. In E. Tulving & W. Donaldson (Eds.), *Organization and memory* (pp. 198-246). New York: Academic Press.

Rummer, R. (1995). *Kognitive Beanspruchung beim Sprechen: Experimentelle Untersuchungen zur ereignisbezogenen Sprachproduktion* [Cognitive load in speaking: Experimental studies on the event-related language production]. Unpublished doctoral thesis, University of Mannheim, Germany.

Russo, J. E., Johnson, E. J., & Stephens, D. L. (1989). The validity of verbal protocols. *Memory and Cognition, 17*, 759-769.

Sacerdoti, E. D. (1974). Planning in a hierarchy of planning spaces. *Artificial Intelligence. 5*, 115-135.

Sachs, J. (1967). Recognition memory for syntactic and semantic aspects of connected discourse. *Perception and Psychophysics, 2*, 437-442.

Sacks, H., Schegloff, E., & Jefferson, G. (1974). A simplest systematics for the organization of turn-taking for conversation. *Language, 50*, 696-735.

Safire, W., & Safir, L. (1992). *Good advice on writing.* New York: Simon & Schuster.

Salovey, P., & Haar, M. D. (1990). The efficacy of cognitive-behavior therapy and writing process training for alleviating writing anxiety. *Cognitive Therapy and Research, 14*, 515-528.

Sanders, T. (1992). *Discourse structure and coherence.* Unpublished doctoral dissertation, Tilburg University.

Sanders, T., & Wijk, C. van (1994). Procedures voor Incrementele Structuur-Analyse: Uitleg en toepassing op verklarende teksten [Procedures for Incremental Structural Analysis: An explanation and application on explanatory texts]. In A. Maes, P. van Hauwermeiren, & L. van Waes (Eds.), *Perspectieven in Taalbeheersingsonderzoek* (pp. 191-203). Dordrecht: ICG.

Sanders, T., & Wijk, C. van (1996). PISA - A procedure for analyzing the structure of explanatory texts. *Text, 16,* 91-132.

Sanders, T., Janssen, D., Pool, E. van der, Schilperoord, J., & Wijk, C. van (1996). Hierarchical text structure in writing products and writing processes. In H. van den Bergh & G. Rijlaarsdam (Eds.), *Writing research: Theories and methods.*

Sanders, T., Spooren, W., & Noordman, L. (1992). Toward a taxonomy of coherence relations. *Discourse Processes, 15,* 1-35.

Sanders, T., Spooren, W., & Noordman, L. (1993). Coherence relations in a cognitive theory of discourse representation. *Cognitive Linguistics, 4,* 93-133.

Santa, J. L. (1977). Spatial transformations of words and pictures. *Journal of Experimental Psychology: Human Learning and Memory, 3,* 418-427.

Sarason, I. G. (1984). Stress, anxiety, and cognitive interference: Reactions to tests. *Journal of Personality and Social Psychology, 51,* 929-938.

Sarason, I. G., Sarason, B. R., Keefe, D. E., Hayes, B. E., & Shearin, E. N. (1986). Cognitive interference: Situational determinants and traitlike characteristics. *Journal of Personality and Social Psychology, 51,* 215-226.

Sattath, S., & Tversky, A. (1977). Additive similarity trees. *Psychometrica, 42,* 319-345.

Sawyer, R., Graham, S., & Harris, K. R. (1992). Direct teaching, strategy instruction, and strategy instruction with explicit self-regulation: Effects on learning disabled students' compositions and self-efficacy. *Journal of Educational Psychology, 84,* 340-352.

Scardamalia, M., & Bereiter, C. (1985). The development of dialetical processes in composition. In D. Olson, N. Torrance, & A. Hildyard (Eds.), *Literacy, language, and learning: The nature and consequences of reading and writing* (pp. 307-329). New York: Cambridge University Press.

Scardamalia, M., & Bereiter, C. (1987). Knowledge telling and knowledge transforming in written composition. In S. Rosenberg (Ed.), *Advances in applied psycholinguistics* (pp. 143-175). Cambridge, UK: Cambridge University Press.

Scardamalia, M., Bereiter, C., & Goelman, H. (1982). The role of production factors in writing ability. In M. Nystrand (Ed.), *What writers know; The language, process, and structure of written discourse* (pp. 173-210). New York: Academic Press.

Scardamalia, M., Bereiter, C., & Steinbach, R. (1984).Teachability of reflective processes in written composition. *Cognitive Science, 8(2):*173-190.

Scarlett, C. M. (1989). *Children's understanding of written language before teaching instruction.* Unpublished doctoral dissertation, University of London.

Schank, R., & Lebowitz, M. (1980), Levels of understanding in computers and people. *Poetics, 9,* 251-273.

Schewe, A., & Froese, V. (1987). Relating reading and writing via comprehension, quality, and structure. *Research in literacy: Merging perspective*, National Reading Conference.

Schilperoord, J. (1993, July). *Grammatical Constructions and Micro-planning in Written Language Production*. Paper presented at the Third Cognitive Linguistic Conference, Leuven.

Schilperoord, J. (1996). *It's about time; Temporal aspects of cognitive processes in text production*. Unpublished doctoral dissertation, Utrecht University.

Schilperoord J., & Janssen, D. (1993). De "text produced so far" in het schrijfproces. *Tijdschrift voor Taalbeheersing, 15*, 266-285.

Schneider, W., & Detweiler, M. (1987). A connectionist/control architecture for working memory. In G. H. Bower (Ed.), *The psychology of learning and motivation* (Vol. 21, pp. 54-119). New York: Academic Press.

Schriver, K. A. (1987). *Teaching writers to anticipate the reader's needs: Empirically based instruction*. Unpublishd doctoral dissertation. Carnegie Mellon University.

Schriver, K. A. (1988). *Teaching writers how to plan: Which planning heuristics work best?* Paper presented at the meeting of the American Educational Research Association, St. Louis, MO.

Schriver, K. A. (1995, June). *Document design as rhetorical action*. Belle van Zuylen Lecture Series, Utrecht, Netherlands: University of Utrecht (available from Faculteitsbureau, Kromme Nieuwegracht 46, 3512 H.J, Utrecht.

Schriver, K. A. (1996, in press). *Dynamics in document design*. New York: Wiley.

Schriver, K.A., Hayes, J. R., & Steffy, A. (1994). *Designing drug education literature: A real audience speaks back*. National Center for the Study of Writing and Literacy: Briefs on Writing, *1(1)*, 1-4.

Schvaneveldt, R. W. (Ed.) (1990). *Pathfinder associative networks: Studies in knowledge organization*. Norwood, NJ: Ablex.

Schvaneveldt, R. (1992, November). *Pathfinder analysis*. Paper given at the annual meeting of the Psychonomic Society, Washington, DC.

Searle, J. R. (1969). *Speech acts: An essay in the philosophy of language*. Cambridge: Cambridge University Press.

Severinson Eklundh, K., & Kollberg, P. (1993). Translating keystroke records into a general notation for the writing process. In L. Ahrenberg (Ed.), *Papers from the third Nordic conference on text comprehension in man and machine*. Dept. of Computer and Information Science, Linkping University, Sweden.

Sexton, M., Harris, K.R., & Graham, S. (1995). *Strategy instruction in planning with students with learning disabilities: Effects on writing and attributions*. Manuscript submitted for publication.

Shanahan, T. (1984). Nature of the reading writing relation: An exploratory multivariate analysis. *Journal of Educational Psychology, 76*, 466-477.

Sharples, M. (1985). *Cognition, computers and creative writing*. Chichester: Ellis Horwood.

Sharples, M. (1994). Computer support for the rhythms of writing. *Computers and Composition, 11(3)*, 217–226.

Sharples, M., & O'Malley, C. (1988). A framework for the design of a writer's assistant. In J. Self (Ed.), *Artificial intelligence and human learning*. London: Chapman and Hall.

Sharples, M., & Pemberton, L. (1988). *Representing writing: An account of the writing process with regard to the writer's external representation*. [Cognitive science research paper No. 119]. Brighton: University of Sussex.

Sharples, M., & Pemberton, L. (1992). Representing writing: External representations and the writing process. In P. O. B. Holt & N. Williams (Eds.), *Computers and writing: State of the art*. (pp. 319–336). Oxford: Intellect.

Sharples, M., & van der Geest, T. (Eds.) (1996). *The new writing environment: Writers at work in a world of technology*. London: Springer-Verlag.

Sharples, M., Clutterbuck, A., & Goodlet, J. (1994). A comparison of algorithms for hypertext notes network linearization. *International Journal of Human-Computer Studies, 40*, 727–752.

Sharples, M., Goodlet, J., & Pemberton, L. (1992). Developing a writer's assistant. In J. Hartley (Ed.), *Technology and writing: Readings in the psychology of written communication* (pp. 209–220). London: Jessica Kingsley.

Shepard, G. M. (1994). *Neurobiology* (3rd ed.). New York: Oxford University Press.

Shepard, R. N. (1962). The analysis of proximities: Multidimensional scaling with an unknown distance function. *Psychometrika, 27*, 125-140.

Shepard, R. N. (1978). The mental image. *American Psychologist, 33*, 125-137.

Shimron, J. (1993). The role of vowels in reading: A review of studies in English and Hebrew. *Psychological Bulletin, 114*, 52-67.

Siegler, R. S., Adolph, K., & Lemaire, P. (1995). Strategy choices across the lifespan. Paper presented at Carnegie Cognitive Symposium, "Implicit Memory and Metacognition."

Simon, H. A., & Hayes, J. R. (1976). The understanding process: Problem isomorphs. *Cognitive Psychology, 8*, 165-190.

Smagorinsky, P. (1989). The reliability and validity of protocol analysis. *Written Communication, 6*, 463-479.

Smagorinsky, P. (Ed.) (1994). *Speaking about writing. Reflections on research methodology*. Thousand Oaks, CA: Sage Publications.

Smolensky, P. (1986). Information processing in dynamical systems: Foundations of harmony theory. In D. E. Rumelhart & J. L. McClelland, (Eds.), *Parallel Distributed Processing*. Cambridge, Mass: MIT Press.

Snow, R. E. (1980). Aptitude processes. In R. E. Snow, P. A. Frederico & W. E. Motague (Eds.), *Aptitude, learning and instruction. Vol. 1 Cognitive process analyses of aptitude*. Hillsdale, NJ: Lawrence Erlbaum Associates.

Snow, R. E., & Yalow, E. (1982). Education and intelligence. In R. J. Sternberg (Ed.), *Handbook of human intelligence*. Cambridge: Cambridge University Press.

Solberg, S., & Nevo, B. (1979). Preliminary steps towards an Israeli standardization of the Peabody Test. *Megamot, 3*, 407-413 [in Hebrew].

Sommers, N. I. (1980). Revision strategies of student writers and experienced adult writers. *College Composition and Communication, 31,* 378-388.

Sperling, M. (1991). *High school English and the teacher-student writing conference: Fine tuned duets in the ensemble of the classroom.* (Occasional Paper No. #26). Berkeley, CA: Center for the Study of Writing.

Spilka, R. (1990). Orality and literacy in the workplace: Process- and text-based strategies for multiple audience adaptation. *Journal of Business and Technical Communication, 4 (1),* 44-67.

Spilka, R. (1993). Moving between oral and written discourse to fulfill rhetorical and social goals. In R. Spilka (Ed.), *Writing in the workplace. New research perspectives* (pp. 71-83). Carbondale: Southern Illinois University Press.

Spivey, N. N. (1984). *Discourse synthesis: Constructing texts in reading and writing.* [Outstanding Dissertation Monograph Series]. Newark, DE: International Reading Association.

Spivey, N. N. (1992). Discourse synthesis: Creating texts from texts. In J. R. Hayes, R. E. Young, M. L. Matchett, M. McCaffrey, C. Cochran, & T. Hajduk (Eds.), *Reading empirical research studies: The rhetoric of research* (pp. 469-509). Hillsdale, NJ: Lawrence Erlbaum Associates.

Spivey, N. N., & King, J. R. (1987). Readers as writers composing from sources. *Reading Research Quarterly, 24,* 7-26.

Sproull, L., & Kiesler, S. (1986). Reducing social context cues: Electronic mail in organization communication. *Management Science, 32,* 1492-1512.

Stallard, C. K. (1974). An analysis of the writing behavior of good student writers. *Research in the Teaching of English, 8,* 206-218.

Stanovich, K. E. (1993). Does reading make you smarter? Literacy and the development of verbal intelligence. *Advances in Child Development, 24,* 133-180.

Stefic, M. (1981a). Planning with constraints. *Artificial Intelligence, 16,* 111-140.

Stefic, M. (1981b). Planning and meta-planning (MOLGEN: Part 2). *Artificial Intelligence, 16,* 141-170.

Stein, N. L., & Glenn, C. G. (1979). An analysis of story comprehension in elementary school children. In R. Freedle (Ed.), *New directions in discourse processing.* Norwood, NJ: Ablex.

Stein, V. (1992). How we begin to remember: Elaboration, task and the transformation of knowledge. Unpublished doctoral dissertation, Carnegie Mellon University.

Steinberg, E. R. (1986). Protocols, retrospective reports, and the stream of consciousness. *College English, 48,* 697-712.

Stoddard, B., & MacArthur, C. (1993). A peer editor strategy: Guiding learning disabled students in response and revision. *Research in the Teaching of English, 27,* 76-103.

Stone, I. (1978). *The origin.* New York: Doubleday.

Stratman, J., & Hamp-Lyons, L. (1996). Reactivity in concurrent think out loud protocols. In P. Smagorinsky (Ed.) *Verbal reports in the study of writing.* Newbury Park, CA: Sage.

Stratman, J. F., & Hamp-Lyons, L. (1994). Reactivity in concurrent think-aloud protocols. Issues for research. In P. Smagorinsky (Ed.), *Speaking about writing: Reflections on research methodology* (pp. 89-112). [Written Communication Series 8]. Thousand Oaks, CA: Sage.

Strong, W. (1973). *Sentence combining; A composing book.* New York: Random House.

Sulzby, E. (1985). Children's emergent reading of favorite storybooks: A developmental study. *Reading Research Quarterly, 20,* 458-481.

Sulzby, E., Barnhart, J., & Hieshima, J. (1989). Forms of writing and rereading from writing: A preliminary report. In J. Mason (Ed.), *Reading and writing connections* (pp. 31-63). Needham Heights, MA: Allyn and Bacon.

Swaney, J., Janik, C., Bond, S., & Hayes, J.R. (1991). Editing for comprehension: Improving the process through reading protocols. In E. R. Steinberg (Ed.), *Plain language: Principles and practice.* Detroit: Wayne State University Press.

Temple, C., Nathan, R., & Burris, N. (1982). *The beginning of writing.* Boston: Allyn and Bacon.

Thorndyke, P. W. (1977). Cognitive structures in comprehension and memory of narrative discourse. *Cognitive Psychology. 9,* 77-110.

Tidwell, P. S. (1992). Using cognitive structure measures to revise text: Diagnosis and repair of reader's mis- and missing conceptions. Unpublished doctoral dissertation, University of Georgia.

Tidwell, P. S. (1989). *Improving written material: An empirical test of passages revised by E. D. Hirsch.* Unpublished master's thesis, University of Georgia.

Tolchinsky Landsmann, L., & Karmiloff-Smith, A. (1992). Children's understanding of notations as domains of knowledge versus referential-communicative tools. *Cognitive Development, 7,* 287-300.

Tolchinsky Landsmann, L., & Levin, I. (1985). Writing in preschoolers: An age related analysis. *Applied Psycholinguistics, 6,* 319-339.

Tolchinsky Landsmann, L., & Levin, I. (1987). Writing in four to six year olds: Representation of semantic and phonological similarities and differences. *Journal of Child Language, 14,* 127-144.

Torrance, M., (1996). Is writing expertise like other expertise? In G. Rijlaarsdam, H. van den Bergh & M. Couzijn (Eds.), *Writing research: Theories, models and methodology.* Amsterdam: Amsterdam University Press.

Trigg, R. H., & Suchman, L. A. (1989). Collaborative writing in Notecards. In R. McAleese (Ed.), *Hypertext: theory into practice* (pp. 45-61). Norwood, NJ: Ablex.

U. S. Air Force Reserve Officers' Training Corps. (1985). *U. S. Air Power: Key to deterence.* Maxwell Air Force Base, Montgomery, AL: U. S. Air Force.

van der Hoeven, J. (1996). Writing performance, writing competence and writing processes. In G. Rijlaarsdam, H. van den Bergh & M. Couzijn (Eds.), *Writing research: Theories, models & methodology.* Amsterdam: Amsterdam University Press.

van der Mast, N. P. (1996). Adjusting target figures downwards: On the collaborative writing of policy documents in the Dutch government. In M.

Sharples & Th. van der Geest (Eds.), *The New writing environment: Writers at work in a world of technology*. London: Springer Verlag.

van der Pool, E. (1995). *Writing as a conceptual process. A text-analytical study of developmental aspects.* Unpublished doctoral dissertation, Katholieke Universiteit Brabant.

Van Dusen, L. M. (1988). Factors influencing text retention and comprehension: An analysis of text features. Unpublished doctoral dissertation, University of Georgia.

Van Galen, G. P. (1991). Handwriting: Issues for a psychomotor theory. *Human Movement Science, 10,* 165-191.

Velez, L. (1994). Interpreting and writing in the laboratory: A study of novice biologists as novice rhetors. Unpublished doctoral dissertation. Carnegie Mellon University.

Velichkovsky, B. (1994). Sprache, Evolution und die funktionale Organisation der menschlichen Erkenntnis [Language, evolution, and the functional organization of human cognition]. In H. J. Kornadt, J. Grabowski & R. Mangold-Allwinn (Eds.), *Sprache und Kognition — Perspektiven moderner Sprachpsychologie* (pp. 113-131). Heidelberg: Spektrum Akadamischer Verlag.

Vipond, D. (1993). *Writing and psychology.* Westport, CT: Praeger.

Voth, T., & Graham, S. (1995). [The effects of goal setting and strategy facilitation on the expository writing performance of junior high students with learning disabilities]. Unpublished raw data.

Vygotsky, L. S. (1962). *Thought and language.* (E. Haufmann & G. Vakar, Eds. and Trans.). Cambridge, MA: MIT Press.

Waes, L. van (1988). *Writing business letters with and without a word processor.* Paper presented at the International Convention of the Association for Business Communication, Indianapolis.

Waes, L. van (1991a). *De computer en het schrijfproces. De invloed van de tekstverwerker op het pauze- en revisiegedrag van schrijvers* [The computer and the writing process. The influence of the text processor on the pauzing and revision behavior of writers]. Enschede: WMW Pubikaties.

Waes, L. van (1991b). *De computer en het schrijfproces. De invloed van de tekstverwerker op het pauze-en revisiegedrag van schrijvers* [The computer and the writing process. The influence of the word processor on the pausing and revision behavior of writers]. Enschede: WMW Publikaties.

Waes, L. van (1992). The influence of the computer on writing profiles. In H. P. Maat & M. Steehouder (Eds.), *Studies of functional text quality* Amsterdam: Rodopi.

Waes, L. van, & Van Herreweghe, L. (1995). Computerprotokolle in der Schreibprozeßforschung. Der Gebrauch von *Keytrap* als Beobachtungsinstrument. In E.M. Jakobs, D. Knorr & S. Molitor-Lübbert (Hrsg.), *Wissenschaftlige Tekstproduktion. Mit und ohne Computer.* Frankfurt A.M.: Peter Lang.

Walker, W.H., & Kintsch, W. (1985). Automatic and strategic aspects of knowledge retrieval. *Cognitive Science, 9,* 261-283.

Wallace, D.L., & Hayes, J.R. (1991). Redefining revision for freshmen. *Research in the Teaching of English, 25,* 54-66.

Wallace, I. (1971). *The writing of one novel*. Richmond Hill, Ontario: Simon & Schuster.

Wallesch, C. (1983). Schreiben — Physiologische Grundlagen und pathologische Erscheinungsformen [Writing — physiological basis and pathological manifestation]. In K. B. Guenther & H. Guenther (Eds.), *Schrift, Schreiben, Schriftlichkeit* (pp. 133-141). Tuebingen: Niemeyer.

Waters, G. S., Rochon, E., & Caplan, D. (1992). The role of high-level speech planning in rehearsal: Evidence from patients with apraxia of speech. *Journal of Memory and Language, 31*, 54-73.

Watson, D., & Clark, L. A. (1984). Negative affectivity: The disposition to experience aversive emotional states. *Psychological Bulletin, 96*, 465-490.

White, E. M. (1985). *Teaching and assessing writing*. San Francisco, CA: Jossey-Bass.

White, E. M. (1994). *Teaching and assessing writing*, (2nd ed.). San Francisco, CA: Jossey-Bass.

Wigfield, A. (1994). The role of children's achievement values in the self-regulation of their learning outcomes. In D. Schunk & B. Zimmerman (Eds.), *Self-regulation of learning and performance: Issues and educational applications* (pp. 101-124). Hillsdale, NJ: Lawrence Erlbaum Associates.

Wijk, C. van (1992). Information analysis in written discourse. In Verhoeven, L. & Jong, J. de (Eds.), *The construct of language proficiency* (pp. 85-99). Amsterdam: Benjamins.

Wijk, C. van (1995, May). *Levels of competence in writing*. Paper presented at the 5th European Workshop on natural language generation. Leiden, The Netherlands.

Williamson, M. M., & Pence, P. (1989). Word processing and student writers. In B. K. Britton & S. M. Glynn (Eds.), *Computer writing environments: Theory, research, and design*. Hillsdale, NJ: Lawrence Erlbaum Associates.

Wine, J. D. (1980). Cognitive-attentional theory of test anxiety, In I. G. Sarason (Ed.), *Test anxiety: Theory, research, and applications* (pp. 349-385). Hillsdale, NJ: Lawrence Erlbaum Associates.

Winograd, T., & Flores, F. (1986). *Understanding computers and cognition: A new foundation for design*. Norwood, NJ: Ablex.

Winsor, D. A. (1989). An engineer's writing and the corporate construction of knowledge. *Written Communication, 6*, 270-285.

Wishbow, N. (1988). *Studies of creativity in poets*. Unpublished doctoral dissertation, Carnegie Mellon University.

Witte, P., & Cherry, R. D. (1994). Think-aloud protocols, protocol analysis, and research design: An exploration of the influence of writing tasks on writing processes. In P. Smagorinsky (Ed.), *Speaking about writing: Reflections on research methodology* (pp. 20-54). [Written Communication Series 8]. Thousand Oaks, CA: Sage.

Wohl, A. (1986). *Adaptation of Marie Clay's test of Concepts About Print*. Unpublished manuscript. [in Hebrew].

Wood, C. C. (1992a). *Intermediate and mediating representations in knowledge acquisition & collaborative writing*. [Collaborative Writing Research Group Rep. 4]. University of Sussex.

Wood, C. C. (1992b). *A cultural-cognitive approach to collaborative writing.* [Cognitive science res. paper CSRP 242]. University of Sussex.

Wood, C. C. (1993). *A cognitive dimensional analysis of idea sketches.* [Cognitive sciences res. paper CSRP 275], University of Sussex.

Wright, P., Creighton, P., & Threlfall S. M. (1982). Some factors determining when instructions will be read. *Ergonomics, 25,* 225-237.

Yanay, Y., & Porat, S. (1987). Hebrew orthography and spelling: An ancient problem and a proposed solution. *Mada,* 31, 18-22. [in Hebrew].

Yin, R. K. (1994). *Case study research: Design and methods* (2nd ed.). Thousand Oaks, CA: Sage.

Zasloff, T. (1984). *Diagnosing student writing: Problems encountered by college freshmen.* Unpublished doctoral dissertation, Carnegie Mellon University.

Zimmerman, B. (1989). A social cognitive view of self-regulated academic learning. *Journal of Educational Psychology, 81,* 329-339.

Zutell, J. (1992). An integrated view of word knowledge: Correlational studies of the relationships among spelling, reading and conceptual development. In S. Tempelten & D. R. Bear (Eds.), *Development of orthographic knowledge and the foundations of literacy: A memorial festschrift for Edmund H. Harderse* (pp. 213-230). Hillsdale, NJ: Lawrence Erlbaum Associates.

AUTHOR INDEX

Subject Index

—A—

Action line, 257-258. 266-268
Actors, 309-311, 313-322
Advanced performance, 259, 267
Affect, 1, 4-5, 7, 9, 146
Alphabet, 75, 274, 278
Analysis and synthesis, 137-138. 146
Assessment, 54, 61, 95, 94, 100, 136, 155, 174. 177, 286, 291, 340, 375
Assignment adaptation, 115-116
Audience, 4-5, 10, 21, 24-25, 30, 39, 43-44, 50-52, 95-96, 103, 110, 128-129, 171, 177, 195, 240, 245, 314-315, 321-322, 348, 363
Automatic processes, 189, 205, 363
Auxiliary systems, 79-81, 86-89

—B—

Balance, 10, 50, 54, 335
Brainstorming, 23, 46, 148, 347, 354, 367, 369, 375, 379
Break, 167-168, 175-176, 178, 185

—C—

Case studies, 6, 165-166, 258, 310, 312-314, 317, 319-322
Central executive, 8, 57-59, 62-65, 67-70, 79, 93, 97, 99-101, 160.
Central capacity, 63-65, 67-70
Cognitive activities, 107-122, 124-125, 127, 133, 146-157, 205,

207-210, 213-215, 217, 219-223, 226
Coherence, 61, 80, 88-89, 103, 251, 253, 256, 264, 267. 323-324, 326-328
Collaboration, 6, 140, 148, 171, 275, 309-310, 314, 317, 319, 353, 359-360
Comprehension, 2, 13-15, 20, 57-58, 61, 71, 77, 93-101, 287-289, 303, 323-327
Concepts about print, 272, 287-290
Conceptual space, 127-132, 143-144, 146-147
Concordance, 183
Concurrent verbal protocol, 150, 156, 159, 233-236, 239-240, 242, 249
Connectionist, 160
Consolidation, 174
Consonantal writing, 272-279, 281-292
Constraints, 21, 30-31, 41, 48, 93-94, 97-100, 127-133, 136, 139, 142-143, 145-147, 150, 164, 195, 230, 279, 295, 307, 311, 338, 348-349, 367
Contemplation, 127-128, 134, 144, 146
Creativity, 127-130, 132-137, 142, 144, 146-149, 191
Cultural differences, 5

—D—

Decision making, 8, 13, 20-21, 58
Deletion, 152, 167-169, 173-174, 179-180, 185, 238, 261, 292

—R—

—S—

Lightning Source UK Ltd.
Milton Keynes UK
UKHW03f0750230418
321474UK00015B/461/P